Applications for COMPUTERS AND INFORMATION PROCESSING

William M. Fuori
Louis V. Gioia
Nassau Community College
Garden City, NY 11530

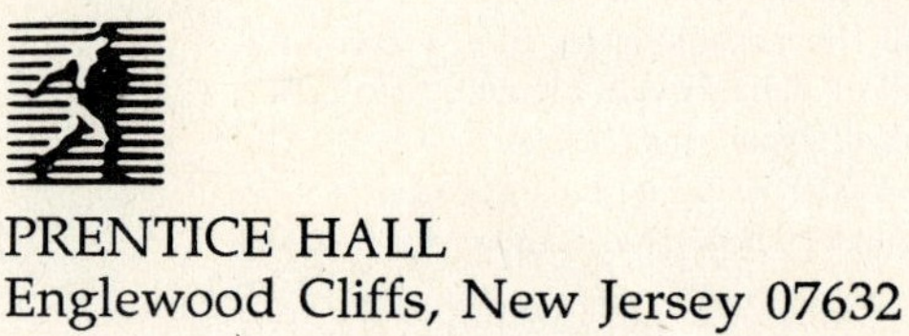

PRENTICE HALL
Englewood Cliffs, New Jersey 07632

Library of Congress Cataloging-in-Publication Data

Fuori, William M.
Applications for computers and information processing / William M. Fuori, Louis V. Gioia. -- 3rd ed.
p. cm.
Includes index.
ISBN 0-13-173675-2
1. Application software. 2. WordPerfect (Computer program) 3. Lotus 1-2-3 (Computer program) 4. dBase III plus (Computer program) I. Gioia, Louis V. II. Title.
QA76.76.A65F86 1991
005.36--dc20 90-22016
CIP

Editorial/Production Supervision: MAI Publishing
Prepress Buyer: Trudy Pisciotti
Manufacturing Buyer: Bob Anderson

Printed in the United States of America

10 9 8 7 6 5 4 3 2

ISBN 0-13-173675-2

Prentice-Hall International (UK) Limited, *London*
Prentice-Hall of Australia Pty. Limited, *Sydney*
Prentice-Hall Canada Inc., *Toronto*
Prentice-Hall Hispanoamericana, S.A., *Mexico*
Prentice-Hall of India Private Limited, *New Delhi*
Prentice-Hall of Japan, Inc., *Tokyo*
Simon & Schuster Asia Pte. Ltd., *Singapore*
Editora Prentice-Hall do Brasil, Ltda., *Rio de Janeiro*

To my wife Elizabeth and our children, Elizabeth E. and Michael T., for the patience, consideration, and understanding you have exhibited toward my writing endeavors over the past twenty years.

To the memory of Ellen Fuori, my mother.

W.M.F.

To Ellen, Kristine, and Amy and to my parents, Gloria, Michael, Ann, and Thomas: Thank you for your patience, understanding, and inspiration.

L.V.G.

Contents

4 dBASE III PLUS *Organizing Your Records*

Preface

The first two editions of this text were a huge success. They were adopted nationally and internationally by universities, two-year colleges, and vocational schools. We felt the attraction came in large part from the option that these editions provided the instructor—hands-on computer experience. Through the use of tutorials and other computer exercises, students became excited and encouraged as they learned first hand of the magic and power of a computer. Therefore, in this third edition, we have expanded the hands-on aspect of the package by providing increased tutorial coverage in a more convenient, easier to use book.

Packaged Software Tutorials

During the last few years, there has been rapid growth in the use of prewritten or packaged software. Now that prewritten software has developed to the point where applications like word processing, electronic spreadsheets, database management systems, and computer graphics are relatively friendly, more and more people from all walks of life are learning how to use these programs. Packaged software is available for use with computers of all sizes, from giant supercomputers to tiny micros.

Experience has shown that a course that teaches students about computers and does not demonstrate how to use them can sometimes be quite dull and uninspiring. Most would agree that the best way to learn about a foreign land is not simply to read about it but to see, touch, smell it—in short, to experience that land. Packaged software has made it possible for the average person to experience the power and magic of the computer—without a great expenditure of time or energy.

The following tutorials on the use of DOS, WordPerfect, Lotus 1-2-3, and dBASE III PLUS provide simple, easy-to-use, keystroke-by-keystroke instructions on how to use the packages in typical business applications. Each tutorial introduces the inexperienced user to the package with an absolute minimum of fuss and bother and explains quickly and easily the necessary information. The explanations are informal, and the text emphasizes general principles rather than the features of any particular package.

We have field-tested the tutorials and have purposely designed them so that a maximum of learning can take place with a minimum of time. Of course, it is best for each student to go through each session while seated at a computer, but, if a computer is not available, each tutorial can still be used profitably and effectively as a computer simulation exercise.

Software Versions

A successful software package must be timely, competitively priced, error free, and appeal to a large user base. Regardless of how ideal a product is when it is first introduced, it must accommodate changing user needs, technological innovations, and so on, if it is to remain desirable. These periodic updates result in newer versions of the software. Each newer version generally provides all the capabilities of previous versions plus new and enhanced features. These software additions and enhancements often are accompanied by increased hardware requirements.

Thus, before using or purchasing a software package, you should determine the capabilities of the version being considered and verify that it is one of the most recent versions available. In addition, if using the latest version of the software will require that you update your hardware, you must carefully weigh the advantages of the new version against the increased hardware costs.

Each of the tutorials that follow represents a recent version of the software package and is identified by version number.

Instructor's Resource Package

Instructor's Resource Manual

To aid the instructor in structuring the course to fit the interests and backgrounds of his or her students, a resource manual is available to adopters of this book and its companion text. This manual includes suggestions and outlines for presenting DOS, word processing, electronic spreadsheets, and database software.

Test Bank

A computerized test bank containing more than 3000 questions that can be used by the instructor in the preparation of examinations is available. Questions are organized and presented by section and are graduated according to level of difficulty. Each section contains a number of objective questions that are drawn from the corresponding section in the text. In each section the questions presented first test a student's factual recall of basic terms and concepts; the questions presented next test for a more detailed knowledge of the text material; and the questions presented in conclusion test a student's ability to reason the answer based on a knowledge and understanding of the text material. The instructor is free to choose questions that are consistent in depth and level with the presentation of this material in class.

Microcomputer disks containing these questions are provided to adopters of the package.

Study Guide

To assist the student in understanding and learning the material presented in the text and this applications book and to make the learning experience more enjoyable, a study guide is available. It contains exercises that require the student to use software packages of the type presented in the tutorials. Each exercise is designed to reduce anxiety, increase motivation, and provide a useful and meaningful experience for the student on a self-paced, independent-learning basis. The exercises are of two types:

1. Performance Exercises—distinct and clearly delineated tasks that can be carried out using the data files provided.
2. Project Descriptions—descriptions of complete projects that can be fun to complete and of immediate benefit to the student.

Acetates and Transparency Masters

Full-color acetates and black-line, text-correlated transparency masters are provided to visually and dramatically enhance the instructor's classroom presentation. These represent the illustrations most often selected and used by instructors during the field-testing of the text.

Acknowledgements

A special word of thanks to our colleagues at Nassau Community College for their contributions, helpful suggestions, and encouragement.

Dr. William Fuori
Louis V. Gioia

Applications for COMPUTERS AND INFORMATION PROCESSING

1

THE DOS OPERATING SYSTEM
Speaking to the Supervisor

This tutorial will help you get acquainted with DOS, your personal computer's disk operating system. DOS is a collection of programs that help you to communicate with your computer. DOS accepts your commands and interacts with the hardware to carry them out. DOS commands are used to manage files and run applications software.

Objectives

Upon completing this tutorial, you will be able to:

- Boot your computer system
- Get and use a disk directory
- Copy individual files and entire disks
- Create, change, and delete a subdirectory
- Describe and use many other DOS internal and external commands
- Format a disk
- Create, rename, and delete files
- Display and print out files
- Create a batch file

Follow the Blue

As you follow along, any procedures you must carry out or entries you must make will be printed in blue, whereas all computer responses will appear as if they were written by a typewriter. Type only entries or follow only directions that appear in blue. A ❑ appears at the right of the first line of each sequence of commands you must enter. Check the box when you have completed the instruction as a way of keeping track of your progress as you proceed through the tutorial.

Whenever a special key (any key other than a letter, digit, or special character) is shown printed in blue, you must tap or momentarily depress that key. For example, if the [Enter] key were printed in blue, you would be expected to momentarily depress the [Enter] key (see Fig. T1-1).

FIGURE T1-1
Standard and Enhanced Keyboard Showing the [Enter] Key.

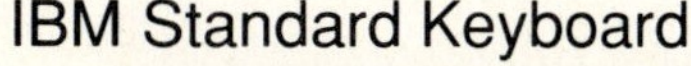

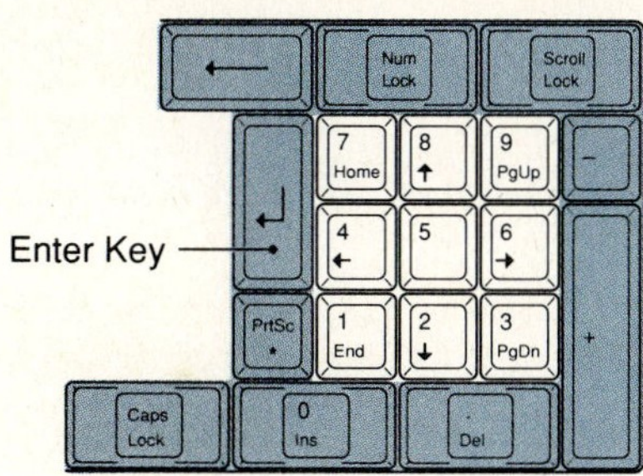

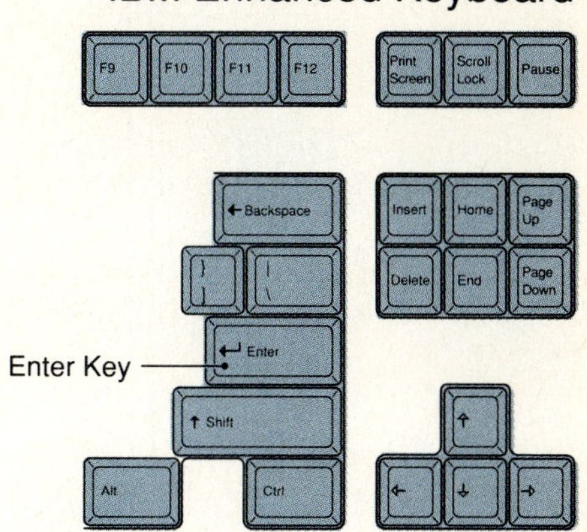

In some special cases, it will be necessary for you to press *and hold down* one special key while momentarily depressing another. To indicate this, the special key or keys to be pressed and held will be printed slightly lower and attached by a thin line to the key to be tapped. If the series of keys

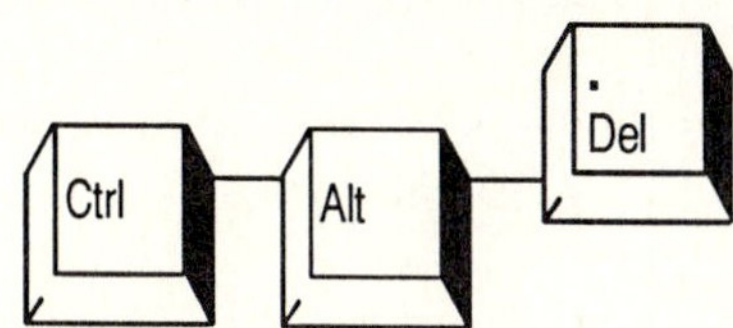

were printed in blue, you would be expected to press and hold down the [Ctrl] and [Alt] keys, press the [Del] key, and then release all three keys.

You will also find it necessary to enter combinations of text and special keys. For example, if the entry

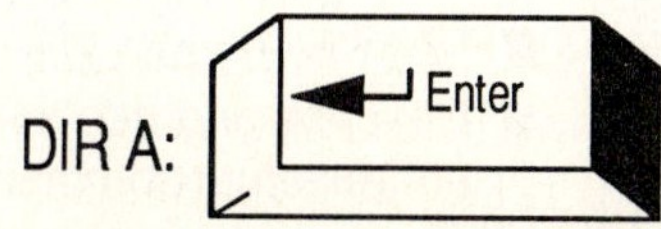

were printed in blue, you would be expected to type **DIR A:** and then depress the [Enter] key.

Required Hardware

Some computer labs have several computers connected to a single printer via a switch box. If this is the case in your laboratory, ask your instructor or lab assistant how to use the switch box correctly.

The microcomputers in your lab generally will look like the PC shown in Figure T1-2. The disk drives, central processing unit, and memory are all housed in the **system** or **processor unit**. Your **monitor**, or **display**, sits on top of the processor. Your microcomputer may be equipped with one or two **floppy disk drives**. If your system has one floppy disk drive and a **hard**, or **fixed**, **disk**—a large-capacity storage device that is not portable as a floppy disk is—some of the procedures you carry out and some of your displays may be slightly different from what is presented in this tutorial.

Your microcomputer may also have a printer attached to it. It will be useful in providing hard copy of your output. We will use it later in the tutorial.

FIGURE T1-2
Typical Two Floppy-Drive System.

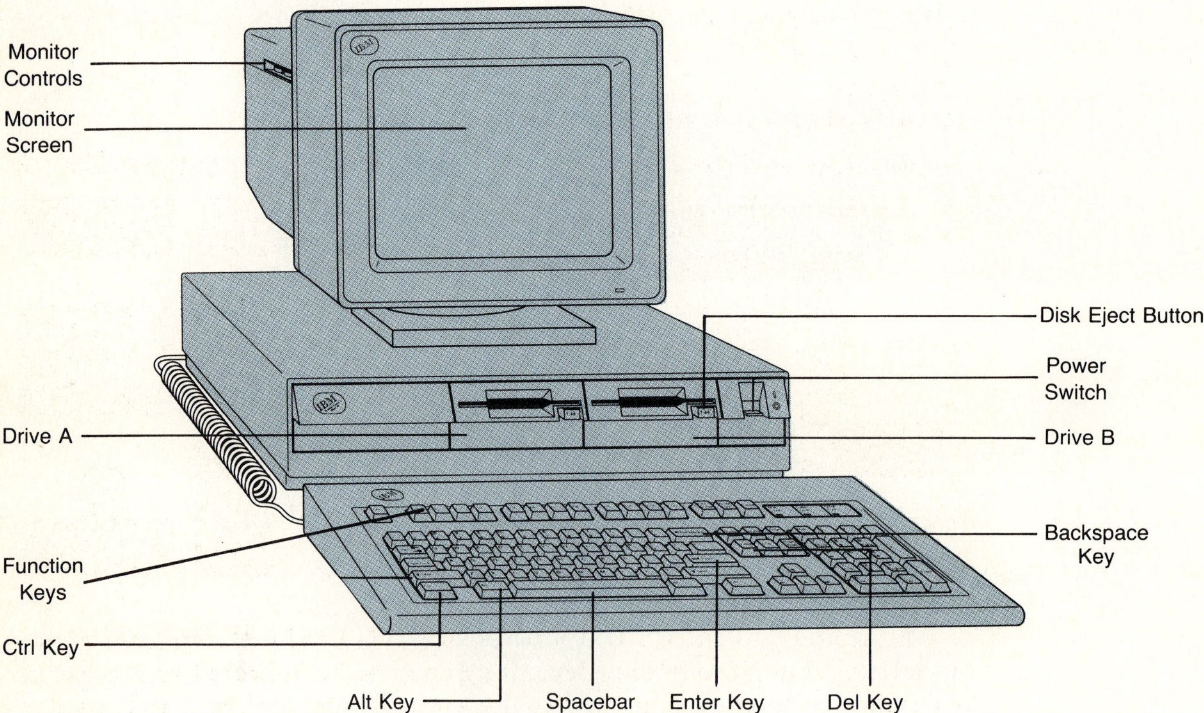

Required Software

If your computer system is not equipped with a hard drive, obtain a copy of **DOS Version 3.3** and a **Learning disk** from your instructor or laboratory assistant for use with this tutorial. If your computer system is equipped with 5¼-inch disk drives, you will be given two disks, one labeled **DOS Startup disk**, the other labeled **DOS Operating disk**. If your computer system uses 3½-inch disk drives, you will be given a single **DOS Startup/Operating disk**.

For purposes of this tutorial, when we refer to the *DOS/Startup disk*, we will mean either the 5¼-inch *DOS Startup disk* or the 3½-inch *DOS Startup/Operating disk*. Similarly, when we refer to the *DOS/Operating disk*, we will mean either the 5¼-inch *DOS Operating disk* or the 3½-inch *DOS Startup/Operating disk.*

If your computer is equipped with a hard disk, a version of DOS will already be installed on it. The particular version of DOS that has been installed will be displayed when you start up the computer system. If the installed version of DOS is 3.3 you need only obtain a *Learning disk* from your instructor. However, if the installed version of DOS is other than 3.3, obtain *DOS Version 3.3* and a *Learning disk* from your instructor and follow the instructions for a floppy disk system.

You will also need two blank floppy disks. Speak to your instructor or the laboratory assistant to determine the disk size appropriate for the computers you will be using. For identification purposes, we will call these disks your **Work disks**.

Forewarned Is Forearmed

Always make backup copies of your disks. You never know what might happen to your originals. Having a backup ensures that your work is protected. You will learn the DOS commands needed to back up your work later in this tutorial.

The floppy disks you will be using are not indestructible. They are nothing more than thin pieces of coated plastic containing magnetically recoded information. If not properly cared for, the information on them can be damaged or lost. They are particularly vulnerable to heat, sunlight, magnetic fields, and other similar environmental conditions. Figure T1-3 illustrates some simple but important don'ts to keep in mind when working with floppy disks.

FIGURE T1-3
Important DON'TS To Remember When Working with Floppy Disks.

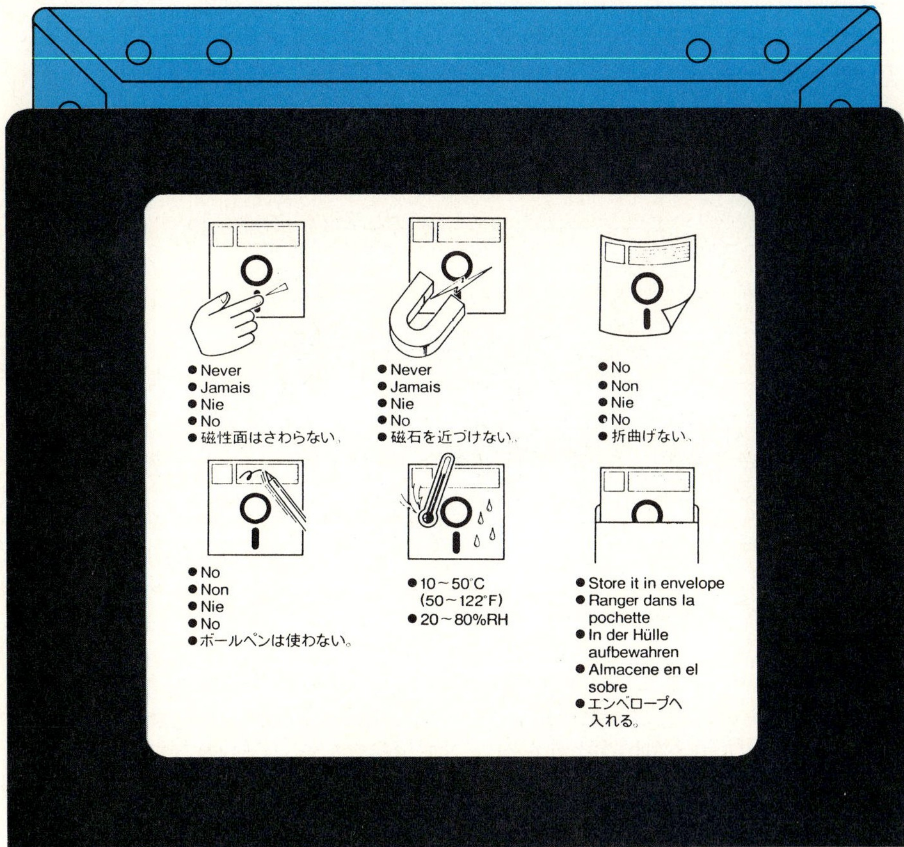

Part I DOS Fundamentals

In Part I of this tutorial we investigate the DOS concepts and commands that are essential if you are to communicate effectively with your computer. One to two hours will be needed to complete Part I.

How To Proceed

You don't have to finish this tutorial at one sitting. During your computer session, you can stop at any time—just turn your computer off and remove your disks. When you want to continue, simply insert the DOS/Startup disk into the A: drive (the one on the left or, on some systems, the drive at the top) and a Work disk into the B: drive (the one on the right or, on some systems, the one at the bottom) and boot the computer, as described shortly.

About Your Keyboard

It is important for you to become familiar with your keyboard. Computer keyboards, in general, resemble typewriter keyboards (see Fig. T1-4). However, they have additional keys that can be used to direct the actions of your computer. Some of the useful keys, along with a description of their functions, are provided in Table T1-1.

FIGURE T1-4
IBM Standard and Enhanced Keyboards.

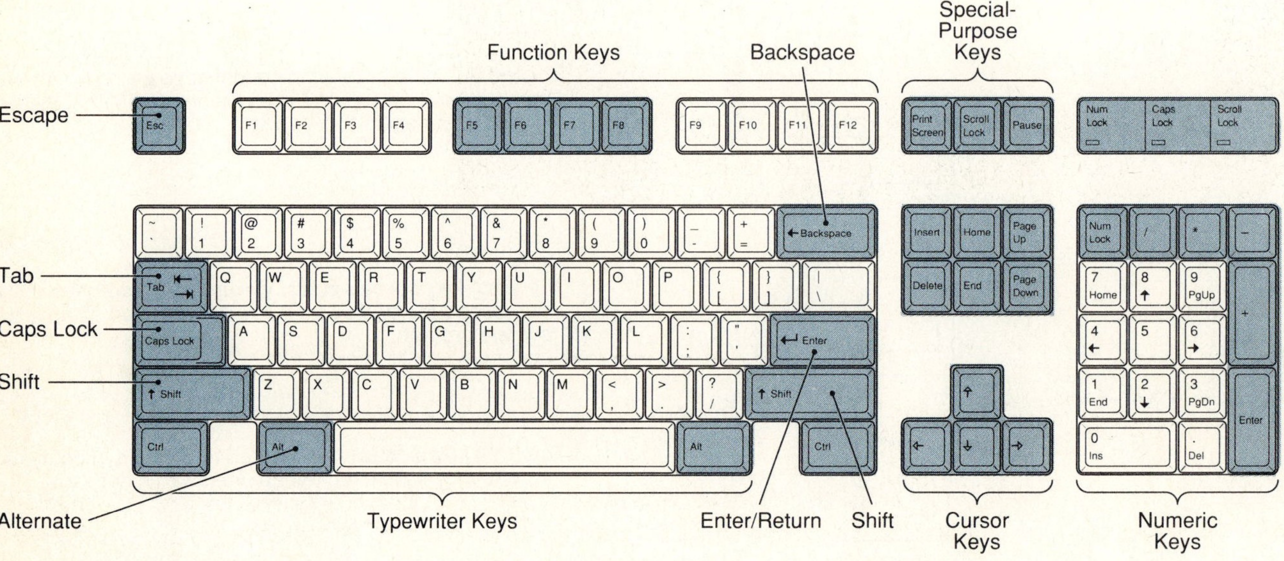

TABLE T1-1
Useful Keyboard Keys

Key	Function
8 ↑ 2 ↓ 4 ← 6 →	The four Arrow keys move the cursor up, down, left, or right one character or line at a time without altering text in any way.
← Enter	The [Enter] key transmits a line to the microprocessor.
Backspace	The [Backspace] key moves the cursor to the left one place (similar to the Left Arrow key). As you press the [Backspace] key, a character to the left is erased. If your command contains an error and you already pressed the [Enter] key, just *RETYPE* the command correctly.
Caps Lock	The [Caps Lock] key toggles the keyboard between uppercase and lowercase. Toggle it on if you desire capital letters. Toggling it again will return the keyboard to lowercase mode. It has no effect on the nonletter keys. DOS commands are not affected by case, but we suggest you toggle the [Caps Lock] key on so that your commands will appear in capital letters.
Shift — PrtSc *	Prints the image appearing on your display screen.
Ctrl — PrtSc *	Causes DOS to print everything that appears on the screen from this point on. This will continue until [Ctrl]-[Print Screen] is depressed again.
Esc	The [Esc] key cancels a line you typed if you haven't yet depressed the [Enter] key. Pressing [Enter] returns the system prompt.
Ctrl	The [Ctrl] key (sometimes referred to by the symbol ^) has no effect by itself but must be used with other keys.

TABLE T1-1
(Continued)

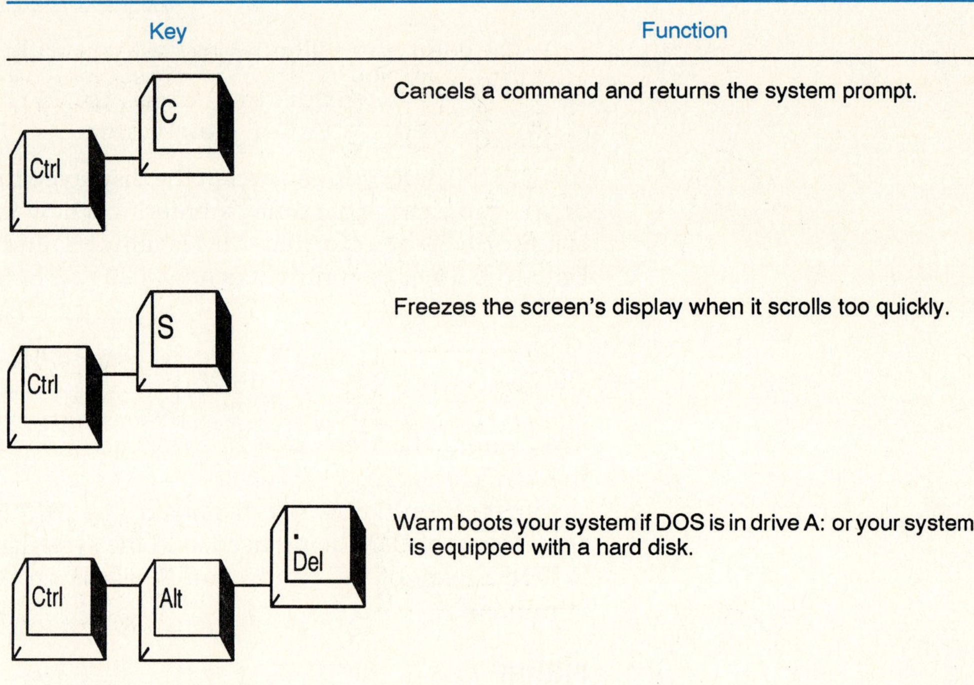

Key	Function
Ctrl – C	Cancels a command and returns the system prompt.
Ctrl – S	Freezes the screen's display when it scrolls too quickly.
Ctrl – Alt – Del	Warm boots your system if DOS is in drive A: or your system is equipped with a hard disk.

We will be describing other important keyboard keys as we use them in this tutorial.

Starting the Computer—The Boot Process

Starting a microcomputer is known as the **boot process**. There are two ways to boot your computer, the cold boot and the warm boot.

The Cold Boot

Don't be alarmed if you see a different date displayed or other activity taking place on your display screen. Your instructor or laboratory assistant may have programed DOS to log in the correct time and date automatically or perhaps to display your college's logo. If this is the case, follow any special instructions given to you by your instructor or laboratory assistant for booting your system. Then, skip to the section "The [Caps Lock] Key" of this tutorial on page 9 and proceed normally.

With the power still turned off, turn on your display screen if it is equipped with a separate power switch. This switch is generally located at the front or on the side of the monitor.

Pick up your DOS/Startup disk by the top edge with your thumb on the label. Now slide it into drive A:, close the door, and turn the computer on. The computer will begin by initiating a self-test. Shortly thereafter, it will sound a beep to indicate that the self-test was successful.

A program contained in ROM (read-only memory) is now executed. Execution of this program accesses your DOS/Startup disk and a portion of the operating system known as the boot is loaded into RAM (random-access memory). This program then pulls a larger portion of DOS from the DOS disk into RAM "by its bootstraps."

You should now see the display

```
Current date is Tue 09-10-1991
Enter new date (mm-dd-yy):
```

You can accept the date displayed by pressing the [Enter] key, or you can change the date by entering a new date in MM-DD-YY format. Assuming today's date is September 10, 1991, enter

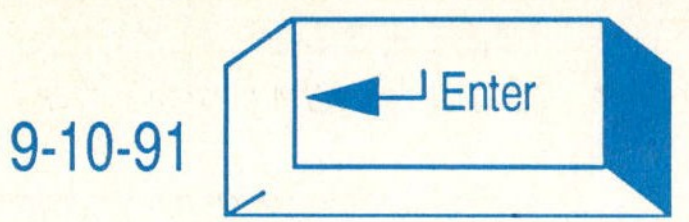

The computer will now prompt you with:

```
Current time is 16:20:02.19
Enter new time:
```

As with the date, you can accept the displayed time by pressing the [Enter] key, or you can change the time by entering a new time in HH:MM:SS format (HH is hours in 24-hour format, MM is minutes, and SS is seconds and is optional). Enter the time, assuming it is now 4:20 P.M. Enter

This enters the time as 4:20 P.M. Since no seconds were entered, they are initialized to zero.

You should now see displayed **The IBM Personal Computer DOS** logo, the version of DOS being used, and the system prompt **A>** (see Fig. T1-5). This is DOS's way of informing you that it is on the job and awaiting your next command.

FIGURE T1-5
Screen of Boot Process with A> at the Bottom.

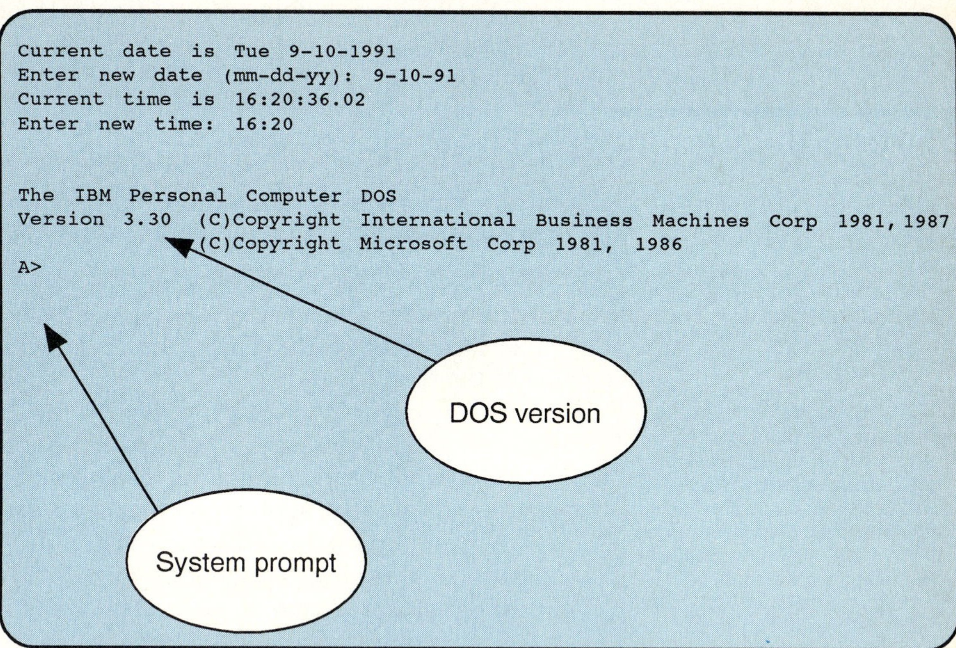

If your computer does not start correctly or your screen does not appear as shown in Figure T1-5, perform a warm boot as described next and follow the DOS prompts.

The Warm Boot

If the computer is already turned on, simply insert your DOS/Startup disk into the A: drive. With your left hand hold down the [Ctrl] and [Alt] keys, and with your right hand tap the [Del] key (see Fig. T1-6).

FIGURE T1-6
Keyboards Showing Placement of Ctrl, Alt, and Del Keys.

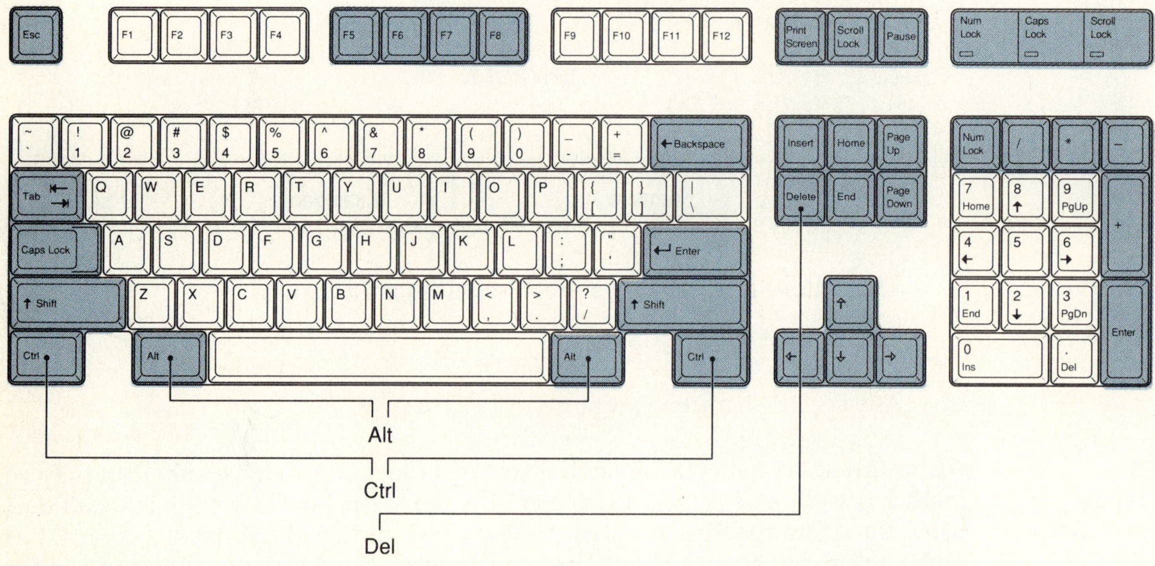

If at any future time, you become "stuck" and desire to get back to A>, you can always place your DOS/Startup disk in drive A:, hold down the [Ctrl] and [Alt] keys, and tap the [Del] key. This will give you the system prompt A>; then you can start over. Knowing how to warm boot your computer will be very useful as you go through this tutorial.

The [Caps Lock] Key

Because capital letters are larger and easier to read on the screen, many users type only capitals. Once you press the [Caps Lock] key, all letters will be typed in CAPITALS. To get out of this mode and back to lowercase, just press the [Caps Lock] key again. DOS does not care if you use uppercase or lowercase.

To simplify matters, press

The nonletter keys, such as 4 and $, still have two meanings. To type the upper symbol, you must always use the [Shift] key (see Fig. T1-4).

so your commands will be in capital letters.

How DOS Works with Disks and Files

Computers store programs and data in files for future access. Program files direct the computer to carry out tasks or procedures, and data files contain the numbers or text the programs need to do what you want done. These files are stored on floppy or hard disks. A single floppy disk can contain from one to literally hundreds of files. The information about the files on a disk is stored in the **disk directory**. Disk directories include information about each file such as the file name, its size, its location in the file allocation table, the time and date that it was created, and a few special file attributes.

File Names

Each file is identified by a **file name**. A file name consists of two parts: the **filename**, which contains up to 8 characters, and an **extension** (optional) of up to 3 characters set off by a period:

PAYROLL.DAT

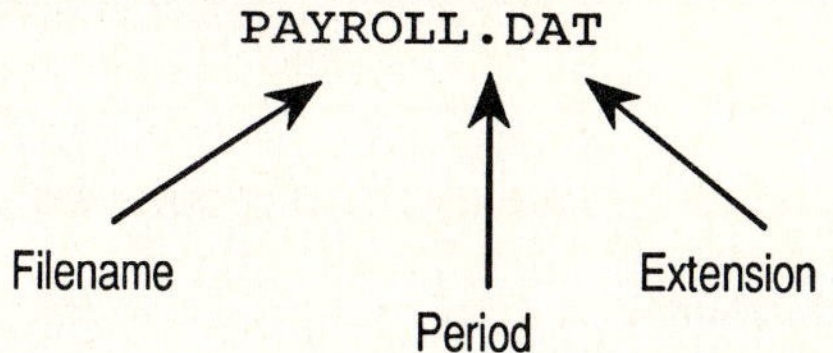

Earlier versions of IBM's PC DOS are generally more restrictive with respect to characters allowed.

The following characters are allowed in a file name:

The letters A-Z
The digits 0-9
Any special character except . " / \ [ ] : | < > + = ; ,

Drive Specifier and Default Drive

Although not considered an actual part of a file name, a **drive specifier** may be included with a file name to identify the drive on which the file is located. If used, the drive specifier must precede the file name and consist of a drive letter and a colon. No spaces should appear between the drive specifier and the file name. For example, specifying

A:PAYROLL.DAT

would tell DOS to search for the file PAYROLL.DAT on drive A:. However, if no drive specifier is provided, as in

PAYROLL.DAT

DOS will look for the file on the current, or **default, drive**—the drive specified in the system prompt. That is, if the DOS system prompt displayed is A>, the default drive is drive A:, and this is where DOS will search for the file. Or, if the system prompt displayed is B>, the default drive is B:, and this is where DOS will search for the file.

Changing the Default Drive

DOS provides us with the ability to change the default drive if we wish. To see how this is done, let's change the default drive from drive A: to drive B:. Before

Don't forget to type a colon (:) after the disk drive letter. To get a colon, you must hold the [Shift] key and simultaneously press the [; :] key. If you inadvertently use a semicolon instead of a colon, the default drive will not change.

we do this, however, we must place a disk in this drive so that DOS can verify that the drive is present and ready for use. Therefore, insert your Learning disk in drive B: and close the door. Now, to change the default drive to B: just enter:

❑

B: is now the current disk drive, as indicated by the system prompt B>. Change back to drive A: as the default drive. Enter

❑

The File Allocation Table (FAT)

The **file allocation table (FAT)** contains the official record of the disk's format and maps out the location of the sectors used by the files on the disk. DOS uses the FAT to keep track of disk-space usage. Because of the importance of the FAT, DOS maintains two copies of it on every disk.

File Attributes

File attributes relate to the type of file and how it can be used. For example, files can be specified as read-only or hidden. **Read-only** files can be read but not written over. **Hidden files** cannot be seen by ordinary DOS operations. That is, if we asked DOS to list all the files on a disk, it would not list any files with a hidden attribute even though the file is actually present. Some software manufacturers include hidden files on their disks for security purposes or so that you cannot accidentally delete the files.

Internal and External Commands

Each time you boot your computer, you pull a small part of DOS into RAM. This portion stays in RAM throughout your session with the computer and contains what are known as **internal commands**. Even if you remove your DOS disk from drive A:, you can still use internal commands. However, turn off your computer and the internal commands are erased from RAM. Boot the system, and they are returned to RAM awaiting your use.

Because DOS commands take up valuable storage space in RAM, the less frequently used DOS commands are not stored in RAM. These commands are stored outside of RAM and are referred to as **external commands**. Each external command appears on the DOS/Startup or Operating disk as a program file with a COM or EXE extension. A program file with a COM or EXE extension can be called into action, or **executed**, simply by entering its filename; the extension need not be specified. For example, by entering the filename DISKCOPY, you direct DOS to access the file DISKCOPY.COM from your DOS/Operating disk and carry out the set of instructions stored therein. Thus when you issue a DOS external command, you are actually directing DOS to access and execute the specific set of instructions stored on the DOS/Startup or Operating disk in a program file of the same name.

Therefore, whenever you use an external DOS command, make certain that your DOS/Startup or Operating disk is in a disk drive. If it is in a drive other than the default drive, a drive specifier naming this drive must precede the DOS external command.

Let's begin by examining some DOS internal commands.

Some Useful Internal Commands

The VER Command

Software developers must constantly improve and enhance their products to remain competitive in the marketplace. Each new release of a product is identified by a higher version number. IBM, for example, has identified its most recent releases of DOS as 3.0, 3.1, 3.2, 3.3, and 4.0. To determine the version of DOS with which your computer was booted, enter

❑

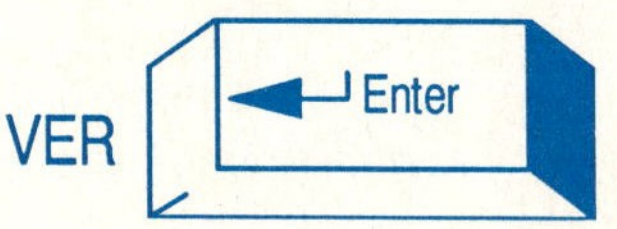

If you enter a DOS command incorrectly, you will most likely see the message *Bad command or file name* and be returned to the A> prompt. Simply reenter the command correctly.

As you can see, the version number of the DOS you loaded into RAM when you booted your computer is displayed. If you are using Version 3.3,you should see the display

```
IBM Personal Computer DOS Version 3.30
```

The DATE Command

The **DATE** internal command can be used to check or change the date logged into your computer at boot-up. Enter

❑

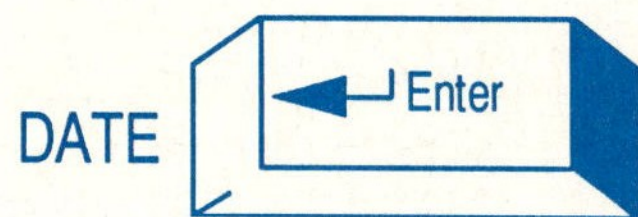

If you logged in with the date September 10, 1991, you should see the display

```
Current date is TUE 9-10-1991
Enter new date(mm-dd-yy):
```

You can change this date by entering a new one in the prescribed format or leave it unchanged by simply depressing the [Enter] key. Press

❑

and you should be back at the A> prompt.

The TIME Command

You can also check or change the current time by using the **TIME** internal command. To check the time, enter

❑

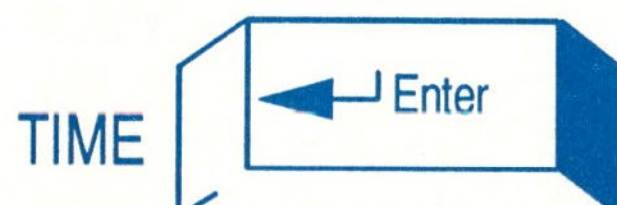

Assuming you entered the time 16:20 when you started your computer, you should see a computer prompt similar to

```
Current time 16:22:50.04
Enter new time:
```

As with the DATE command, you can change the time by entering a new time in the prescribed format or leaving it unchanged by depressing the [Enter] key. Press

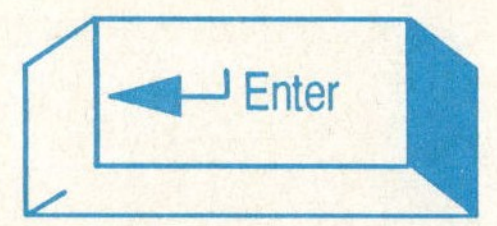

and return to the A> prompt.

The CLS Command

Now let's clear the screen of the previous entries and responses. This is a job for the **CLS** internal command. To see how it works, enter

Now your display screen should be completely blank except for the system prompt A> that appears at the top of the screen.

The DIR Command

Earlier we learned that the names of the files on a disk are kept in the disk directory, along with other pertinent information, such as the size of the file, the date, and time it was created. Let's take a peek at the directory of your DOS/Operating disk. This is a job for DOS's internal command **DIR**. Insert your DOS/Operating disk in drive A: and type

The DIR command will not list any files with a hidden attribute.

This command lists each file on the disk. But, because there were so many files on this disk, they scrolled on and off the screen before you could read them. When the screen stops scrolling, you should see the bottom portion of the list, as shown in Figure T1-7.

For each file on the disk, the DIR command lists the filename, extension, size in bytes, date, and time it was created or last updated. For clarity, no period is shown between the filename and its extension, if any.

You are probably wondering how you can view the beginning of the directory. This can be done several ways. One way is to cause the DIR command to pause or cancel by using your keyboard keys. *This method can be used for any DOS command*. The keys you press depend upon which keyboard you are using (see Fig. T1-4). Table T1-2 provides the information about how you can pause or cancel a DOS command.

TABLE T1-2
DOS Pause and Cancel Keys

Keyboard Type	To Pause	To Cancel
Standard	Press and hold [Ctrl]: then tap [Num Lock]. (Use the Space bar to continue listing).	Press and hold [Ctrl]; then tap [Scroll Lock]. (This is also called [Ctrl]-[Break].)
Enhanced	Press [Pause]. (Use the Space bar to continue listing.)	Press and hold [Ctrl]; then press [Pause]. (This is also called [Ctrl]-[Break]).

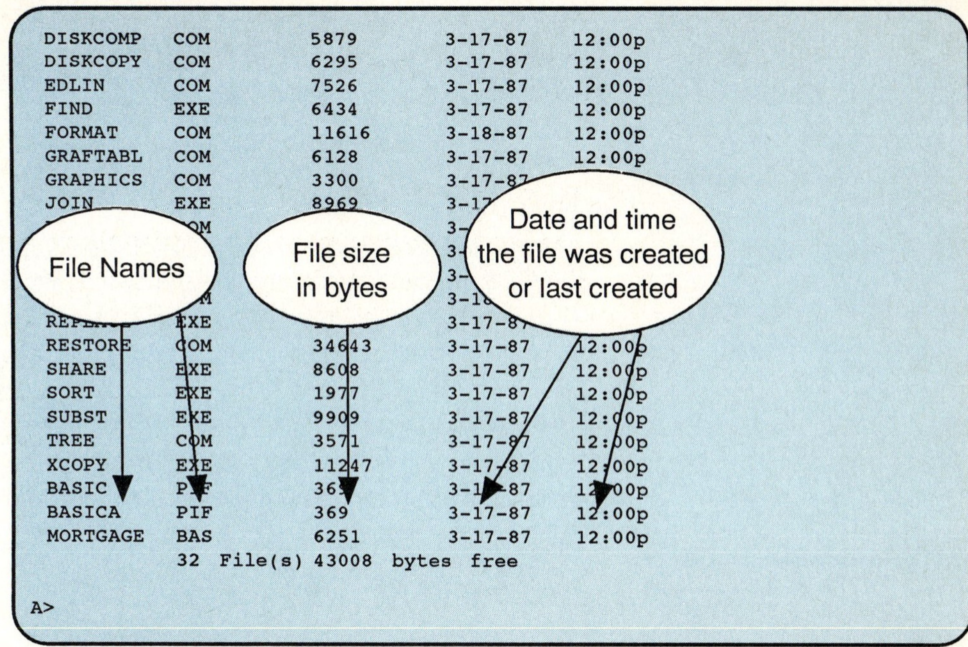

FIGURE T1-7
Directory of DOS disk.*

Another way we can cause the DIR command to pause is to specify the /P option. Enter

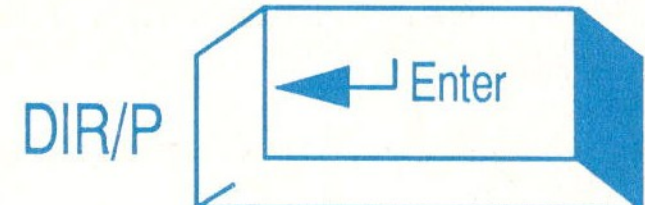

❑

As you can see, the /P option causes the display to *pause* after 23 lines have been displayed, allowing us to read one screen before proceeding to the next. Depressing any key will display another 23 lines, and so on until the entire directory has been displayed. To complete your directory listing, depress

❑

Before we move on, let's clear the screen. Enter

❑

Another possibility exists if we have a large number of files and wish to see the file names but not the size or creation dates of the files. Enter

❑

---

*Because you may be using a different version of DOS than 3.3, the files you see on the display may be different from what is shown here.

The / W parameter produces a five-column-*wide* display of the directory. Note, however, that the file size, date, and time of creation are now omitted (see Fig. T1-8).

FIGURE T1-8
Wide Directory of DOS Disk.

```
A>DIR/W

 Volume in drive A has no label
 Directory of  A:\

APPEND   EXE   ASSIGN   COM   ATTRIB  EXE   BACKUP  COM   BASIC  COM
BASICA   COM   CHKDSK   COM   COMMAND COM   COMP    COM   DEBUG  COM
DISKCOMP COM   DISKCOPY COM   EDLIN   COM   FIND    EXE   FORMAT COM
GRAFTABL COM   GRAPHICS COM   JOIN    EXE   LABEL   COM   MORE   COM
PRINT    COM   RECOVER  COM   REPLACE EXE   RESTORE COM   SHARE  EXE
SORT     EXE   SUBST    EXE   TREE    COM   XCOPY   EXE   BASIC  PIF
BASICA   PIF   MORTGAGE BAS
       32 File(s)     43008 bytes free

A>
```

Wild Cards

Wild card characters enable you to execute commands in an abbreviated form. The two wild cards used in DOS are * and ?.

The Asterisk (*)

The * character may be used as the main file name and/or the extension; it has the effect of saying *accept all characters here*. For example, expanding on the previous examples of the DIR command, * .COM stands for *any* file that has the extension COM. Enter

This will cause the computer to display *all* files located on the A: drive that have the extension COM (see Fig. T1-9).

The wild card can also be used when you are looking for a particular file but know only a portion of the name. Enter

This will cause all files on the disk in the A: drive to be displayed that have a name beginning with the letter S and any extension (see Fig. T1-10).

What do you think executing DIR A:*.* will cause to happen? It will do the same thing as DIR A:—list all files on the disk in the A: drive.

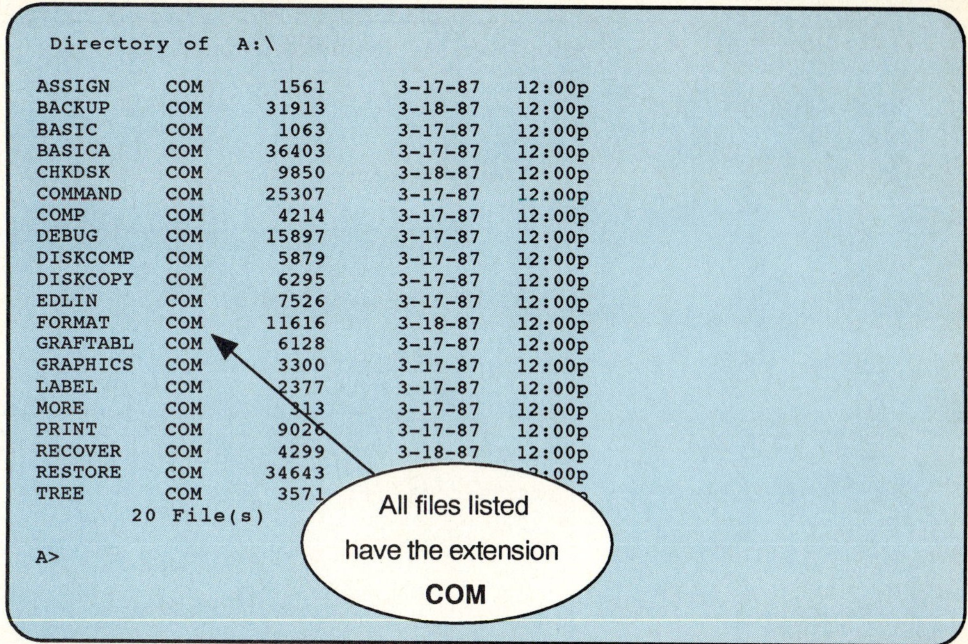

```
 Directory of  A:\

ASSIGN     COM        1561      3-17-87    12:00p
BACKUP     COM       31913      3-18-87    12:00p
BASIC      COM        1063      3-17-87    12:00p
BASICA     COM       36403      3-17-87    12:00p
CHKDSK     COM        9850      3-18-87    12:00p
COMMAND    COM       25307      3-17-87    12:00p
COMP       COM        4214      3-17-87    12:00p
DEBUG      COM       15897      3-17-87    12:00p
DISKCOMP   COM        5879      3-17-87    12:00p
DISKCOPY   COM        6295      3-17-87    12:00p
EDLIN      COM        7526      3-17-87    12:00p
FORMAT     COM       11616      3-18-87    12:00p
GRAFTABL   COM        6128      3-17-87    12:00p
GRAPHICS   COM        3300      3-17-87    12:00p
LABEL      COM        2377      3-17-87    12:00p
MORE       COM         313      3-17-87    12:00p
PRINT      COM        9026      3-17-87    12:00p
RECOVER    COM        4299      3-18-87    12:00p
RESTORE    COM       34643
TREE       COM        3571
        20 File(s)

A>
```


FIGURE T1-9
Directory of All Files with the Extension COM.

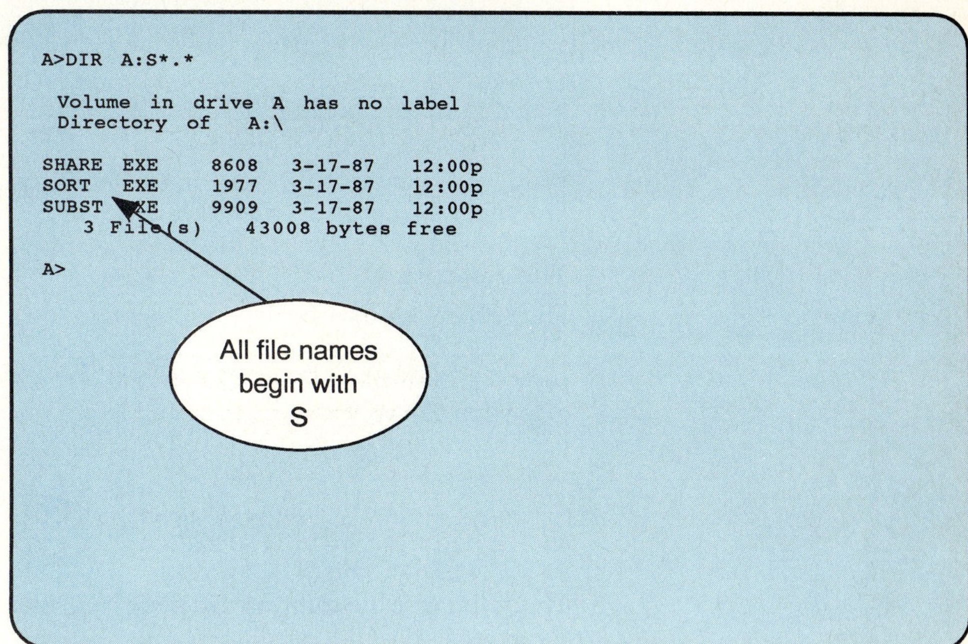

```
A>DIR A:S*.*

 Volume in drive A has no label
 Directory of   A:\

SHARE  EXE     8608   3-17-87    12:00p
SORT   EXE     1977   3-17-87    12:00p
SUBST  EXE     9909   3-17-87    12:00p
    3 File(s)    43008 bytes free

A>
```


FIGURE T1-10
DIR of All Files That Begin with the Letter *S*.

The Question Mark (?)

The ? wild card has the effect of saying *accept any character in this position.* For example, to get a list of all directory entries having file names of four characters, beginning with SO and ending with T, and having *any* character in the third position and an EXE extension, enter the command ❑

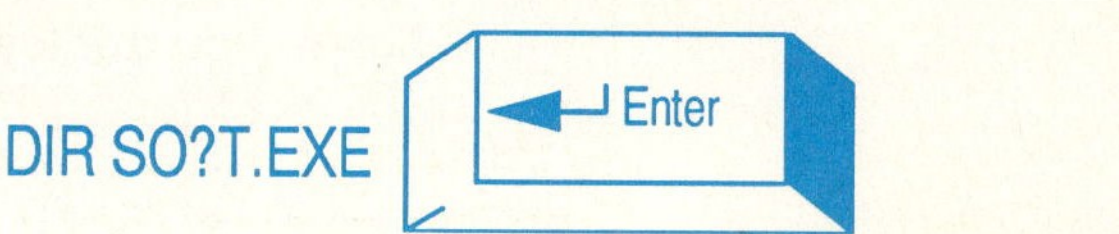

DOS will respond with the screen shown in Figure T1-11.
Let's play with this wild card. Enter

❑

and your screen should contain the display shown in Figure T1-12. This same result could have been achieved using the * wild card and what command? If you answered DIR DISK*.COM [Enter], you would be correct.

FIGURE T1-11

DIR of Files with Names of the Form SO?T.EXE.

```
A>DIR SO?T.EXE

 Volume in drive A has no label
 Directory of  A:\

SORT   EXE   1977   3-17-87   12:00p
  1 File(s)  43008 bytes free

A>
```

FIGURE T1-12

DIR of All Files with Filenames Beginning with DISK and Having the Extension COM.

```
A>DIR DISK????.COM

 Volume in drive A has no label
 Directory of  A:\

DISKCOMP COM    5879    3-17-87   12:00p
DISKCOPY COM    6295    3-17-87   12:00p
       2 File(s)    43008 bytes free

A>
```

The wild card characters can be used with most DOS commands. In particular, they are very useful when used with DIR, COPY, and DEL. When used with the DIR command, they can help you locate a file on a disk while knowing only part of the file name.

Printing the Screen

If you hold the [Shift] key down and press the [Print Screen] key, the current contents of the screen will be sent to the printer.

If you hold the Control key [Ctrl] down and depress the [Print Screen] key, you activate your printer and anything displayed on the screen from that point on will also be printed. To deactivate the printer, press [Ctrl]-[Print Screen] again.

Additionally, if you follow up a DOS command with the symbols **>PRN**, any output that would have been displayed will be directed to your printer. Lets try this. If you have a printer, turn it on. If your computer is connected to a printer via a switch box, be sure the switch box is set to your computer. If you are having trouble, ask your instructor or the laboratory assistant for help. If you would like to print, enter

DIR/W A:>PRN

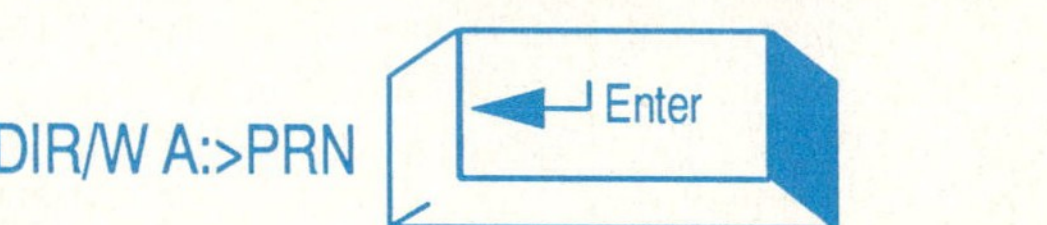

❑

Otherwise continue reading.

If you decided to print, your printer should be printing a wide directory of the disk in the A: drive. When you are finished, remove the output from your printer and clear your screen by entering

CLS

❑

Formatting a Disk

When DOS writes on a disk, data is placed in concentric circular areas called **tracks**. Each track is then subdivided into a fixed number of segments called **sectors** (see Fig. T1-13).

Before DOS can write to a disk, you must prepare it for use by writing the tracks and sectors boundaries on the disk. This process is referred to as **formatting** the disk.

OK. Let's clear the screen and format the disk. Enter

CLS

❑

If you attempt to access an unformatted disk, DOS will issue a command such as

```
General Failure error
 reading drive B
Abort, Retry, Fail?
```

This message indicates that DOS cannot read your disk. If you see such a message, enter an A to abort.

Now, let's format a disk. Formatting is accomplished by the DOS external command **FORMAT**. Place your DOS/Startup disk in drive A: and a blank unformatted disk in drive B:; Enter

❑

This command, as all DOS commands, may be entered in either uppercase, or lowercase letters. The computer will respond with:

```
Insert new diskette for drive B:
and strike ENTER when ready
```

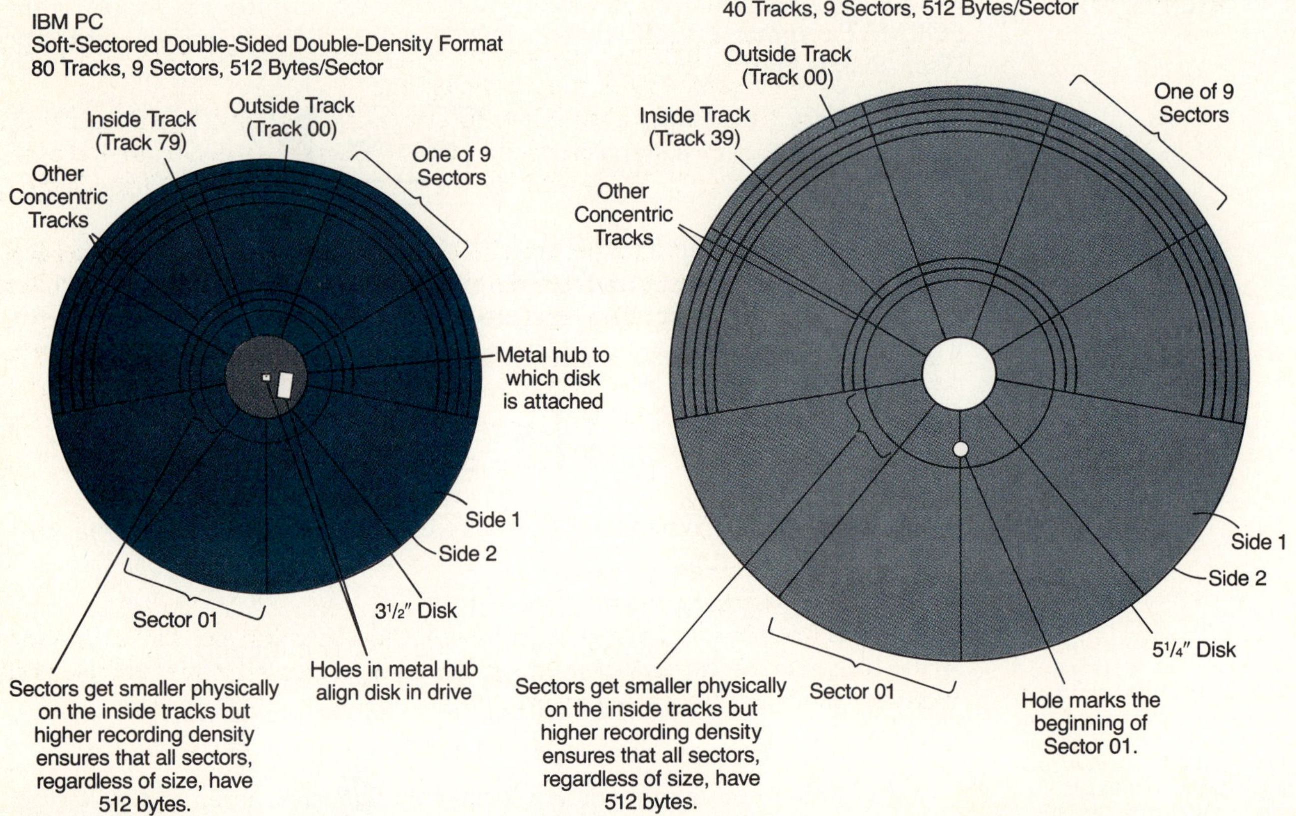

FIGURE T1-13
The Format of a Disk.

You should already have a blank disk in drive B:, but if you don't, place a blank disk in B: and press

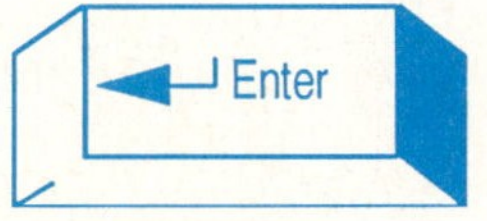

❑

The disks will begin to whirl, and the computer will start formatting your disk. When it finishes formatting, it will display

```
Format complete

    362496 bytes total disk space
    362496 bytes available on disk

Format another (Y/N)?
```

These figures will differ if you are formatting a high-capacity disk or if your disk contains bad sectors. Assuming we don't wish to format another disk, enter

❑

Congratulations! You just created your Work disk. Remove it from drive B:, label it "Work disk," and reinsert it in drive B:.

Creating a Bootable Disk While Formatting

Often it is desirable to create a disk that can be used to boot the system as well as to store files. This can be accomplished by adding the /S option to the FORMAT command. Verify that the DOS/Startup disk is in drive A: and your Work disk is in drive B:; enter

❑

The computer will respond with:

```
Insert new diskette for drive B:
and strike ENTER when ready
```

Since your Work disk is already in drive B:, simply press

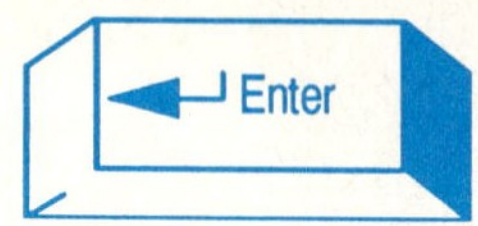

❑

to begin formatting. When DOS finishes formatting, it will report the results

```
Format complete
System transferred

     362496 bytes total disk space
      78848 bytes used by system
     283648 bytes available on disk

Format another (Y/N)?
```

Notice that we formatted the same disk twice. A floppy disk can be formatted many times. This is one way of clearing a disk of all stored information. Just remember, each time a disk is formatted, *all information previously stored on it will be lost.* If you're ever in doubt as to the contents of a disk, use the DIR command to list its contents before formatting it. You never can tell if important files exist on a disk until you look.

Assuming you do not wish to format another disk, enter

❑

Note that for this version of DOS, 78,848 bytes were used by the system. A directory of this disk will show the file COMMAND.COM but not the hidden files. This will be true for all bootable disks; only the number of bytes will vary, depending on the version of DOS you are using.

This disk now contains the DOS internal commands and can be used to boot your computer. If you wish to verify that the disk is bootable, place it in drive A: and warm boot your system by using the [Ctrl], [Alt], and [Del] keys. If you do so, be sure to enter the correct date and time. Then, move your Work disk to drive B: and insert your DOS/Startup disk back in drive A:.

Adding a Volume Label While Formatting

With the /V option of the FORMAT command, you can format a disk and also record a **volume label** on it. DOS refers to disk names as volume labels. To format a disk, copy the system and enter a volume label, place the DOS/Startup disk in the A: drive and your Work disk in the B: drive, and enter

❑

Respond to the FORMAT prompts as before. After DOS reports the results of formatting the disk, it will issue the additional prompt

```
Volume label (11 characters, ENTER for none)?
```

Enter *your last name* as the volume label

And, in response to the prompt

```
Format another (Y/N)?
```

enter

Now, when you ask DOS for a directory of this disk, your name will also be displayed. To see this, enter

and observe your name appears after the words, *Volume in drive B is.*

If your instructor collects your disk to verify your work, there is no need to write your name on the label. A DIR will tell your instructor whose disk is being graded, provided you created a volume label using your name.

The COPY Command

To copy a file from one place (device) to another, we use the DOS internal command **COPY**. It can be used to copy files from one disk to another or to the same disk, to copy from the console (keyboard) to disk, and to use COPY to print a file. Let's investigate some of these uses now.

COPY from Disk to Disk

To copy one or more files or even an entire disk to another disk using the COPY command, you must place the disk containing the file to be copied in one drive and the disk onto which this file is to be copied in another drive. The process is not dependent on which disk is placed in which drive.

When a COPY command is issued, DOS will direct the computer to read the **source file**—the file listed first and the file to be copied. If a drive is specified, the source file will be read from that drive; otherwise it will be read from the default drive.

The source file is then written to the **target file**—the file listed second and the file to be created. If a drive is specified for the target file, the source file will be copied to that drive; if none is specified, the source file will be copied to the default drive. If no file name is specified for the target file, the source file name will be assumed.

Let's check it out and copy the file REMARK1.BAT from your Learning disk to your Work disk. Place your Learning disk in drive A: and your Work disk in drive B:; enter

After a moment of disk activity, the file REMARK1.BAT will be copied from the disk in drive A: to the disk in drive B:.

DOS will confirm the success of the operation by displaying the message

```
1 File(s) copied
```

As you use DOS commands more and more, you will get a feel for what is happening simply by listening to the disk activity and watching the drive lights. If you observed these items during the execution of the above command, you would have heard the source drive whirl and seen it light momentarily, confirming that the source file was being read. This would have been followed by similar activity from the target drive, confirming that the target file was being written.

Examples of COPY commands and their meanings appear in Table T1-3.

If you misspell the name of the source file or name a source file not contained on the source disk, DOS will issue the message

```
... file not found
0 File(s) copied.
```

To rectify this, either correct your spelling or replace the source disk with one containing the source file and repeat the command.

TABLE T1-3
Valid and Invalid Examples of COPY Statement Usage

COPY Statement	Meaning
COPY A:FILE1.A B:FILE1.A	Copies file FILE1.A from drive A: to drive B: and assigns the copy the same name.
COPY A:FILE1.A B:	Copies file FILE1.A from drive A: to drive B: and assigns the copy the file name FILE1.A. As you can see, this is preferred over the above COPY command because there is less to type.
COPY FILE1.A FILE2.A	Copies file FILE1.A from the default drive to the default drive and assigns the copy the new name FILE2.A. This is how to make a copy of a file located on the same disk as the original.
COPY FILE1.A FILE1.A	Is *Illegal* because this attempts to copy a file onto itself.
COPY FILE1.A A:FILE1.A	Copies file FILE1.A from the default drive to drive A:. This would be illegal if the default drive were drive A:, since it would attempt to copy a file onto itself.
COPY A: B:FILE1.A	Is *Illegal* because no source file was specified.
COPY A;REM1.TXT B:	Is *Illegal* because you must use a colon after the drive letter.
COPY A:*.COM B:	Copies all files on drive A: with the file extension COM to drive B:. As you can see, wild cards can be very useful.
COPY B:MYFILE.* A:	Copies files from drive B: with the filename MYFILE and having any or no extension to drive A:.
COPY A:*.* B:	Copies all visible files (no hidden files) from drive A: to drive B:. You can use this to make quick backup copies of your disks. Never forget this one.

COPY from Console (Keyboard) to Disk

You can also use the COPY command to copy a file from the console or display screen to disk. For example, to initiate a copy from the screen to your Work disk, place your Work disk in drive B: and enter

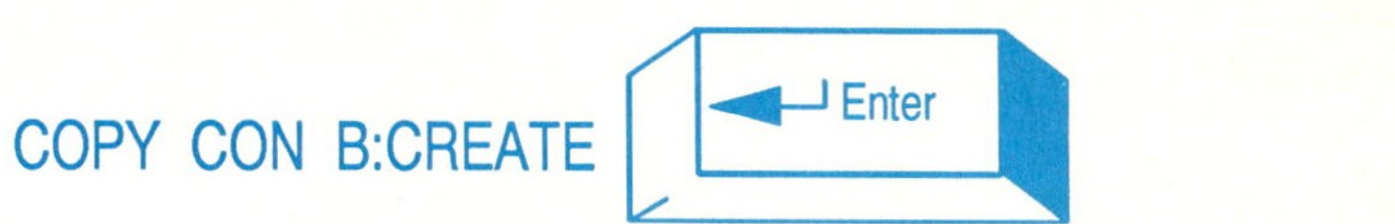

❏

Before you press the [Enter] key to move to the next line, check the contents of the line you are on and remove any typing, spelling, and spacing errors. For example, if you have spelled something wrong, correct it by using the [Backspace] key. If you press the [Enter] key and then discover an error, BREAK out of the COPY command by pressing [Ctrl]-[Break]. Then start the process over from the very beginning.

Notice that for the first time you pressed the [Enter] key and DOS took no action except to move the cursor to the next line. Actually, when you pressed the [Enter] key, you told DOS to prepare to copy whatever is displayed on the console or screen, character for character, to the file CREATE on drive B:. Let's type something to be copied. Enter

THIS IS THE FIRST FILE I EVER CREATED.

❏

After you enter these two lines, press the **[F6] Function key** to mark the end of the file and then the [Enter] key to save it. (*Note*: Do not type an F and a 6.) Do it now. ❑

The drive light on drive B: will go on momentarily, indicating your file is being written on that disk, and you should see

```
1 File(s) copied
```

Congratulations! You have successfully created your first file. If you don't believe it, enter ❑

to see the file name CREATE displayed in the directory of your Work disk.

To really be certain your file has been faithfully created, type its contents on your display screen. Enter the command ❑

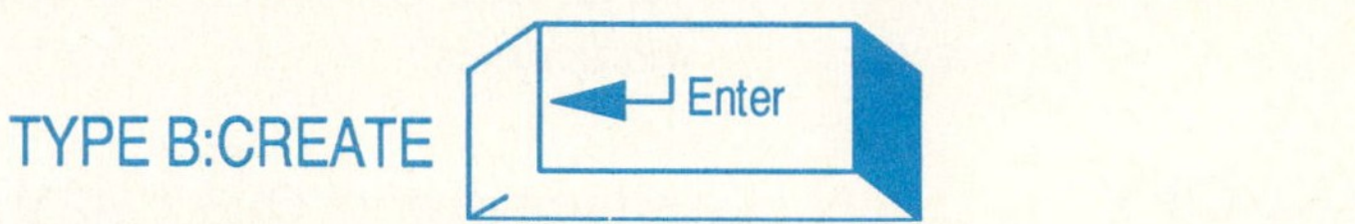

to which the computer responds

```
THIS IS THE FIRST FILE I EVER CREATED.
IT WASN'T SO BAD.
```

If you discover an error, repeat the process of creating and saving the batch file.

Using COPY To Print a File

Would you like a permanent copy of your first file to save as a keepsake? One way of getting a printout is to copy the file to the printer, known to DOS as PRN. Check that your printer is on and type ❑

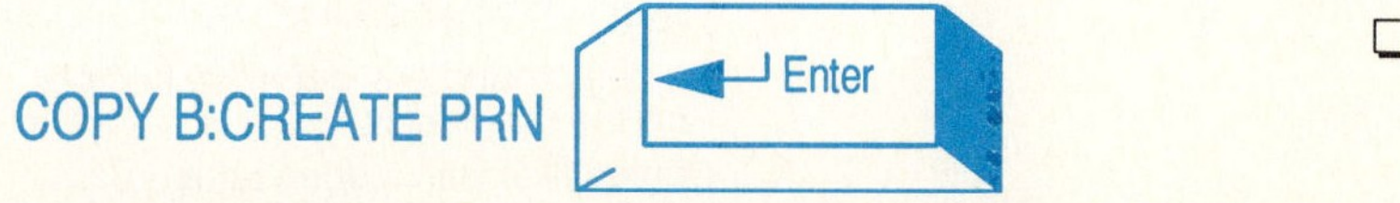

and your file will be printed. Tear off the page and it's yours.

Using COPY To Combine Files

The COPY command can also be used to combine two or more files into a single new file. For example, if you wanted to combine the monthly sales files SALES.JAN, SALES.FEB, SALES.MAR into a single sales file for the first quarter, SALES.Q1, you could enter

COPY SALES.JAN+SALES.FEB+

If no target file is specified, the combined file will be stored in the file named first; it will replace the previous contents of that file. Thus, if the target file SALES.Q1 had not been specified, the combined file would have replaced the previous contents of SALES.JAN.

COPY and Hidden Files

Table T1-3 illustrates the versatility of the COPY command. It is a very powerful yet flexible command. It does, however, have a limitation—it cannot copy a file with a *hidden* attribute. If you must copy a hidden file, you have two alternatives: (1) Use the DOS command DISKCOPY (it will be discussed next) to duplicate the entire disk exactly, including hidden files, or (2) use one of the many routines available outside of DOS to remove the hidden attribute and make the file visible.

The DISKCOPY Command

An alternate way of copying all files from one disk to another—that is, from the *source disk* to the *target disk*—is with the command **DISKCOPY**. Because this is an external command and is not stored in RAM, the DOS/Operating disk must be placed in the default drive before this command is issued. Once entered, the DISKCOPY routine will confirm the placement of the source and target disks. When the DISKCOPY is completed, both disks will be *identical, including any hidden files.*

DISKCOPY Versus COPY *.*

Although both DISKCOPY and COPY *.* copy all files listed in the directory of the source disk to the target disk, they differ in several important ways (see Table T1-4).

TABLE T1-4
Comparison of COPY *.* and DISKCOPY Commands

Feature	DISKCOPY	COPY *.*
Command type	External	Internal
Writes over files previously contained on the target disk	Yes	No
Automatically formats the target disk.	Yes	No
Copies around any defective sectors on the target disk	No	Yes
Copies files with hidden attribute	Yes	No

Would you like to try DISKCOPY? Why not. Let's make a copy of your Work disk. Place your DOS/Operating disk in drive A: and a new disk (not your Work disk) in drive B:, and call up the A> prompt. Now enter

❑

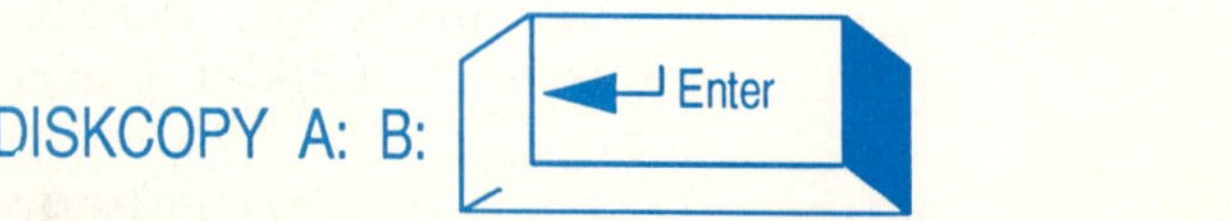

Depending on the version of DOS you are using, you should see a prompt similar to:

```
Insert SOURCE diskette into drive A:
Insert TARGET diskette into drive B:
Press any key when ready  . . .
```

In response, place your Work disk in drive A:; the target disk has already been installed in drive B:. Now press

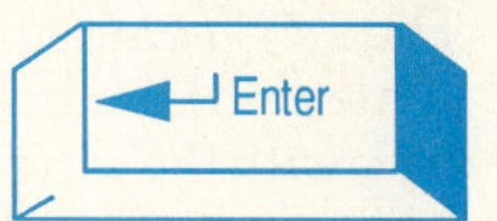

to start the copy process. When the process is completed, your computer responds with

```
Copy another diskette (Y/N)?
```

Assuming you do not wish to use this command again, respond by typing

N

and DOS will display the familiar A>. Remove the disk from drive B: and label it "Temp Disk."

DISKCOPY may not be used with disks of different sizes or capacities or with hard disks. If your computer has only one drive, you can use the command DISKCOPY A: A: to carry out the aforementioned procedures.

A word of caution: Because the DISKCOPY command erases everything previously stored on the target disk, it is a good practice to **write-protect** the source disk before the operation begins in case you accidently insert the disks in the wrong drives. 5¼-inch floppy disks have a **write-protect notch** on the right side as you look at the label, whereas 3½-inch disks employ a **write-protect switch**, a rectangular cutout to the top right as you look at the label (see Fig. T1-14). Covering the notch on a 5¼-inch disk or opening the switch on a 3½-inch disk write-protects the disk. While write-protected, a disk can only be read.

FIGURE T1-14
File-Protecting Floppy Disks.

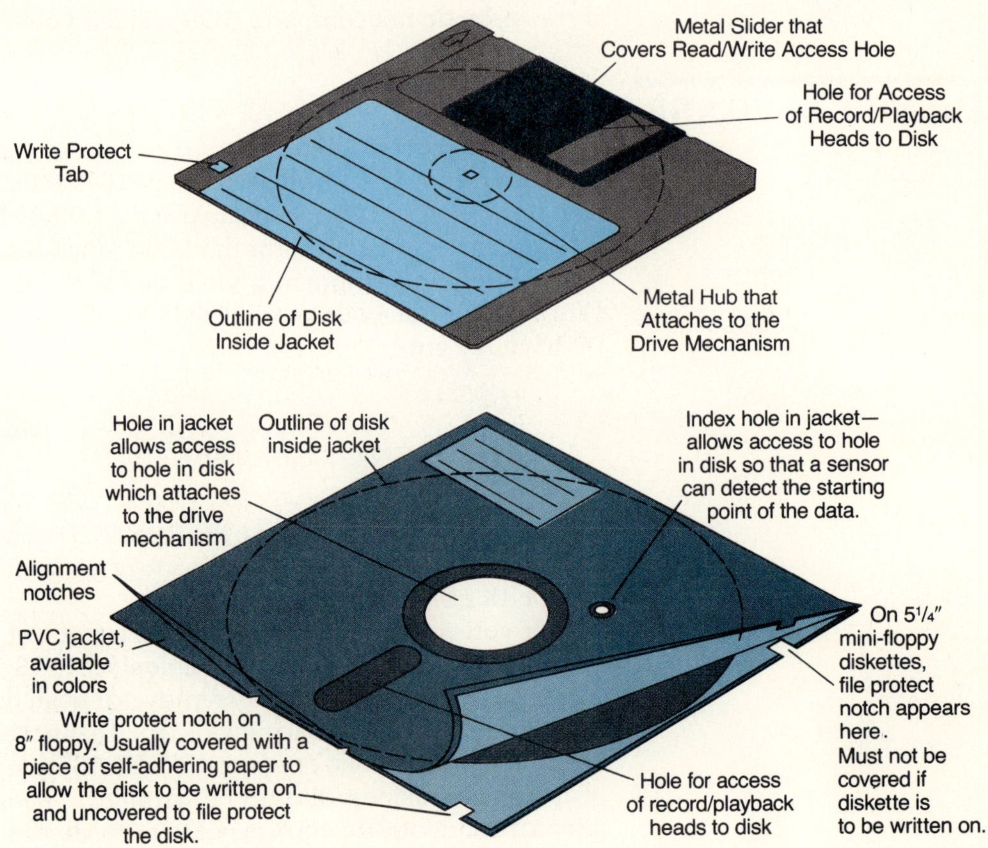

The DISKCOMP Command

The DOS command **DISKCOMP** (Disk Compare) allows you to compare the contents of two disks to assure that they are identical. Let's compare your Work disk with the copy of the Temp disk you produced earlier using the DISKCOPY command. Begin by placing your DOS/Operating disk in drive A: and your Temp disk in drive B:. Enter the command

❑

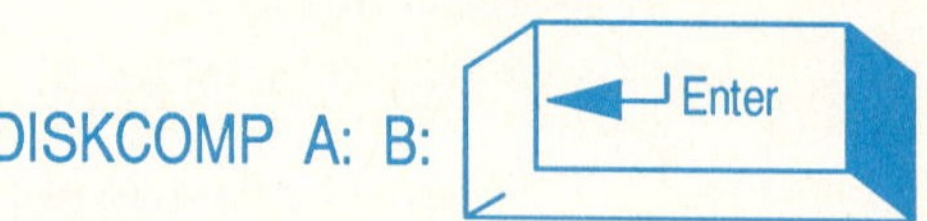

When you see the prompt

```
Insert FIRST diskette in drive A:
Insert SECOND diskette in drive B:
Press any key when ready    . . .
```

replace the DOS/Operating disk in drive A: with your Work disk and press any key.

If the copies are identical, you should see the message

```
Diskettes compare ok
Compare more diskettes? (Y/N)?
```

Type:

N ❑

If the disks do not compare, DOS will tell you.

The DEL or ERASE Command

Eventually, your disk will become so full that there is no room for new files. To remove unwanted files, you can use the **DEL** or **ERASE** command. These two internal commands perform the same functions.

To test this command, we'll delete the file REMARK1.BAT from your Work disk. Place your Work disk in the B: drive and the DOS/Operating disk in drive A:; enter

❑

When the disk activity ceases, the file will be gone. No message will be printed confirming this fact. Take a directory of your Work disk and verify that REMARK1.BAT was deleted.

If you accidently delete a file, all is not lost. The good news is that it can generally be restored. This is possible since DOS does not actually erase the file when it deletes it. DOS simply removes it from the directory making it temporarily inaccessible. The bad news is that it cannot be restored with DOS. This can be done only with one of several UNERASE programs available separately (a program no business should be without). The important thing to remember after an accidental deletion is not to write anything new on the disk until after the accidentally deleted file has been restored or that file might be written over and permanently lost.

You can also use wild cards to assist in deleting files. But, because of their global implications, extreme care should be exercised when using wild cards with the DEL or ERASE command. Let's use the wild card * to delete *all* the files on your Temp disk. Inser the Temp disk in drive B: and enter

❑

Realizing this is a drastic move, DOS requests verification that this is what you really want to do. It does so with the prompt

```
Are you sure (Y/N)?
```

In our case we're sure, aren't we? With a little apprehension, enter

❑

and DOS will give you back the system prompt A>.

Before moving on, clear the display screen.

CHKDSK—A Useful Command

CHKDSK is an external DOS command that analyzes the file allocation table (FAT) and determines, among other things, how much disk space is assigned to files and how much is free. Let's give it a try. But first, since this is an external DOS command, make certain that your DOS/Operating disk is in drive A: then enter

❑

You should see a display similar to that of Figure T1-15.

The exact numbers displayed on your screen may vary from those shown, depending on the version of DOS you are using, the memory in your computer, and the storage capacity and physical condition of your floppy disk.

The first four lines of output provide information about your floppy disk. In the first line we see that the total disk capacity is 362,496 bytes. For our purposes, 1 **byte** is capable of storing one character of information. The next line tells us that there is one hidden file. You may recall that a hidden file cannot be seen by ordinary DOS operations. This file occupies no space since it is reserved by DOS for a special purpose. Next we see that there are 32 user files present, and these files occupy 319,488 bytes (remember different versions of DOS will have a different number of user files). **User files** are ones that we can see by name when we take a directory of the disk. In general, user files are program or data files.

Since it is likely that you are an inexperienced computer user, it will be hard for you to determine how big or small a file is. Thus, we suggest that you follow a simple rule of thumb—if you have less than 50,000 bytes of free space on a disk, do not attempt to store any new files or add to existing files on that disk.

Notice that on the DOS/Operating disk, the majority of the total disk space is taken up by user files. What user files? The program files that facilitate DOS external commands.

The CHKDSK command also tells us how much free space is available on a disk and in memory. The amount of free space available on a disk will determine whether or not you can save new files or add to files that are already stored on the disk.

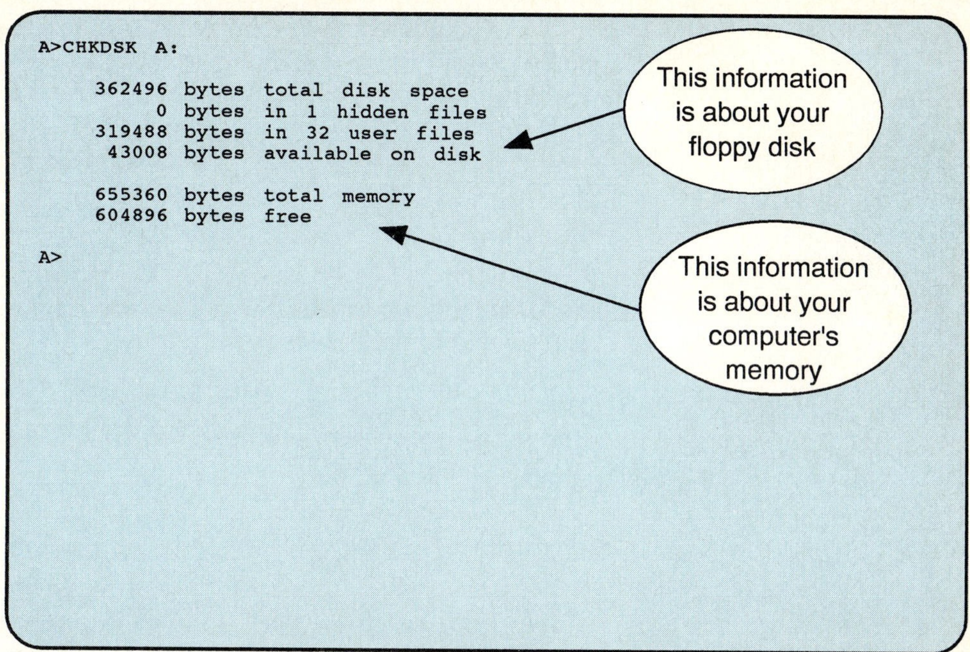

FIGURE T1-15
The Screen Display Produced by a CHKDSK Command.

If, when you execute the CHKDSK command, you see a line stating that you have a number of bytes in **bad sectors**, don't be alarmed. This simply alerts you to the fact that one or more areas of that disk are not usable. This can happen occasionally, but it should not happen often. If this happens with a new disk, return it to the place of purchase.

The last two lines displayed by the CHKDSK command indicate that 655,360 bytes of total memory are available to DOS and that 604,896 bytes are free for your use. By taking the difference of these two numbers, we see that 50,464 bytes of our total memory are being used. What do you think might be stored in this space?

If you said DOS internal commands, you would be correct. These commands were placed in memory when you booted your system. Only a minimum of essential DOS commands are stored internally in order to keep free as much memory as possible.

The CHKDSK *.* Option

After a disk has been in use for some time, new files will have been added and old files deleted. Modified files will have been increased or decreased in size. Space freed up by modified or deleted files becomes available for storing new files. If this process continues for any period of time, the free space available on the disk will not be in adjacent or contiguous blocks of bytes but in disjointed blocks. Now, when DOS writes a file to this disk, it may be forced to use blocks of free space that are widely dispersed about the disk. The result is a **fragmented file.**

The greater the fragmentation of files, the more the disk performance drops and the slower it reads and writes. Therefore, it is a good practice to test for fragmented files occasionally and, if they are present, remove them. The ***.*** option of the CHKDSK command can be used to locate fragmented files on a disk. To see how this option works, enter

❑

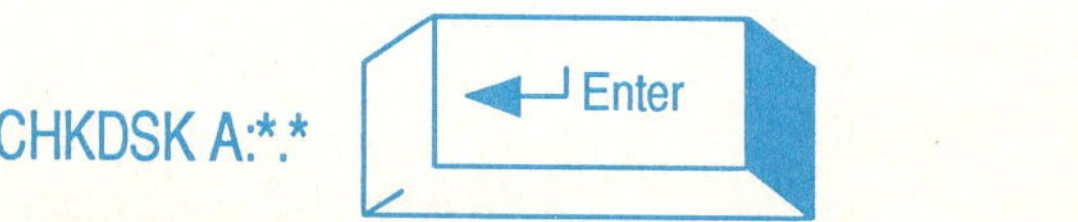

You should see a display similar to that shown in Figure T1-15 but with the added line

```
All specified file(s) are contiguous.
```

This indicates that each file is stored in adjacent or contiguous blocks and that no files are fragmented. Had one or more fragmented files been present, you would have seen the name of each fragmented file followed by the number of noncontiguous blocks in that file.

Once it has been determined that a disk contains fragmented files, there are a number of ways to correct the situation. For our purposes, the simplest of these is to copy all the files from the old floppy to a new floppy disk. The files will be stored contiguously on the new disk, automatically. The old disk can then be formatted and reused.

Other Commonly Used DOS Commands

The TYPE Command

Any time you want to see the *contents* of a file, you could use the **TYPE** command. This is an internal command and has the general format

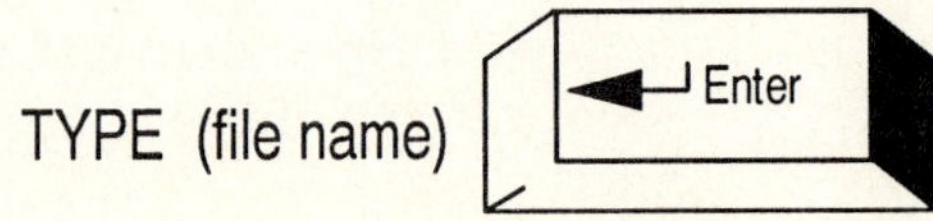

If the file name has an extension, it must be stated when using this command. To test this command, place your DOS/Operating disk in drive A: and your Learning disk in drive B:; enter

❑

You should see the screen shown in Figure T1-16.

FIGURE T1-16
The Screen Display of File REMARK1.BAT Using a TYPE Command.

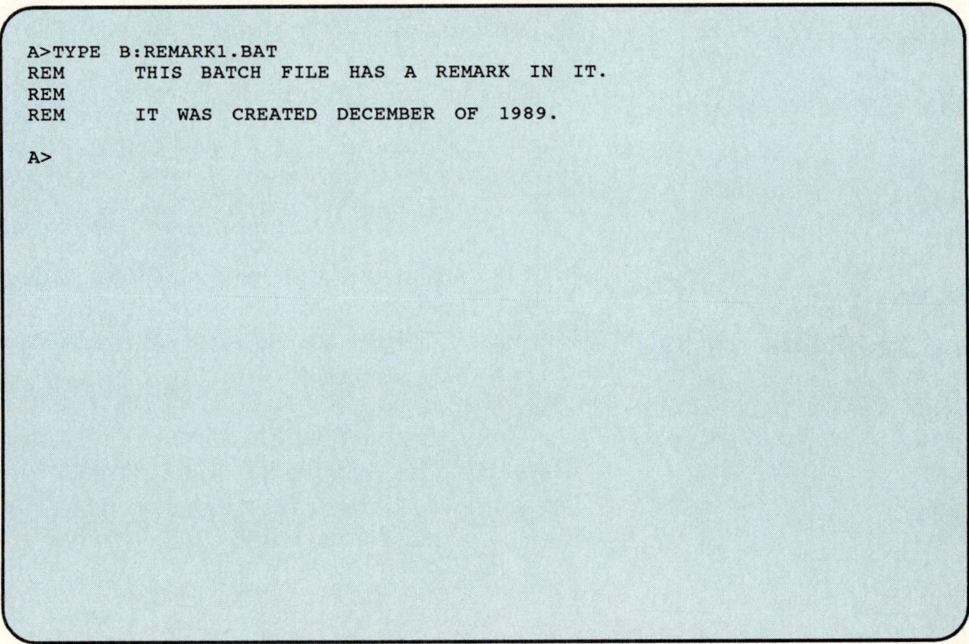

This is the display of a batch file, a special command file about which you will learn more later. Notice that the display of this file is very legible, but this will not always be the case. The contents of files with the extensions BAT, DOC, and TXT are generally legible, whereas displaying the contents of files with the extensions COM and EXE will produce gibberish. It all depends on the form in which the computer stored the file in the first place. Let's try displaying a file with an extention EXE. Verify that your DOS/Operating disk is in drive A:, clear your display screen, and enter

❑

See what we mean? Gibberish!

The REN Command

The **REN** internal command renames DOS files. For example, executing the command REN B:FILE1.DOC NEWFILE would rename the file FILE1.DOC, NEWFILE.

Let's experiment and rename the file REMARK1.BAT that is located on your Learning disk. Place your Learning disk in drive B:, clear your screen, and enter

❑

and the file REMARK1.BAT is renamed NEWNAME.BAT. It's that simple. DOS does not produce a specific message confirming the name change. Therefore, if you have any doubts that the operation was carried out successfully, take a directory of the disk. Take a directory of Learning disk now.

For practice, let's change the name back to REMARK1.BAT. Enter

❑

and take a directory of your Learning disk to verify the change.

The COMP Command

To compare two *files* to see if they are identical, we use the **COMP** (Compare) external command. The COMP command will first compare the files with respect to size. If they are different sizes, the computer will respond with

```
Files are different sizes
```

If the files are the same size, DOS will compare the files, byte by byte, and display the location and content of all bytes that differ, if any. If the files are identical, COMP will display the message

```
Files compare ok
```

Let's compare the file REMARK1.BAT on the Learning disk with the file REM1.BAT located on the same disk. Before we begin, insert your DOS/Operating disk into drive A: and your Learning disk into drive B:, and obtain the A> prompt. Now, enter

❑

to which DOS will respond

```
Enter primary file name
```

DOS is requesting the file name of the first file. Our response is to enter

and DOS counters with

```
Enter 2nd file name or drive id
```

Our response to this prompt will depend on several factors. If the second file has the same name as the first but resides on a different drive, we only have to provide the drive designation. Or, if the second file has a different name, we must provide this name and the file designator only if the second file is *not* on the default drive.

In our case, since the files have different names and since the second file does not reside on the default drive, the appropriate response would be to enter

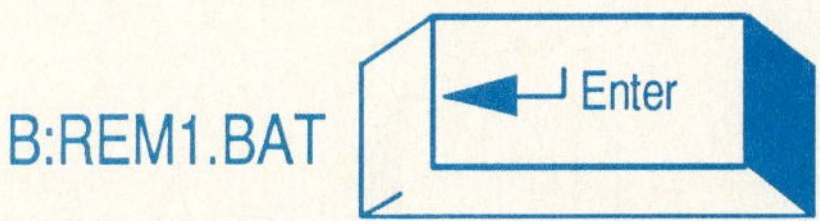

DOS will now initiate the comparison. The result should be

```
B:REMARK1.BAT and B:REM1.BAT
Eof mark not found
Files compare ok
Compare more files (Y/N)?
```

Type

N

to terminate the operation.

DOS Editing Keys

When you type a line and press the [Enter] key, DOS puts a copy of the line in a temporary storage area called the **input buffer**. The line is placed in the buffer so that you can change it or use it again. This eliminates the need to completely reenter the line.

The DOS edit keys are used to edit the line in the input buffer. The function of each editing key is described in Table T1-5.

TABLE T1-5
DOS Editing Keys

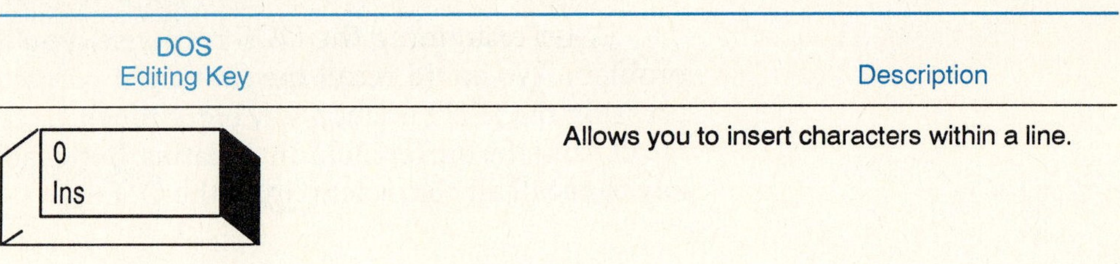

DOS Editing Key	Description
0 Ins	Allows you to insert characters within a line.

TABLE T1-5
(Continued)

DOS Editing Key	Description
Del	Deletes one character in the input buffer. The character in the buffer is not displayed, and the cursor does not move.
Esc	Cancels the line currently being displayed. Pressing the [Enter] key returns you to the system prompt. The buffer is erased.
F1 or 6 ➔	Displays one character from the buffer each time it is pressed.
F2 (char)	Displays all characters in the buffer up to a specified character.
F3	Displays all characters in the buffer.
F4 (char)	Deletes all characters up to but not including the specified character.
F5	Accepts the line you edited as the current buffer line.

Let's see how using these Function keys can save time and keystrokes and eliminate possible new errors when editing a DOS command. Get to the B> prompt and enter

❑

After examining the DOS response, you'll realize there was a typo. No problem. We could recall the first eight correctly typed characters by simply pressing the [F1] Function key eight times, once for each character we wish to recall from the buffer including blanks. Better still, we can use the [F2] Function key to recall all characters up to the O. Enter

and see displayed

```
TYPE REM
```

Now, type an A to correct the O incorrectly entered. We could complete the entry by pressing the [F1] Function key seven times, or we could simply press the [F3] Function key once to accept the remaining characters from the buffer. Press

once. You should now see

```
TYPE REMARK1.BAT
```

Now, tap

to execute the command. Your screen should be similar to that shown in Figure T1-16.

Part II Advanced DOS Concepts

In this section, we investigate some advanced DOS commands. This section can be omitted without affecting your ability to complete subsequent tutorials in any way. Approximately one hour will be needed to complete Part II.

Working with Subdirectories

The large storage capacity of high-density floppy disks and fixed or hard drives often makes it advisable to organize these media into subdirectories. A **subdirectory** is a *file* that contains directory entries identical in form to those found in the main or **root directory** (so called because all branches or subdirectories emanate from it). For example, if your computer system is equipped with a 20-megabyte hard drive, you might create one subdirectory for your DOS external commands, another for your Lotus 1-2-3 program and data files, and still another for your computer games. You might even further subdivide your LOTUS subdirectory into PROGRAM and DATA subdirectories and further subdivide your GAMES subdirectory into EDUC, WAR, and OTHER subdirectories. Then, if you need access to a DOS external command, you would go to the DOS subdirectory; if you wish to play an educational computer game, you would go to EDUC subdirectory of the GAME subdirectory; and so on. Without subdirectories, you could easily exceed the number of files allowed in the root directory or overwrite a file used by one application with a file having the same name but used by another application.

Although your computer may not be equipped with a high-density floppy or hard disk, you can get some experience working with subdirectories using a standard floppy disk. Let's see how its done. Place your DOS / Operating disk in the A: drive and your Work disk in the B: drive, and clear your display screen. Now, enter

to change the default drive to B:.

The MD or MKDIR Command

The DOS external command to make a subdirectory is **MD** or **MKDIR**. Both commands perform the same function—they create a subdirectory. Let's create a subdirectory of the root directory. We'll call it GAME. Enter

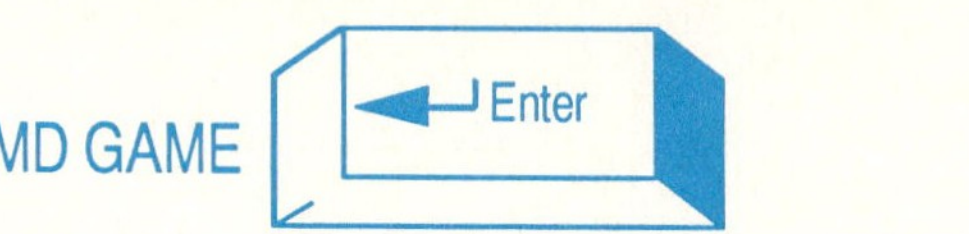

Now, take a directory to see the effect of this command. Enter

Among other things, you will see an entry similar to

```
GAME          <DIR>       09-10-91    6:00p
```

depending on the time and date you do this. Notice the presence of the <DIR> designation. This indicates that this entry is not a program or data file but a subdirectory. You will see a <DIR> designation for each subdirectory of the root directory. This entry immediately will follow the subdirectory name and extension, if any.

What do you think might be accomplished if we were now to enter the command MD GAME\EDUC? The answer is, it would create the subdirectory EDUC of the subdirectory GAME of the root directory.

The CD or CHDIR Command

The **CD** or **CHDIR** command changes the current directory to a different subdirectory or to the root directory. To change from the current or root directory to the GAME subdirectory, enter

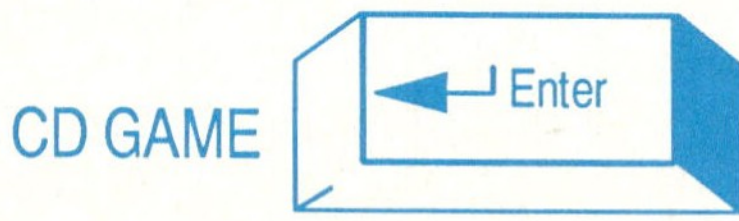

Name the Subdirectory in the System Prompt

How can we be certain that we actually changed the current directory to the subdirectory GAME? One way to always know what subdirectory you're in is to have this information displayed as part of the system prompt. This can be accomplished with the DOS internal command PROMPT. Let's change the system prompt to include the name of the current directory. Enter

and you should now see the new system prompt

```
B:\GAME>
```

The B: indicates the default drive, the backslash, \, refers to the root directory, and GAME specifies the current subdirectory. Similarly, the prompt B:\GAME\EDUC would indicate that you are in the EDUC subdirectory of the GAME subdirectory of the root directory of drive B:. We will discuss shortly the PROMPT command and its uses in greater detail.

Let's clear the screen and then take a directory of our newly created subdirectory. Enter

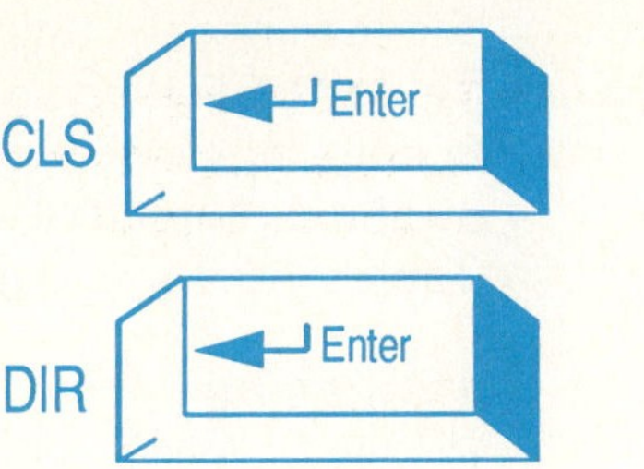

You should see Figure T1-17.

FIGURE T1-17
Directory of the Subdirectory GAME.

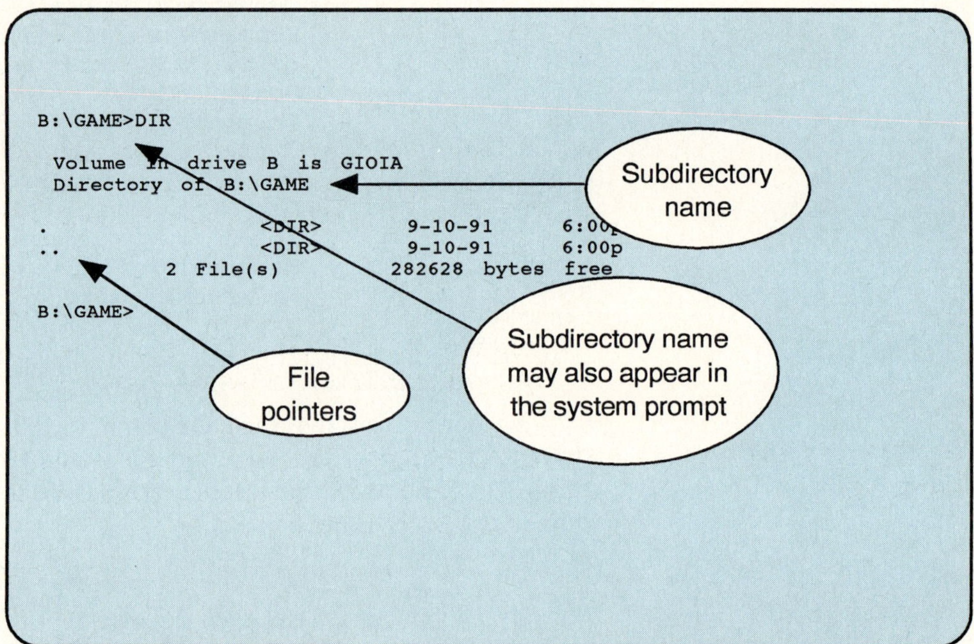

If you look toward the top of your display, you can see that GAME is the current directory. The first two things you see after the volume and subdirectory name are one and two dots, each followed by <DIR>. These are called file pointers and appear in every subdirectory. Their use is beyond the scope of this tutorial. Suffice it to say that each time you create a subdirectory, these two entries will appear. They cannot be removed unless you remove the entire subdirectory.

Express Return to the Root Directory

DOS makes it very easy for us to restore the root directory as the current directory from any subdirectory on a disk; you only need to enter

and DOS speeds us back to the root directory and issues the new system prompt

```
B:\>
```

The PROMPT Command

The **PROMPT** command allows you to change the system prompt to include the current date, time, default drive, directory, DOS version number, and so on. Table T1-6 lists some of the options that can be specified in a system prompt. To change the system prompt, simply enter the keyword PROMPT followed by the string of characters you would like printed, or a $-character combination from Table T1-6. More than one option may be selected.

TABLE T1-6
Prompt Options and Result

Option	Result
String of characters	Displays the string of characters.
$d	Displays the current date.
$t	Displays the current time.
$p	Displays the current directory of the default drive.
$v	Displays the DOS version number.
$n	Displays the default drive letter.
$g	Displays the > character.
$l	Displays the < character.
$b	Displays the | character.
$q	Displays the = character.
$-	Ends the current line and starts a new one.
$ (blank)	Resets the prompt to the normal DOS prompt.
$ (any character other other than one of the above)	Suppresses the prompt.

Earlier we saw that the DOS command **PROMPT PG** would cause the drive letter, current directory, and a > symbol to appear. What prompt do you think would be produced after executing PROMPT SMILE$_$N$G? Let's find out. Enter

and you will see the prompt

```
SMILE
B>
```

Experiment with this command to see what combination of options you like best. When you finish experimenting, you can return the system prompt to normal by entering

with no options.

The RD or RMDIR Command

The **RD** or **RMDIR** command is used to remove a subdirectory. However, before a subdirectory can be removed, all files except the file pointers . and .. must be deleted, and the subdirectory to be removed cannot be the current directory. *A subdirectory cannot be removed if it contains any files or other subdirectories or if it is the current directory.* We could remove the GAME subdirectory since it contains no files and is not the current directory. Let's remove it. Enter

❑

DOS will not display any message if the operation is carried out successfully. However, if DOS is unable to remove the directory, it will display the message

```
Invalid path, not directory,
or directory not empty
```

Before leaving this section, use the DIR command to verify that the subdirectory GAME was removed from your Work disk; then clear your screen.

Table T1-7 summarizes subdirectory-related internal commands.

Subdirectories are rarely used with floppy disks and almost always used with fixed or hard disks.

TABLE T1-7
Subdirectory-Related Internal Commands

Command	Action Taken
CD	Changes the current directory.
CD\	Changes the current directory to the root directory.
MD	Makes a subdirectory.
PROMPT PG	Changes the system prompt to display the subdirectory you are in, followed by the symbol >.
RD	Removes a subdirectory.

How To Create Your Own DOS Commands—Batch Files

Occasionally, you might find it necessary to execute the same sequence of DOS commands repeatedly. For example, suppose you must frequently prepare disks for distribution. Specifically, you want to format and copy the program CALC.COM onto each disk. Each time you wanted to do this, you would have to type several commands. A better way is to create a batch file that will do it for you.

A **batch file** is a program file containing one or more DOS commands. All batch files must have a filename and be assigned the extension BAT. For argument's sake, let's name the batch file we're about to create MYFIRST.BAT and store it on your Work disk. To create this batch file, we'll use the COPY command. Earlier we saw how this command can be used to copy a file from the console to a disk. This is the procedure we will use to create our batch file. Place your Work disk in drive B:, and enter

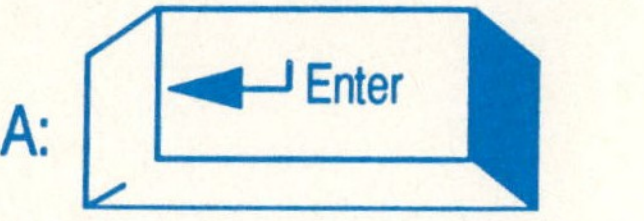

❑

Enter the command

COPY CON B:MYFIRST.BAT [Enter]

The only response from DOS will be to place the cursor at the beginning of the next line. Now let's create something on the console to be copied. Enter

Before you press the [Enter] key to move to the next line, check the contents of the line you are on and remove any typing or spelling and spacing errors. For example, if you spell something wrong, correct it by using the [Backspace] key. If you press the [Enter] key and then discover an error, BREAK out of the COPY command by pressing [Ctrl]-[Break]. Then start the process over from the very beginning.

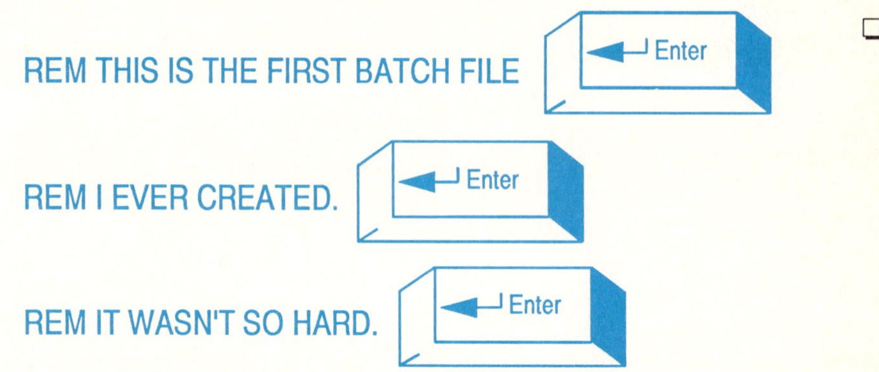

To mark the end of our batch file and to save it, press

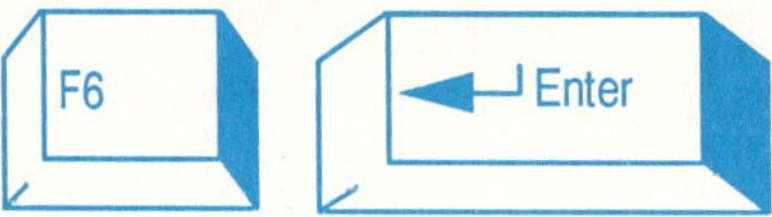

The drive light on drive B: will go on momentarily, indicating your file is being written on that disk, and you should see

```
1 File(s) copied
```

The REM or REMARK Command

The **REM** or **REMARK** command is used to place a comment in a batch file. DOS ignores the words that appear after REM. Thus, you can use the REM statement to describe what the batch file is doing or perhaps to give instructions to the person executing the batch file.

To execute, or run a batch file, simply type its name. There is no need to include the extension BAT. However, you must specify the drive if the file is not located on the default drive. Let's execute this simple batch file. Clear your screen. Now, enter

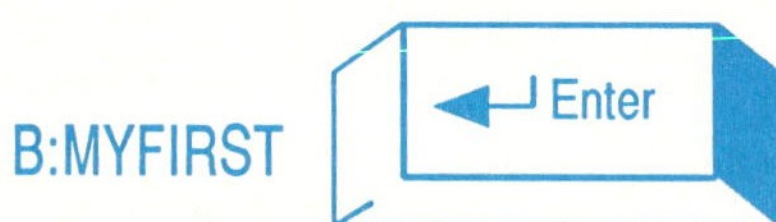

After some disk activity, you will see

```
A>REM THIS IS THE FIRST BATCH FILE

A>REM I EVER CREATED.

A>REM IT WASN'T SO HARD.

A>
A>
```

Now we'll create a batch file that contains some more useful DOS commands. If necessary, place your Work disk in drive B:, insert your DOS/Operating disk in drive A:, and then enter

COPY CON B:MYSECOND.BAT Enter

The sequence of instructions we are about to enter will, when executed, direct DOS to display the version of DOS used to start your computer, display the current subdirectory, and change the system prompt. Enter

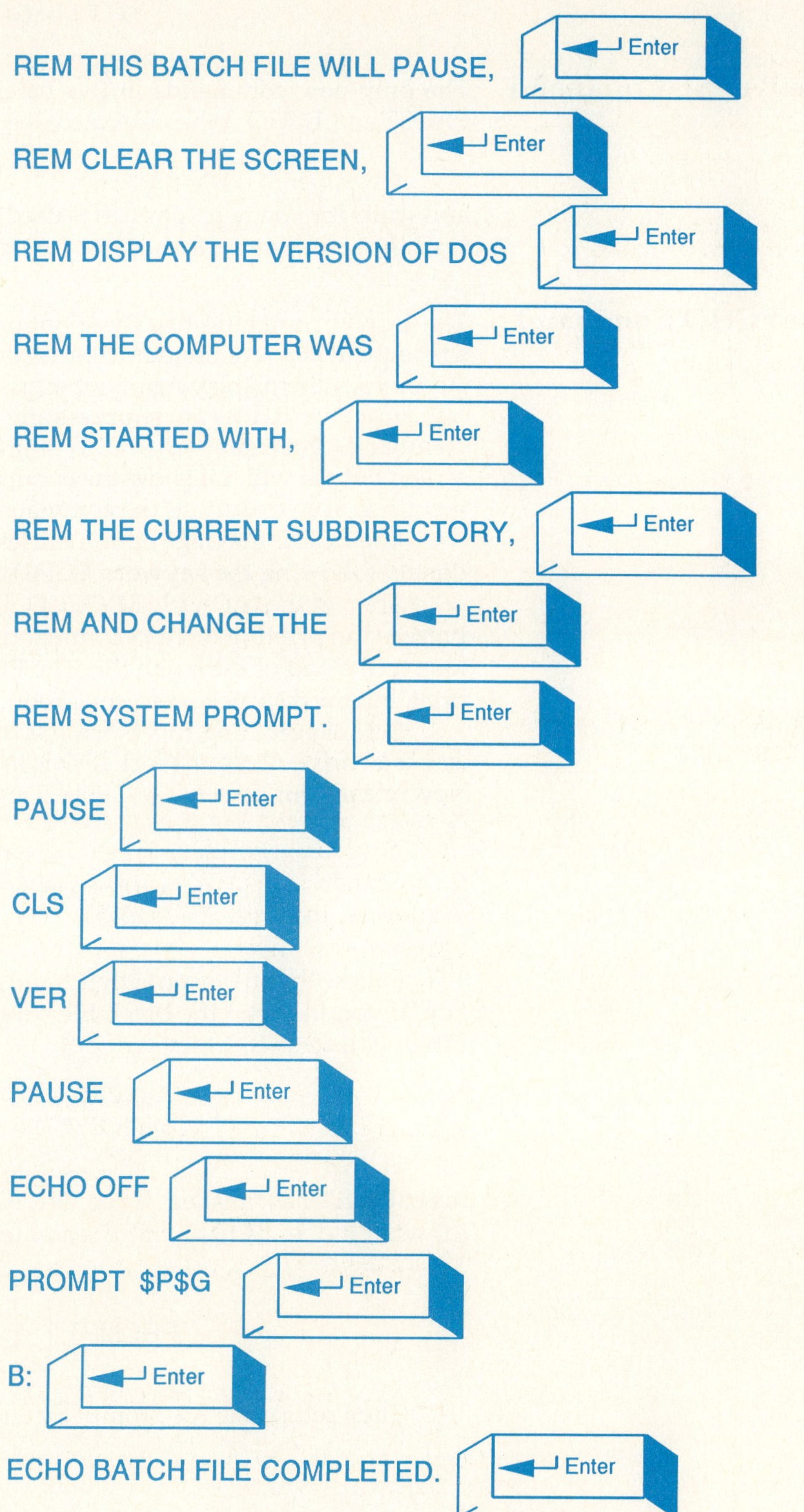

To mark the end of the file and save it, press

❏

DOS will issue the confirmation

```
1 File(s) copied
```

The PAUSE Command

The only new commands in this batch file that we haven't seen before are PAUSE and ECHO. When executed, the **PAUSE** command displays the message

```
Strike a key when ready...
```

and waits for you to respond. It is used when you want to give the user time to read the screen or perform some function before proceeding.

The ECHO Command

The ECHO command has three options. **ECHO ON**, the default, causes the subsequent DOS commands to be displayed as they are carried out. **ECHO OFF** suppresses the displaying of subsequent DOS commands as they are carried out. However, it does not suppress any displays resulting from executing these commands. For example, if a DIR command is executed after an ECHO OFF, the screen output will not show the command but will show the directory listing resulting from executing the command.

The **ECHO message** option causes the message string of characters immediately following the keyword ECHO to be displayed.

Thus in the batch file MYSECOND.BAT, the ECHO OFF command suppresses the printing of DOS commands from the PROMPT PG, on the next line, to the end of the batch file. The ECHO command on the last line will not print, but the display it produces—BATCH FILE COMPLETED.—will be printed.

Before executing this batch file, make certain that your DOS/Operating disk is in drive A:, your Work disk is in drive B:, and you have the A> prompt. Now, clear your screen and enter

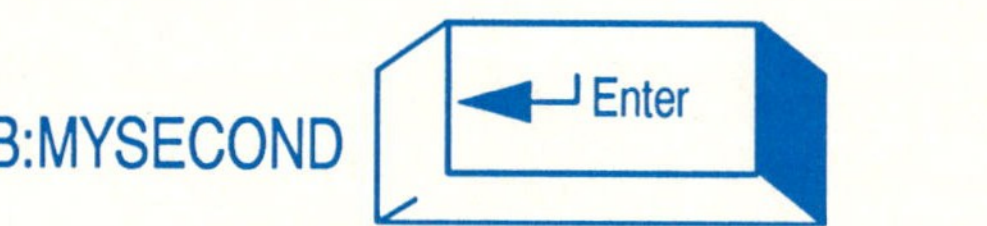

❏

Follow the on-screen activity, and respond to each PAUSE by pressing any key. If you like, run the batch file several times to get a feel for what it does. When you see

```
A>ECHO OFF
BATCH FILE COMPLETED.
B:\>
```

the batch file has finished. If you like, run the batch file several time to get a feel for what it does. When you're ready to move on, enter

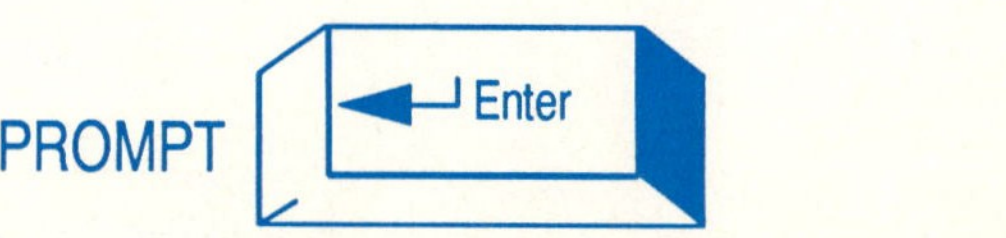

❏

Then return the A> prompt by entering

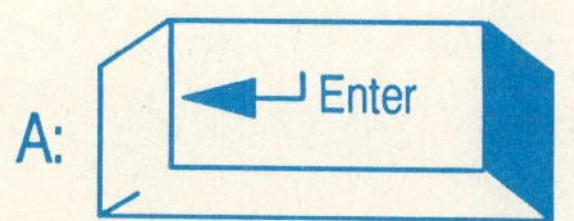

Customizing the Start-Up Procedure

AUTOEXEC.BAT is a special batch file. It is special in that DOS searches for it on your system disk before doing a normal start-up. If DOS finds this special file, it will execute the procedures contained in this file rather than performing its own start-up. AUTOEXEC.BAT can be used to display information, set the system prompt, change directories, automatically start an application program, and so on. Let's assume that we want to create an AUTOEXEC.BAT batch file on your Work disk that will display your name, instruct you to insert your Work disk in drive B:, change the prompt, change the default drive to B:, produce a directory of the disk in drive B:, and then change the default drive back to A:. To accomplish this, place your Work disk in drive A: and, if necessary, change the default drive to A:. Now, enter

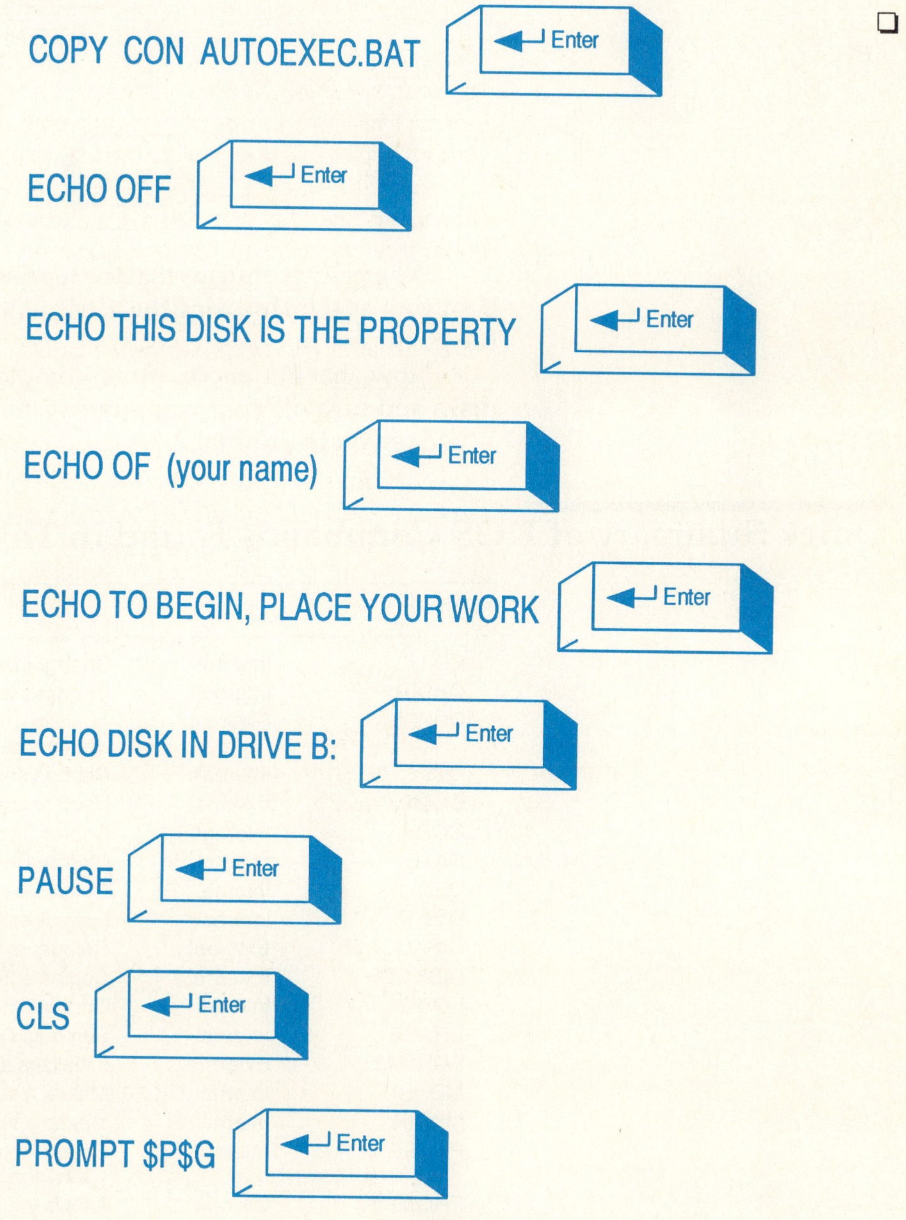

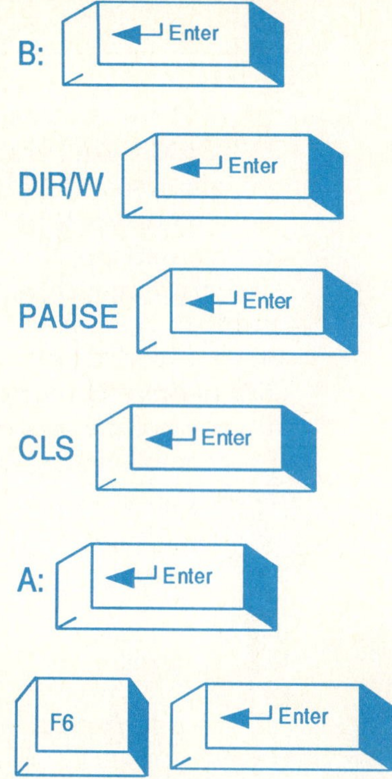

When DOS confirms that the file has been copied to your Work disk, warm boot your system by using the [Ctrl], [Alt], and [Del] keys and watch your batch file go into action.

Now, having successfully completed this DOS tutorial, remove your disks and turn off your computer system and monitor, if necessary.

See you in Tutorial 2.

Quick Summary of DOS Commands Found in This Tutorial

Command	Type	Action
CD	Internal	Changes the current directory (same as CHDIR command).
CHDIR	Internal	Changes the current directory (same as CD command).
CHKDSK	External	Analyzes the directories and files located on a disk in a specified drive.
CLS	Internal	Clears your display screen.
COMP	External	Used to compare two files.
COPY	Internal	Copies files from disk to disk.
DATE	Internal	Displays the current date, and permits you to enter any date.
DEL	Internal	Deletes a file or files from a disk.
DIR	Internal	Lists directory entries.
DISKCOMP	External	Compares entire disks including hidden files.
DISKCOPY	External	Copies entire disk including hidden files.
ECHO	Internal	Controls the displays of batch commands.
ERASE	Internal	Same as DEL.
FORMAT	External	Initializes a disk for computer use.
MD	Internal	Makes a subdirectory (same as MKDIR command).
MKDIR	Internal	Makes a subdirectory (same as MD command).
PAUSE	Internal	Causes the screen to pause until you direct DOS to continue.
PROMPT	Internal	Allows you to change the symbol for the system prompt.
RD	Internal	Removes a subdirectory (same as RMDIR command).
REM	Internal	Tells DOS to ignore the words that follow it on a line.

Command	Type	Action
REN	Internal	Renames a file.
RMDIR	Internal	Removes a subdirectory (same as RD command).
TIME	Internal	Displays the current time, and permits you to enter any time.
TYPE	Internal	Displays the contents of a file on your display.
VER	Internal	Displays the version of DOS used to boot the system.

DOS Command Summary

DOS Commands

<table>
<tr><th>Command</th><th>Function</th></tr>
<tr><td>[d:][path]ASSIGN [x[=]y[. . .]]</td><td>Routes requests to a different drive</td></tr>
<tr><td>[d:][path]ATTRIB [+|-R][d:][path]filename[.ext][/s]</td><td>Marks a file as read-only or archive</td></tr>
<tr><td>[d:][path]BACKUP d:[path][filename[.ext]]
d:[/S][/M][/A][/D:mm-dd-yy][/T:hh:mm:ss][/F]
[/L[:[d:][path]filename[.ext]]]</td><td>Backs up disk files</td></tr>
<tr><td>BREAK [ON I OFF]</td><td>Checks for control break</td></tr>
<tr><td>CHDIR [d:][path]
or
CD [d:][path]</td><td>Changes current directory</td></tr>
<tr><td>[d:][path]CHKDSK
[d:][path][filename[.ext]][/F][/V]</td><td>Checks disk and reports status</td></tr>
<tr><td>CLS</td><td>Clears the display screen</td></tr>
<tr><td>[d:][path]COMP [d:][path][filename[.ext]]
[d:][path][filename[.ext]]</td><td>Compares files</td></tr>
<tr><td>COPY [/A][/B][d:][path]filename[.ext][/A][/B]
[d:][path][filename[.ext]][/A][/B][/V]
or
COPY [/A][/B][d:][path] filename[.ext][/A][/B]
[+[d:][path]filename[.ext][/A][/B]. . .]
[d:][path][filename[.ext]][/A][/B][/V]
or
COPY[/A][/B][d:][path] filename[.ext][/A][/B]
[+[[,,]d:][path] filename[.ext][/A][/B]. . .]
[d:][path][filename[.ext]][/A][/B][/V]</td><td>Copies files</td></tr>
<tr><td>CTTY device-name</td><td>Changes to an auxiliary console</td></tr>
<tr><td>DATE [mm-dd-yy] I [dd-mm-yy] I [yy-mm-dd]</td><td>Enters date</td></tr>
<tr><td>DEL [d:][path]filename[.ext]</td><td>Deletes files</td></tr>
<tr><td>DIR [d:][path][filename[.ext]][/P][/W]</td><td>Lists file names</td></tr>
<tr><td>[d:][path]DISKCOMP [d: [d:]][/1][/8]</td><td>Compares diskettes</td></tr>
<tr><td>[d:][path]DISKCOPY [d: [d:]][/1]</td><td>Copies diskettes</td></tr>
<tr><td>ERASE [d:][path]filename[.ext]</td><td>Erases files</td></tr>
<tr><td>[d:][path]EXE2BIN [d:][path]filename[.ext]
[d:][path][filename[.ext]]</td><td>Converts .EXE files to .COM format</td></tr>
<tr><td>[d:][path]FASTOPEN d:[=nnn]...</td><td>Allows for fast accessing of files</td></tr>
<tr><td>[d:][path]FDISK</td><td>Prepares fixed disk for DOS</td></tr>
<tr><td>[d:][path]FIND[/V][/C][/N] "string" [[d][path]
filename[.ext]. . .]</td><td>Searches files for strings of text</td></tr>
<tr><td>[d:][path]FORMAT [d:][/S][/1][/8][/V][/B][/4]
[/N:xx][/T:yy]</td><td>Formats diskettes or fixed disks</td></tr>
<tr><td>[d:][path]GRAFTABL</td><td>Loads character table</td></tr>
<tr><td>[d:][path]GRAPHICS[printer type][/R][/B]</td><td>Prints graphics display screen</td></tr>
<tr><td>[d:][path]JOIN[d: d:\directory][/D]</td><td>Connects a drive to a directory on another drive to produce a single directory structure</td></tr>
<tr><td>[d:][path]KEYBUK
or
[d:][path]KEYBGR
or
[d:][path]KEYBFR
or
[d:][path]KEYBIT
or
[d:][path]KEYBSP</td><td>Loads a keyboard program</td></tr>
</table>

DOS Commands

Command	Function
[d:][path]LABEL [d:][volume label]	Creates, changes, or deletes a volume
MKDIR [d:]path or MD [d:]path	Creates a subdirectory
[d:][path]MODE LPT #[:][n][,[m][,P]] or [d:][path]MODE n or [d:][path]MODE [n],m[,T] or [d:][path]MODE COMn[:]baud[,parity[,databits[stopbits[,P]]]] or [d:][path]MODE LPT#[:]=COMn	Sets mode on printer/display
[d:][path]MORE	Displays a screenful of data
PATH[[d:]path[[;][d:][path]. . .]]	Searches directories for commands or batch files
[d][path]PRINT[/D:device][/B:buffsiz] [/U:busytick][/M:maxtick][/S:timeslice] [/Q: quesiz][/C][/T][/P] [[d:][path][filename[.ext]...]	Prints and queues data files
PROMPT [prompt-text]	Sets new prompt
[d:][path]RECOVER [d:][path]flename[.ext] or [d:][path]RECOVER d:	Recovers files from disk
REN[AME] [d:][path]filename[.ext] filename[.ext]	Renames files
[d:][path]RESTORE d: [d:][path]filename[.ext][/S][/P]	Restores backup files from one disk to another disk.
RMDIR [d:]path or RD [d:]path	Removes a subdirectory
[d:][path]SELECT xxx yy	Selects the keyboard layout and date and time format
SET [name=[parameter]]	Inserts strings into the command processor's environment
[d:][path]SHARE[/F· filspace][/L:locks]	Loads support for file sharing
[d:][path]SORT [/R][/+n] d:	Sorts text data
[d:][path]SUBST[d: d:path][/D]	Uses a different drive specifier to refer to another drive or path
[d:][path]SYS d:	Transfers DOS
Time [hh:mm:[:s[.xx]]]	Enters time
[d:][path]TREE [d:][/F]	Displays all directory paths
TYPE [d:][path]filename[.ext]	Displays file contents
VER	Displays DOS version number
VERIFY [ON I OFF]	Verifies data
VOL [d:]	Displays volume identification

Batch Commands

Command	Function
[d:]filename[.BAT][parameters]	Executes batch file
CALL[d:][path]filename	Calls another batch file from within a batch file
ECHO [ON|OFF|message]	Inhibits screen display
FOR %%variable IN (set) DO command	Interactively executes commands
GOTO label	Transfers control to line following the label
IF [NOT] condition command	Conditionally executes commands
PAUSE [remark]	Provides a system wait
REM [remarks]	Displays remarks
SHIFT	Shifts command lines

CONFIG.SYS Commands

Command	Function
BREAK = [ON I OFF]	Sets BREAK = ON or OFF
BUFFERS = x	Sets number of buffers DOS will allocate
COUNTRY = xxx	Specifies date and time format for a given country
DEVICE = [d:][path]filename[.ext]	Installs a device driver
FCBS = m, n	Sets number of control blocks that can be open concurrently
FILES = x	Sets maximum number of files that can be open concurrently
LASTDRIVE = x	Sets maximum number of drives that can be accessed
SHELL = [d:][path]filename[.ext]	Loads a top-level command processor
STACKS=n,s	Allows you to override the defalt stack

EDLIN Commands

Command	Function
[n]A	Appends lines
[line],[line],line[,count]C	Copies lines
[line][,line]D	Deletes lines
E	Ends edit, saves changes
[line]I	Inserts lines
[line][,line]L	Lists lines
[line],[line],lineM	Moves lInes
[line],[line]P	Lists pages
Q	Quits edit
[line][,line][?]R[string][[F6]string]	Replaces text
[line][,line][?]S[string]	Searches text
[line]T[d:]filename[.ext]	Transfers lines
[n]W	Write lines

Exercises

1. What command or commands would you use to do the following?
   a. Find out how much RAM space you have available.
   b. Copy a disk from B: to A:.
   c. Delete all the files from a disk in the A: drive.
   d. Rename a file from FILE1 to FILE2.
   e. Compare the files OLDFILE.SYS and NEWFILE.SYS.
   f. Copy hidden files.
   g. Change to the root directory.
   h. Place a comment in a batch file.
   i. Change the current date.
   j. Determine the version of DOS used to start your computer.
2. Answer each of the following with either true or false.

   _______ a. Disks are formatted into tracks and sectors.

   _______ b. Internal commands are loaded into memory at the time of booting and remain in memory until the power is turned off.

   _______ c. The source disk is the disk to be copied.

   _______ d. When you turn off the power, you lose everything that was stored on your disk.

   _______ e. The COPY command can be used to copy all files, including the hidden ones that may exist on a disk.

   _______ f. A warm boot is accomplished by pressing the [Ctrl]-[Alt]-[Del] keys.

_______ g. DIR with the /P option is useful for long directories.

_______ h. A file name may include a space imbedded between two characters.

_______ i. DIR H*.* will list all files that have an * as a file extension.

_______ j. A new blank disk need not be formatted if it is to hold only data.

_______ k. No two DOS files can have the same name and be stored in the same directory.

_______ l. COMP is an internal DOS command.

_______ m. The ERASE command functions differently from the DEL command.

_______ n. It is not possible to print a hard copy of a batch file.

_______ o. All versions of DOS have the same number of bytes occupied by internal commands.

_______ p. It is OK to copy a file onto itself.

3. For the following matching questions, write the number of the phrase that best completes the lettered item in the first column.

a.	_______	*	1. Places an end-of-file marker in a batch file.
b.	_______	BAT	2. Clears your display screen.
c.	_______	>PRN	3. A wild card character that will match one character only.
d.	_______	CD\	4. The batch file extension.
e.	_______	TYPE	5. Displays the next entry in a keyboard buffer when pressed.
f.	_______	F3	6. Used to obtain a hard copy of the output from certain DOS commands.
g.	_______	F6	7. Changes the current directory to the root.
h.	_______	F1	8. A wild card character that will match up to eight characters in a name.
i.	_______	CLS	9. Used to display the contents of a file on your display screen.
j.	_______	?	10. Displays the entire contents of the keyboard buffer when pressed.

4. Describe what each of the following commands does.

   a. CD\
   b. COPY A:F1 A:F2
   c. DISKCOPY A: A:
   d. PAUSE
   e. DEL B:*.*
   f. REN A:GGG.G B:FFF.F
   g. COPY CON B:GIOIA.BAT
   h. DIR/W
   i. DIR B:*.?SS
   j. COPY B*.* B:
   k. FORMAT B:/S
   l. CHKDSK B:*.*
   m. VER>PRN
   n. COPY CON CONFIG.SYS
   o. MD DBASE
   p. COPY B:SCOTT A:NANCY
   q. RD DBASE

Hands-On Activities

1. Assuming you have a DOS/Startup disk in the A: drive and a Work disk in the B: drive, carry out each of the following:
   a. Get a directory of your Work disk.
   b. Copy the file FORMAT.COM from your DOS/Startup disk to your Work disk.
   c. Copy all files from the DOS disk having the extension EXE to your Work disk.
   d. Display a wide directory of your Work disk.
   e. Get a hard copy of the wide directory of your Work disk.
   f. Delete the files you copied in steps b and c from your Work disk.

2. Using DOS commands, specifically indicate how each byte of space on your DOS/Startup disk is being used. For example, how many bytes are free? How many bytes are in user and hidden files? How many bytes are in bad sectors?

3. Create a bootable disk that will allow you to use the following external DOS commands:

   DISKCOPY
   FORMAT
   CHKDSK
   COMP

   Hint: To do this, you will need your DOS/Startup and Operating disk and a blank disk (formatted or otherwise). Be sure to format your disk first with the /S option.

4. Create and run a batch file called SAMPLE1 that will execute the following sequence of DOS commands, in the order shown.
   a. Display a comment with your name and address.
   b. Pause and clear the screen.
   c. Check the version of DOS being used.
   d. Pause and clear the screen.
   e. Determine if the disk in the B: drive has files that are fragmented.

   Be sure to save this batch file on your Work disk.

5. Create and run a batch file that will provide a directory of all batch files that exist on your Work disk. Name this batch file AUTOEXEC.BAT. Then, copy all previously created batch files to this boot disk. Boot your computer with the boot disk you just created. Comment on what happened.

6. Create and run a batch file that will display a menu. The menu should provide the following options:

Option	Action To Be Taken
a.	Display a width directory of the disk in the A: drive.
b.	Display a width directory of the disk in the B: drive.
c.	Change the prompt symbol to your name.
d.	Change the prompt symbol back to the system prompt.

   The user of the batch file should see the menu displayed when the batch file name is typed. Then the user should be able to select one of the four options and have the option executed. To accomplish this, four additional batch files will have to be created in addition to the batch file needed to create the menu to carry out each action. These batch files should be saved on the disk containing the menu batch file. Thus, a total of five batch files should be created, one to display the main menu and one for each of the four options. *Hint*: Option c can be created using the PROMPT command followed by a space and then your name as the prompt option.

7. Create a subdirectory of your Work disk called BAT. Copy all files from the root of your Work disk to BAT. Create a subdirectory of BAT called FAT. Copy all batch files found in BAT to FAT. When you are finished, remove all subdirectories and their contents.

8. Create your own AUTOEXEC.BAT file designed specifically to help you with your course. Save it on your boot disk. Print a hard copy of it, and store it in a safe place.

2

WORDPERFECT 5.1
Your Magic Pencil

WordPerfect is currently one of the most popular word processing programs available. It is a trademark of the WordPerfect Corp., 288 West Center St., Orem, UT 84057.

To assist you in learning WordPerfect, we have provided this easy-to-follow, step-by-step tutorial. This tutorial will also help you to work with other word processing packages since most of the concepts described here are common to them as well. However, to reap the greatest possible benefit from this tutorial, you should complete each step on your computer using the WordPerfect software package. Even if you do not have a computer available, you will still benefit from the detailed explanations provided.

This tutorial will take approximately two hours to complete.

Objectives

This tutorial is intended to introduce you to WordPerfect. It describes the virtues of the package and will teach you some basic operations. You will learn to:

- Enter text
- Rearrange text
- Get a printout
- Perform basic editing operations
- Save a file
- Spell check text

Before You Begin

Review the material concerning word processing in Chapter 12.

Follow the Blue

As you follow along, any procedures you must carry out or entries you must make will be printed in *blue* whereas all computer responses will appear as if they were written by a typewriter. *Type only entries or follow only directions that appear in blue.* A ❑ appears at the right of the first line of each sequence of commands you must enter. Check the box when you have completed the instruction as a way of keeping track of your progress as you proceed through the tutorial.

Whenever a special key (any key other than a letter, digit, or special character) is shown printed in blue, you must tap or momentarily depress that key. For example, if the key

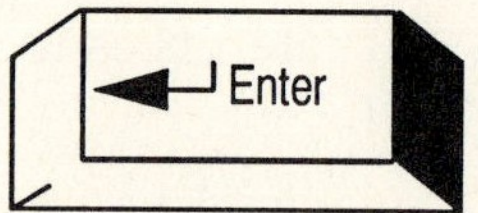

were printed in blue, you would be expected to momentarily depress the [Enter] key.

In some special cases, it will be necessary for you to press *and hold down* one special key while momentarily depressing another. To indicate this, the special key or keys to be pressed and held will be printed slightly lower and attached by a thin line to the key to be tapped. If the series of keys

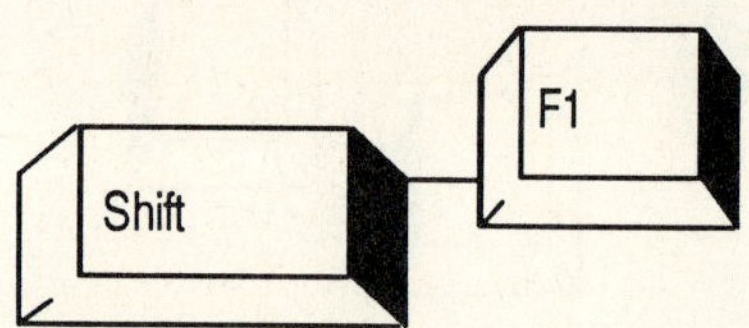

were printed in blue, you would be expected to press and hold down the [Shift] key, tap the [F1] Function key, and release the [Shift] key.

You will also find it necessary to enter combinations of text and special keys. For example, if the entry

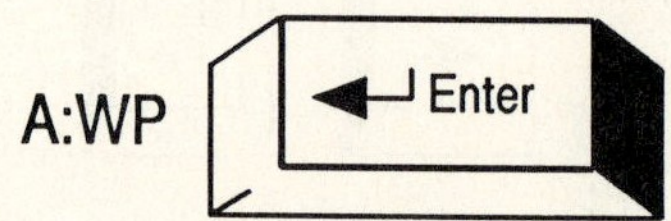

were printed in blue, you would be expected to type **A:WP** and then depress the [Enter] key.

Version 5.1 Versus Version 5.0

This tutorial is designed for use with **WordPerfect Version 5.1** but can also be used with Version 5.0. Athough there are some differences between these versions (and we will point them out when they occur), their impact on this tutorial is minimal.

Required Hardware

We assume your microcomputer is equipped with two floppy disk drives of capacity 720K or larger. WordPerfect Version 5.0 can be run from 360K drives. If your system is equipped with a hard drive and WordPerfect 5.0/5.1 is stored on the hard drive, some of the procedures we describe may differ slightly. When hardware-related differences arise, we will point them out.

Required Software

If your computer system *is not* equipped with a hard drive, obtain a copy of **DOS** version 2.1 (2.0 for WordPerfect 5.0) or *higher* and a copy of **WordPerfect** from your instructor or laboratory assistant before proceeding. Your WordPerfect system may be contained on one or two disks. If it is contained on two disks, they should be labeled **WordPerfect 1** and **WordPerfect 2**. If it is contained on one disk, it should be labeled **WordPerfect 1&2**. You also will need the **Speller** disk.

If your computer *is* equipped with a hard drive, DOS and the required WordPerfect files are, in all likelihood, stored on it. Thus, you do not need to obtain any other software.

We suggest that you format a floppy disk so you can save your work when finished. Formatting a disk prepares it so that the computer can write data onto it. Every disk must be formatted before it can be used. If you are not familiar with this process, refer to the DOS tutorial. Henceforth, your Work disk will mean a formatted floppy disk.

For the remainder of this tutorial, unless specifically stated otherwise, all references to WordPerfect will apply both to Version 5.0 and to Version 5.1.

Special Keys

The use of special keys can greatly simplify the task of creating documents with WordPerfect. Some of the more commonly used ones are listed next. You should familiarize yourself with them.

Special Keys	Function
Alt + =	When you press and hold the [Alt] key and type =, the WordPerfect 5.1 pull-down menu system is displayed at the top of your screen. This is not an option with Version 5.0.
8 ↑, 2 ↓, 4 ←, 6 →	The four Arrow keys move the cursor up, down, left, or right one character or line at a time without altering any text.
Backspace	The [Backspace] key moves the cursor to the left one place each time it is pressed (similar to the Left Arrow key), but in the process it erases a character.
Caps Lock	The [Caps Lock] key toggles the keyboard between uppercase and lowercase. Toggle it on if you desire capital letters. Toggling it again will return the keyboard to the lowercase mode.
F1	The [F1] Function key is used to cancel or back out of a procedure one step at a time. It can also be used to restore erased text.

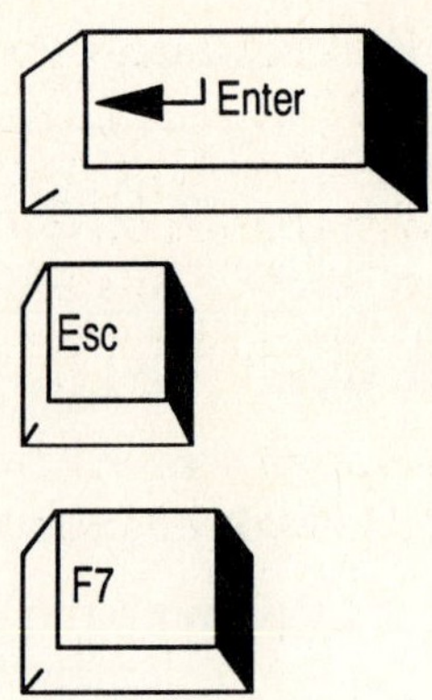

The [Enter] key either transmits a line to memory or ends a short line.

The [Esc] key can be used to repeat a keystroke a specified number of times. It can be used to move the cursor right or left a specified number of characters or up or down a specified number of lines or pages.

When editing a document, the [F7] Function key (commonly called the Exit key) is used to save and exit or simply to exit the document. When carrying out a procedure, pressing the Exit key will return you to the previous screen, or to the Editing screen. In some cases, the Exit key is pressed several times to return to the Editing screen.

Getting Started with WordPerfect 5.1

Installation

Before WordPerfect can be used, it must be installed. To install WordPerfect means to adjust it to your printer, monitor, and mouse, if you have one. This process is normally done once. We assume that the installation procedures have already been carried out for you by your instructor or laboratory assistant. However, if you must install WordPerfect, consult the WordPerfect manuals for specific details.

Starting Your Computer and WordPerfect

The method for starting your computer will vary depending on whether you have a two-disk drive system or a hard drive and one floppy disk drive. If you have a hard disk, skip to the section titled "Starting Your Computer and WordPerfect from a Hard Drive"; otherwise read on.

Starting Your Computer and WordPerfect from a Floppy Disk Drive

Be sure that your computer is turned off before you begin.

Place your DOS/Startup disk in disk drive A: (the left-hand drive, or top drive) and your Work disk in the drive B: (the right-hand drive, or bottom drive). Be sure the drive doors are closed. Locate your computer's power switch or switches. Turn on your computer.

In a few moments you will hear some disk activity. Then either you will be requested to enter the correct date and time, or the correct date and time will automatically be entered for you. If you are requested to enter the correct date and time, do so now; otherwise read on.

You should now see the familiar system prompt

WordPerfect depends on DOS for the correct date and time. Thus, always be sure to enter the correct date and time when you start your computer if prompted to do so. Computer systems equipped with clock calendars will automatically have the correct date and time logged in when they are started. In this case, it is not necessary for you to enter the date and time.

A>

Remove the DOS disk from drive A:, and replace it with your WordPerfect 1 disk (or WordPerfect 1&2 disk). Any files that you create will be stored on the disk in drive B:; so place a formatted Work disk in the B: drive now. Let's get started. Enter

❑

You should now see

B>

displayed on your screen. Let's continue. Type

❑

In a moment you see the WordPerfect copyright screen immediately followed by the message

`Insert diskette labeled "WordPerfect 2" and press any key`

Replace the WordPerfect 1 disk with the WordPerfect 2 disk (the above message will not appear and no replacement is needed if WordPerfect 1&2 are stored on one disk). Press

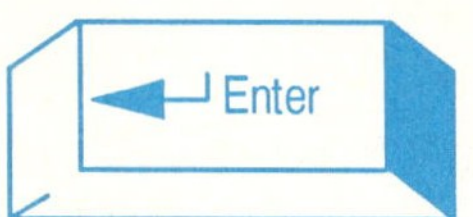

❑

and a moment later the **Editing screen** shown in Figure T2-1 will appear.

FIGURE T2-1
The WordPerfect Editing Screen.

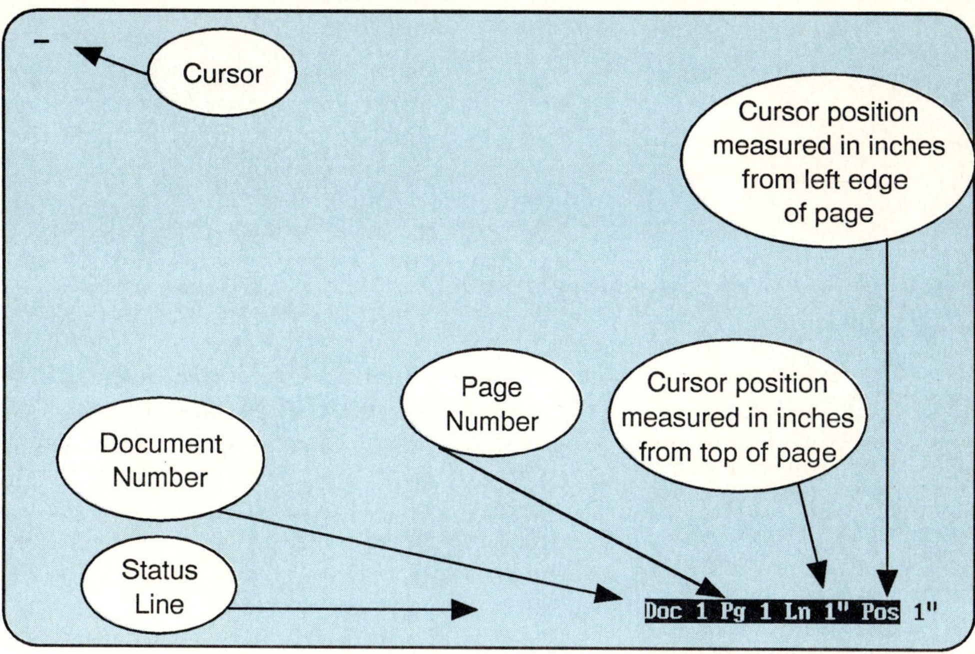

If you see the message *Are other copies of WordPerfect currently running? (Y/N)*, you should type **N** to advance to the Editing screen. This message will appear it you exit WordPerfect the wrong way.

Congratulations! You have successfully started WordPerfect. Now, skip to the section titled "The Editing Screen."

Starting Your Computer and WordPerfect from a Hard Drive

Be sure that your computer is turned off before you begin. There is no need to place the DOS disk in the A: disk drive because DOS should already be stored on the hard disk.

Locate your computer's power switch or switches. Turn on your computer.

In a few moments you will hear some disk activity. If you are requested to enter the correct date and time, do so; otherwise read on.

WordPerfect depends on DOS for the correct date and time. Thus, always be sure to enter the correct date and time when you start your computer if prompted to do so. Computer systems equipped with clock calendars will automatically have the correct date and time logged in when they are started. In this case, it is not necessary for you to enter the date and time.

You should see the familiar system prompt

To start WordPerfect, change the current directory to the subdirectory that contains the WordPerfect program files. For example, if your WordPerfect files are stored in a subdirectory called WP51, from the C> prompt you would type **CD WP51 [Enter]**. If you will be saving your work on a floppy disk drive, place your Work disk in either your A: or B: disk drive.

Now enter ❑

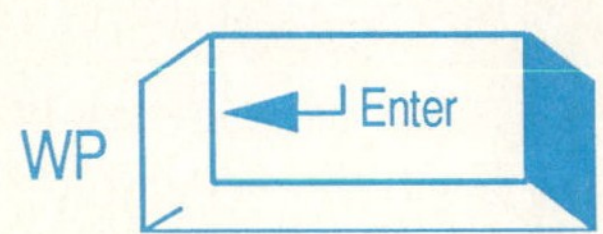

In a moment you will see the WordPerfect copyright screen, and then the Editing screen shown in Figure T2-1 should appear.

Congratulations, you have successfully started WordPerfect.

The Editing Screen

When you begin WordPerfect, you are provided with a clean screen, referred to as the **Editing screen**. There are several important settings and information areas provided in the Editing screen. Each is described in Table T2-1.

TABLE T2-1
The Editing Screen

Setting/Area	Meaning
Cursor	The cursor, the blinking underscore, is used to indicate your position within the document.
Status line	The Status line at the bottom is used to present messages and warnings to the user and to indicate the position of the cursor. In addition, when you save a document, the Status line will display the document name as long as you are working on it.
Doc 1	WordPerfect permits you to work on two documents at once. The Doc setting indicates that you are currently editing Document 1 of 2.
Pg 1	This indicates the current page number. A WordPerfect page is 11 inches long. However, WordPerfect automatically allows 1 inch of extra space for the top and bottom margin. This reduces the actual area in which text can appear.
Ln 1"	This indicates the position of the cursor measured in inches from the top of the page. Ln 1" means the cursor is located on a line that is 1 inch from the top of the page.
Pos 1"	This indicates the position of the cursor measured in inches from the left edge of the page. WordPerfect automatically provides a left and right margin of 1 inch. Thus, a Pos of 1" indicates that your text will be entered beginning at 1 inch from the left edge of your page.

A printed page does not have the same dimensions as a screen page. Approximately two screen pages equal one printed page.

The settings displayed in the Status line are WordPerfect's default settings. This means that WordPerfect initially sets them for you. Later in this tutorial you will learn how to change the default (initial) settings.

The Template

WordPerfect offers you great power and versatility once you become familiar with the program. To assist you in using WordPerfect effectively during this familiarization and learning process, WordPerfect provides a number of **key-activated commands** that specify the additional key or keys you must depress to accomplish a particular task. Each command is concerned with all options of a particular type. For example, there is a Help command, a Block command, a Print command, a Spell command, and a Format command, to name just a few.

WordPerfect keeps the commands in reserve until you need them. In this way you are not distracted by information that, at the moment, is of no value. To access WordPerfect's operational commands, you must become familiar with the keyboard template.

When you've finished this tutorial and exit WordPerfect, *don't forget to remove your template and return it to your instructor or laboratory assistant.*

WordPerfect provides two keyboard templates, one designed for the standard IBM keyboard and the other for the enhanced keyboard. This template is WordPerfect's main menu. Position the template on your keyboard as shown in Figure T2-2.

FIGURE T2-2
Placing WordPerfect's Templates on Your Keyboard.

WordPerfect® for the IBM® Personal Computers	Shell	Spell	Screen	Move	*Ctrl*	Text In/Out	Tab Align	Footnote	Font	*Ctrl*	Merge/Sort	Macro Def		
Column Left/Right — Home ← →	Thesaurus	Replace	Reveal Codes	Block	*Alt*	Mark Text	Flush Right	Columns/Table	Style	*Alt*	Graphics	Retrieve		
Compose — 2; Delete to End of Ln/Pg — End/PgDn; Delete Word — Backspace	Setup	• Search	Switch	• Indent •	*Shift*	Date/Outline	Center	Print	Format	*Shift*	Merge Codes	Macro		
Hard Page — Enter; • Margin Release — Tab; Pull down Menus — -; Screen Up/Down — -+(num); Word Left/Right — ← →	Cancel	• Search	Help	• Indent		List	Bold	Exit	Underline		End Field	Save	Reveal Codes	Block
	F1	*F2*	*F3*	*F4*		*F5*	*F6*	*F7*	*F8*		*F9*	*F10*	*F11*	*F12*

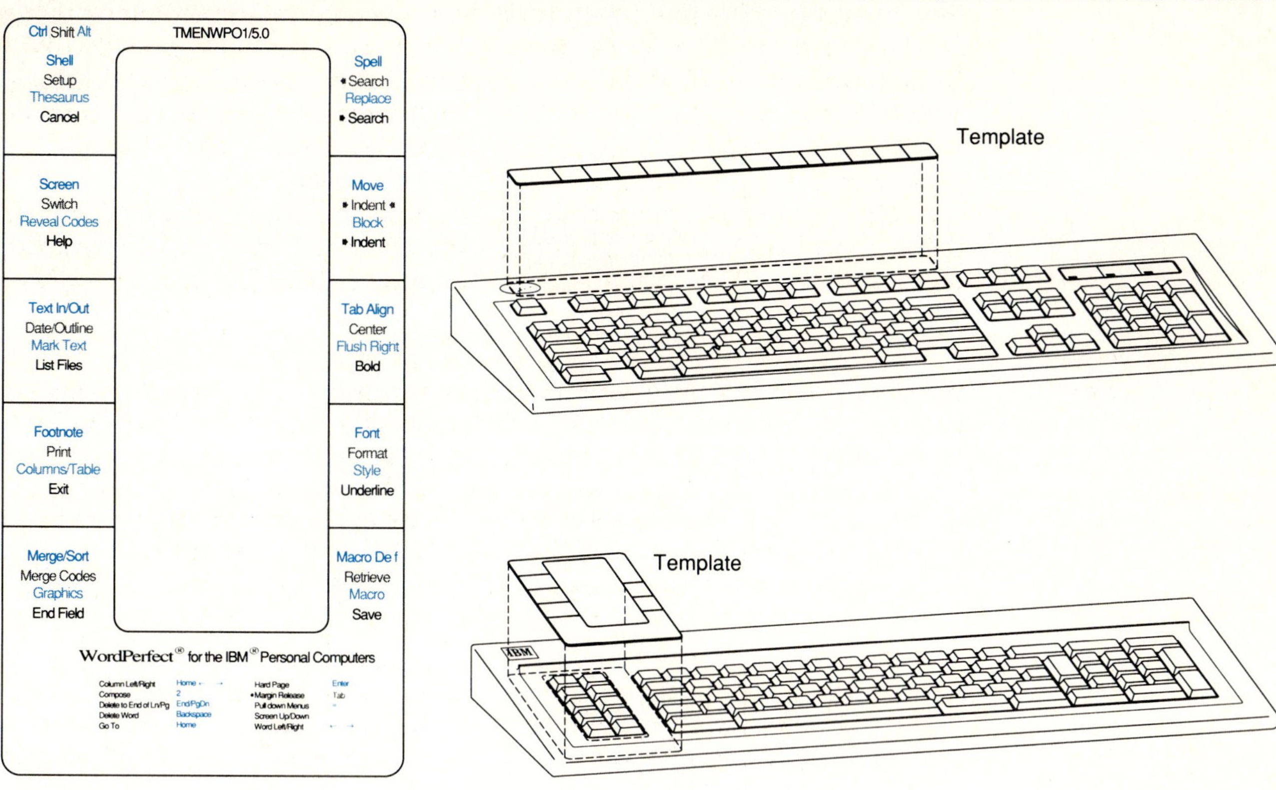

The template you see in Figure T2-2 is the Version 5.1 template. The Version 5.0 template has a few *visible* differences. Some of these differences are listed in Table T2-2.

TABLE T2-2
Versions 5.0 and 5.1 Template Differences

Version 5.0 Entry	Version 5.1 Entry
List Files	List
Math/Columns	Columns/Table
Merge R	End Field

To select most commands from the menu, you must first depress either the [Ctrl], [Shift], or [Alt] key and then depress the Function key associated with the desired command. To help you with these associations, the keyboard template is color coordinated. Each of the [Ctrl], [Shift], and [Alt] keys is assigned a color—red, green, and blue, respectively—that is displayed at the top left of the template designed for the standard keyboard or in two columns of the template designed for the enhanced keyboard. The commands adjacent to each Function key are then coordinated with the colors of the [Ctrl], [Shift], and [Alt] keys. Each Function key may also be used alone. Commands initiated by depressing the Function key only are printed in black.

For example, to invoke the Move command you must first depress the [Ctrl] key and, while holding down this key, press the [F4] Function key. Notice that both the [Ctrl] key and the word *Move* are color coded the same. To invoke the List (List Files for Version 5.0) command, you would press the [F5] Function key only, since the command List (List Files) is displayed in *black* (just as the [F5] Function key is on your keyboard).

Aside from the commands listed on your template, there are other little tidbits provided. For example, information concerning cursor movement and deletion of text can be found at the bottom or to the right of the template, depending on the type of template you are using.

Pull-Down Menus

WordPerfect Version 5.1 supports the use of pull-down menus. These menus contain the full complement of WordPerfect features. To access the pull-down menus, simply press and hold the [Alt] key and tap =. To select features from the pull-down menus, you use the Arrow keys and press the [Enter] key. Pull-down menus are removed by either completing a command or by pressing the Cancel key, [F1], until the menus are removed.

We do *not* use pull-down menus in this tutorial.

Mouse Support

To install a mouse while you are viewing the WordPerfect 5.1 Editing screen, you must activate the **Setup** command. Press and hold the **[Shift]** key then press the **[F1]** function key. Select **1** for **Mouse** by typing 1, then select **1** for **Type** by typing 1. Select the manufacturer of your mouse from the list provided by placing the cursor on your selection and type **1**. To exit and save your installation, press the **Exit** key, **[F7]**, to return to the Editing Screen.

WordPerfect Version 5.1 users have the option of working with a pointing device commonly referred to as a **mouse**. In WordPerfect the computer mouse allows you to reposition the cursor in your document and to perform editing functions such as copying, moving, and deleting blocks of text. In addition, the mouse can be used to activate the pull-down menus and to select a command from the menu. A mouse must be installed to work with WordPerfect before you can use it.

The mouse is activated by moving it. To move the cursor while using a mouse, move the mouse; a rectangular indicator will appear. Move the indicator to the desired position in your document, and then press the *left* mouse button once. To activate the pull-down menus, press the *right* mouse button once. Pressing the right button a second time removes the pull-down menus. The mouse is temporarily deactivated when you press a keyboard key.

A computer mouse is *not* used in this tutorial.

The Help Command

WordPerfect is ready and willing to provide you with assistance at all times. Clearly you will need the greatest help with the command structure when you first start using the package and the least help when you become familiar with the package. The designers of WordPerfect recognize this fact and provide you with help as you need it.

To activate the Help command, press

❑

Read the information displayed, and pay careful attention to the message at the very bottom of your display screen. WordPerfect is looking for a specific help file.

If WordPerfect 1&2 are stored on one disk or if you have a hard disk, no such message will be displayed and the next step is not necessary. Skip to the sentence below that is worded "Let's get some help." Otherwise, remove your Work disk from drive B:, and insert your WordPerfect 1 disk.

Now enter the letter of the disk drive containing the WordPerfect 1 disk. Type

B ❑

Let's get some help. Press

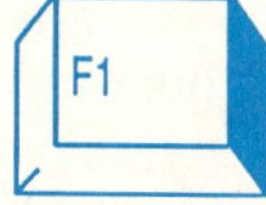

❑

FIGURE T2-3
Cancel Help Screen.

Figures T2-3 through T2-5 will be slightly different for WordPerfect 5.0.

```
Cancel

     Cancel
     Cancels the effect or operation of any function key that displays a prompt
     or menu.  It will also stop the operation of a macro or merge before it is
     finished.

     Undelete
     When no other function is active, this key undeletes (restores) up to
     three deletions.  A deletion is any group of characters or codes erased
     before the cursor is moved.  WordPerfect temporarily inserts the most
     recent deletion at the cursor position.  You can then restore the text or
     display the previous deletion.

Selection: 0                                          (Press ENTER to exit Help)
```

You are now looking at a description of the first Function key, Cancel. Read it now. This screen will appear each time you follow the preceding procedures and press the [F1] Function key.

Once you are in the Help command, simply press the key or keys corresponding to the command or desired action for which you are seeking help. For example, let's get some help on the Move command. Press

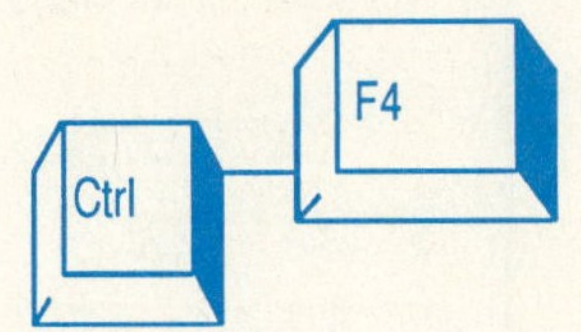

You should now see Figure T2-4.

FIGURE T2-4
The Move Help Screen Displayed in Response To Depressing the [Ctrl]-[F4] Keys.

```
Move

     Lets you move, copy or delete text.  You can then move to another place in
     the document or to a document in the second editing screen and retrieve
     the text.  You can also append a block of text to a file on disk.

     You must first highlight the text you want to move, copy, etc.  You can
     either use the Block feature to highlight the desired text, or let the
     Move key automatically highlight the current sentence, paragraph, or page.

     1 - Block On

     2 - Block Off




Selection: 0                                        (Press ENTER to exit Help)
```

Once you have finished reading the information, you can exit Help by pressing the [Enter] key or you can read another help screen. Let's read one more. Press

You should now see Figure T2-5.

Not bad. This can really be fun. You could probably spend days reading all the Help screens provided by WordPerfect. Well, we don't want you spending days reading Help screens.

Exit The Help Command

To exit Help, press

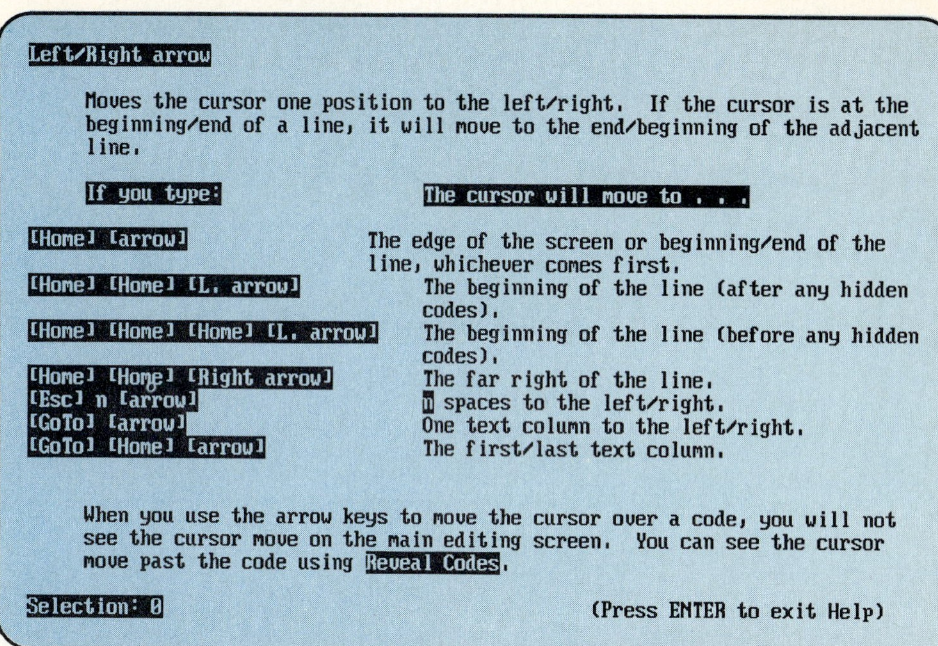
Left/Right arrow

Moves the cursor one position to the left/right. If the cursor is at the beginning/end of a line, it will move to the end/beginning of the adjacent line.

If you type:	The cursor will move to . . .
[Home] [arrow]	The edge of the screen or beginning/end of the line, whichever comes first.
[Home] [Home] [L. arrow]	The beginning of the line (after any hidden codes).
[Home] [Home] [Home] [L. arrow]	The beginning of the line (before any hidden codes).
[Home] [Home] [Right arrow]	The far right of the line.
[Esc] n [arrow]	n spaces to the left/right.
[GoTo] [arrow]	One text column to the left/right.
[GoTo] [Home] [arrow]	The first/last text column.

When you use the arrow keys to move the cursor over a code, you will not see the cursor move on the main editing screen. You can see the cursor move past the code using Reveal Codes.

Selection: 0 (Press ENTER to exit Help)

FIGURE T2-5
The Right Arrow Help Screen Displayed by WordPerfect.

If necessary, remove the WordPerfect 1 disk from drive B:, and replace it with your Work disk.

Before You Begin to Type

Creating a document involves more than simply typing it. All too often, in the interest of getting the job done, we give too little thought to how the document will look when it is printed. However, the appearance of a document may ultimately determine its effectiveness.

Before you begin to type, several important factors should be considered. First, you should consider a design for your document. Then, determine if your word processor can accommodate your design. In many cases it may be necessary to customize your word processor to implement the design you have chosen.

Let's look at what should be done before you begin to type.

Design Your Document

Although an in-depth presentation on document design is beyond the scope of this tutorial, we will point out the prerequisites for achieving a good design.

A good design will make your document attractive and easy to read. To achieve a good design, a few basic questions must be answered:

Who is your audience?
What do you want to say to them?
How will you say it?

The first question, Who is your audience?, is answered by knowing your readers. For example, the vocabulary level, margin size, and line spacing will be different for a personal letter than it will be for a physical science term paper. The personal letter will incorporate an average vocabulary level and convey a friendly feeling. Wide margins and plenty of space between lines will lend to this feeling. On the other hand, an impersonal feeling will transmit through the highly technical vocabulary used in the term paper. The reason is that the reader of the term paper is interested in the topic and doesn't care if lines and lines of cold facts appear on each page.

The next question, What do you want to say to them?, can be answered by knowing your topic. For example, if you have to write a report on the advantages and disadvantages of traveling by bus as opposed to commercial airline make sure you research both sides thoroughly. This could involve actually traveling by bus and plane to the same destination. Doing so would answer any critic who challenges your material based on your lack of travel experience.

The final question, How will you say it?, is answered by knowing your hardware and software. No matter how well you know your audience or how well you understand the topic, if you don't have the software to produce your design, or the hardware to print it, your efforts will be wasted. Accordingly, you must know the capabilities and limitations of your word processor and target printer.

In conclusion, if you know your reader, topic, and hardware and software, you are likely to create an effective and aesthetically pleasing looking document.

Identify Your Target Printer

No matter what design you incorporate or how powerful your word processor, if your printer can't produce the document you create, your work is for naught. Hours can be spent preparing a document only to have your printer produce a poor facsimile. For example, you may decide that a phrase should be emphasized with the *italic style*. After applying the style to your phrase, you discover that your printer cannot produce words in the italic style. Now you must choose another style. This scenario can be avoided by *knowing the capabilities and limitations* of your target printer. Your instructor, laboratory assistant, or the printer manuals can provide this information.

WordPerfect cannot print unless a printer is installed. Once installed, the printer must be selected as the **target printer** for your document. To identify your target printer, select the **Print** command. Press

❑

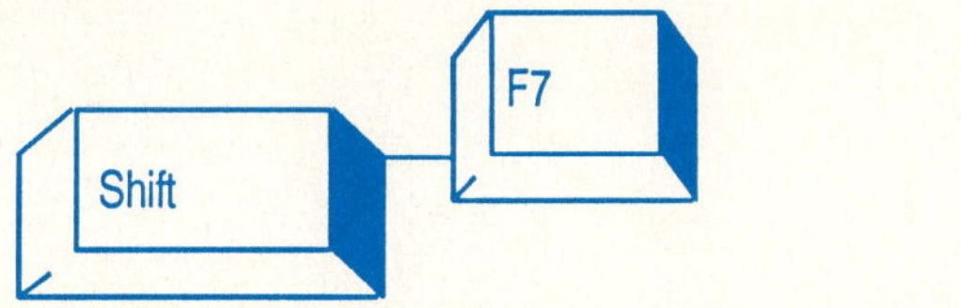

You should now see Figure T2-6.

Look to the right of the Option S, *Select Printer*. You should see *Standard Printer*. This is the generic target printer we installed on our copy of WordPerfect. You are probably looking at a different target printer. For example, you may be looking at *IBM ProPrinter II* or possibly *Epson LQ-1500*. Regardless, if a printer has been installed and selected as the target printer, you should see its name on your display screen.

If you have several printers installed to work with WordPerfect and you decide to change the target printer, you should do so *before* you begin to type.

If two or more printers have been installed to work with your copy of WordPerfect, you can *change the target printer* by selecting **S** from the Print command. Then place the cursor on the new target printer and type **S**. To save the change, press the Exit key, [F7].

To exit the Print command, press the Cancel key, [F1]. Press

❑

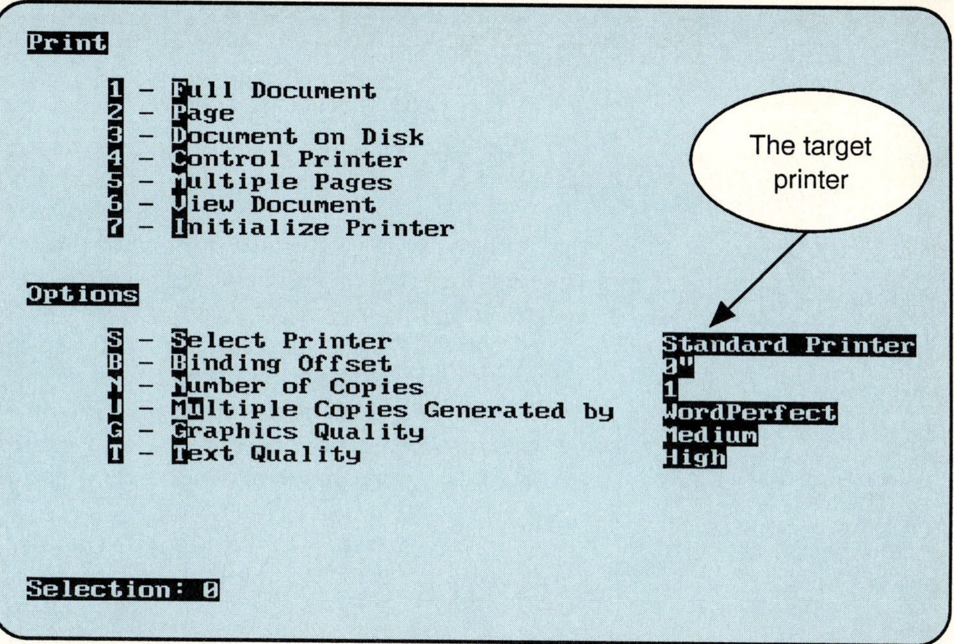

FIGURE T2-6
The Print Command.

Version 5.0 users will see a slightly different display. Specifically, the *Multiple Pages* Print option is replaced by *Type Through*, and the *Multiple Copies Generated by* option is not present.

Set Your Margins

When designing a document, you must determine the size of the *image area*, the area on a page into which all text and graphics will be contained. The positioning of the margins determines the **length** and **number** of lines of text in your image area. In addition, margins establish the boundaries within which your text will be aligned when you reformat your document after either inserting and/or deleting characters. Thus it is imperative that you set your margins before you begin typing.

WordPerfect automatically assumes a left margin and right margin of 1 inch. These settings are referred to as **default margin settings**. If you are satisfied with the default margin settings, there is no need to change them. However, if you want to increase or decrease the size of your image area, you must change them.

The **Format** command is used to change the default margin settings. To invoke this command, examine the template and locate Format. Do you see that you must hold down the [Shift] key while you press the [F8] Function key? OK, let's do it. Press

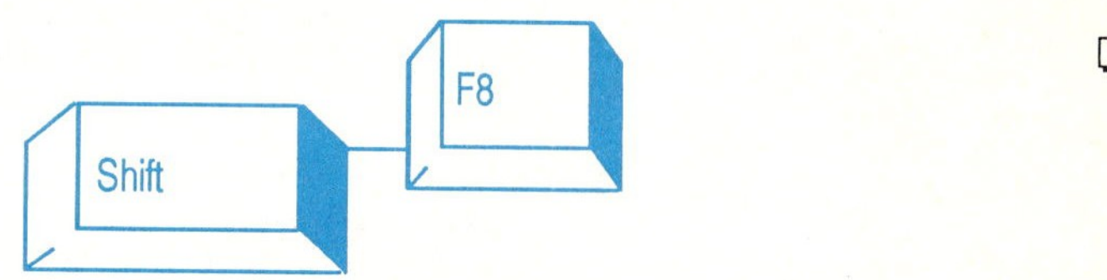

❑

You should see the Format command as displayed in Figure T2-7.

To change the left and right margin settings, select the Line option, **1**. Type

1 ❑

You now should see Figure T2-8.

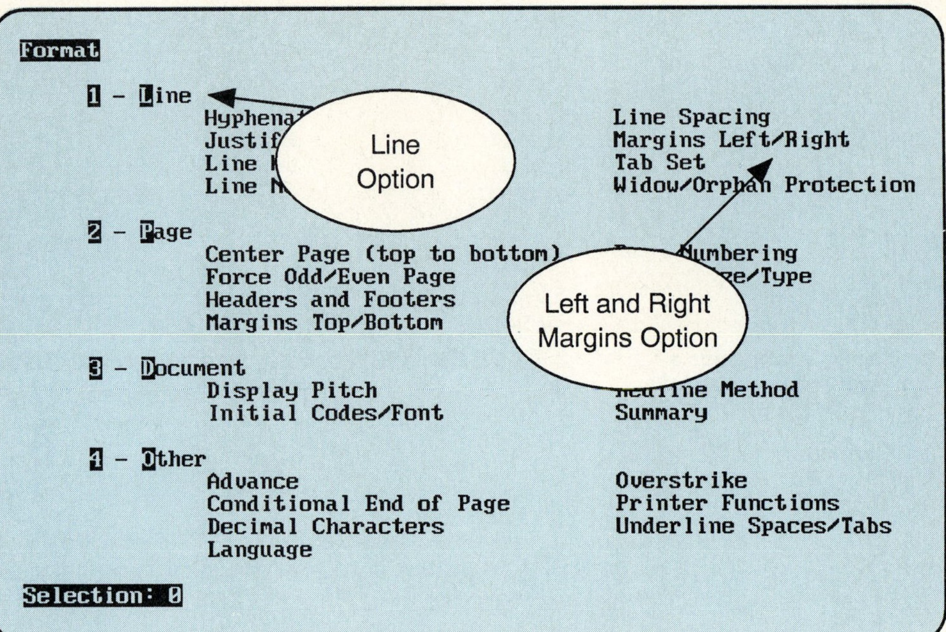

Version 5.0 users should see the additional entry *New Page Number* found under Option 2, *Page*.

FIGURE T2-7
The Format Command.

FIGURE T2-8
The Line Option of the Format Command.

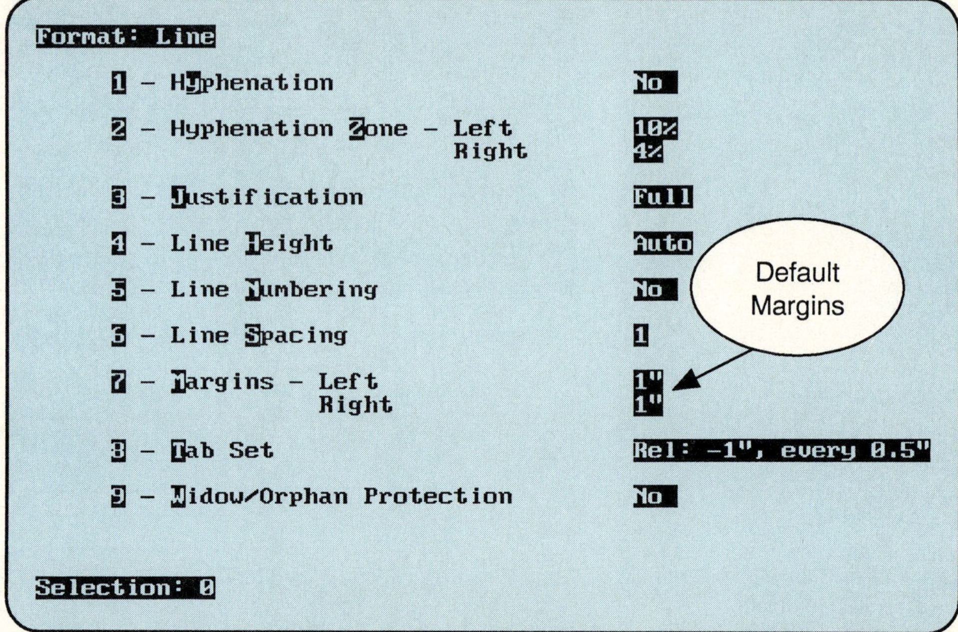

Version 5.0 users will see a different *Tab Set* setting.

Let's select the *Margins* option to change both left and right margins to 1.5 inches. Enter

7

1.5

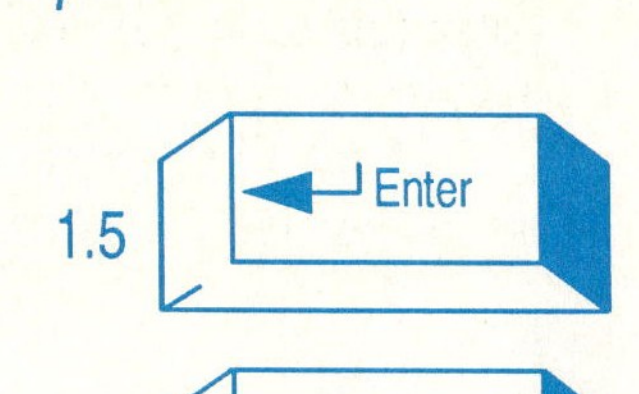

1.5

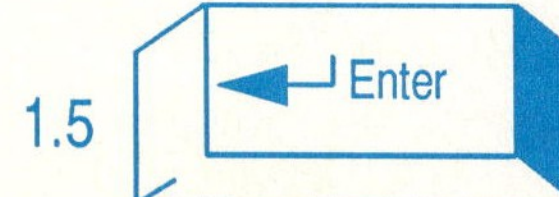

Remember, if you enter a command and want to exit without changing any setting, press the Cancel key, [F1], until you return to the Editing screen.

To register your change, press the Exit key. Press

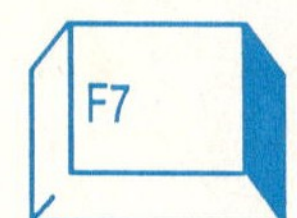

Check the **Pos** indicator to the bottom right of the screen. If *1.5"* is displayed, pat yourself on the back. You have successfully changed the default margin settings.

Now that you have changed your margins once, it should be a simple matter to do it again. Let's change them back to their original default settings of 1 inch left and 1 inch right. Are you ready? Enter

You should see the Format command, as displayed in Figure T2-7. To change the left and right margin settings, select the **Line** option, **1**. Type

1

You now should see Figure T2-8, including the changes we incorporated above.

Let's select the *Margins* option and change both the left and right margin back to 1 inch. Enter

7

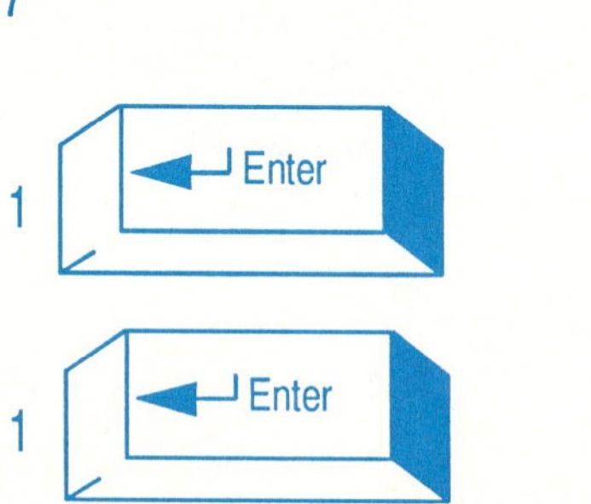

To register your change, press the Exit key. Press

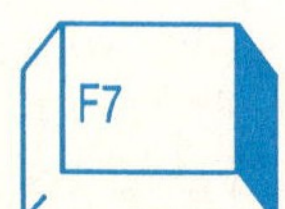

Check the **Pos** indicator to the bottom right of the screen. If *1"* is displayed, you've finished the task. Let's move on.

Set Your Tabs

To ensure consistent text alignment throughout your document, always check your tab stops. If necessary, change them to your specifications, but do so before you begin typing.

WordPerfect provides default tab stops every half inch. To look at them, we must use the same Format command we used to set the margins. Press

❑

You should see the Format command, as displayed in Figure T2-7. To check the tab stops, use the Line option, **1**. Type

1 ❑

You now see Figure T2-8. To select the *Tab set* option, type

8 ❑

You should now see Figure T2-9.

FIGURE T2-9
The Tab Set Menu.

Version 5.0 users will see a slightly different screen.

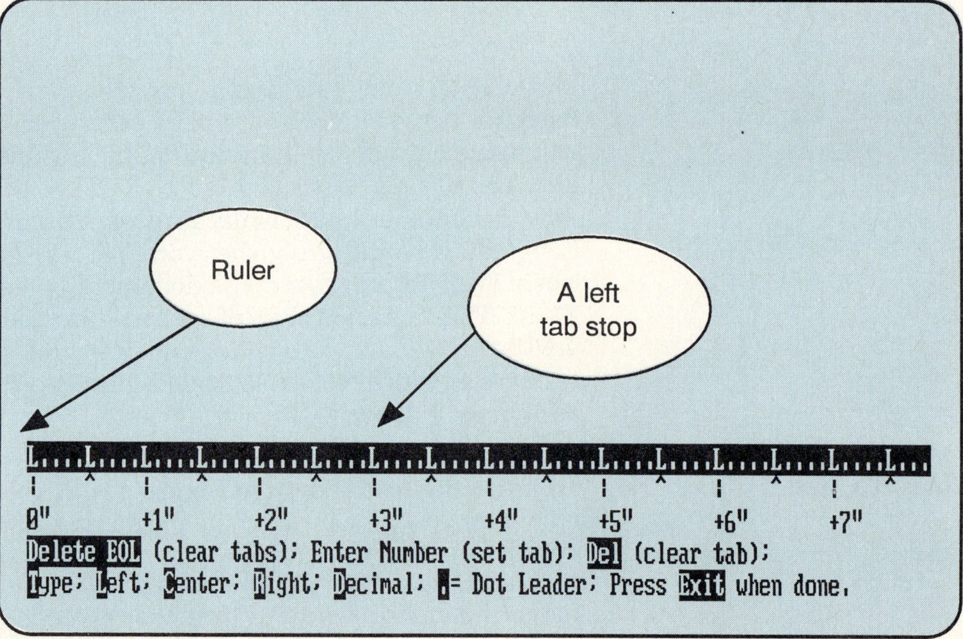

As you can see from Figure T2-9, WordPerfect displays a ruler and labels it in inches in increments of one-tenth of an inch. A left tab stop, identified by *L*, is placed every half inch. This means that when you press the [Tab] key, the character at the cursor, or character you are about to type, will end up at the first tab stop encountered beginning at the position of the cursor when the [Tab] key was initially pressed. In addition, the character is Left-aligned against that tab stop.

To remove a tab stop, place the cursor under it and then press the [Del] key. To add a tab stop, place the cursor in the desired position in the ruler and type an L.

To avoid having the cursor stop unnecessarily when the [Tab] key is pressed, it may be necessary to delete all tab stops and set only those you find useful. To delete all tabs from the cursor position to the end of the line, press and hold the [Ctrl] key then press the [End] key. This keystroke sequence is referred to as **Delete EOL**. Once all tabs are cleared, individual tabs can be set. This procedure can be very useful when creating a résumé.

To exit the Format command and save your tab stops, press the Exit key, [F7], until you are in the Editing screen. Since we have not changed anything, press the Cancel key three times. Press

❑

We know you have been awaiting patiently your chance to show how well you type. So let's begin typing.

Entering Text

If you have done everything correctly, the cursor should appear at the 1 " Position. Any text entered will be entered at the cursor position. The cursor will move ahead of you, indicating the position into which the typed character will go.

The moment has finally arrived. You are ready to create a document. Longfellow would envy the word processing power you are about to unleash. Well, let's get at it. The document you are to create is shown in Figure T2-10. The design is that of a simple business letter and will serve as the vehicle by which you will learn firsthand some of the many and varied features of WordPerfect. We will accept WordPerfect's default margins, tabs, and target printer.

How to Enter Text

To enter the text shown in Figure T2-10, you just type, spelling errors and all; when you type beyond the right margin, WordPerfect does a **wordwrap**. Wordwrap is a word processing automatic carriage-return feature. As you type and the cursor reaches the end of a line, wordwrap will automatically move the cursor (and any text that exceeds the right margin) down to the next line. For wordwrap to work properly, do not use the [Enter] key except *when you want to end a line before the right margin or when you wish to begin a new paragraph*. Each time you press the [Enter] key, a "hard" carriage return is inserted—only you can't see it unless you reveal the hard carriage-return **code** by using the WordPerfect command **Reveal Codes**. Codes are commands that tell WordPerfect and your printer what to do. Whenever you press the [Enter] key or execute a command like Format, WordPerfect inserts codes into your document. The Reveal Codes command displays these codes. To activate Reveal Codes, you need only press and hold the [Alt] key while pressing the [F3] Function key.

All lines are justified automatically. This means that when printed, the document will have even left and right margins, regardless of what the screen version of your document looks like.

Ms Sally Mathews
14 Woodhill Lane
Hollywood, CA 38223

Dear Sally,

You have been a valued member of the Stretch-n-Smith Health Spa for one year. We know, Sally, you are aware of the many benefits that our orgamization has to offer. Now is the time for you to reew. Stretch and I value your participation. We would like you to know, Sally, that the cost to our old members has not increased. If you would like to continue your membership, please fill out and return the enclosed membership registration form.

Also, this Saturday afternoon is the annual meeting of the Body Builders of America Club. We hope to see you there.

Sincerely,

J.P. Miller
Manager

cc L.V. Smith

FIGURE T2-10
Simple Business Letter Containing Errors.

To get capital letters, just hold down the [Shift] key and type your letter.

If you make a mistake typing a character, simply press the [Backspace] key. Each time you press this key, the character to the left of the cursor is deleted. Don't press the [Tab] key; it will not be needed.

Now enter the document exactly as you see it, including the errors. If you make additional errors, don't worry; you'll correct them later.

When you are finished, your document may look different than ours. For example, the word *for* located at the beginning of our line 2 may appear at the end of your line 1. Also, your lines may be longer than ours. Do you know why? One reason may be your target printer. Is it different than ours?

If your document does look different than ours, *do not* attempt to edit the text that appears in each of its lines to match Figure T2-10.

Cursor Movement

There are going to be times when you will wish to jump from one line, paragraph, or even one page of text to another. (You may already have encountered some cases while typing in the sample text.) This is accomplished by moving the cursor to the new position.

There are many keys and combinations of keys that can be used to move the cursor within a document. Some are included on the keyboard template, and others are included in Table T2-3. In general, you can expect to use from one to three keys to move the cursor to a particular location within your document.

TABLE T2-3
Cursor-Movement Keys

Key	Cursor Movement
8 ↑	Moves the cursor up one line
2 ↓	Moves the cursor down one line
4 ←	Moves the cursor one character to the left
6 →	Moves the cursor one character to the right
Ctrl – 4 ←	Moves the cursor one word to the left
Ctrl – 6 →	Moves the cursor one word to the right
7 Home, 8 ↑ or - *	Moves the cursor to the top of the screen
7 Home, 2 ↓ or + *	Moves the cursor to the bottom of the screen

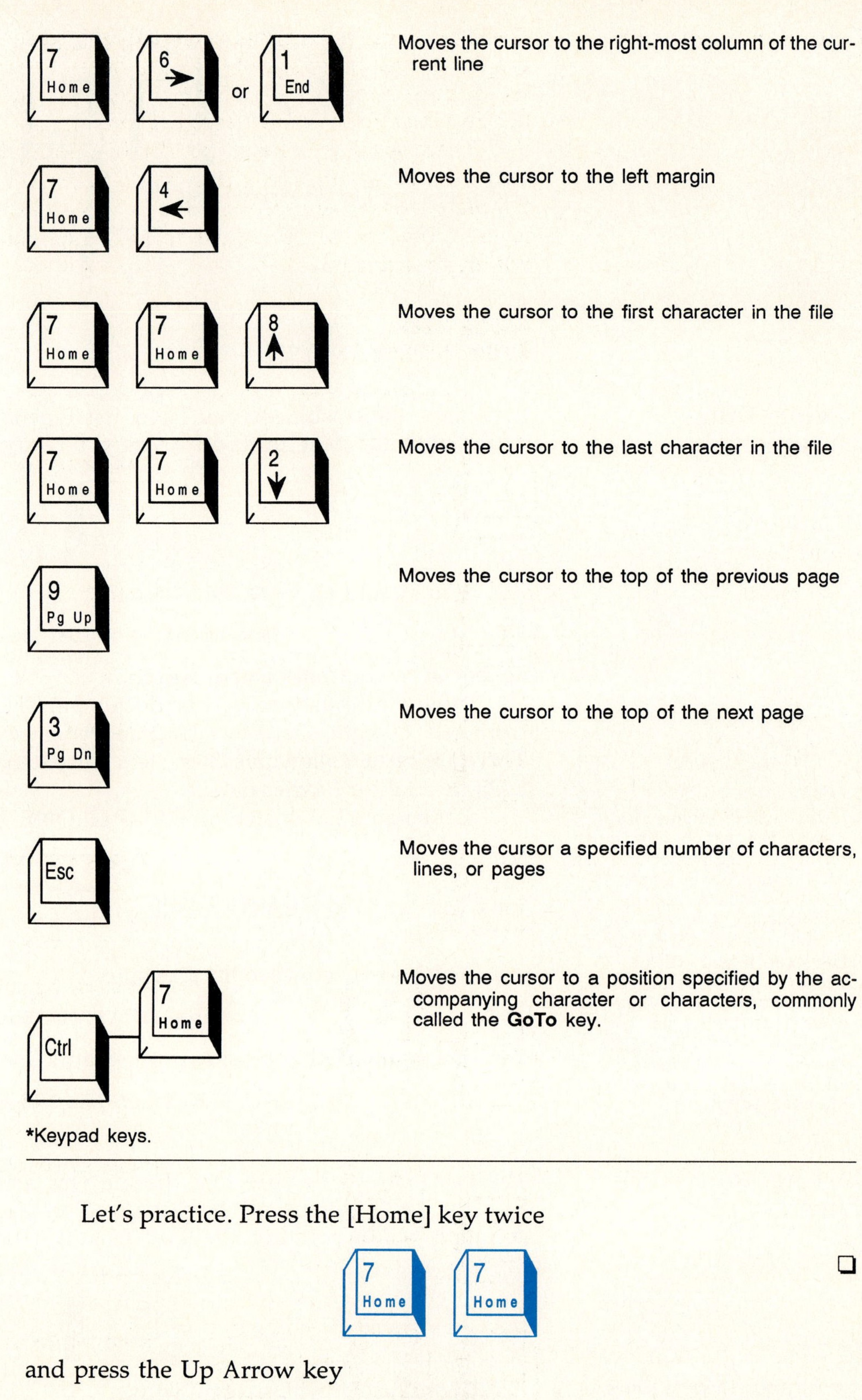

*Keypad keys.

Let's practice. Press the [Home] key twice

7 Home 7 Home ❑

and press the Up Arrow key

8 ❑

You are at the beginning of your file. Now press the [Home] key twice

❑

and press the Down Arrow key

❑

to go to the end of your file.

Saving Your Document

Let's save the document you have just typed. This is a very simple, but extremely important, procedure. Are you ready? Depress the **Save** key

❑

You should now see the message

```
Document to be saved:
```

appear at the bottom of your screen.

Now you must name your document. The name you choose must be from one to eight characters long and begin with a letter of the alphabet. There are certain allowable characters and extensions permitted. Consult the DOS tutorial for further details.

If you will be saving to a drive other than B:, you must qualify the file name with the drive name. For example, if you have a hard disk and are saving to the A: drive, you should type A:SAMPLE.ONE. However, if you will be saving to the WordPerfect subdirectory of your hard drive, you could type C:\WP51\SAMPLE.ONE, assuming the subdirectory to which you are saving your file is C:\WP51.

Let's name the document **SAMPLE.ONE**. Enter

❑

You should now see the message

```
Saving B:\SAMPLE.ONE
```

and in a moment, the left side of the Status line should display

```
B:\SAMPLE.ONE
```

Listing Your Work Files

The best way to be sure that the file was actually saved with the name SAMPLE.ONE is to list all the files saved on the disk in drive B:. This can be accomplished by pressing the **List** (**List Files** for Version 5.0) key, [F5]. Press

❑

If you want to see a listing of a different directory, type the directory name followed by a colon, :. For example, to see a listing of the files stored on the disk in the A: drive, type A: to the preceding message and then press the [Enter] key.

WordPerfect will respond with

```
Dir B:\*.*          (Type = to change default Dir)
```

Since we do want a directory of the disk in drive B:, press

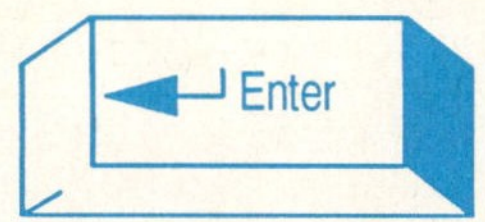

❑

If SAMPLE.ONE is the only file on your diskette, you will see Figure T2-11.

FIGURE T2-11
Listing of Files Saved on the Diskette in Drive B:.

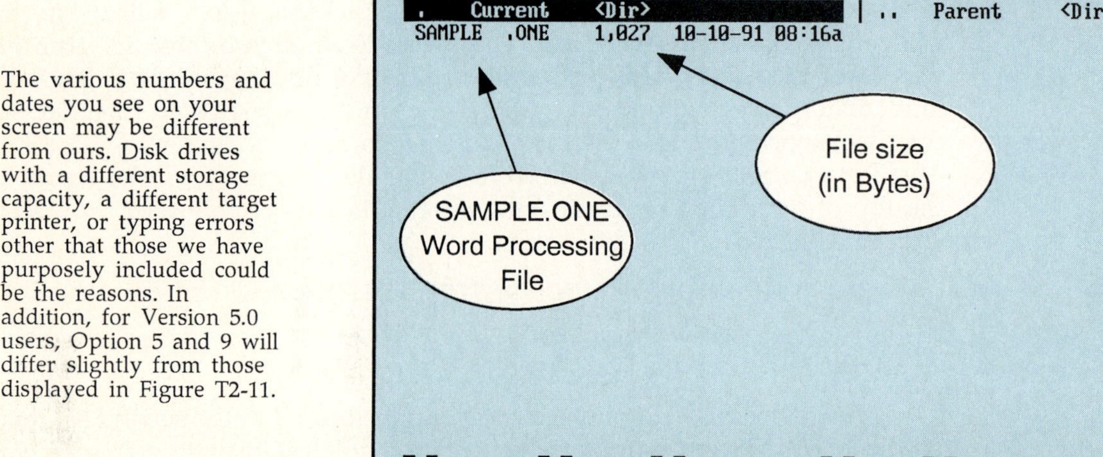

The various numbers and dates you see on your screen may be different from ours. Disk drives with a different storage capacity, a different target printer, or typing errors other that those we have purposely included could be the reasons. In addition, for Version 5.0 users, Option 5 and 9 will differ slightly from those displayed in Figure T2-11.

To exit from the List (List Files) command, press

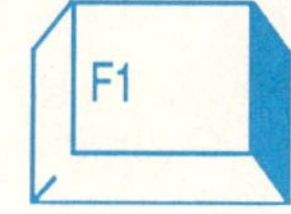

❑

Correcting Errors

If you make a typographical error (should we say *when* you make a typographical error?), you will first have to move the cursor to the location of the transgression. The template and your keyboard will help you to choose the correct commands to help you salvage your work. Your template is a guide and first aid kit all rolled into one.

Deleting

The [Del] key on your keyboard deletes the character at the cursor position. For example, if you meant to type "bar" but mistakenly entered "barf," you would have to remove the *f*. Simply move the cursor to the letter *f* and press the [Del] key to erase it. Not only does this erase the *f*, but it would move the remaining characters on the line to the left one position. Thus, if the line had been typed

"Members! You are becoming negligent in paying your barf bills."

deleting the *f* would result in

"Members! You are becoming negligent in paying your bar bills."

If you are simply replacing one character with another, you need not delete the old character first. You can type the correct character over the incorrect one replacing it. For example, if "barf" had been typed where "bark" was intended, move the cursor under the *f*, press the [Ins] key, and then type in a *k*. This will cause the *k* to replace the *f*—provided the Insert feature is off. The Insert feature is turned off by pressing the [Ins] key. The Status line displays the word *Typeover* in the lower left corner when Insert is off. If Insert is on, the name of your document is displayed in the Status line.

If you did not turn off Insert, typing a *k* would cause the word to be expanded to read "barkf," which is not what you want. To go back into the Insert mode, simply press the [Ins] key again.

As mentioned earlier, depressing the [Backspace] key will delete the character to the left of the cursor. This is handy when you catch an error that was just typed and want to change it before continuing. In our example, if immediately after typing *f* you noticed your mistake, you could then depress the [Backspace] key to erase the *f* and then continue typing.

Let's correct some of the errors in our document. Move the cursor to the top of your file by pressing the [Home] key twice followed by the Up Arrow key. Press

❑

Notice the misspelled word *orgamization* located in the second sentence of the body of your sample letter. Correct this by using what you have learned above. Don't be afraid; go ahead. Use the Arrow keys to move your cursor under the *m* in *orgamization* and make the correction. Don't forget to use the [Ins] key to change from insert to typeover mode.

That's great. We knew you could do it. Now, let's see how you would delete whole words and complete lines of text. Table T2-4 explains how.

TABLE T2-4
Key Combinations For Deleting Words and Lines

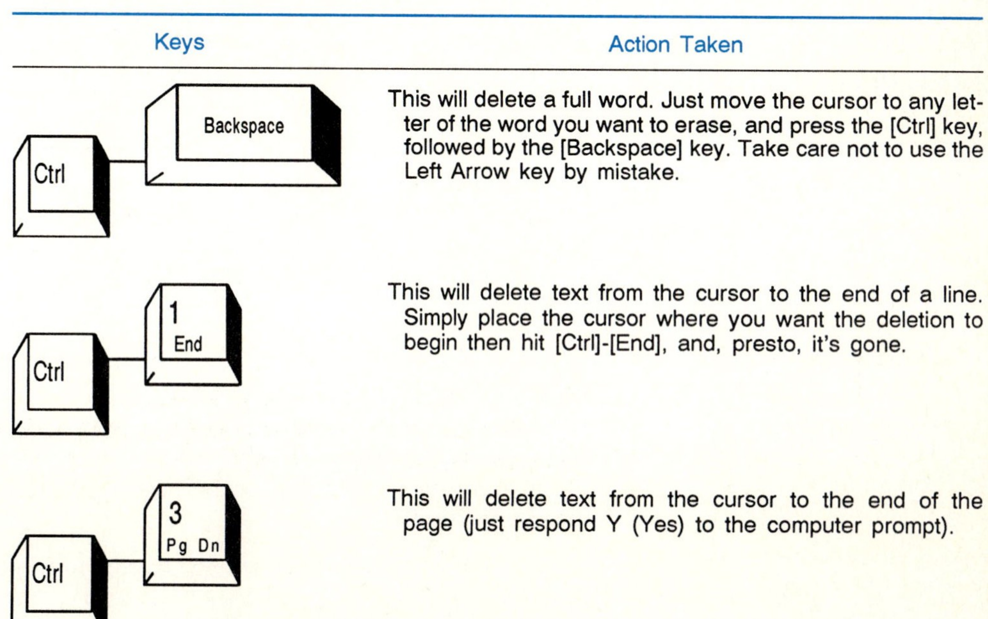

Keys	Action Taken
Ctrl – Backspace	This will delete a full word. Just move the cursor to any letter of the word you want to erase, and press the [Ctrl] key, followed by the [Backspace] key. Take care not to use the Left Arrow key by mistake.
Ctrl – 1 End	This will delete text from the cursor to the end of a line. Simply place the cursor where you want the deletion to begin then hit [Ctrl]-[End], and, presto, it's gone.
Ctrl – 3 Pg Dn	This will delete text from the cursor to the end of the page (just respond Y (Yes) to the computer prompt).

This will delete a blank line. Just place the cursor at the beginning of the blank line you want deleted, and press the [Del] key.

Inserting

You will recall that pressing the [Ins] key will toggle in and out of the Insert mode. To insert text, that is, to "squeeze" something into your document, you must be in the Insert mode or get into it (in this mode the file name is displayed in the Status line to the lower left of your screen). If you see the word *Typeover* in the Status line, then you must get back to the Insert mode by pressing the [Ins] key. Make sure that you are in the Insert mode. Very good! Now lets try making some insertions within our sample letter.

Find the word *reew* located at the end of the third sentence of the body of your sample letter. Change "reew" to "renew," and add the words *your membership.* To insert the letter *n,* move the cursor to the character before which you want *n* inserted (under the second *e* in *reew*) and type

n ❑

Now move the cursor to the period right after *renew.* At this point type

your membership ❑

Did you forget to insert a space before you typed the word *your*? If you did, move the cursor to the *y* in *your* and depress the Space bar.

To insert a blank line, place the cursor where you want the line to appear and press the [Enter] key.

Undeleting Text

There will be times when you delete text that should not have been deleted in the first place. WordPerfect saves the three most recent deletions of any type (a deletion is any group of erased characters). Does this mean that if you delete something by mistake, you can bring it back into your document? It sure does. Here is how it works. Move the cursor to the *S* in the word *Sally* at the top of your document. Now delete the word by depressing and holding the [Ctrl] key followed by the [Backspace] key.

❑

Sally is gone. But wait, you made an error. You need *Sally* exactly where it is. No problem. If necessary, use the Arrow keys to position the cursor where you want *Sally* returned, and press

❑

You should now see Figure T2-12.

Notice that the word *Sally* is restored, but it is also highlighted. To remove the highlight, type

1 ❑

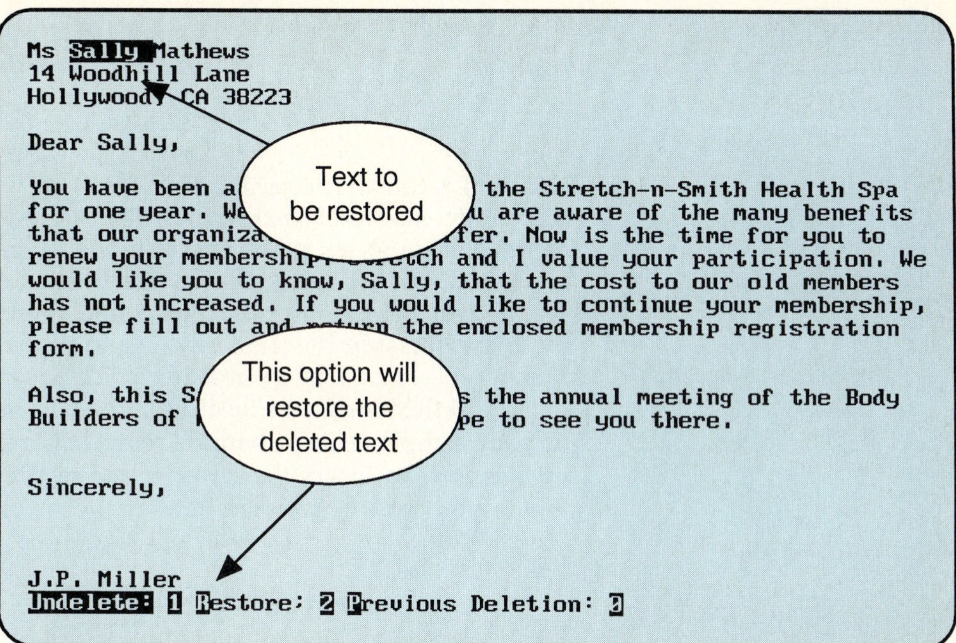

FIGURE T2-12
The Undelete Key.

Reforming Text

Reforming a Paragraph

After making changes to your text, chances are that some of the letters you've inserted and deleted have caused the right margin in your paragraph to become ragged and unaligned. You need help. After editing a line of text, to realign your paragraph within your margins, simply press the Down Arrow key and WordPerfect will automatically reform your text from the cursor position down to the end of the paragraph.

Hyphenation

Should your text require hyphenation, you will have to turn hyphenation on. To turn hyphenation on, position the cursor at the top of the first page to start hyphenation, then execute the Format command by holding down the [Shift] key while pressing the [F8] Function key. Then type 1 twice followed by Y (Version 5.0 users type 1 twice followed by 3), and press the Exit key, [F7]. This action will insert an invisible hyphen-on code within your document. After pressing the [F7] Function key, hyphens will be inserted automatically where needed.

If you decide to hyphenate, WordPerfect will split a word by placing a soft hyphen on the current line and continue the remaining characters of the word on the next line as hyphenation is needed. The hyphen is referred to as a soft hyphen because it has meaning only when it is the last character on a line. If you were to later reform the paragraph so that the soft hyphen moved away from the right margin and the parts of the split word recombined, the soft hyphen would no longer appear when the text is printed.

If you manually hyphenate, don't just type a minus to hyphenate. Instead, manually insert a soft hyphen. To accomplish this, press the [Ctrl] key and type a minus [–] sign where you want a hyphen inserted in a word.

To turn hyphenation off at any location within your document, you must insert a hyphen-off code. This can be done using the Format command. Hold down the [Shift] key, and press the [F8] Function key; then type a 1 twice followed by an N (Version 5.0 users press 1 three times), and press the Exit key, [F7]. This option will remain in effect until changed by inserting a hyphen-on code.

Paragraph Indents

If you would like a paragraph indented from the left margin, use the Indent key, or command, [F4]. When pressed, the cursor will move to the first tab stop to the right of its position in the line. All text typed from that point on will be aligned at the tab stop until the [Enter] key is pressed. When the [Enter] key is pressed, the cursor will return to the left-margin setting.

You should know the difference between the Tab and Indent functions. You press the [Tab] key to indent only the first line of a paragraph. To indent the entire paragraph, press the [F4] or Indent key.

Let's try the Indent command. We will use your sample letter and indent paragraph 2. Move the cursor to the beginning of paragraph 2, under the *A* in *Also*. Press

❑

You should now see Figure T2-13.

FIGURE T2-13
The Indent Key Applied To Paragraph 2.

```
Ms Sally Mathews
14 Woodhill Lane
Hollywood, CA 38223

Dear Sally,

You have been a valued member of the Stretch-n-Smith Health Spa
for one year. We know, Sally, you are aware of the many benefits
that our organization has to offer. Now is the time for you to
renew your membership. Stretch and I value your participation. We
would like you to know, Sally, that the cost to our old members
has not increased. If you would like to continue your membership,
please fill out and return the enclosed membership registration
form.

     Also, this Saturday a                  meeting of the
     Body Builders of Amer                  ee you there.

Sincerely,


J.P. Miller
B:\SAMPLE.ONE                        Doc 1 Pg 1 Ln 3.67" Pos 1.5"
```

Text is indented from this point on

To remove the Indent command and restore our paragraph to its original state, we will use Reveal Codes. Place the cursor under the *A* in *Also* if it is not already there. Press

❑

This action splits your screen horizontally. The top portion contains the text in the immediate vicinity of the cursor without codes revealed, whereas the bottom portion contains both the text and codes (see Fig. T2-14).

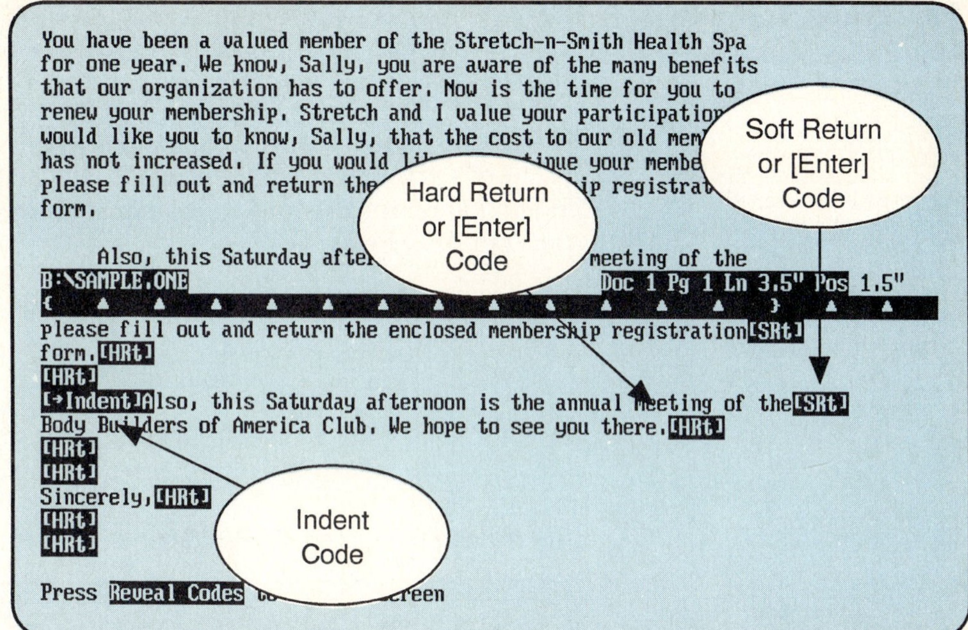

FIGURE T2-14
Reveal Codes Displaying the Indent Code.

Look at the bottom portion of the screen, to the left of the *A* in *Also*. You should see

[→Indent]

This is the code for Indent. To delete it, if necessary, place the cursor under the *A* in *Also*. Then press the [Backspace] key

❑

Presto, its gone! Did you notice how your text reformed to the left margin?

To escape from Reveal Codes, use [Alt]-[F3] a second time. Press

❑

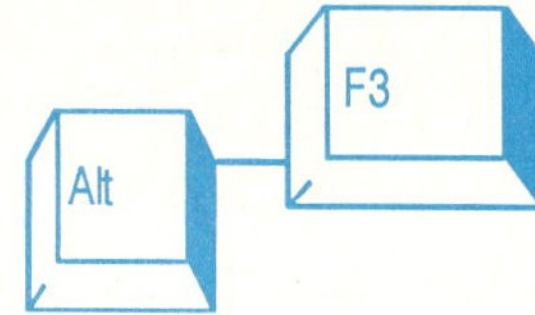

To remove a format option that you no longer want, reveal its code by using Reveal Codes. Use the [Backspace] key or the [Del] key to remove the code, and then escape from Reveal Codes.

Saving and Retrieving a Document

Save and Resume

As you write your document, it's always a good idea to "take out insurance" by saving a copy of your work every once in a while. Many are the poor users who, after hours of entering text, are horrified to learn that because of some freak accident or oversight their text is lost. The Save key, [F10], will allow you to breath easier as you type away.

Since you have already named and saved your document, pressing the

[F10] Function key now will do a save and resume operation. The computer will save a copy of your document on the disk named just before the file name at the bottom of your screen. Let's save your file now. Press

❑

In response to the message

Hard-disk users may see A:\SAMPLE.ONE or C:\WP\SAMPLE.ONE displayed instead of B:\SAMPLE.ONE.

`Document to be saved: B:\SAMPLE.ONE`

press

❑

and WordPerfect will begin looking for your document. Once it finds the document, it will ask if you want to replace the saved copy of SAMPLE.ONE with the current copy. The message displayed by WordPerfect Version 5.1 (5.0 is slightly different) is

`Replace B:\SAMPLE.ONE? No (Yes)`

Since we do want to replace the old version, type

❑

After some disk activity, you are back in business.

Save and Exit

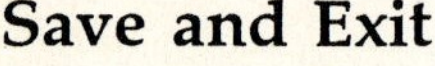

There will be occasions when you wish to save your document and leave WordPerfect until you can resume your work at some future date. At times, you may want to exit WordPerfect without saving your document. In either case, *you should always exit WordPerfect using the Exit key, [F7].*

Let's see how this save and exit procedure would be carried out. Initiate the Exit command by pressing

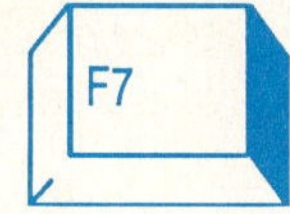

❑

The message

Some of the messages displayed by WordPerfect Version 5.0 will be slightly different than those shown in this section, which correspond to Version 5.1.

`Save document? Yes (No)          (Text was not modified)`

appears. Press

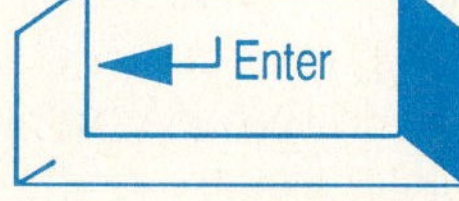

❑

to see the message

Hard-disk users will probably not see B: displayed. Instead, A: or C:\WP51\ may appear.

`Document to be Saved: B:\SAMPLE.ONE?`

Press

❑

Now you will be presented with the option to replace your copy on disk with the most recent copy located in your computer's memory.

```
Replace B:\SAMPLE.ONE? No (Yes)
```

Type

Y ❑

WordPerfect responds with

```
Saving B:SAMPLE.ONE    Yes
```

then

```
Exit WP? No (Yes)      (Cancel to return to document)
```

At this point you may wish to vary from the save and resume procedure. Check with your instructor to determine if he or she would like you to exit WordPerfect. To remain in WordPerfect, simply press the [Enter] key; otherwise, to exit WordPerfect, type

Y ❑

and you are out of WordPerfect and back at the system prompt. If you chose not to exit WordPerfect, you should be viewing the blank Editing screen (see Fig. T2-1).

Retrieving a Document

If you want to resume work on a document previously saved to disk, the procedure is straightforward.

First, if you exited WordPerfect before, now bring it back up by following the procedures we provided in the section titled "Starting Your Computer and WordPerfect." Otherwise read on.

Once you are in the Editing screen, you can retrieve a document from disk (and bring it back into the computer's memory), by using the **Retrieve** command. To execute Retrieve, hold down the [Shift] key and press the [F10] Function key. Press

❑

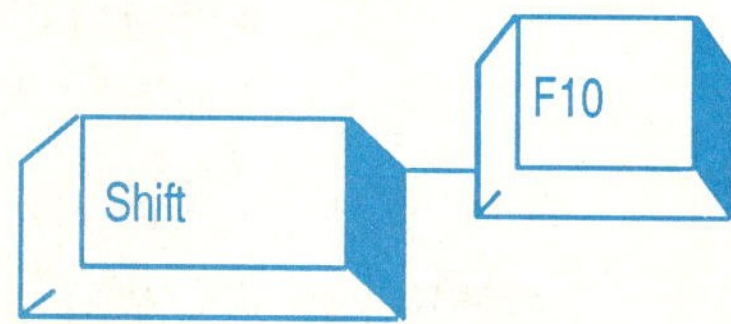

In response to the prompt, type the name of your document:

❑

Hard-disk users will probably replace the disk drive specification B: with A: or C:\WP51\.

Now you can continue working on your masterpiece.

Retrieving Documents Produced by Other Versions of WordPerfect

A WordPerfect Version 4.2 file can be converted to Version 5.0 format by retrieving ([Shift]-[F10]) the Version 4.2 file into Version 5.0 and then saving it. Similarly, a WordPerfect Version 4.2 or 5.0 file can be converted to Version 5.1 by retrieving ([Shift]-[F10]) the 4.2 or 5.0 file into Version 5.1 and then saving it. Some Version 4.2 codes may not convert to Version 5.1 codes. In these cases, WordPerfect will replace the code with a comment.

WordPerfect Version 5.1 files can be converted to Version 4.2 or 5.0 files using the Text In/Out feature ([Ctrl]-[F5]).

Basic Block Operations

If you want to move, copy, or delete blocks of text (characters, words, parts of lines, whole lines, paragraphs, parts of paragraphs, pages, and parts of pages, for example), WordPerfect provides a way. In order for block operations to work, the beginning and end of the text you want to work with must be marked. What is marked is referred to as a **block** of text. A block of text can be a single character, an entire document, or anything in between.

Marking a Block

To mark a block of text, move the cursor to the first character in the text to be marked and press and hold the [Alt] key while pressing the [F4] Function key. This will turn on the *Block-on* message in your Status line. To complete marking the block, simply position the cursor immediately after the last character in the text to be marked. If the end of the block is also the end of a paragraph, move the cursor to the beginning of the line following the paragraph. That's it.

Let's mark the first paragraph of your sample letter so that we can move it. To do this, move the cursor to the first letter in your first paragraph, *Y* in *You,* and press

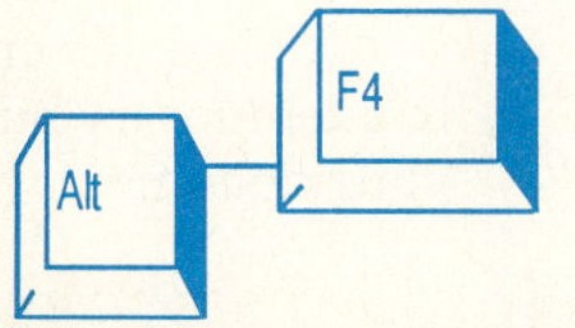

❑

The *Block-on* message should be flashing at the bottom left of your screen. Now, let's mark the end of the block. Use the Down Arrow key to move the cursor to the first position of the line following the paragraph. Your first paragraph is now marked (see Fig. T2-15).

To cancel or unmark a marked block, press the Cancel key, [F1].

FIGURE T2-15
The Sample Letter with the First Paragraph Blocked (Highlighted).

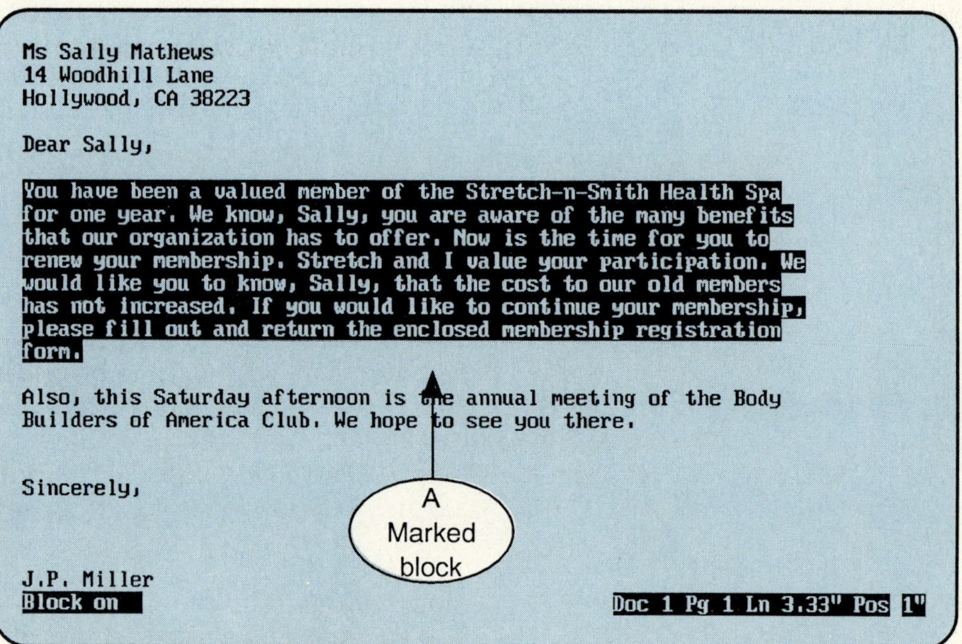

Ms Sally Mathews
14 Woodhill Lane
Hollywood, CA 38223

Dear Sally,

You have been a valued member of the Stretch-n-Smith Health Spa
for one year. We know, Sally, you are aware of the many benefits
that our organization has to offer. Now is the time for you to
renew your membership. Stretch and I value your participation. We
would like you to know, Sally, that the cost to our old members
has not increased. If you would like to continue your membership,
please fill out and return the enclosed membership registration
form.

Also, this Saturday afternoon is the annual meeting of the Body
Builders of America Club. We hope to see you there.

Sincerely,

J.P. Miller
Block on   Doc 1 Pg 1 Ln 3.33" Pos 1"

Moving a Block

To move a block, you must first mark it as we just did. Then, you must call up the Move command. Call up the Move command by pressing

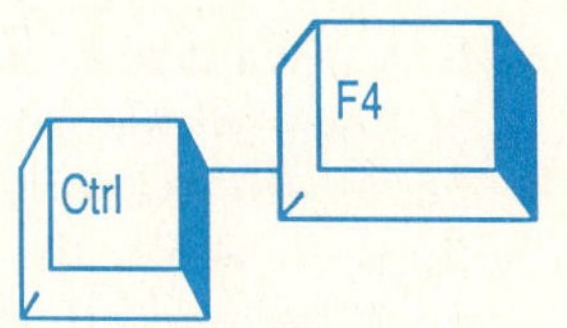

❑

The message

`Move: 1 Block; 2 Tabular Column; 3 Rectangle: 0`

should appear at the bottom of your display.

Select the Block option by typing

1 ❑

The following message will be displayed:

`1 Move; 2 Copy; 3 Delete; 4 Append: 0`

Type

1 ❑

Presto, the entire block is gone. Well, not completely. You see, it is stored in a temporary buffer waiting to be brought back to some other place within your document. Notice the message at the bottom of your display

`Move cursor;  press Enter to retrieve.`

Let's move it now.

Move to the beginning of the second blank line after your last paragraph (the one beginning with "Also, this . . .). Now depress

❑

and, with the speed of light, your paragraph is moved to its new location and deleted from its old location (see Fig. T2-16).

Notice that there are no longer two blank lines between the last line of text and the salutation. Let's insert a blank line now. Move the cursor to the *S* of *Sincerely.* Press

❑

This causes all text from the cursor on to be moved down one line.

Notice also that there are extra blank lines at the beginning of the letter. This resulted from the fact that the blank lines before and after the moved block of text are now together. Move the cursor to one of these blank lines, and delete it by pressing

❑

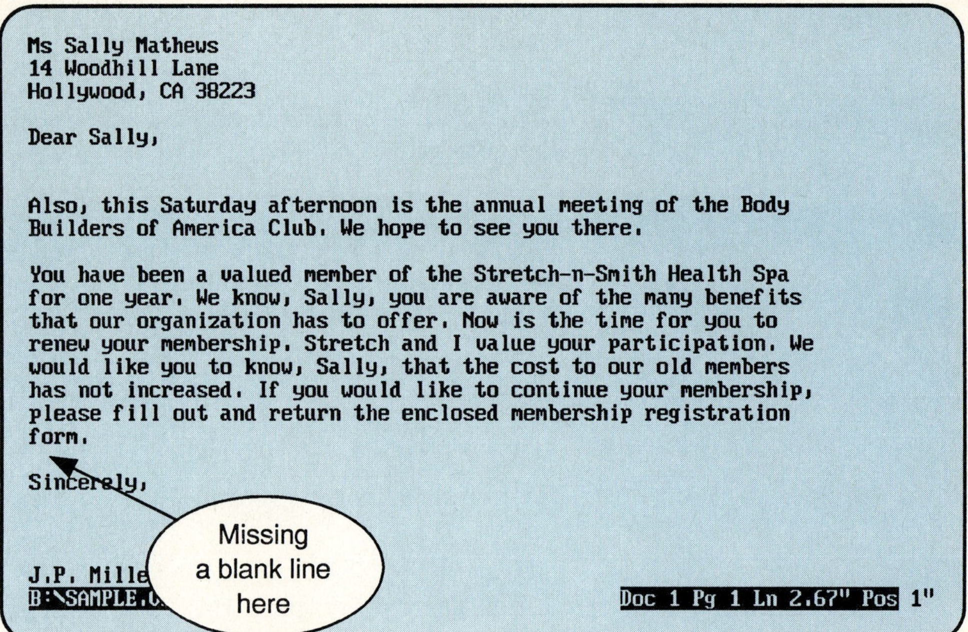
Ms Sally Mathews
14 Woodhill Lane
Hollywood, CA 38223

Dear Sally,

Also, this Saturday afternoon is the annual meeting of the Body Builders of America Club. We hope to see you there.

You have been a valued member of the Stretch-n-Smith Health Spa for one year. We know, Sally, you are aware of the many benefits that our organization has to offer. Now is the time for you to renew your membership. Stretch and I value your participation. We would like you to know, Sally, that the cost to our old members has not increased. If you would like to continue your membership, please fill out and return the enclosed membership registration form.

Sincerely,

J.P. Mille
B:\SAMPLE.C
Doc 1 Pg 1 Ln 2.67" Pos 1"

FIGURE T2-16
Moved Block.

Copying a Block

Copying a block of text is similar to moving it. To copy your paragraph to another location of your document, the Copy option is selected from the Move command. When you copy a block of text, you do not delete it from its original position; instead, you duplicate it in a new position.

Position the cursor at the beginning of the paragraph just moved (under the *Y* in *You*), and direct WordPerfect to mark the block that will include the entire paragraph. Do you remember what to do? That's right; hold down the [Alt] key and press the [F4] Function key. Press

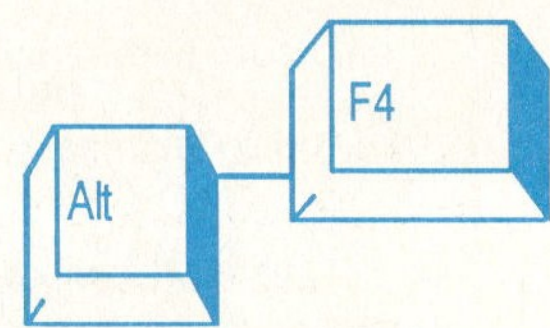

❑

The *Block-on* message is now flashing at the bottom left of your screen. Now, move the cursor to the beginning of the line immediately after the paragraph to be marked. Your paragraph is now marked.

Enter the Move command by holding down the [Ctrl] key and pressing the [F4] Function key. To do this, depress

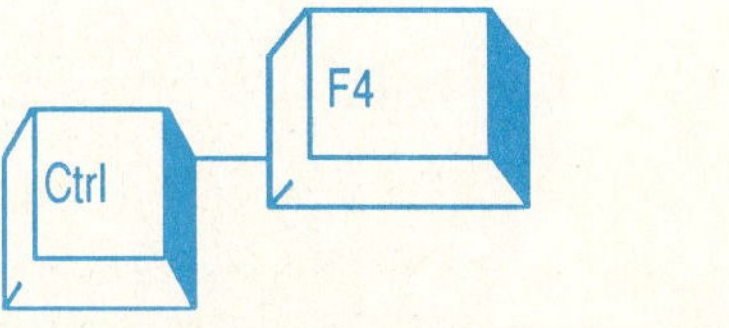

❑

You should now see the Move menu. Select the Block option by typing

1 ❑

The following message will be displayed

```
1 Move; 2 Copy; 3 Delete; 4 Append: 0
```

Type

2 ❑

Notice that the paragraph has not been removed from your document. The message

`Move cursor;   press Enter to retrieve.`

informs us that we must indicate where the copy will go. Let's copy the paragraph into its original position. Move the cursor to the beginning of the blank line immediately under "Dear Sally." Then depress

❑

You should now see Figure T2-17.

FIGURE T2-17
Screen After the Paragraph Has Been Copied.

```
Ms Sally Mathews
14 Woodhill Lane
Hollywood, CA 38223

Dear Sally,
You have been a valued member of the Stretch-n-Smith Health Spa
for one year. We know, Sally, you are aware of the many benefits
that our organization has to offer. Now is the time for you to
renew your membership. Stretch and I value your participation. We
would like you to know, Sally, that the cost to our old
has not increased. If you would like to continue you
please fill out and return the enclosed membersh
form.

Also, this Saturday afternoon is the annual meet
Builders of America Club. We hope to see you there

You have been a valued member of the Stretch-n-Smith Hea
for one year. We know, Sally, you are aware of the many benefits
that our organization has to offer. Now is the time for you to
renew your membership. Stretch and I value your participation. We
would like you to know, Sally, that the cost to our old members
has not increased. If you would like to continue your membership,
please fill out and return the enclosed membership registration
B:\SAMPLE.ONE                                Doc 1 Pg 1 Ln 1.83" Pos 1"
```

Identical paragraphs appear after the copy command is completed

You should have two copies of the original first paragraph, one at the beginning of the letter (the one you just copied) and one at the end of the letter (the one previously moved).

Notice that the blank line under "Dear Sally" is missing. Let's put it back now. Position the cursor under the *Y* of *You,* and press

❑

Deleting a Block

Once you mark a block, you can delete it with the touch of a key. That's right. All you have to do is press the [Del] key. If you respond to WordPerfect's query with *yes,* the block is gone.

Let's delete one copy of the duplicate paragraph from our text. Assume that we want the paragraph at the end of the letter deleted. How would you do this? Did you realize that you can't delete it immediately because it is not marked. Mark it now. Position the cursor under the first character in the block to be marked. Press

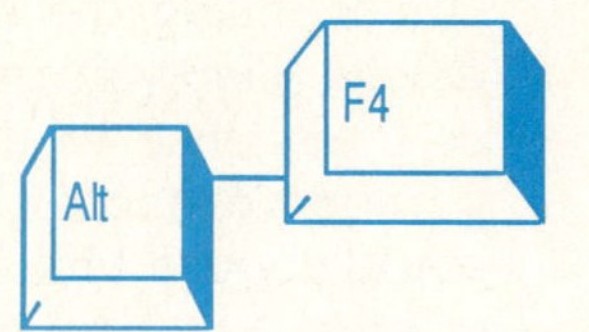

❑

Now move the cursor to the beginning of the line after the paragraph. The paragraph should now be marked. All that remains is to press

❑

The message

```
Delete  Block?  No  (Yes)
```

appears at the bottom of you screen.

Since we want to delete the block, type

❑

Version 5.0 users will see *"(Y/N) No"* displayed after *"Delete Block?"*.

That's it; its gone. Your display should be as shown in Figure T2-18.

FIGURE T2-18
Document After the Last Paragraph Has Been Deleted.

```
Ms Sally Mathews
14 Woodhill Lane
Hollywood, CA 38223

Dear Sally,

You have been a valued member of the Stretch-n-Smith Health Spa
for one year. We know, Sally, you are aware of the many benefits
that our organization has to offer. Now is the time for you to
renew your membership. Stretch and I value your participation. We
would like you to know, Sally, that the cost to our old members
has not increased. If you would like to continue your membership,
please fill out and return the enclosed membership registration
form.

Also, this Saturday afternoon is the annual meeting of the Body
Builders of America Club. We hope to see you there.


Sincerely,

B:\SAMPLE.ONE                                  Doc 1 Pg 1 Ln 4" Pos 1"
```

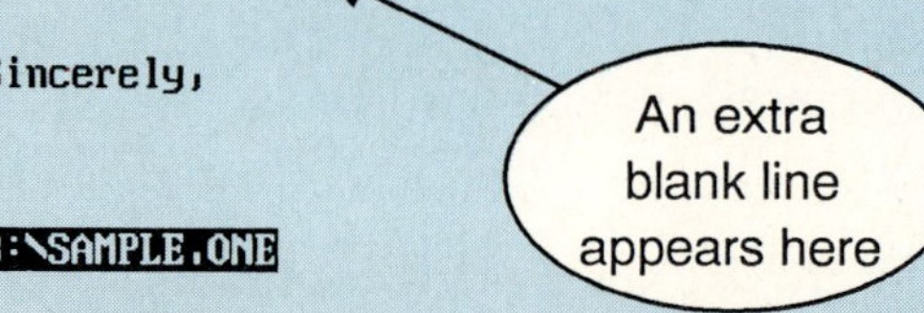

If you delete a block of text and immediately discover that you should not have done so, use the Cancel key, ([F1]), to undelete the block.

Finish up by removing the extra blank line before the salutation. Since the cursor is correctly positioned at one of these blank lines, we only need to press

❑

and the extra line is gone.

Quickly Moving, Copying, or Deleting

If you are either moving, copying, or deleting complete lines, paragraphs, or pages in your document, you can bypass the Block command and use only the Move command to carry out your action. To do this, you first move the cursor inside the line, paragraph, or page that you want to cut, copy, or delete. Then you enter the Move command and select the appropriate option. A 1 response would mark the sentence you are in, a 2 would mark the paragraph, and a 3 would mark the page. Then, after selecting 1, 2, or 3, you could choose Move (1) to move text. You could select Copy (2) to keep the original text, and make a copy of it for later insertion into your document. And, finally, you could select Delete (3) to delete the text.

Search and Replace

Let's assume you would like to send this same letter to Mary Mathews of the Stretch-n-Smith Health Spa. A global **search and replace** could be used to change the name from Sally to Mary. To change every occurrence of Sally to Mary, we must first decide if we will search from the top down or the bottom up, since the command differs depending on the direction of search.

We can replace only text while searching in a forward direction, so we will search from the top down. Move the cursor to the top of the document by pressing

❑

To activate the Replace command, press

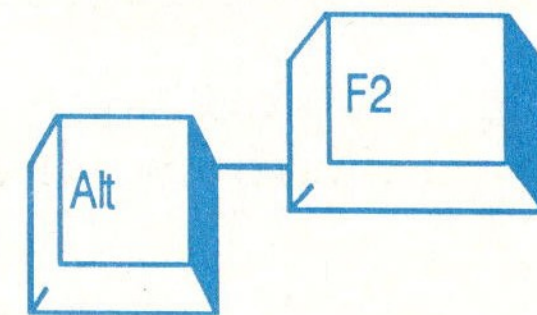

❑

and the display shown in Figure T2-19 should appear.

You must decide if you want the option to confirm each replacement or if you would rather have WordPerfect do it. Let's confirm each replacement ourselves, so type

Now enter the string of characters you want to replace. Since we want *Sally* replaced, you should type

Sally ❑

To invoke the Search command, press

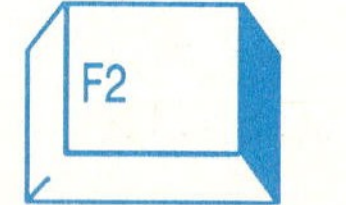

❑

and you should see message

```
Replace with:
```

displayed at the bottom of your screen. Now enter the new string of characters or codes. Type

Mary ❑

Version 5.0 users will see *(Y/N) No* displayed in places where *No (Yes)* appears.

```
Ms Sally Mathews
14 Woodhill Lane
Hollywood, CA 38223

Dear Sally,

You have been a valued member of the Stretch-n-Smith Health Spa
for one year. We know, Sally, you are aware of the many benefits
that our organization has to offer. Now is the time for you to
renew your membership. Stretch and I value your participation. We
would like you to know, Sally, that the cost to our old members
has not increased. If you would like to continue your membership,
please fill out and return the enclosed membership registration
form.

Also, thi                   n is the annual meeting of the Body
Builders                    hope to see you there.

Sincerely,


J.P. Miller
w/Confirm? No (Yes)
```

Confirm Option

FIGURE T2-19
The Replace Menu.

At last, the search and replace can begin. Activate the search by pressing

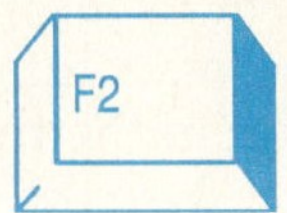

❑

WordPerfect should locate and identify the first occurrence of *Sally* immediately and issue the prompt

`Confirm?   No  (Yes)`

Respond with *yes* because you want to replace *Sally* with *Mary*. Type

Y ❑

and you should see Figure T2-20.

To continue, you must press either Y for *yes*, or N for *no* each time WordPerfect finds *Sally*. When there are no more occurrences of *Sally* in your document, you can continue with another command or key in more text. Go ahead and make all the necessary replacements until you are at the end of your document. Type Y to all prompts in order to replace all occurrences of *Sally*. It shouldn't be necessary to reform your text because this is done automatically by WordPerfect.

To be certain that you don't lose your work as the result of an accidental power loss or other problem, save it now. If you've forgotten how to do this, refer to the section entitled "Save and Resume," page 74.

Styling Your Document

Before your document is printed, you will want to add some finishing touches to it. Let's examine some WordPerfect commands that, when used properly, will enhance the appearance of your document.

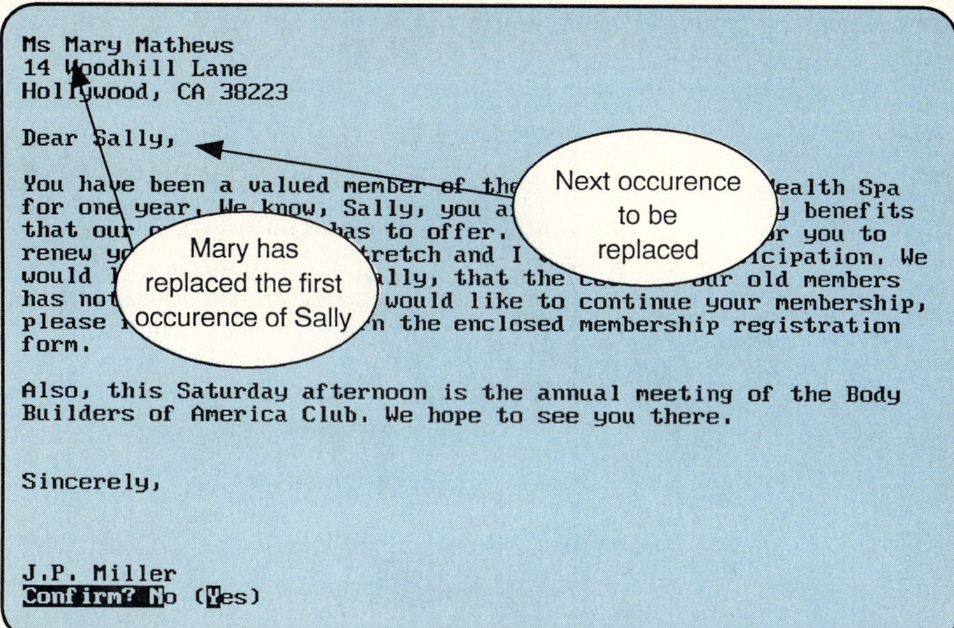

FIGURE T2-20
First Find of Sally.

Adding Boldface

Boldface is a character style that results in a darker, heaver print such as the first word in this sentence. It is effective for emphasizing words. They just seem to jump up at you from the page as you read them. To illustrate the use of boldface, let's assume that we want to put into boldface the word *Now* in the third sentence of our document.

Use the Arrow keys to move the cursor to the *N* in *Now*. Since the text we wish to put into boldface already exists, we must begin by blocking it. (This step would not be necessary if you were entering new text.) To mark the beginning of the block, press

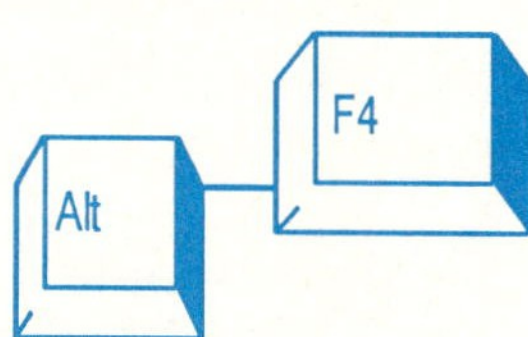

To mark the end of the block, move the cursor to the space after the word *Now*. The block is now marked. To put the block into boldface, press

If you have a color monitor, the blocked characters should appear in a different color; otherwise they will be highlighted.

If you want to remove the boldface style from a word, use Reveal Codes ([Alt]-[F3]) to reveal the **[BOLD]** code, move the cursor to the code and then delete the code.

It is never a good idea to use boldface excessivly. Use it sparingly, or risk having its effectiveness diminished.

Note that it was not necessary to turn off the boldface. This is because we were putting existing text into boldface. If we were typing new text, we would have to press the [F6] Function key before we begin typing and again after we type the last character to be put into boldface. However, no blocking is necessary in this case.

Underscoring Text

As with the **boldface** character style, text can be underscored for emphasis, as it has been in this sentence. WordPerfect provides for a number of variations of underscoring. We will investigate one of these, single-line continuous. The technique is similar to that used with boldface, except that we use the [F8] Function key instead of the [F6] Function key.

To see how this works, let's assume that we wish to underscore the words *the cost to our old members has not increased.* As with boldface, since the text already exists, we must begin by blocking the text to be underscored. Move the cursor to the *t* in *the.* Mark this by pressing

❑

Move the cursor to the period after the word *increased.* The block is now marked. Press

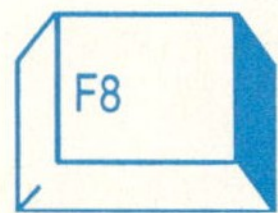

❑

to underscore the block (see Fig. T2-21).

FIGURE T2-21
The Sample Document with the Word *Now* Typed in Boldface and the Phrase *the Cost to Our Old Members Has Not Increased* Underscored.

"The cost to our old members has not increased" may appear on your monitor underscored with dashed or solid lines or in color or reverse video without any underscore. These differences are possible because of the variety of monitors that may be used with WordPerfect. Different hardware will display the screen version of the underscore differently. However, when you print the sample letter, the phrase will be underscored no matter what monitor you are using.

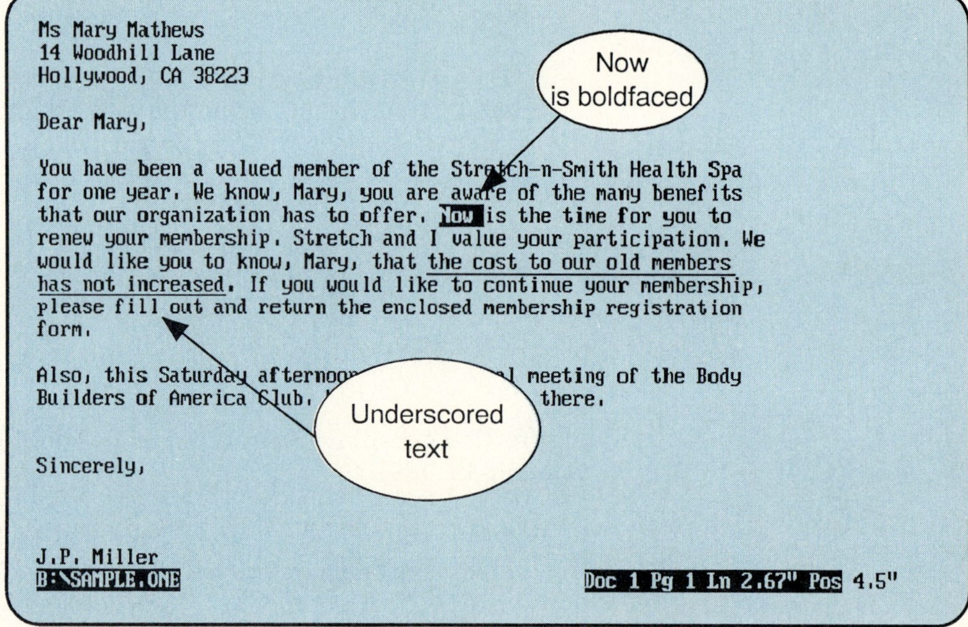

Ms Mary Mathews
14 Woodhill Lane
Hollywood, CA 38223

Dear Mary,

You have been a valued member of the Stretch-n-Smith Health Spa for one year. We know, Mary, you are aware of the many benefits that our organization has to offer. **Now** is the time for you to renew your membership. Stretch and I value your participation. We would like you to know, Mary, that the cost to our old members has not increased. If you would like to continue your membership, please fill out and return the enclosed membership registration form.

Also, this Saturday afternoon ... l meeting of the Body Builders of America Club. ... there.

Sincerely,

J.P. Miller

B:\SAMPLE.ONE Doc 1 Pg 1 Ln 2.67" Pos 4.5"

Note that, as with boldface, it was not necessary to turn off the underscore. This is necessary only when you are entering new text.

Adding the Date to a Document

If you forgot to enter the current date when you started your computer, you can do it now, while in WordPerfect. To accomplish this, you must use the Shell command [Ctrl]-[F1]. When executed, select the *Go to Dos* option, *1*. This places you in DOS. When you are in DOS, type Date and enter the correct date according to DOS specifications. When you are finished, type EXIT to return to WordPerfect.

Provided you entered the current date correctly when you started your computer, the Date/Outline (Date for Version 5.0) command, [Shift]-[F5], is used to retrieve the current date into your document.

Let's enter the current date. Move the cursor to the top of your document. Press

We will place the current date two lines above the first line of text and flush with the right margin. To accomplish this, press

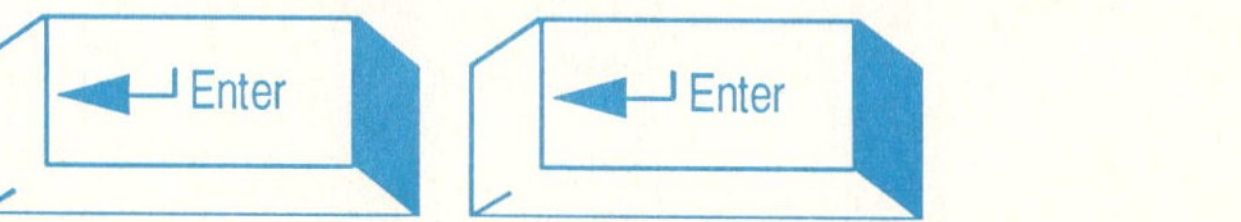

This provides the two blank lines. Move the cursor to the top of your document again. Press

To place the date flush with the right margin, we use the Flush Right command, [Alt]-[F6]. Ready, press

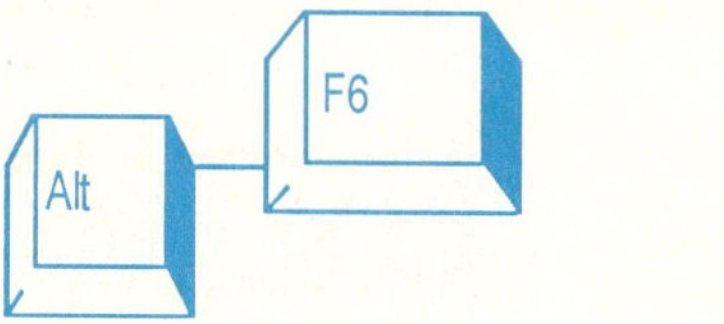

Notice that the cursor jumps to the right. To enter the date, press

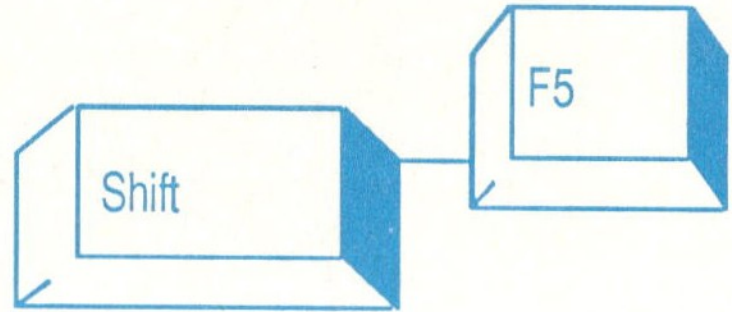

Now type

1

Figure T2-22 displays your letter as it would appear had today's date been October 10, 1991.

To be certain that you don't lose your work as the result of an accidental power loss or other problem, save it now. If you've forgotten how to do this, refer to the section entitled *"Save* and *Resume,"* page 74.

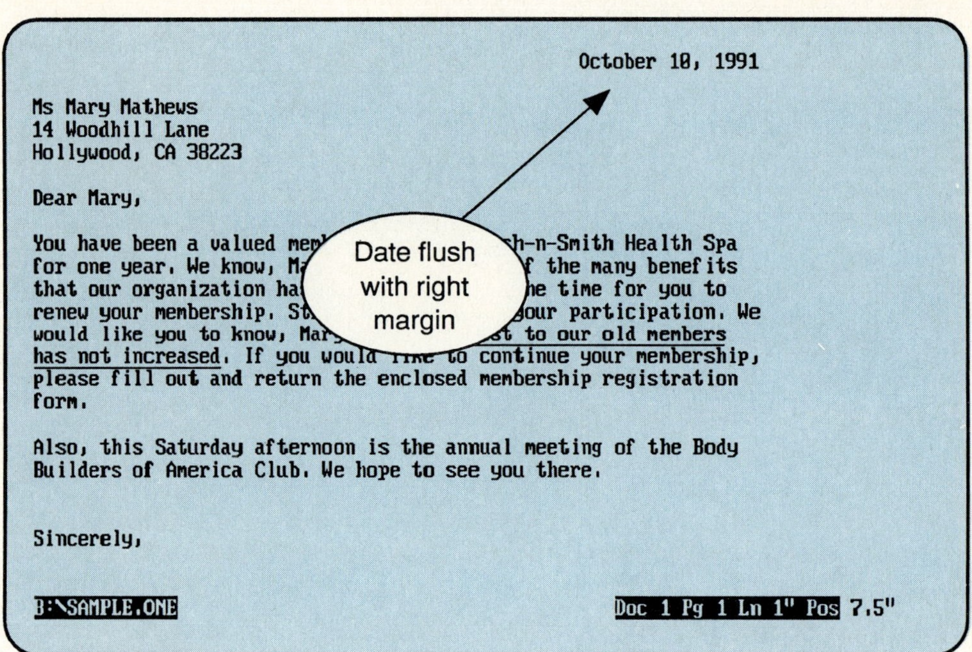

FIGURE T2-22
Current Date Displayed Flush Right.

Printing Your Document

Once you have saved your document and your printer is hooked up and ready to go, you are all set to print a permanent copy of your document. Check to see that the top of the paper in the printer is lined up with the printer head.

If your printer is connected to several computers via a printer connect box, be sure the connect box is set for your computer before you begin.

To print, we select the Print command, [Shift]-[F7]. Press

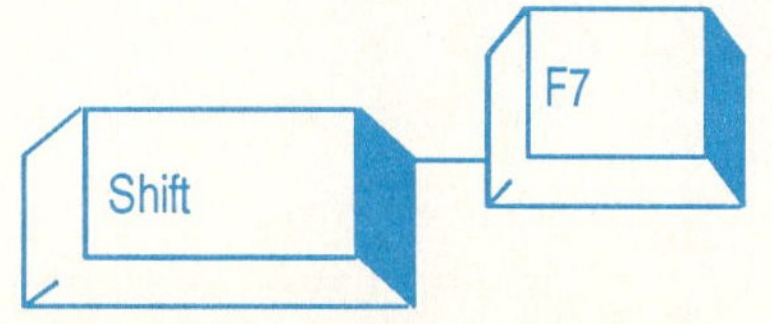

❑

and you will see the Print command options. They are also shown in Figure T2-6 on page 60.

To get a printed copy of the full document you are currently working on, you need to type 1. Are you ready? Well, go for it. Type

1 ❑

Excellent! Your printer is printing the letter you see in Figure T2-23.

October 10, 1991

Ms Mary Mathews
14 Woodhill Lane
Hollywood, CA 38223

Dear Mary,

You have been a valued member of the Stretch-n-Smith Health Spa for one year. We know, Mary, you are aware of the many benefits that our organization has to offer. **Now** is the time for you to renew your membership. Stretch and I value your participation. We would like you to know, Mary, that <u>the cost to our old members has not increased.</u> If you would like to continue your membership, please fill out and return the enclosed membership registration form.

Also, this Saturday afternoon is the annual meeting of the Body Builders of America Club. We hope to see you there.

Sincerely,

J.P. Miller
Manager

cc L.V. Smith

FIGURE T2-23
Finished Letter, Including Changes.

Starting a New Document from an Old One

Some of the messages in this section displayed by WordPerfect Version 5.0 will be slightly different in appearance but not in content.

The process of exiting an old document to begin a new one is very similar to the save and exit procedure we discussed earlier. As with the save and exit procedure, we must begin with the Exit command. Press

❑

The message

```
Save document? Yes (No)    (Text was not modified)
```

appears. Press

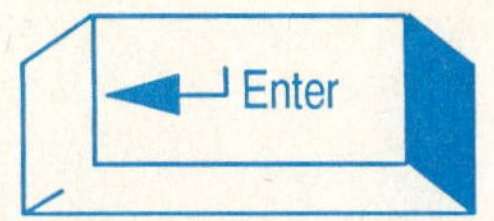

❑

to see the message

Hard-disk users will probably not see B: displayed in this message. Instead, A: or C\WP51 may appear.

`Document to be Saved: B:\SAMPLE.ONE?`

Press

❑

Now you will be presented with the option to replace your copy on disk with the most recent copy located in your computer's memory.

`Replace B:\SAMPLE.ONE? No (Yes)`

Type

Y ❑

WordPerfect responds with

`Saving B:SAMPLE.ONE   Yes`

and then

`Exit WP? No (Yes)     (Cancel to return to document)`

At this point you deviate from the save and exit procedure. If you want to begin a new document, type N or simply press the [Enter] key; otherwise type Y, and you will return to DOS. Type

N ❑

and WordPerfect provides you with a clean Editing screen with which to begin your new document.

Checking Spelling

Spelling errors very often creep into written material. WordPerfect's spell checker will scan every word in your text, checking to see if it matches any word in its dictionary. If it finds some phonetically similar words, it will present them to you, at which point you can choose one to insert into your document. If a similar word is not found, you always have the option of editing the word, adding it to your dictionary, or simply skipping over it.

Proper names and abbreviations generally will not appear in the WordPerfect dictionary. Also, the spell checker will not tell you if you are using the wrong word. For example, if you typed "four example" instead of "for example," the word *four*, although incorrectly used, is nevertheless spelled correctly.

In order to see how the WordPerfect spell checker works, we must first create a document with some misspellings. You should be looking at a clean Editing screen. Now begin typing the document shown in Figure T2-24. Type exactly what you see, misspellings and all.

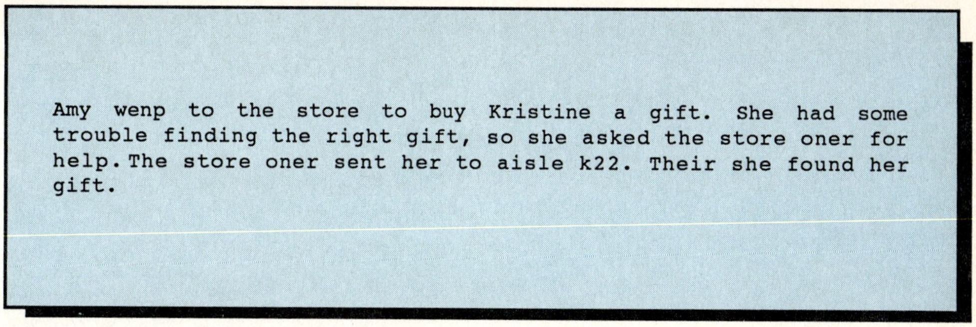

```
Amy wenp to the store to buy Kristine a gift. She had some
trouble finding the right gift, so she asked the store oner for
help. The store oner sent her to aisle k22. Their she found her
gift.
```

FIGURE T2-24
Document To Spell Check.

Now that you have typed this brief document, let's spell check it. If you are using a floppy drive system, remove your Work disk, place the WordPerfect Speller disk in drive B:, and proceed. If you have a hard disk, the Speller should already be copied onto it and no action is necessary.

Accessing the Spell Checker

Press

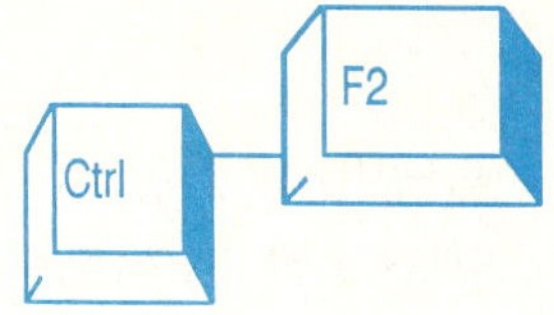

❑

If a message appears indicating that a Speller file is *not found*, check to see if the Speller disk is in drive B:. Then type 1 B: and press the [Enter] key.

If all goes well, your screen should look just as Figure T2-25 does.

FIGURE T2-25
Spell Command Options.

```
Amy wenp to the store to buy Kristine a gift. She had some
trouble finding the right gift, so she asked the store oner for
help. The store oner sent her to aisle k22. Their she found her
gift.

Check: 1 Word; 2 Page; 3 Document; 4 New Sup. Dictionary; 5 Look Up; 6 Count: 0
```

The document option will affect the entire document

Version 5.0 users will see a slightly different screen.

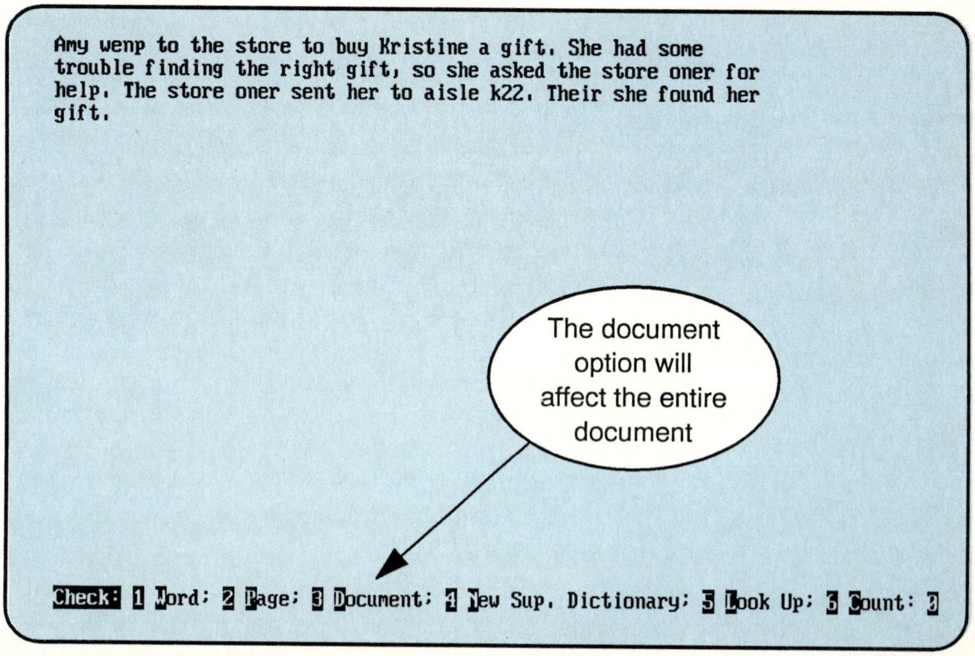

You now must select the Document option, since you want to spell check the entire document, type

3 ❑

and the spell checker will go into action.

Figure T2-26 displays the first suspect word, *wenp*.

FIGURE T2-26
First Flagged Word.

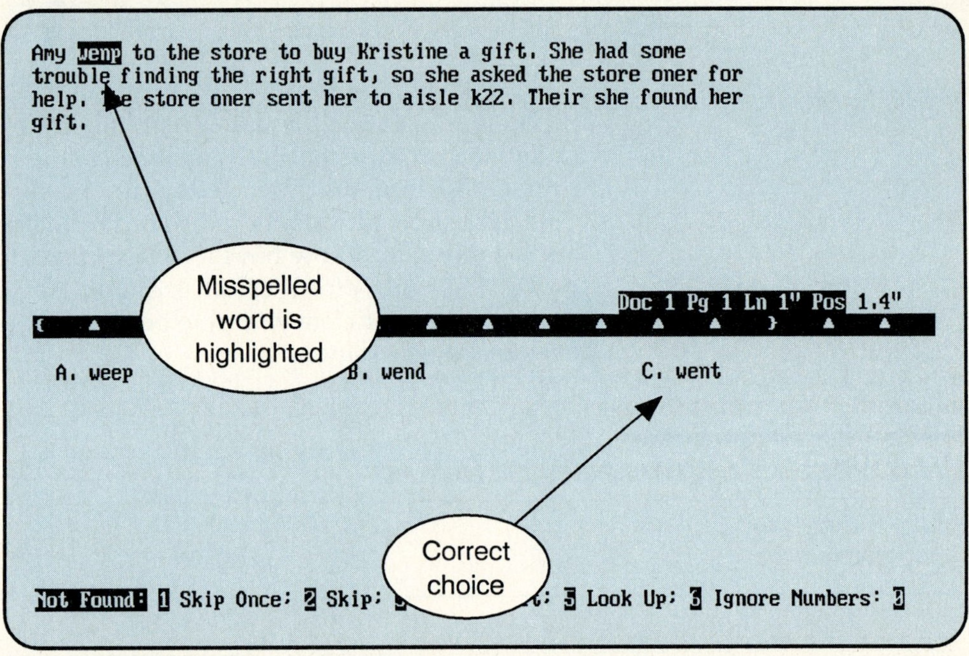

All you have to do is enter the letter C, identifying the correctly spelled word, and the incorrectly spelled word is replaced automatically.

Notice that the word *Kristine* is now flagged, but *Amy* wasn't, even though both are proper names. There are two reasons for this. First, Amy is a typical proper name, so it is included in the WordPerfect dictionary. Second, although also a typical proper name, Kristine is usually spelled with a C. We know that Kristine is an acceptable spelling, even though it is not a typical one that is usually found in dictionaries. Therefore, we will choose the Skip option displayed at the bottom of the screen so that we can skip over Kristine, and proceed to the next spelling error. Type

Use *Skip* as opposed to *Skip Once* when you want WordPerfect to skip all remaining occurrences of a flagged word.

2 ❑

Continue spell checking your document until all words have been examined and corrected, where necessary. Then, in response to the prompt

```
Word count:39                    Press any key to continue
```

press

❑

to exit the Spell command. Did you notice *Their* should have been *There*? A spell checker can't do everything for you.

If necessary, replace the Speller disk with your Work disk.

Exiting WordPerfect

You must always exit WordPerfect by using the Exit command. Never turn off your computer until you exit properly. To exit WordPerfect, depress

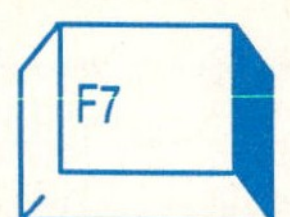

❑

If you want to save the document you are working on, you can; otherwise follow the prompts until you are back at the B> system prompt. Choose your course of action, and then follow it.

This short introduction to WordPerfect should be enough to get you off and running. You now have a basic but sound understanding of what word processing with WordPerfect is about. As you use this software package, your speed, proficiency, and expertise will cause you to wonder how you ever managed without it.

WordPerfect Command Summary

Cursor Control

Key	Function
↓	Line down
↑	Line up
Ecs *n*, ↑ or ↓	Up or down *n* lines
←	One position left
→	One position right
Ecs *n*, → or ←	Right or left *n* spaces
Ctrl ←	Word left
Ctrl →	Word right
Pg Dn	Page down
Pg Up	Page up
+ (numeric keypad)	Screen down
- (numeric keypad)	Screen up
Ctrl-Home, *n*	Go to page n
Ctrl-Home, (any character)	Go to next occurrence of character
Home, Home, ↑	Beginning of file
Home, Home, ↓	End of file
Ecs *n*, command	Repeat command *n* times

Help

Key	Function
[F3], [F3]	Keyboard template
[F3], and key combination	Help on corresponding feature
[F3], first letter of feature	Alphabetic list of features and corresponding keys

Macros

Key	Function
Ctrl-[F10]	Create
Alt-(A through Z)	Invoke
Alt-[F10], macro name	Invoke

Block

Key	Function
Alt-[F4]	Block on
Alt-[F4], Ctrl-[F4], B, M, or C	Move/Copy
Alt-[F4], Ctrl-[F4], B, D	Delete Block
Ctrl-[F4], B, A	Append marked block to the end of a disk
[F10]	Save marked block to a separate disk file
Shift-[F8]	Block protection
[F1]	Block off

Format

Key	Function
Shift-[F8], L, M	Margins l/r
Shift-[F8],L, T	Tabs
Shift-[F8], L, S	Spacing
Shift-[F8],P, M	Top margin

Format

Key	Function
Shift-[F8], P, M	Bottom margin
Shift-[F6]	Center text
Alt-[F6]	Flush right
[F4]	Indent
Shift-Tab	Margin release

Print Enhancements

Key	Function
Ctrl-[F8], S, P, or B	Super/subscript, overstrike
[F6]	Bold on/off
Ctrl-[F7], F or E	Footnotes, endnotes
[F8]	Underline on/off
Shift-[F8], P, H, or F	Headers or footers
Shift-[F8], L, J	Justification off/on
Shift-[F8], P, N	Add page number
Ctrl-[F8], A, D	Double underline
Ctrl-[F8], A, I	Italic
Ctrl-[F8], F	Change font

Search and Replace

Key	Function
[F2]	Search in foward direction
Shift-[F2]	Search in reverse direction
Alt-[F2]	Search and replace

Move, Copy

Key	Function
Alt-[F4], Ctrl-[F4], B, M	Move block
Alt-[F4], Ctrl-[F4], B, C, or D	Copy or delete (cut) a marked block, column, or rectangle
Ctrl-[F4], S	Move/Copy Sentence
Ctrl-[F4], P	Move/Copy Paragraph
Ctrl-[F4], a	Move/Copy Page

File

Key	Function
	General
[F5]	List files key for file management
Shift-[F10] or [F5], 1	Retrieve file from disk
Shift-[F3]	Switch to Document 2
Ctrl-[F1], 1	Temporary exit to DOS
Ctrl-[F5]	Convert DOS text (straight ASCII) files to or from WordPerfect files, file locking
	Saving
[F10]	Save and continue
[F7],Y,Y	Save and exit from WordPerfect

Printing

Key	Function
	General
Alt-[F4], Shift-[F7]	Print marked block
Shift-[F7], P	Print a page from screen
Shift-[F7], F	Print full document from screen
Shift-[F7], D	Print from disk
Shift-[F7], 5	Typewriter mode
	Printer Control
Shift-[F7], 4, C	Cancel a print job
Shift[F7], 4, S	Temporarily stop printer
Shift-[F7], 4	Printer status, job list
Shift-[F7], S	Select printer
Shift-[F7], N	Select number of copies to print

Delete, Undelete

Key	Function
	Delete
Backspace	Delete character left of cursor
Del	Delete character at cursor
Ctrl-Backspace	Delete word
Ctrl-End	Delete to end of line
Ctrl-Pg Dn	Delete to end of page
	Blocks
Ctrl-[F4]	Delete (cut) sentence, paragraph, or page
Alt-[F4], Ctrl-[F4]	Delete (cut) marked block, column, or rectangle
Alt-[F4], Backspace	Quick method of deleting a marked block
	Undelete
[F1]	Undelete any of last three deletions

Utility

Key	Function
Alt-[F1]	Thesaurus
Ctrl-[F2]	Speller
Ctrl-[F3], L	Line drawing
Shift-[F3]	Switch key
Alt-[F5], C	Mark block of text for table of contents
Shift-[F5], T	Date key
Alt-[F3]	Reveal codes
Alt-[F7]	Math/columns key
Ctrl-[F9], S	Sort, select, merge
[F9]	Merge return

Utility

Key	Function
Shift-[F9]	Merge codes
Ctrl-[F10]	Macro: define
Alt-[F10]	Macro: use
Shift-[F5], D	Outline (define)
Shift-[F5], O	Outline on/off
Ctrl-↵	Page break
Alt-[F9], 1	Graphics figures

Exercises

1. What WordPerfect command would you use to accomplish each of the following?
   a. Save and replace a previously named and saved document.
   b. Indent a whole paragraph.
   c. Save and exit.
   d. Reveal all hidden codes.
   e. Change the right margin to 1.5 inches.
   f. Mark a block of text.
   g. Undelete an already deleted word.
   h. Get help.
   i. Insert the current date.
   j. Load a document into memory.

2. Answer each of the following questions with either true or false.
   ______ a. Margins are normally set after a document has been created.
   ______ b. The [Tab] key, when pressed, works the same as the Indent command, when chosen.
   ______ c. Before you begin to type a document, you should consider its design.
   ______ d. When using the Save and Exit command, you will always have to end your WordPerfect session.
   ______ e. A recommended way to exit WordPerfect is with [Ctrl]-[Alt]-[Del], better know as the warm boot.
   ______ f. It is possible to both **boldface and underline** the same text.
   ______ g. If you decide to remove boldface from a word, you have to delete the word first and then type it again without boldface.
   ______ h. To cancel a WordPerfect command before you have completed entering all its options, press the [Esc] key.
   ______ i. A paragraph can be moved without blocking it first.
   ______ j. On-line help is not available with WordPerfect.

3. Describe what each of the following commands or keyboard keys do when executed or pressed in the sequence shown.
   a. [Ctrl]-[→]
   b. [Home][Home]-[↑]
   c. [Shift]-[F7]1
   d. [Ctrl]-[F2]3[Enter]
   e. [Indent]This is the reason why all good men and women seek to run for political office when it is much safer for them not to.[Enter]
   f. [F7]NY
   g. [Ctrl]-[Home]12[Enter]
   h. [Ctrl]-[F4][↓][↓][↓][↓][Del]Y
   i. [Home][←][Del]
   j. [Enter]

4. Complete the following exercises as best you can:
   a. Name the keys that must be depressed in order to save a previously saved document.
   b. What is the purpose of the Menu template?
   c. Describe the function of the Status line.
   d. Explain the difference between pressing the [Tab] key and the Indent key, [F4].
   e. List and discuss what must be done before you can begin to create a document.
   f. Describe the steps necessary to start your computer and WordPerfect.
   g. What is the difference between the Speller option Skip Once and Skip?
   h. Explain the purpose of the Reveal Codes command.
   i. List the steps involved when copying a page of text to a new page.
   j. How would you go about printing your document? Be very specific when listing the steps.

Hands-On Activities

1. Using the sample document found in Figure T2-10, perform the following activities:
   a. Where "Sally Mathews" appears, replace it with "Tommy Carol" and replace every occurrence of "Sally" with "Tommy."
   b. Reset you margins to 1.5 inches and 0.5 inch.
   c. Spell check the document.
   d. Print the final result.

2. Write a letter to a friend describing the course you are taking. Insert the current date flush right. Run the document through the spell checker and print it.

3. Prepare a paper, using WordPerfect, that must be submitted as a required project for a course other than your computer applications course. Submit a printed copy to your computer instructor and to the instructor of the course for which your paper was written.

4. Open a document file called SIMILE.
   a. Set your margins to 0.5 inch and 2 inches, and enter the following:

      Our language is full of everyday comparisons: "red as a rose," "cold as ice," "shy as a mouse." Poets try to communicate ideas in new ways by creating new comparisons.

      There are two basic kinds of comparisons in poetry: similes and metaphors. In a simile two things are compared by using the words *like* or *as* (Language is like a river...). In a metaphor two things are compared by saying that one thing is another (Your voice is a song...).

   b. Save your file SIMILE.
   c. Delete the phrase "Your voice is a song..." and replace it with "The ship is a plough..."
   d. Search the document for the word *comparisons,* and replace each occurrence of this word with the word *analogies.*
   e. Save your edited file and print it out.

5. You will need your Learning Disk 1 to complete this activity.

   In this activity you will use WordPerfect to correct the file MIRACLE2 contained on Learning Disk 1.

   From a clear Editing screen, you will have to place Learning Disk 1 in drive B:. Hard-disk users can place Learning Disk 1 in drive A: or copy the file MIRACLE2 into the WordPerfect subdirectory of your hard disk.

   Use the Retrieve command to retrieve MIRACLE2. Once the file is in the Editing screen, make the following modifications:

a. Set the left margin to 2 inches and the right margin to 1.5 inches.
b. Edit your document to include all the changes, shown in Figure T2-27.
c. Save the edited version and get a printout.

6. Create a document that contains the text portion of Activity 4. Do not follow the directions for Activity 4; simply type them. Be sure that all alignment is correct.

7. Create your résumé. The length should be a minimum of two pages. If you have not accumulated enough information to include in it, make up information. The format should be as follows.
   a. All category names should be on a left margin of 1 inch.
   b. The contents of each category should be indented at the 3.5-inch tab stop. Turned lines should wrap at 3.5 inches.
   c. All category names should be in boldface.
   d. Your name and address should be centered at the top of the résumé. (Use [Shift-][F6] to center.)
   e. Number the pages. To accomplish this, move to the top of your file and then enter [Shift]-[F8]2646[F7]. (Version 5.0 users enter [Shift]-[F8]276[F7].)
   f. Underline all publication names, if present.

   Be sure to spell check and print your résumé.

FIGURE T2-27

Letter Showing Editing.

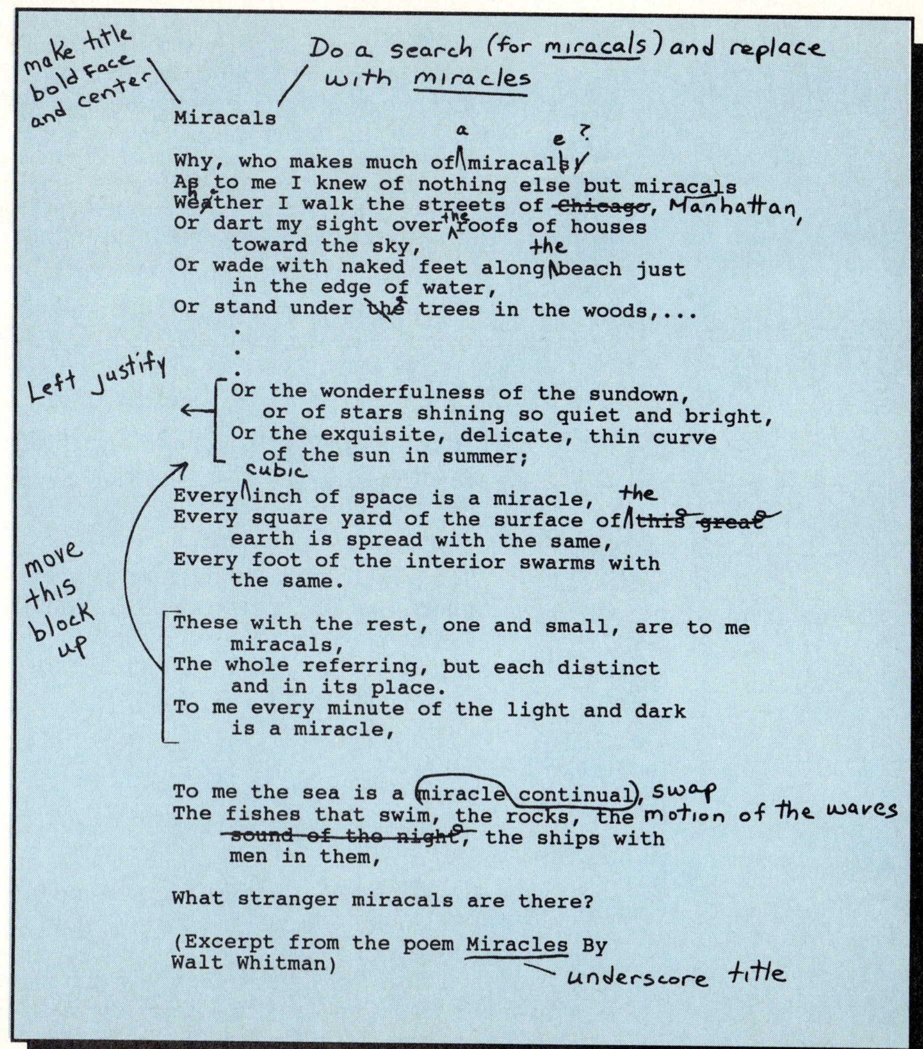

```
Miracals

Why, who makes much of miracals?
As to me I knew of nothing else but miracals
Wether I walk the streets of Chicago,
Or dart my sight over roofs of houses
    toward the sky,
Or wade with naked feet along beach just
    in the edge of water,
Or stand under the trees in the woods,...
    .
    .
    .
Or the wonderfulness of the sundown,
    or of stars shining so quiet and bright,
Or the exquisite, delicate, thin curve
    of the sun in summer;
Every inch of space is a miracle,
Every square yard of the surface of this great
    earth is spread with the same,
Every foot of the interior swarms with
    the same.

These with the rest, one and small, are to me
    miracals,
The whole referring, but each distinct
    and in its place.
To me every minute of the light and dark
    is a miracle,

To me the sea is a miracle continual,
The fishes that swim, the rocks, the
    sound of the night, the ships with
    men in them,

What stranger miracals are there?

(Excerpt from the poem Miracles By
Walt Whitman)
```

3

LOTUS 1-2-3
Managing Your Finances

This tutorial is your step-by-step guide to learning Lotus 1-2-3 as you sit at your computer. We have chosen Lotus 1-2-3 because it is the most powerful spreadsheet program yet devised. Because most of the concepts described here are common to other spreadsheet programs, this tutorial will help you to work with virtually any spreadsheet package. If you do not have immediate access to a computer or to this package, you will still benefit from the detailed explanations and analyses provided.

The tutorial is divided into two parts. Part I, "Creating a Spreadsheet," will familiarize you with the Lotus 1-2-3 working environment. Part II, "Beyond the Spreadsheet," will carry you beyond the basic spreadsheet functions.

Lotus 1-2-3 is a product of the Lotus Development Corporation (Lotus 1-2-3 is a trademark of the Lotus Development Corp., 55 Wheeler St., Cambridge, MA 02142) and has become the single most popular piece of microcomputer software ever written. It is available for virtually every Apple, IBM, or compatible microcomputer system containing at least 320K bytes of memory and two double-sided disk drives or one double-sided disk drive and a hard disk.

Objectives

In this tutorial you will learn how to:

- Design a spreadsheet
- Enter data
- Save a spreadsheet
- Perform "what-if" analysis
- Work with the current date
- Link two 1-2-3 spreadsheet files
- Freely move around the spreadsheet
- Create formulas
- Print a spreadsheet
- Graph a 1-2-3 spreadsheet
- Change the natural order of your data by sorting it
- Create and execute Lotus macro instructions

Before You Begin

Review and familiarize yourself with the material concerning spreadsheet software packages presented in Chapter 13 and the material concerning DOS found in Tutorial 1. Specifically, be sure you review how to boot up your computer, enter the correct date, and copy a file. You will be called upon to preform these procedures in this tutorial.

Follow the Blue

As you follow along, any procedures you must carry out or entries you must make will be printed in *blue* whereas all computer responses will appear as if they were written by a typwriter. *Type only entries or follow only directions that appear in blue.* A ❑ appears at the right of the first line of each sequence of commands you must enter. Check the box when you have completed the instruction as a way of keeping track of your progress as you proceed through the tutorial.

Whenever a special key (any key other than a letter, digit, or special character) is shown printed in blue, you must tap or momentarily depress that key. For example, if the key

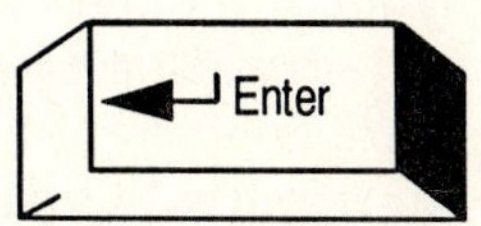

were printed in blue, you would be expected to momentarily depress the [Enter] key.

In some special cases, it will be necessary for you to press *and hold down* one special key while momentarily depressing another. To indicate this, the special key or keys to be pressed and held will be printed slightly lower and attached by a thin line to the key to be tapped. If the series of keys

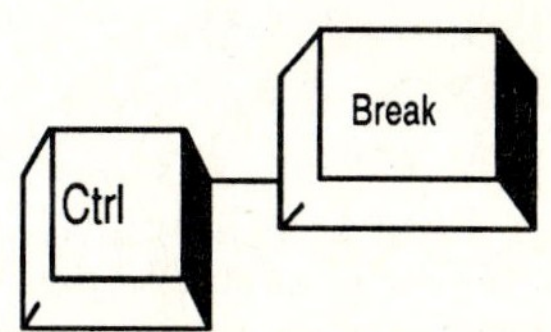

were printed in blue, you would be expected to press and hold down the Control [Ctrl] key, tap the [Break] key, and release the [Ctrl] key.

You will also find it necessary to enter combinations of text and special keys. For example, if the entry

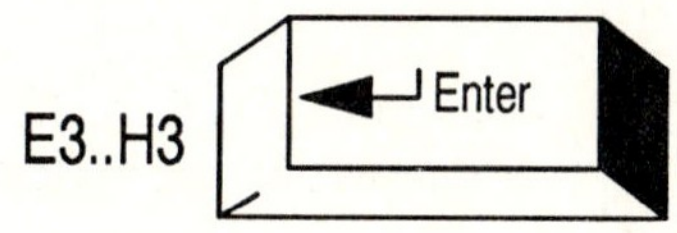

were printed in blue, you would be expected to type **E3..H3** and then depress the [Enter] key.

Required Hardware

This tutorial is written for use with **Lotus 1-2-3 Release 2.2**. Lotus Release 2.2 is specifically designed to work with the IBM PC, XT, PS/2 Models 25 and 30 and with Lotus certified compatibles running under DOS 2.0 or higher. Your computer should be equipped with a minimum of 320 kilobytes of random access memory (256K for earlier releases of Lotus 1-2-3).

For maximum effect, Lotus 1-2-3 should be run from a computer equipped with a hard or fixed disk drive and one floppy disk drive. However, if your computer is equipped with two floppy disk drives, 1-2-3 will still work. Differences in computer hardware will have little effect on what we do in this tutorial. Procedural changes resulting from different hardware configurations will be explicitly noted.

If you would like to obtain a hard copy of your work during this tutorial, you will need a printer.

Required Software

If your computer system is not equipped with a hard drive, obtain a copy of **DOS 2.0** or higher and a copy of the **Lotus 1-2-3 Release 2.2 System Disk** from your instructor or laboratory assistant so that you can start your computer and Lotus 1-2-3.

If you are using an earlier release of 1-2-3, you can still use this tutorial. When differences arise, they will be noted. With earlier versions of 1-2-3, your instructor or computer laboratory assistant may have created licensed copies of the **Lotus 1-2-3 System Disk** that can also boot (start) your computer. This dual-purpose disk will be used by you whenever we ask you to use your DOS disk or Lotus 1-2-3 System Disk. If applicable, obtain a copy of a bootable Lotus 1-2-3 System Disk.

If you are using Lotus 1-2-3 Release 3.0, read the appendix to this tutorial first, then return to this point. *Throughout this tutorial Lotus, 1-2-3, or Lotus 1-2-3 will mean Lotus 1-2-3 Release 2.2.*

You should use an installed version of 1-2-3. When 1-2-3 is installed properly, you can display graphs and print. If your software is new, be certain to follow the installation procedures described in the manual on setting up 1-2-3.

We suggest that you format a floppy disk so you can save your work when finished. Formatting a disk prepares it so that the computer can write data onto it. Every disk must be formatted before it can be used. If you are not familiar with this process, refer to the DOS tutorial. Henceforth, your *Work disk* shall mean a formatted floppy disk.

Part I Creating a Spreadsheet

In this part of the tutorial you will learn to create, modify, save, and print a spreadsheet. It will take you approximately two hours to complete.

Getting Started

The method for starting your computer will vary depending on whether you have a two floppy disk drive system or a hard disk and one floppy disk drive. If you have a hard drive, skip to the section "Starting Lotus from a Hard Drive"; otherwise read on.

Starting Lotus from a Floppy Disk Drive

Be sure that your computer is turned off before you begin.

Place your DOS disk (or bootable Lotus 1-2-3 System Disk for earlier releases of Lotus) in disk drive A: (the left-hand drive, or top drive) and your Work disk in the B: drive (the right-hand drive, or bottom drive). Be sure the drive doors are closed. Locate your computer's power switch or switches. Turn on your computer.

In a few moments you will hear some disk activity. Then either you will be requested to enter the correct date and time, or the correct date and time will automatically be entered for you. If you are requested to enter the correct date and time, do so now.

1-2-3 depends on DOS for the correct date and time. Thus, always be sure to enter the correct date and time when you start your computer. Computer systems equipped with clock calendars will automatically have the correct date and time logged in when they are started. In this case, it is not necessary for you to enter them manually.

You should see the familiar system prompt

A>

To start 1-2-3, place an installed Lotus 1-2-3 System Disk in disk drive A: and place your formatted Work disk in disk drive B:. Enter

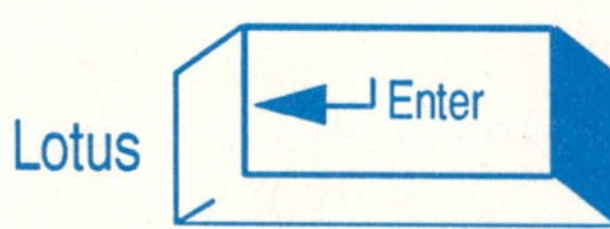

❑

You should now see the **1-2-3 Access System**, as displayed in Figure T3-1.

FIGURE T3-1
1-2-3 Access System.

```
1-2-3  PrintGraph  Translate  Install  Exit
Use 1-2-3

                    1-2-3 Access System
                  Copyright  1986, 1989
              Lotus Development Corporation
                   All Rights Reserved
                       Release 2.2

The Access system lets you choose 1-2-3, PrintGraph, the Translate utility,
and the Install program, from the menu at the top of this screen.  If
you're using a two-diskette system, the Access system may prompt you to
change disks.  Follow the instructions below to start a program.

o  Use → or ← to move the menu pointer (the highlighted rectangle
   at the top of the screen) to the program you want to use.

o  Press ENTER to start the program.

You can also start a program by typing the first character of its name.

Press HELP (F1) for more information.
```

Users of earlier releases of Lotus will see a slightly different Access System.

Now skip to the section "The Worksheet" and continue with the tutorial.

Starting Lotus from a Hard Drive

Be sure that your computer is turned off before you begin. There is no need to place the DOS disk in the A: drive because DOS is already stored on the hard disk.

Locate your computer's power switch or switches. Turn on your computer.

In a few moments you will hear some disk activity. If you are requested to enter the correct date and time, do so; otherwise read on.

1-2-3 depends on DOS for the correct date and time. Thus, always be sure to enter the correct date and time when you start your computer. Computer systems equipped with clock calendars will automatically have the correct date and time logged in when they are started. In this case, it is not necessary for you to enter them manually.

You should see the familiar system prompt

C>

To start 1-2-3, change the current directory to the subdirectory that contains the Lotus 1-2-3 program files. For example, if your 1-2-3 files are stored in a subdirectory called Lotus, from the C> prompt you would type **CD Lotus**

Earlier releases of Lotus 1-2-3 may require that the Lotus System Disk be placed in the A: drive even though a hard disk may be present that contains all Lotus program files.

and press the **[Enter]** key. If you will be saving your work to the floppy disk drive, place your Work disk in either your A: or B: disk drive.

Assuming you have placed yourself in the subdirectory containing the Lotus software, enter

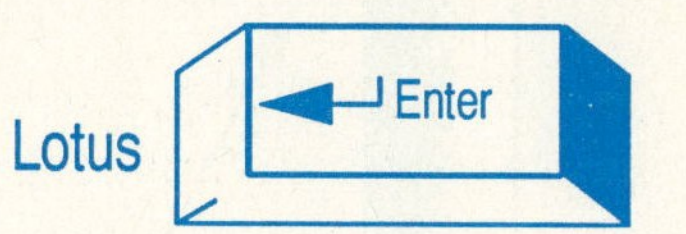

❑

You should now see the 1-2-3 Access System, as displayed in Figure T3-1. Users of earlier releases of Lotus, as well as Release 3.0 users, will see a slightly different Access System.

The Worksheet

You should be viewing the Access System screen shown in Figure T3-1. Because Lotus 1-2-3 is an integrated software package, you must indicate to the program which of the possible options you desire. This Access System screen is currently pointing at the 1-2-3 option. Pressing the [Enter] key will transfer you to a blank **worksheet**. A worksheet is a large work area capable of displaying and storing data. We will use this area to prepare our spreadsheets.

Options not available through the Access System's 1-2-3 environment can be accessed simply by moving the cursor over the desired option with the use of the Left and Right Arrow keys on the keyboard and then by depressing the [Enter] key. Since we will be creating a spreadsheet, position the cursor over 1-2-3, if necessary, and press

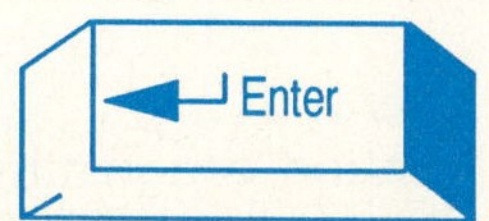

❑

Momentarily, you will see the Lotus copyright. This screen will quickly disappear and be replaced by a blank worksheet. You are actually viewing only a window, or portion (the upper left corner), of a 1-2-3 worksheet (see Fig. T3-2). The full worksheet is 256 columns by 8192 rows, clearly too large to display on a single screen.

Rows, Columns, and Cells

The worksheet is a grid made up of rows and columns. The intersection of each row and column forms a **cell** in which you can store data. Each cell has a unique address that consists of its column letter and row number. For example, A6 identifies the cell at the intersection of Column A and Row 6. Each cell is given an initial capacity of nine characters and may be used to store a *value, label,* or *formula*. The capacity of a cell or group of cells can be increased or decreased, as necessary.

The Control Panel

The **control panel** is located at the top of your worksheet screen. It contains three unnumbered lines of information.

The first line indicates the current position of the **cursor** or **cursor pointer** and describes the contents of the cell being pointed to (highlighted). In the worksheet screen shown in Figure T3-2, the first line of the control panel tells us that the cursor is at cell A1. It also tells us that this cell is empty since nothing appears after the colon.

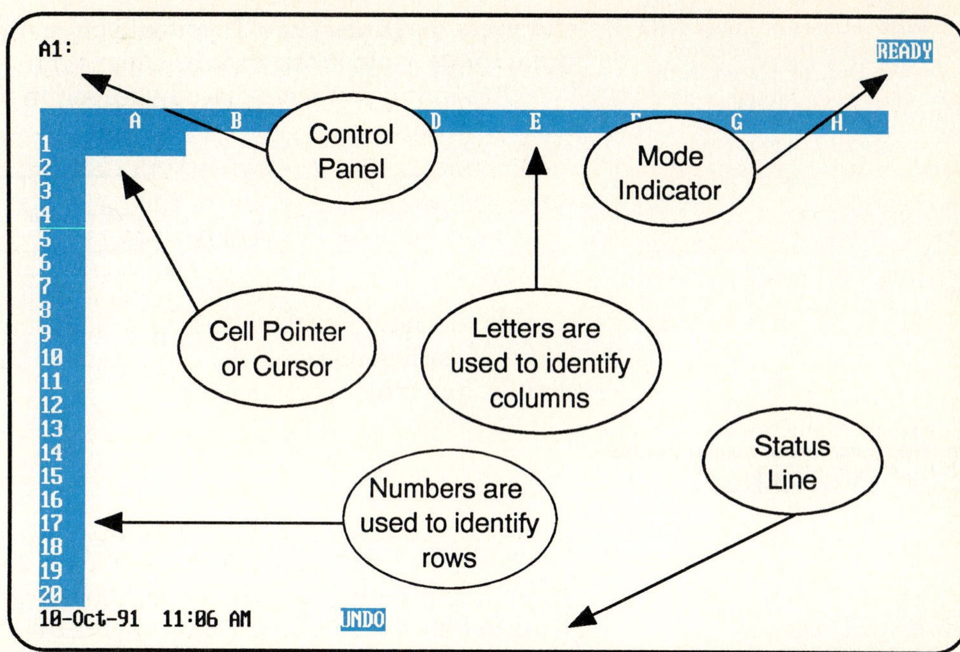

FIGURE T3-2
The Basic Worksheet Screen.

At the right of the first line of the control panel is the **mode indicator.** It tells you the mode, or state, that 1-2-3 is in. In the READY mode, 1-2-3 is waiting for you to issue your next command. When you enter a value into a cell, 1-2-3 changes to the VALUE mode. In the worksheet shown in Figure T3-2, 1-2-3 is in the READY mode awaiting a command.

1-2-3 uses the second and third lines of the control panel to display a menu of available commands and subcommands or to request more information concerning a command you entered. Since you haven't given 1-2-3 any commands, these lines are blank.

The Status Line

The **status line** is the last line on your worksheet screen. At the left it contains a **date-and-time indicator**. If your screen is not showing the correct date and time, you probably did not enter the date and time when you started your computer.

If your date and time are wrong and you wish to correct them, do the following: Enter /S. This will put you in DOS. Now type DATE, change the date, and press the [Enter] key. Then type TIME, change the time, and press the [Enter] key. Finally, type EXIT and press the [Enter] key to return to 1-2-3.

At the right of the status line, 1-2-3 displays one or more **status indicators**. These indicators appear when you use certain special keys or when a particular program condition exists. The first status indicator shown in Figure T3-2 is the **UNDO** indicator.

Releases of 1-2-3 prior to Version 2.2 do not support the Undo feature.

When you first enter a worksheet, Undo is enabled by default and awaits your call to action. Then, each time you create or manipulate data, the Undo feature automatically makes and stores a temporary backup copy of your work. Undo can then be directed to replace the current entries with those contained on the backup copy. Undoing can be initiated by simply holding the [Alt] key down and pressing the [F4] Function key. This is a little detail, but one that will come in handy and is worth remembering.

The status of special 1-2-3 keys, such as [Caps Lock], [Num Lock], [Ins], and [Scroll Lock], is displayed at the right of the status line. For example, if the status of the [Caps Lock] key is *on*, the word CAPS will be displayed and everything you type will be in capital letters. We use capitals extensively in this tutorial. Each time one of these keys is depressed its status is toggled from on to off, or from off to on.

Turn the CAPS indicator on by pressing the [Caps Lock] key, if it is not already on.

Before moving on, be sure your display screen looks like Figure T3-2 with the CAPS indicator on. If it does not, press and hold down the [Ctrl] key and tap the [Break] key, then type /WEY.

Function Keys

Your keyboard is equipped with either 10 or 12 **Function keys**. These keys are located either to the left side of your keyboard or across the top. The name and function of each key is shown in Table T3-1. When pressed, the function associated with the key will be carried out. Basically, these keys are time savers.

TABLE T3-1
Function Keys

Function Key	Name	Function
F1	Help	Provides on-line help
F2	Edit	Used to edit a cell's contents
F3	Name	Displays a listing of range names in POINT mode
F4	Abs	Changes relative addresses to mixed or absolute addresses when in POINT mode
F5	GoTo	Moves the cursor to a specified cell
F6	Window	Moves the cursor between two screen windows

TABLE T3-1
(Continued)

Function Key	Name	Function
F7	Query	Repeats the last data query operation
F8	Table	Repeats the last data table operation
F9	Calc	Recalculates all formulas
F10	Graph	Displays the current graph

Let's Experiment

The cursor may be moved or scrolled by using the four Arrow keys on your keyboard. Pressing the [Home] key, if you have one, brings the cursor to cell A1. Scrolling allows you to construct large spreadsheets that exceed the dimensions of your screen. Moving the cursor to the right eventually results in a display of more columns, and moving it down results in a display of rows that are normally not in view. Remember, the worksheet in 1-2-3 is 256 columns by 8192 rows.

Now is a good time to get a feel for moving the cursor. Scroll the cursor until it displays columns and rows that are normally not in view. Notice how the first line of the control panel changes to reflect the location of the active cell as you scroll.

GOTO Operations

Do not enter the keystrokes *[F5]*. Simply depress the [F5] Function key. This notation applies throughout this tutorial.

Moving the cursor by scrolling can be slow, especially when working with large spreadsheets. To scroll to cell Z200 from cell B8, for example, would take quite a while. This can be accomplished more quickly using the [F5] Function key. Simply depress

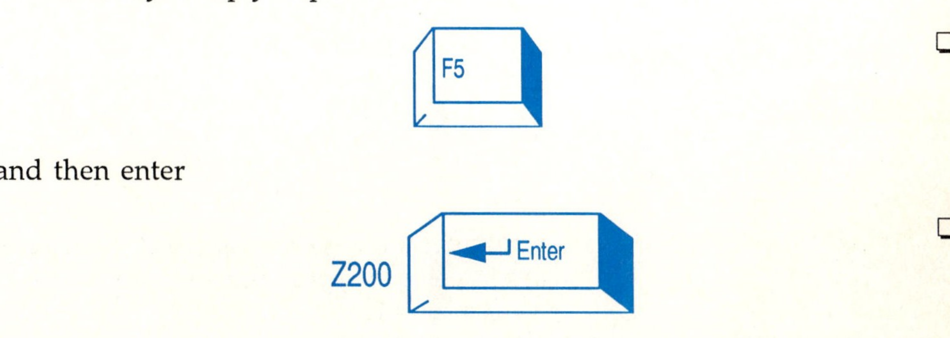

and then enter

How about that—express! Pressing the [F5] Function key issues a GoTo command, an unconditional jump to the cell specified.

Entering Data

Move to cell C1 by entering

and then enter

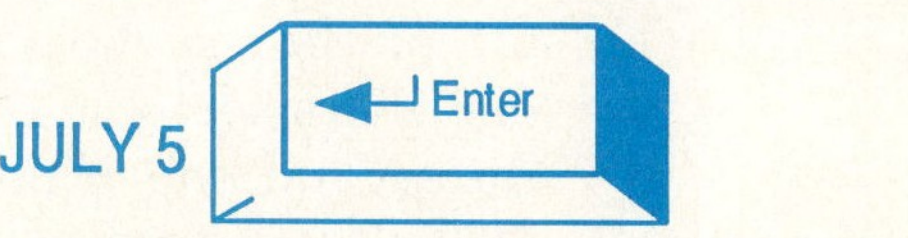

Unless directed otherwise, Lotus 1-2-3 will left-justify a label and right-justify a value within a cell.

Typing JULY 5 will place this label on the edit line. When the [Enter] key is pressed, the label is inserted, left-justified, into cell C1.

Move the cursor to cell D1, and prepare to enter 1776, but do not actually enter it. 1776 is not going to be treated as a number (since it is really part of a label). We must indicate this fact to the computer. We do this by preceding the label with a special label-prefix character. This label prefix identifies what follows as a label and indicates where in the cell it is to be printed. The prefix characters and their meanings are as follows:

Label prefixes are *optional* with labels that do not begin with digits and, when selected, perform the same functions as described previously.

Label Prefix	Meaning
'	Aligns the title on the left side in the cell
^	Centers the title in the cell
"	Aligns the title on the right side in the cell
\	Repeats the character or characters that follow it for the length of the cell

Remember: Type only what is in blue.

Thus, if you were to enter the command

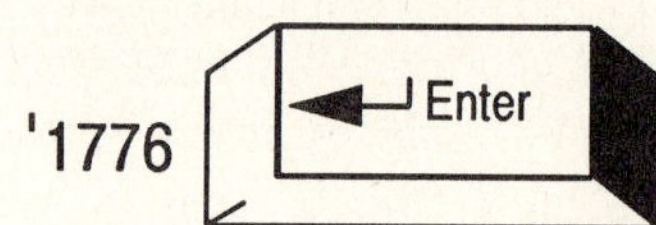

1776 would be placed at the left or left-justified in the current cell (cell specified in the first line of the control panel), whereas if you were to enter

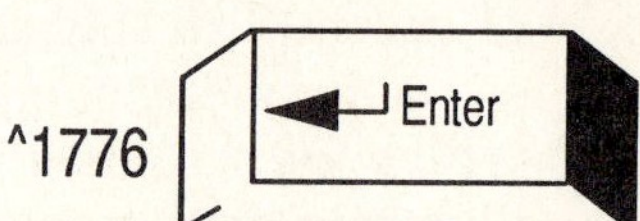

1776 would be centered in this cell. Let us assume that we wish it to be left-justified. Enter

Correcting Errors

If you make a mistake, there are different ways to make the correction. One way to correct errors is simply to reenter the data. Move the cursor back to cell C1 and enter

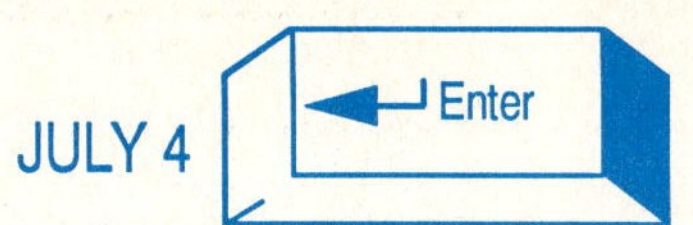

If you catch your mistake before you press the [Enter] key, you can use the Escape [Esc] key or the [Backspace] key. Move the cursor to B6 and type

BUDJET

but don't hit the [Enter] key since we must correct this error.

Pressing the [Esc] key will cancel your label entry and return you to the beginning of the cell. On the other hand, pressing the [Backspace] key (at the top of your keyboard, not to be confused with the Left Arrow key) erases one character—the character immediately to the left of the small cursor on the second line of the control panel. In this case it would erase the character *T*. If you pressed the [Backspace] key two more times, you would erase the next two characters to the left of the cursor (*E* and *J*). Press

[Backspace]
[Backspace]
[Backspace]

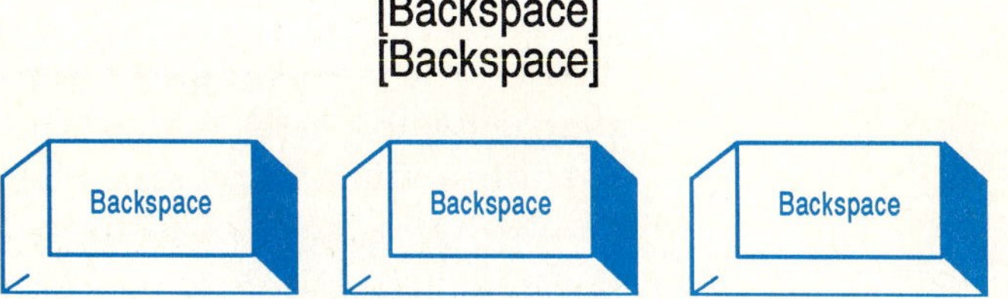

and then enter

to correct this entry.

Before we continue, let's move the cursor to cell A1. A quick way to accomplish this is by pressing the [Home] key. Press

Entering Commands

Suppose that after typing in one or more entries or labels, you decide that you are not satisfied with them and want them deleted. The process required to accomplish this consists of a number of individual but relatively simple steps involving some of 1-2-3's many menus. Because most commands with which we will deal require the use of menus, let us take a moment now to illustrate how menus are used to delete the contents of one or more cells.

To get the attention of 1-2-3 to receive a command, press the Forward Slash key,

This brings up 1-2-3's command menu and changes the mode from READY to MENU (see Fig. T3-3).

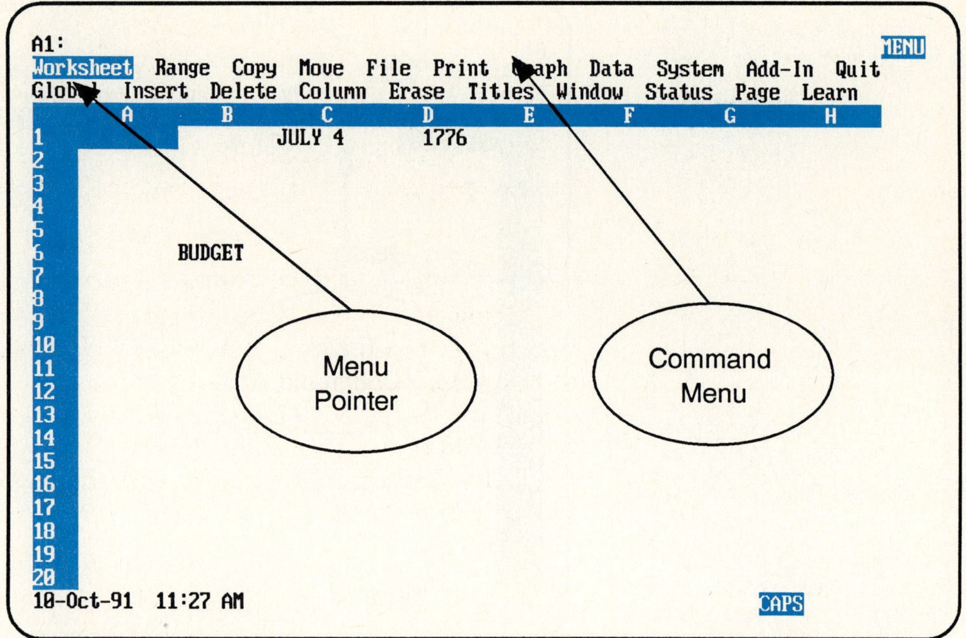

FIGURE T3-3

In this menu, the command Worksheet is highlighted. 1-2-3 uses this highlighted box, or **menu pointer**, to tell you what command it will execute if you press the [Enter] key. The third line of the control panel provides a listing of what subcommands are possible should you press the [Enter] key and implement the Worksheet command. One likely looking subcommand is Delete. However, this subcommand, as all worksheet subcommands, refers to entire rows, columns, or areas of the worksheet and not to selected cells. Therefore, we must look beyond the Worksheet command to the Range command.

To move the menu pointer to the Range command, depress the Right Arrow key

❑

Your screen should now appear as shown in Figure T3-4.

READY Mode

Note that if at any time you feel lost or confused, you can depress the [F1] Function key for help, or, if you desire to go back to the previous screen, you can simply depress the [Esc] key. Pressing this key again will return you to the next previous screen, and so on until you will end up back in the READY mode with the worksheet displayed. You know you're in READY mode by the word READY highlighted in the upper right-hand portion of your screen.

The third line of the control panel shown above indicates the subcommand Erase. This is the one we want, since it will allow us to erase the contents of cells within a *range* that we can specify. Therefore, simply depress

❑

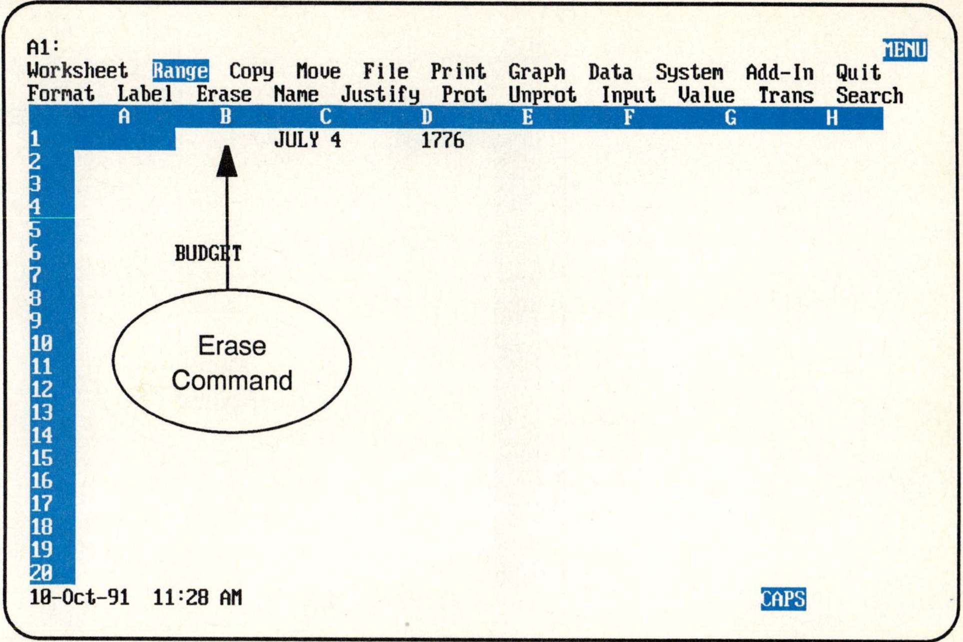

FIGURE T3-4

to activate the Range command. Your screen should now appear as shown in Figure T3-5.

FIGURE T3-5

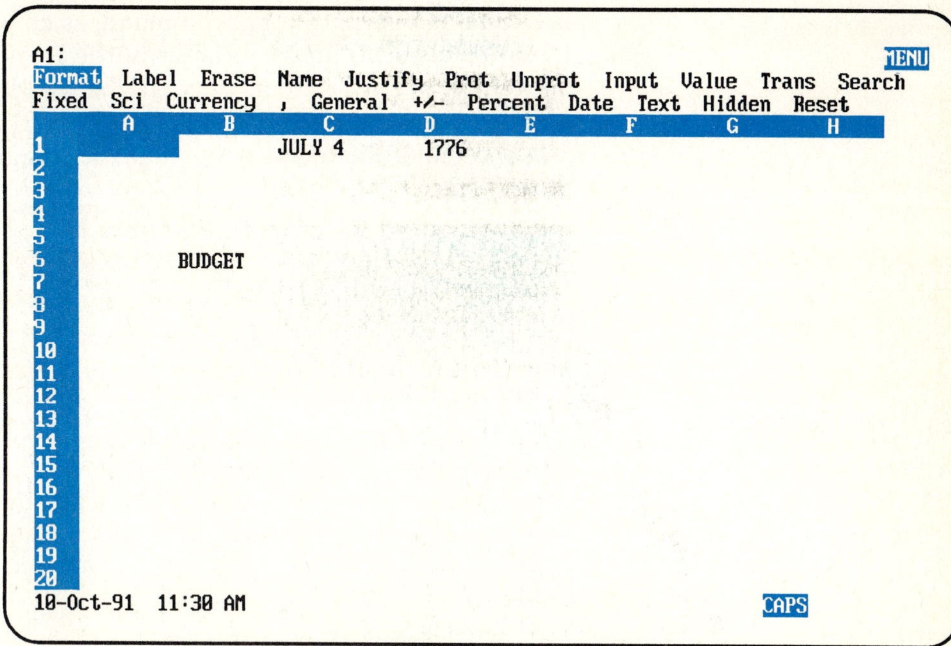

Depress the Right Arrow key twice to highlight the Erase subcommand. (See Fig. T3-6.)

❑

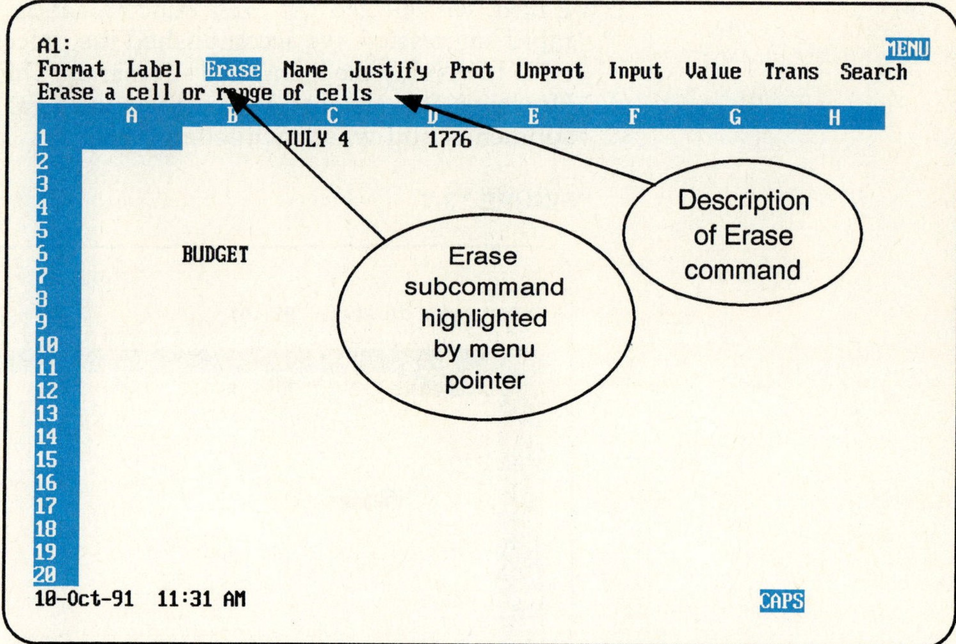

FIGURE T3-6

Notice that the command summary line no longer contains a list of possible subcommands but instead gives a description of what the subcommand Erase does:

`Erase a cell or range of cells`

A description always appears when the lowest-level subcommand has been reached. Since this is what we wish to accomplish, depress

❏

and activate the Erase subcommand. Your screen should now appear as shown in Figure T3-7.

If your display screen is not as shown in Figure T3-7, you will have to depress the [Esc] key until a screen containing the READY mode is indicated at the right of the status line. This indicates that you are back in the worksheet and 1-2-3 is READY for you to issue a command. If your screen doesn't look like the one shown in the figure, depress the [Esc] key until READY is displayed. Then enter /RE.

Using a Command Sequence

Whether you entered the command sequence /RE above or not, it's important that you understand what it means. Basically, it is a form of shorthand in which each character represents a 1-2-3 command or subcommand. Every command sequence must begin with a /. This tells 1-2-3 that you wish to issue a command. 1-2-3 responds by presenting you with its basic command menu from which to choose a command. You may choose any item from this menu by moving the cursor to that item and pressing the [Enter] key, *or* you can accomplish the same thing by typing the first letter of that command without pressing the [Enter] key. By entering the letter *R* next, we selected *Range* from this menu. The Range command, in turn, provided us with a menu of Range subcommands from which to choose. By entering an

E next, we selected the *Erase* subcommand. By entering the /, *R*, and *E* in rapid succession, we accomplished the preceding steps without waiting for 1-2-3 to display the menu and submenus. This is good because it saves time. However, it is also bad because we don't get a chance to see the menus and submenus and what each letter represents.

FIGURE T3-7

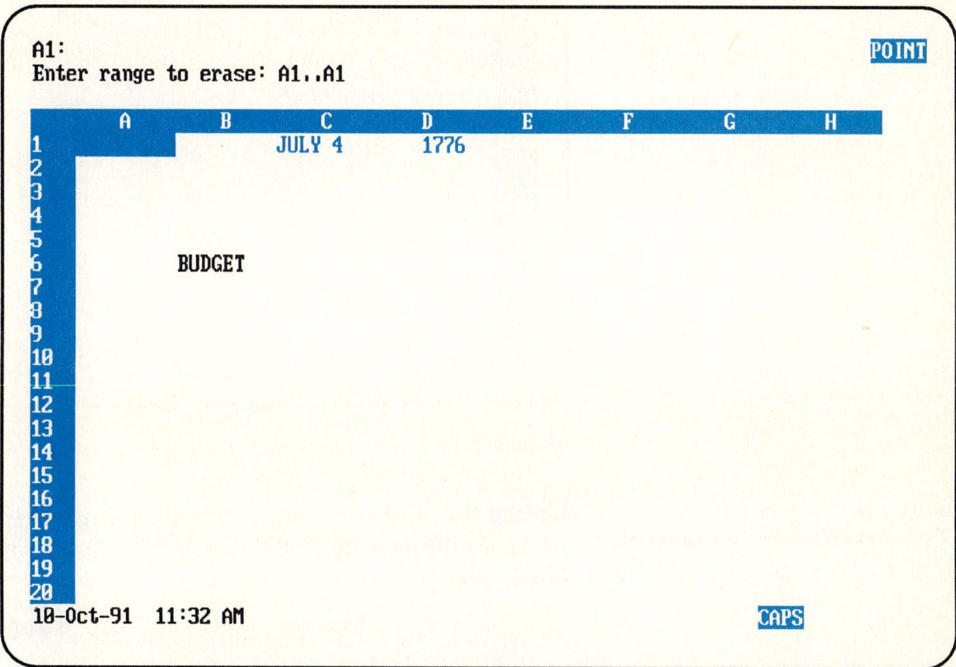

To eliminate this problem, whenever a command sequence is required, we shall *both* identify the menu and submenu items and provide the exact command sequence that you must carry out. Only the command sequence will be printed in blue, since this is what you will actually enter. This would be shown as follows.

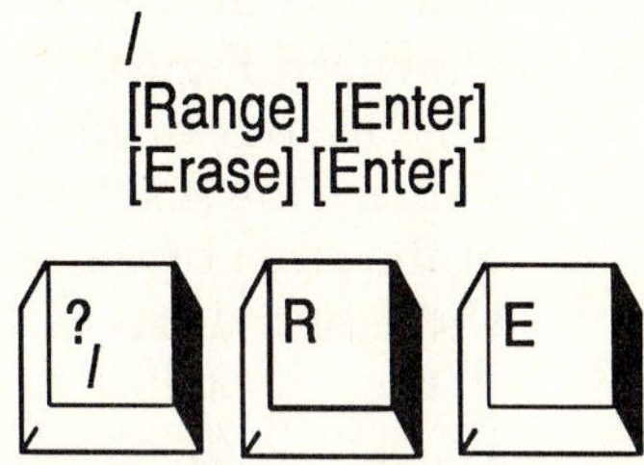

The /, R, and E keys would appear in blue if you actually were to enter this sequence of commands.

Let's continue. We must now specify the range of cells whose contents we want deleted. If we want only the contents of the current or highlighted cell (A1) to be deleted, we simply press the [Enter] key. If, however, we wish a range of cells deleted, we use the Arrow keys to move around the spreadsheet, highlighting each cell that we pass through for future deletion. For example, if we depress the Right Arrow key [→] three times, cells A1 through D1 will be highlighted. If we then depress the Down Arrow key [↓] five times, cells A1 through A6, B1 through B6, C1 through C6, and D1 through D6 will also be highlighted. Depressing the [Enter] key at any time will cause the contents of the highlighted cells to be deleted.

We could also accomplish the same end by directly typing in the address of a single cell or a range of cells. For example, if we had entered

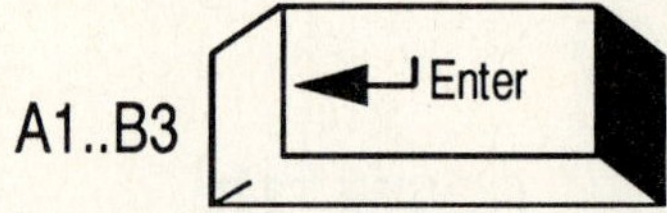

the contents of all cells from A1 through B3 would be deleted. Note, *two dots* between cell addresses are interpreted by 1-2-3 as "through." What cells are included in the range A1 through B3? The answer is all cells within an imaginary rectangle bounded by A1 in its upper left corner and B3 in its lower right corner (A1, A2, A3, B1, B2, B3). The cells specified must be in diagonally opposite corners of the imaginary rectangle. B3..A1, B1..A3, or A3..B1 can also be used to define the same range.

Thus, to delete the labels previously entered into our spreadsheet, enter

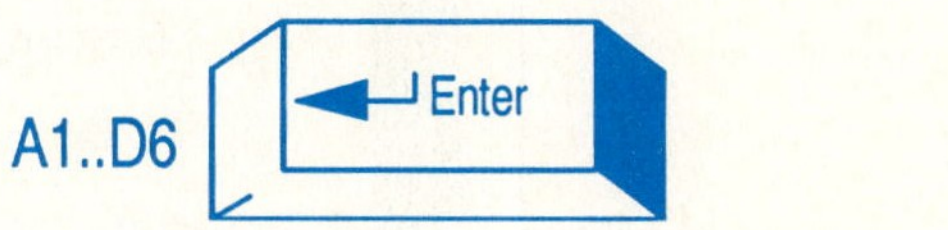

❑

Have you got it? Do you think you're ready to enter your first spreadsheet? Let's do it.

Building a Spreadsheet

An important area of business management is **budget forecasting**. Assume you own a small business and would like to project the growth of your company over the next year. You could start by entering the present budget values for the month of January, as shown in Figure T3-8. Although you could easily fit in the entire year's projection, we will limit our sample to half a year so we have to work only with one window.

We are using a relatively simple spreadsheet to illustrate the capabilities of the Lotus 1-2-3 integrated package. A more detailed and exacting breakdown of costs would be more realistic but is not necessary for our purposes.

Building the Model

Let's assume that we wish to enter the model shown in Figure T3-8. Begin by entering the title. Move your cursor to cell D1 using the Arrow keys and enter

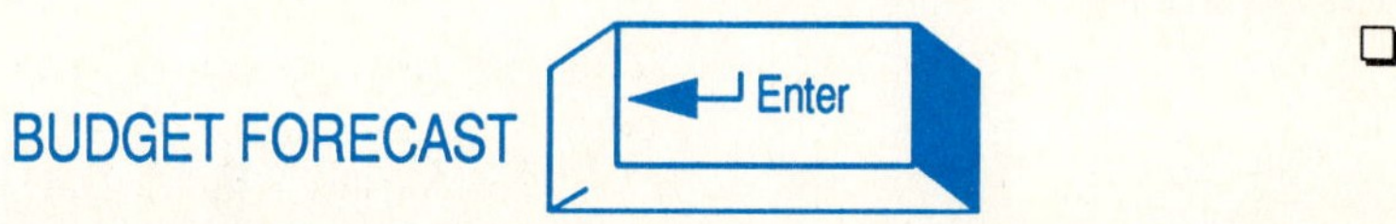

❑

Because each column in 1-2-3 has a default of *nine* positions, this label will not fit in one column width. Thus the first nine characters are entered into cell D1, and the remaining six characters are left-justified in cell E1. The first line of the control panel indicates cell D1 and the entry BUDGET FORECAST, yet the spreadsheet shows BUDGET FO highlighted in cell D1 and RECAST not highlighted in cell E1. This is to make us aware that the program was forced to use more than one cell.

Care should be taken to ensure that the label characters entered in each position begin with a letter or label prefix. Otherwise, the entry will be interpreted as a number and will be right-justified. When numbers are right-justified, the right-most digit is placed in the eighth, or next to last, position of a cell. This ensures that numbers in consecutive cells are always separated by at least one space.

FIGURE T3-8
Spreadsheet for Sample Problem.

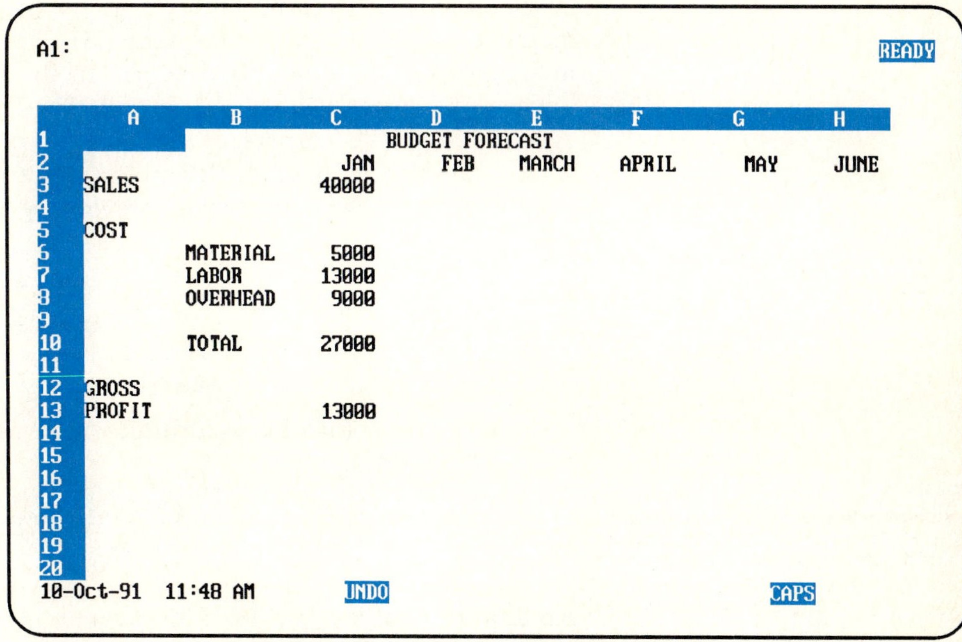

You can now either scroll or jump directly to C2 in order to begin entering the months. Remember, scroll by using the Arrow keys, or jump directly to a location by depressing the [F5] Function key followed by the address of the cell to which you wish to jump.

We could scroll to cell C2 by entering

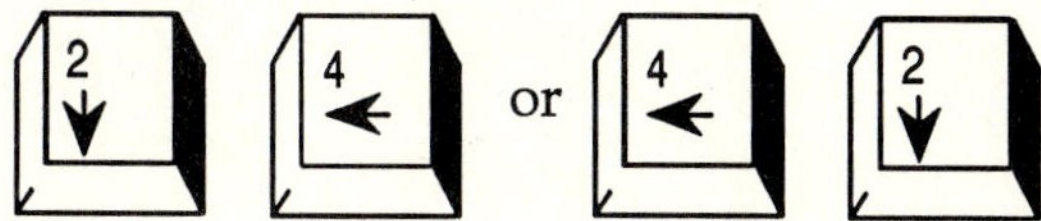

but, for practice, let's jump to cell C2 and enter the label JAN, right-justified. Enter

[F5] C2 [Enter]
"JAN [Enter]

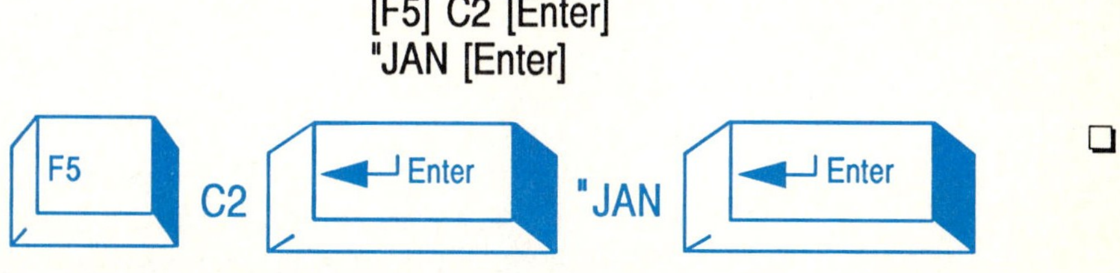

❑

We entered the month label right-justified so that it would be more aligned over the values below it. Remember, values are automatically right-justified. Thus, both the label and the values beneath it will be right-justified.

Now move the cursor to cell A3 and enter the label SALES. Enter

[F5] A3 [Enter]
SALES [Enter]

Notice that although the 'label-prefix was not used with SALES, it was left-justified in the cell. Labels are automatically left-justified if no label prefix is used.

Move to cell C3 and enter the number 40000. Enter

[F5] C3 [ENTER]
40000 [Enter]

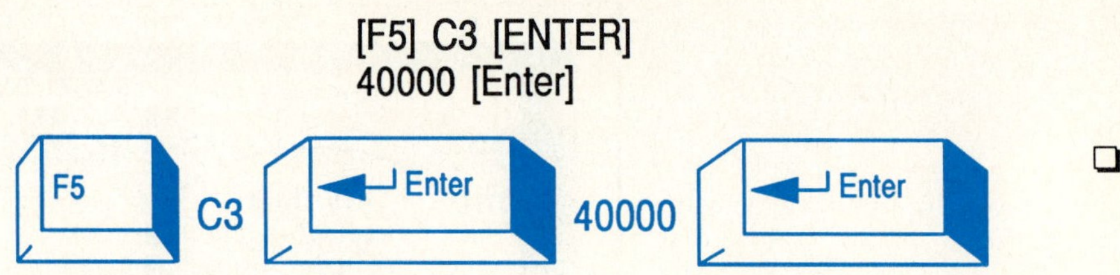

Notice how the number 40000 is entered right-justified in the cell. Numbers are automatically right-justified.

Either scroll or jump to cell A5 and enter COST

[F5] A5 [Enter]
COST [Enter]

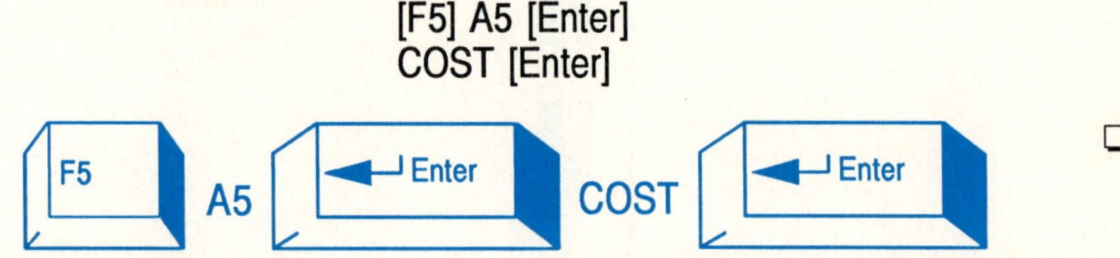

If at anytime you get confused or feel lost, you can get help by depressing the [F1] Function key. Or, if you type a wrong command, 1-2-3 allows you to back up one step by depressing the [Esc] key until the READY mode appears.

Now let's see what you can do on your own. This may take a little time.

Skip down to cell B6 and enter the word MATERIAL. Then move to cell C6 and enter 5000. Continue filling the rest of the spreadsheet until it looks like Figure T3-8.

Stopping Work

If you desire to end your Lotus session at any point, you must **Save** your spreadsheet onto your Work disk. At your next session, you can then **Load** your spreadsheet from your Work disk and resume. If you would like to break now, refer to the sections entitled "Saving a Spreadsheet on Diskette" and "Loading a Spreadsheet File," which appear later in the tutorial.

Making Calculations

Now, let's have the computer perform some calculations for us. To do a budget forecast, you must make assumptions. The first assumption we will make is that the *sales* figures will increase by 1.1 percent each month. Also, we expect *material* and *labor* costs to increase by 1 percent and *overhead* by 1.3 percent every month.

To calculate the SALES figures for succeeding months, we will use the value in cell C3, 40000 (the sales amount for January). Since we are predicting a 1.1 percent increase each month, we must enter a formula into cell D3, that is, D3 equals 1.011*C3 (where 1.1 percent = 0.011). Enter

[F5] D3 [Enter]
1.011*C3 [Enter]

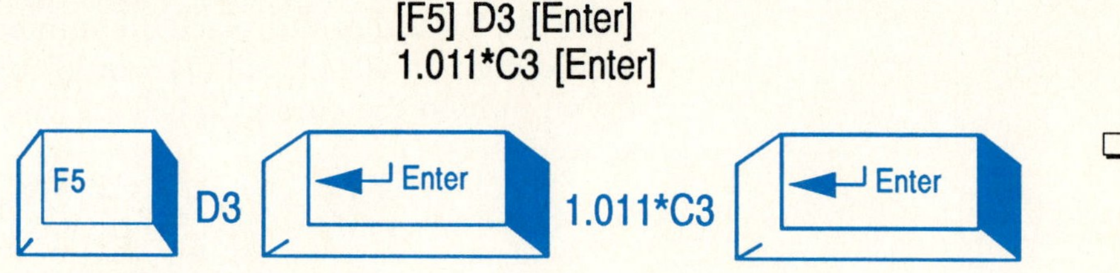

This brings the cursor to cell D3 and fills it with the product of the previous cell, C3, and 1.011 (an increase of 1.1 percent to a total of 40440). (See Fig. T3-9.)

FIGURE T3-9

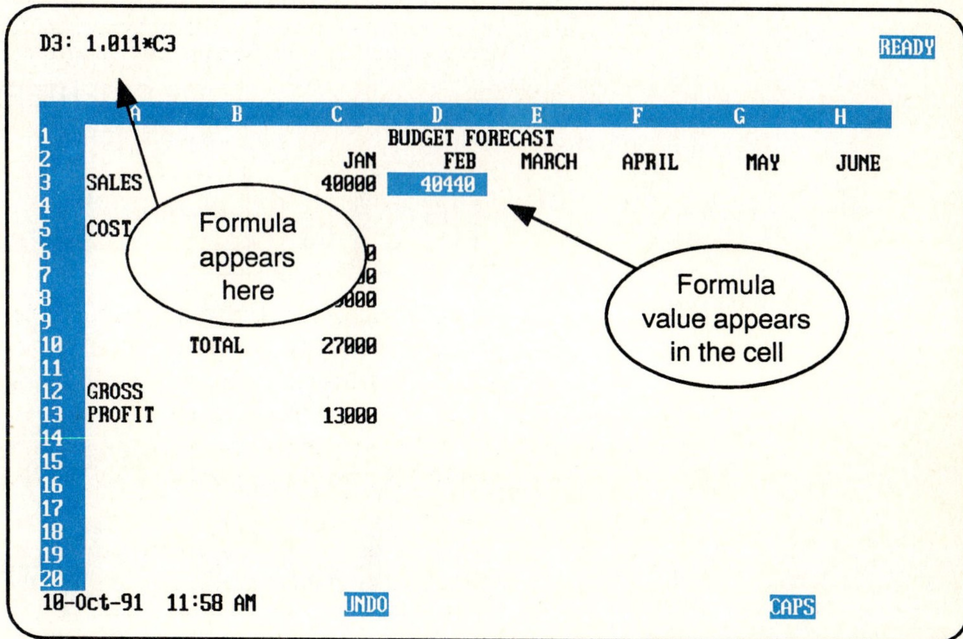

Note that the formula is written 1.011*C3 and not C3*1.011, because the latter begins with a letter and would be interpreted as a label, not a formula. A cell entry beginning with any one of the characters

+
-
.
(
@
#
$

will also be interpreted as a number, formula, or function. That is, the formula +C3*1.011 could also be used.

We could now enter a similar formula for cell E3 (1.011*D3), and so on until cell H3, which would get its value from the formula 1.011*G3. Thus the contents of the cells, beginning with 40000 in cell C3, are determined by the following formulas:

Cell C3	Cell D3	Cell E3	Cell F3	Cell G3	Cell H3
40000	1.011*C3	1.011*D3	1.011*E3	1.011*F3	1.011*G3

If you entered these formulas beginning in cell D3, the computer would store the formulas and place the numeric results in the cell. That is, cell D3 would contain 40440, cell D4 would contain 40884.84, and so on. However, if you moved the cursor to cell D3 (highlighted cell), the status line would show

D3:1.011*C3

indicating the cell address and the formula on which the content 40440 is based.

This procedure is acceptable for a few cells but is too time-consuming if we had to apply it many times. It would be preferable to instruct the computer to follow a pattern in determining the contents of each subsequent cell. But, before we can direct the computer to follow a pattern, we must recognize the pattern. Examining the formula needed in each successive cell, we have

D3 = 1.011*C3
E3 = 1.011*D3
F3 = 1.011*E3
G3 = 1.011*F3
H3 = 1.011*G3

Clearly, the content of each successive cell is obtained by multiplying the constant 1.011 by the value in the cell immediately to the left of the current cell. This is the pattern for which we were looking. All that remains is to tell the computer the pattern and to what cells to apply it. The command that accomplishes this is called Copy. Do you remember how to initiate a command? Yes, you must enter a slash. Press

❑

Your screen should now appear as shown in Figure T3-10.

FIGURE T3-10

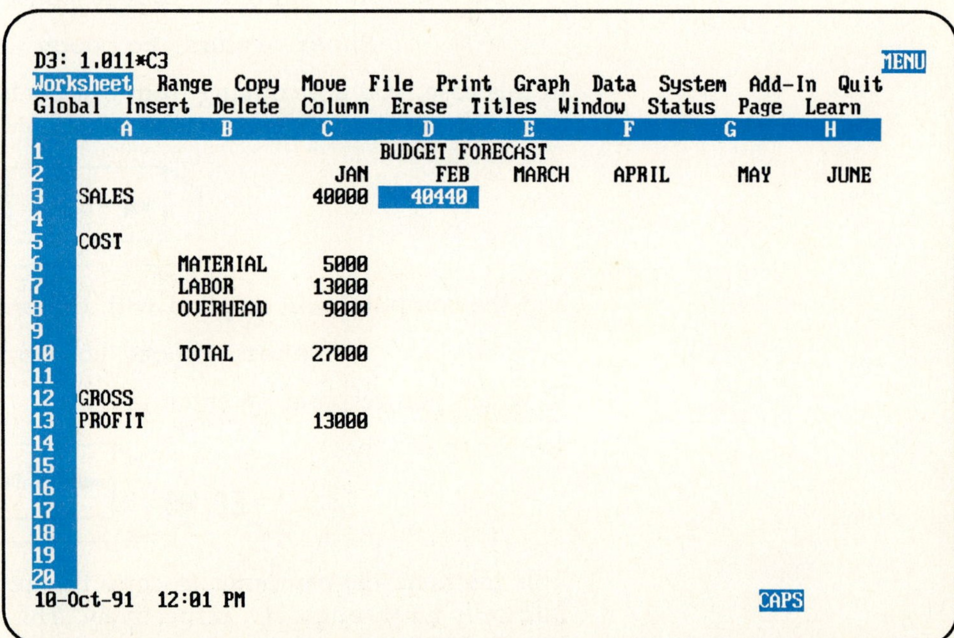

To initiate the [Copy] command, type

This should invoke the screen shown in Figure T3-11.

FIGURE T3-11

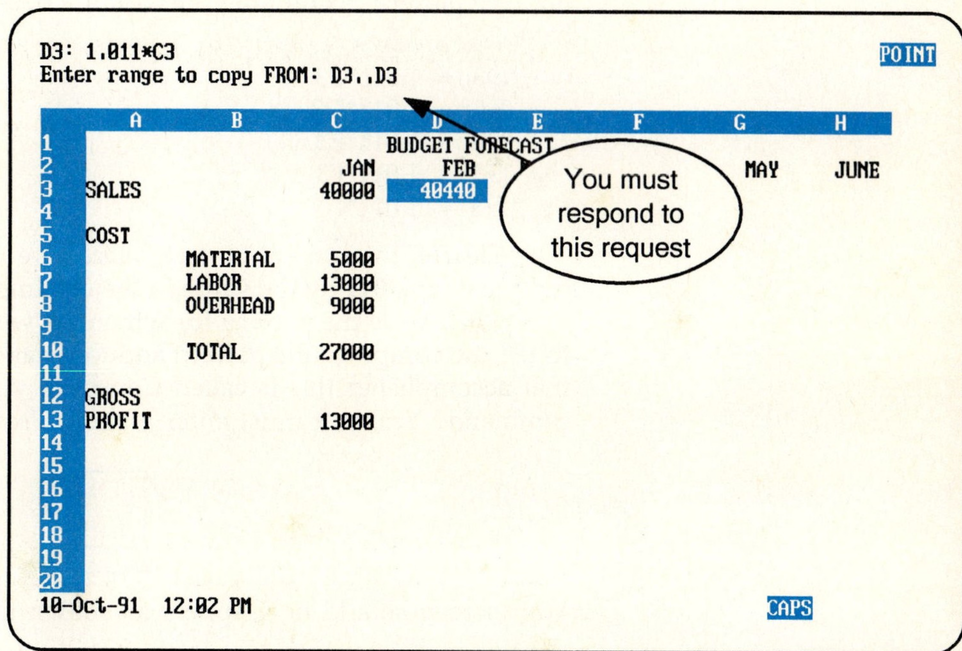

1-2-3 is now waiting for your response to the prompt

```
Enter range to copy FROM: D3..D3
```

In this case, you are copying from cell D3 because it contains the formula. Since this already appears on the screen, you need only press

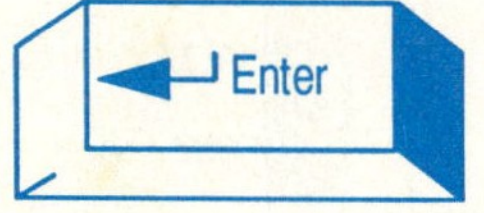

and the computer will respond with the prompt

```
Enter range to copy TO: D3
```

to which you respond by entering

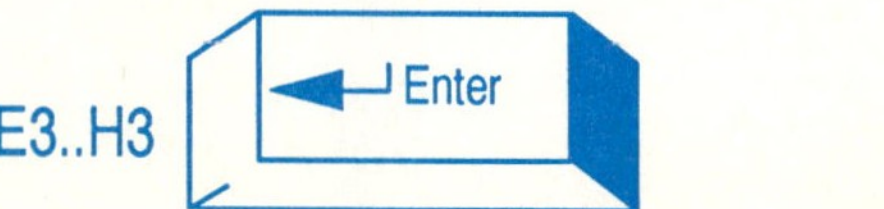

This instructs the computer to copy the generalized formula from cell D3 into cells E3 through H3, respectively. This results in the screen shown in Figure T3-12.

You're doing splendidly! Let's keep going.

Now that you've found the SALES figures, let's consider the cost figures. To calculate the individual MATERIAL, LABOR, and OVERHEAD costs, simply repeat the procedure you used for the sales, being careful to multiply by the correct constant. For the 1 percent increase in material and labor, *multiply by 1.01,* and for a 1.3 percent increase in overhead, *multiply by 1.013.*

FIGURE T3-12

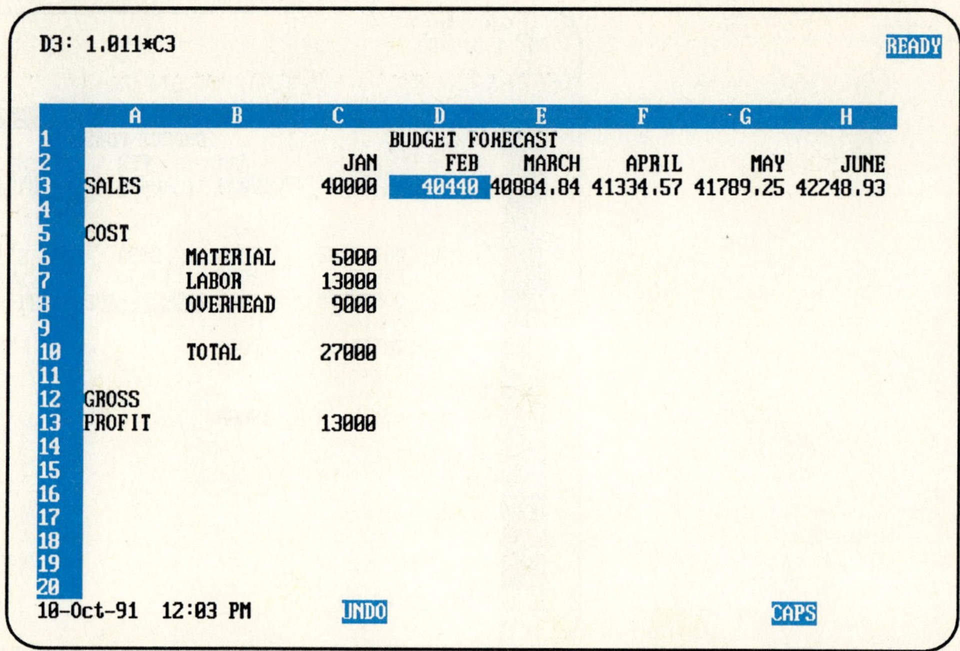

Applying this procedure to determining the MATERIAL costs for each successive month, you would

■ Move the cursor to cell D6:

❑

■ Enter the formula:

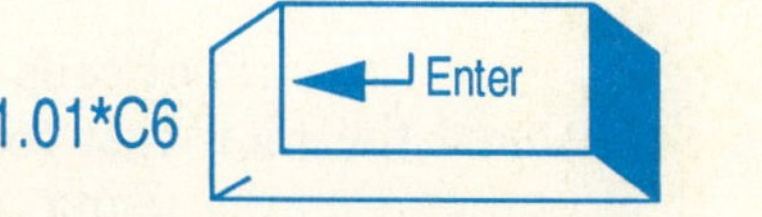

❑

■ Invoke the Copy command, and accept the default range D6:

/
[Copy] [Enter]
[Enter]

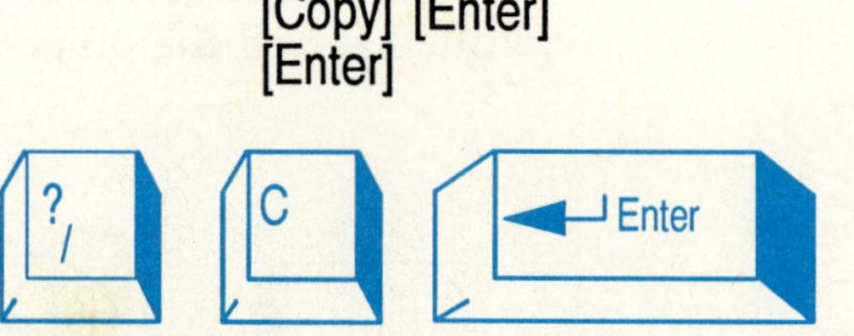

❑

■ Provide the range copied to:

❑

■ Repeat the preceding steps for the LABOR and OVERHEAD rows. Use the constants 1.01 and 1.013 in the LABOR and OVERHEAD formulas, respectively.

Your screen should now appear as shown in Figure T3-13.

FIGURE T3-13

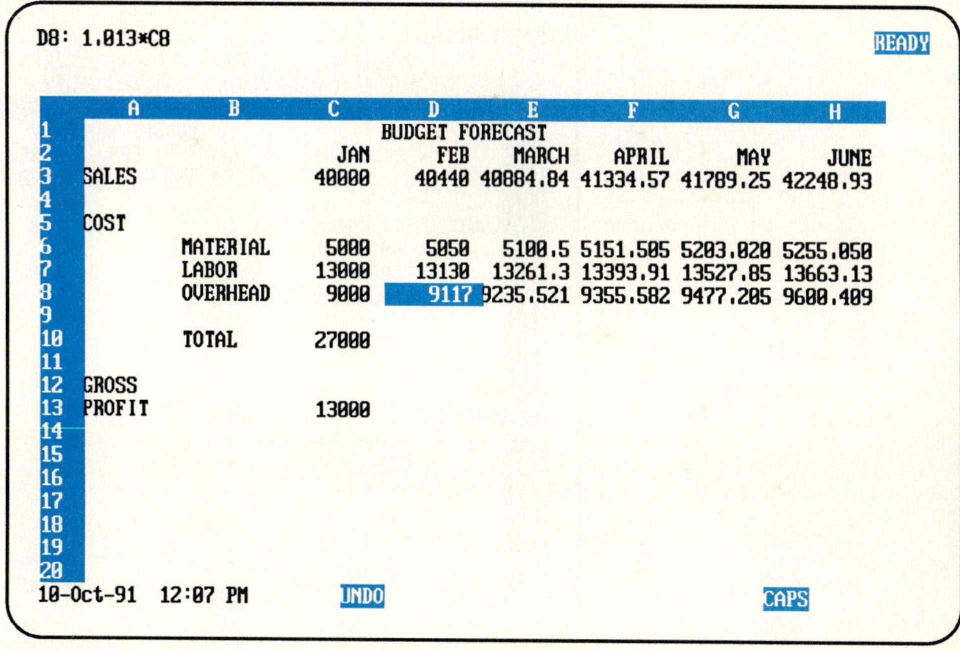
D8: 1.013*C8 READY

	A	B	C	D	E	F	G	H
1				BUDGET FORECAST				
2			JAN	FEB	MARCH	APRIL	MAY	JUNE
3	SALES		40000	40440	40884.84	41334.57	41789.25	42248.93
4								
5	COST							
6		MATERIAL	5000	5050	5100.5	5151.505	5203.020	5255.050
7		LABOR	13000	13130	13261.3	13393.91	13527.85	13663.13
8		OVERHEAD	9000	9117	9235.521	9355.582	9477.205	9600.409
9								
10		TOTAL	27000					
11								
12	GROSS							
13	PROFIT		13000					
14								
15								
16								
17								
18								
19								
20								

10-Oct-91 12:07 PM UNDO CAPS

Finding a Sum

To find the **TOTAL** figures, you could sum up each of the monthly cost columns. Although you can add a series of cells by using the plus sign, using the **@SUM** function is generally faster. Enter the following:

[F5] D10 [Enter]
@SUM(D6..D8) [Enter]

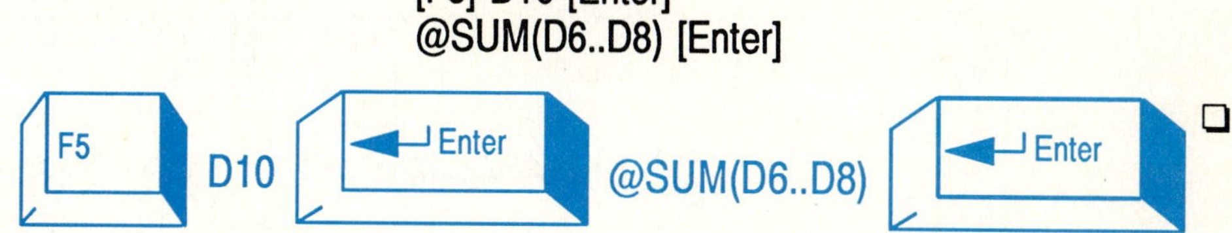

The sum of cells D6 through D8 will be placed into cell D10. You now have the total cost for the month of February. Compute the totals for the other months using @SUM commands. Compare your results with those shown in Figure T3-14.

GROSS PROFIT is found by subtracting TOTAL cost from SALES. The gross profit cell, D13, requires a formula: D13=D3 –D10. This formula can be replicated for all the other months. To accomplish this, enter

[F5] D13 [Enter]
+D3–D10 [Enter]

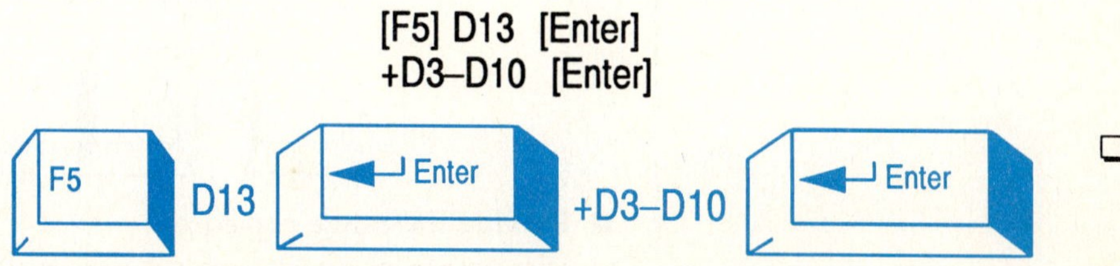

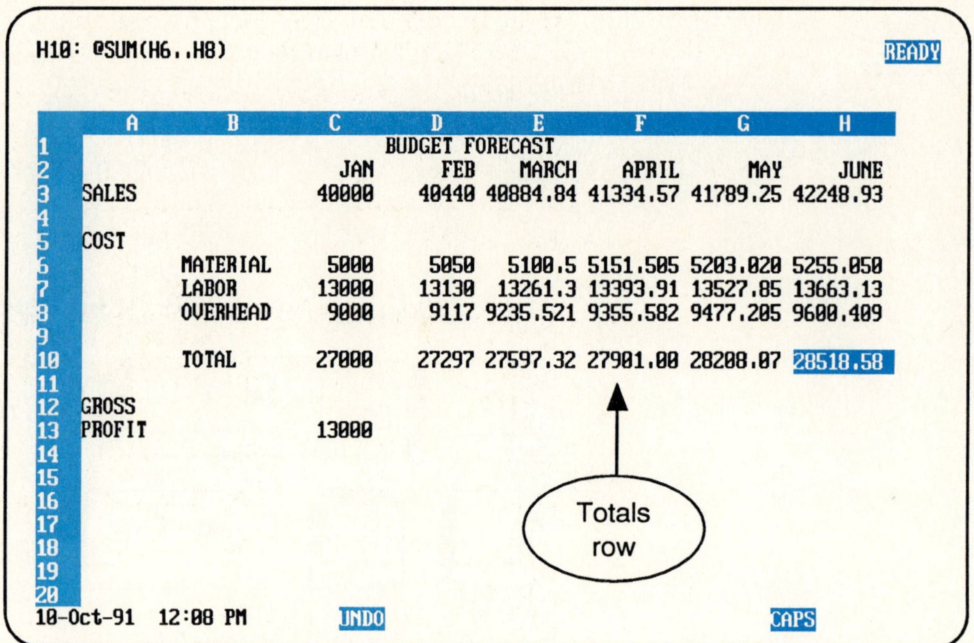

H10: @SUM(H6..H8) READY

	A	B	C	D	E	F	G	H
1				BUDGET FORECAST				
2			JAN	FEB	MARCH	APRIL	MAY	JUNE
3	SALES		40000	40440	40884.84	41334.57	41789.25	42248.93
4								
5	COST							
6		MATERIAL	5000	5050	5100.5	5151.505	5203.020	5255.050
7		LABOR	13000	13130	13261.3	13393.91	13527.85	13663.13
8		OVERHEAD	9000	9117	9235.521	9355.582	9477.205	9600.409
9								
10		TOTAL	27000	27297	27597.32	27901.00	28208.07	28518.58
11								
12	GROSS							
13	PROFIT		13000					
14								
15								
16								
17								
18								
19								
20								

10-Oct-91 12:00 PM UNDO CAPS

FIGURE T3-14

Now use the Copy command to replicate the formula into cells E13 through H13. Remember how you replicated material, labor, and overhead costs?

If your screen looks like Figure T3-15, you've passed your first spreadsheet test with flying colors. Congratulations!

FIGURE T3-15
Completed Sample Spreadsheet.

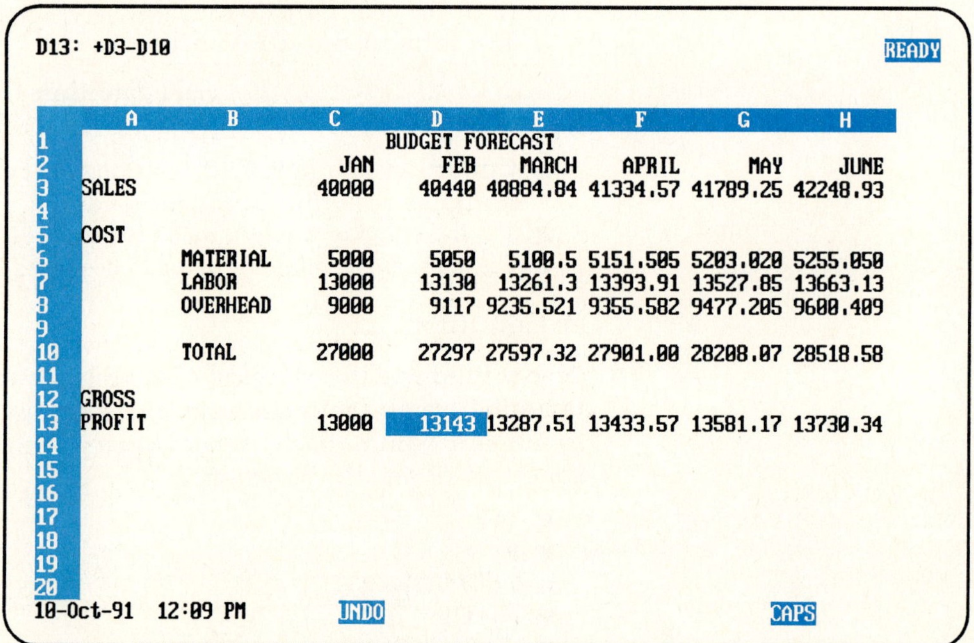

D13: +D3-D10 READY

	A	B	C	D	E	F	G	H
1				BUDGET FORECAST				
2			JAN	FEB	MARCH	APRIL	MAY	JUNE
3	SALES		40000	40440	40884.84	41334.57	41789.25	42248.93
4								
5	COST							
6		MATERIAL	5000	5050	5100.5	5151.505	5203.020	5255.050
7		LABOR	13000	13130	13261.3	13393.91	13527.85	13663.13
8		OVERHEAD	9000	9117	9235.521	9355.582	9477.205	9600.409
9								
10		TOTAL	27000	27297	27597.32	27901.00	28208.07	28518.58
11								
12	GROSS							
13	PROFIT		13000	13143	13287.51	13433.57	13581.17	13730.34
14								
15								
16								
17								
18								
19								
20								

10-Oct-91 12:09 PM UNDO CAPS

If it does not look like the preceding figure, you didn't replicate the GROSS PROFIT formula correctly. If necessary, correct this by entering the following:

[F5] D13 [Enter]
+D3–D10 [Enter]
/
[Copy] [Enter]
[Enter]
E13..H13 [Enter]

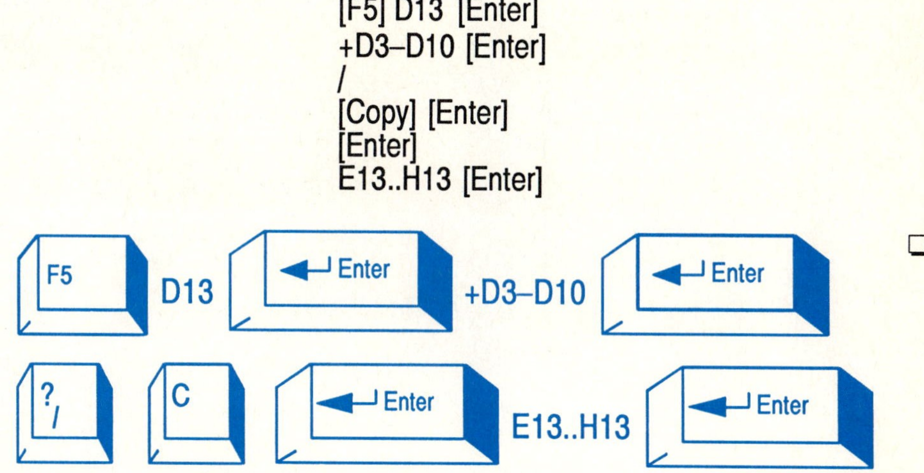

❑

You might consider saving your spreadsheet and taking a well-deserved break. If you choose to do this, review the Save command in the section "Saving a Spreadsheet on Diskette," and the Retrieve command in the section "Loading a Spreadsheet File," both of which appear later in this tutorial.

@IF Function

It is often convenient to specify the contents of one cell in terms of the contents of one or more other cells. For example, we expressed the value in cell D3 in terms of the value in cell C3 (D3=1.011*C3), the value of cell H10 in terms of the values in cells H6 through H8 (H10=@SUM(H6..H8)), and so on. A natural extension of this principal is to specify the contents of one cell in terms of one or more cells *under specific conditions*. Lotus provides this feature in the @IF Function.

The form of the @IF Function is

@IF(condition,T,F)

where

- **Condition** is a specified relationship between two numeric values or formulas resulting in numeric values.
- T is the string or numeric value to be placed in the cell if the condition is true.
- F is the string or numeric value to be placed in the cell if the condition is false.

A Condition

A condition specifies a *logical relationship* between numeric quantities. These quantities can be numeric values or expressions or functions that evaluate to numeric values. Each numeric quantity shown here could be used in the condition of an @IF Function.

- 14.5
- 0
- @SUM(A1..C1)
- C1+D1
- -14.5
- A1*(B1-D2)

Logical relationships are expressed using logical operators. The logical operators you can use are shown in Table T3-2.

TABLE T3-2
Logical Operators

Logical Operator	Condition Being Tested
=	Equal
<	Less than
>	Greater than
< =	Less than or equal to
> =	Greater than or equal to
< >	Not equal to

A condition is comprised of two numeric quantities and a logical operator. The *logical value* of a condition must be either **true** or **false**. It is true if the relationship expressed between the numeric quantities is true; it is false if the expressed relationship is false.

Several conditions and logical values are shown next. The truth values shown are based on the cell values: A1 = 14.5, A2 = 3.5, A3 = 2.0, B1 = 0, B2 = -15, and C1 = 20.

Condition	Logical Value
A1>0	True
B1=B2	False
A1+B2>5	False
@SUM(A1..A3)=C1	True
2.5*A3<>C1+B2	False

To illustrate the use of the @IF Logical Function, let's return to our spreadsheet. Assume that OVERHEAD costs are to be determined as follows:

> If the total cost of material and labor is less than $18,100, overhead is $9,000, otherwise overhead is $9,000 plus 1 percent of the total of material and labor costs.

Move the cursor to cell C8; then let's develop an @IF Function for cell C8. We must begin by expressing the condition *cost plus material is less than* 18,100 (C6+C7<18100). Next, we must include the value of overhead if the condition is *true* (9000). Finally, we must incorporate the value of overhead if the condition is *false* (9000+0.1*(C6+C7)).

Put it all together and enter the formula

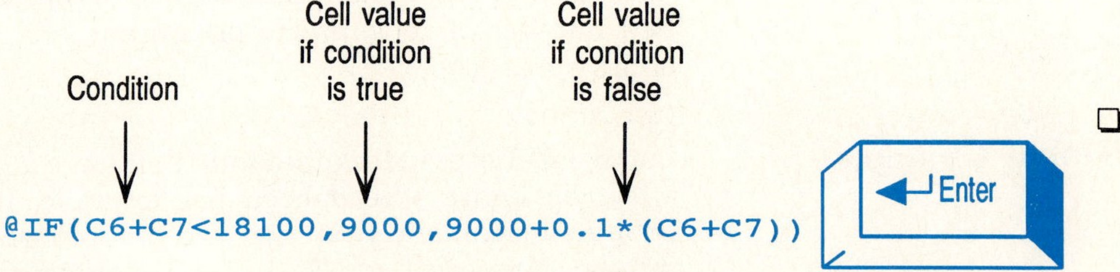

Now, we must replicate this formula into cells D8 through H8. Do you remember how to do this? Enter

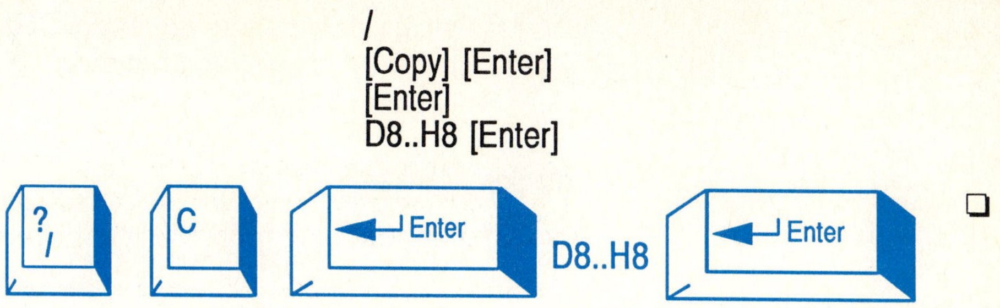

❑

and see the screen shown in Figure T3-16.

FIGURE T3-16
Spreadsheet After Incorporating Logical IF Function.

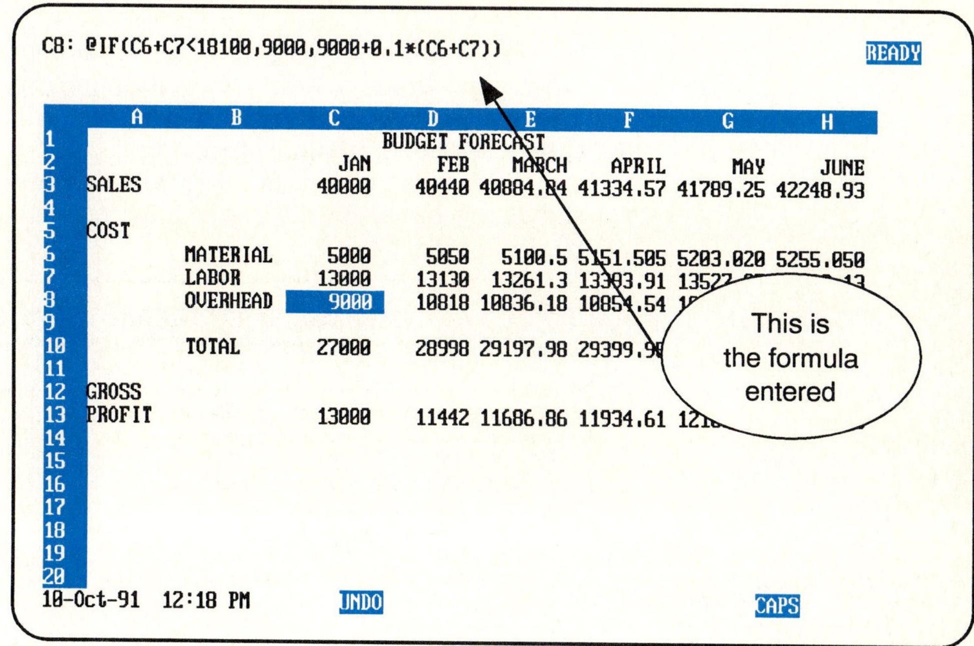

Improving the Appearance of Your Spreadsheet

It is possible to alter the appearance of numbers in a spreadsheet without changing their values. For example, we may choose to have all numbers in a particular row or column appear with a dollar sign, commas, and two decimal places. This can be accomplished with a few simple commands, as we shall see shortly. The important point to remember, however, is that the actual number in storage is not altered; only its appearance in the spreadsheet is affected.

There are two ways that we can accomplish these aesthetic, or cosmetic, changes. We can accomplish them on a limited basis—a single cell, a specified number of cells, a row or column—or on a global basis affecting the entire spreadsheet.

Global Changes

Lotus 1-2-3 provides commands that have a global impact, commands that affect an entire spreadsheet. For example, if the column width isn't big enough to contain your entries, you can reset the column width to any number between 1 and 72. In 1-2-3, a global change in field width causes all column widths to be reset. Let's assume we wish to change all column widths from the default 9 positions to 12 positions.

To do this press

In this screen, the cursor is pointing to Worksheet, making the subcommands listed on the next line Worksheet subcommands. The Global subcommand deserves further investigation. Therefore, depress

to enter the Worksheet command and give access to the Global subcommand. Since the cursor is already positioned over Global, press

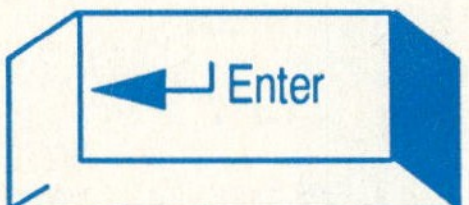

Your screen should now appear as shown in Figure T3-17.

FIGURE T3-17

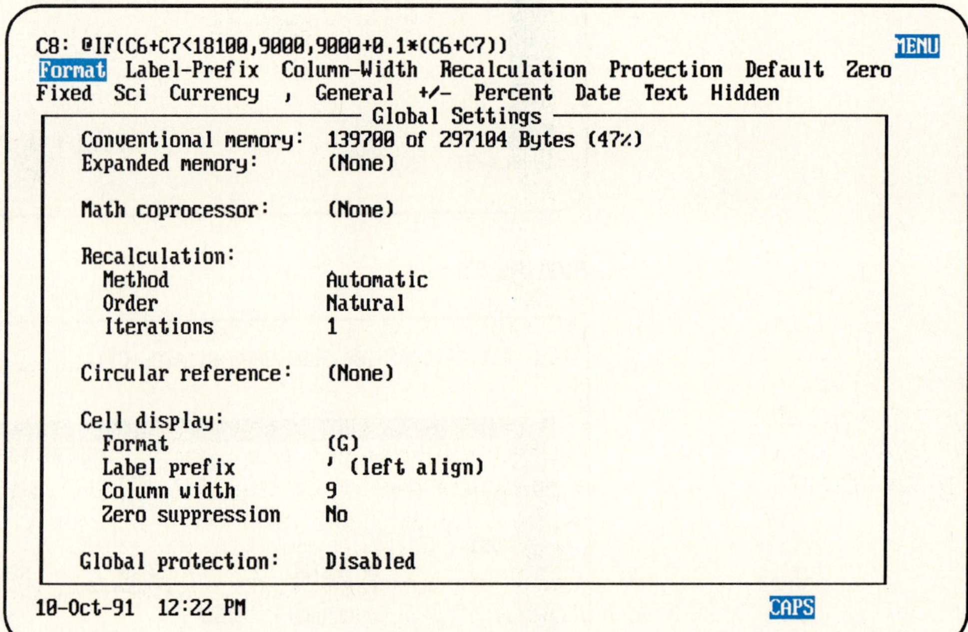

Earlier releases of Lotus do not support the Global Settings sheet you see in Figure T3-17.

Since you wish to change the width of each column in the spreadsheet, move the menu pointer to Column-Width and depress

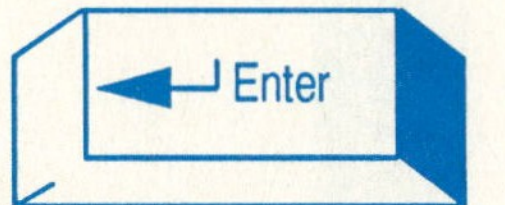

See Figure T3-18.

The prompt tells us to enter a new column width from 1 to 240 characters or to press the [Enter] key to accept the current column width of 9 characters. Enter

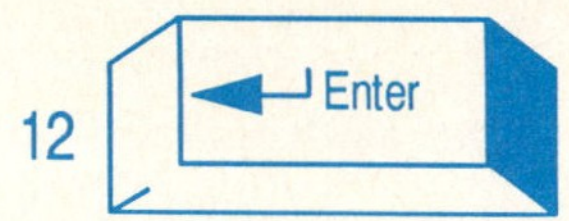

and, like magic, you will see a completely reformatted spreadsheet. See Figure T3-19.

FIGURE T3-18

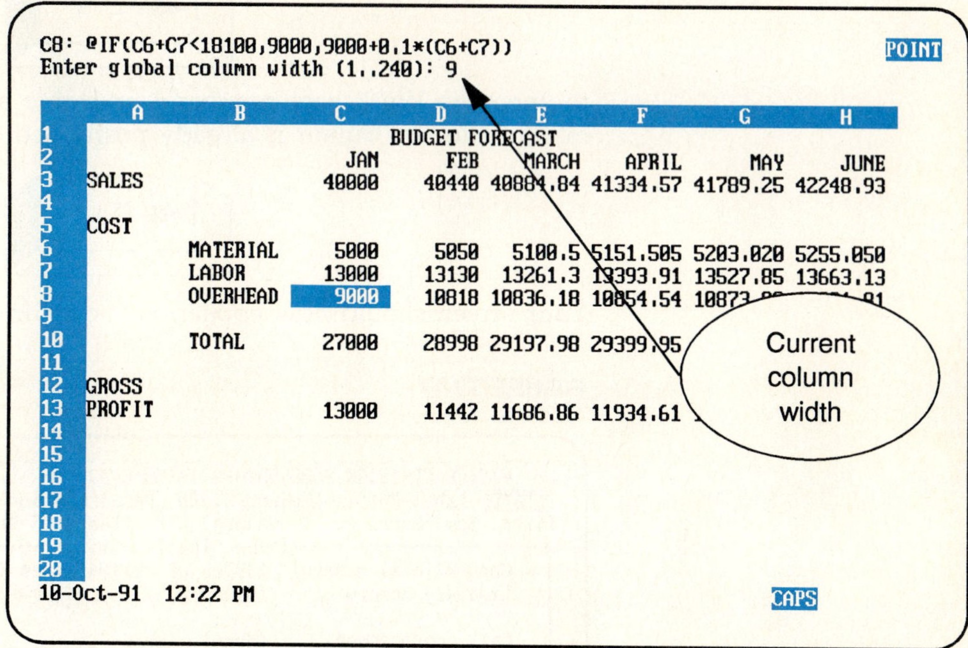

FIGURE T3-19

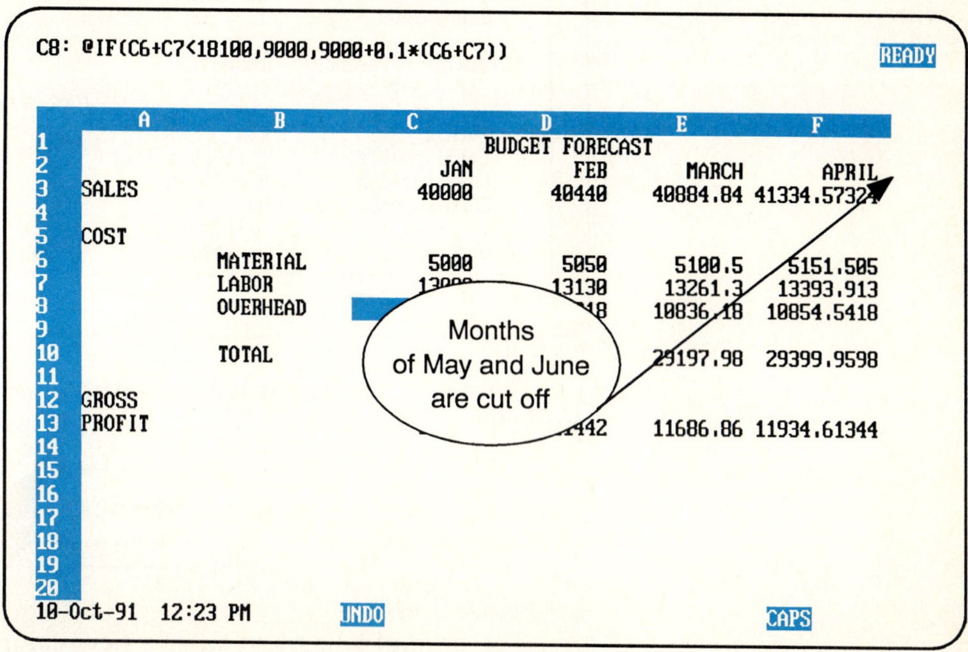

The thing most notable about this new spreadsheet is that we see only the entries for the months of January through April. This is because the window is only 72 positions wide. Our spreadsheet is now 96 positions across. How, then, can we view the entries for May and June? We can move the window by simply moving the cursor to the right beyond the current window, and the window will move to the right with the cursor.

In our spreadsheet, we will use another Global command to convert the values displayed in the spreadsheet to a **dollar-and-cent** format. To accomplish this, enter

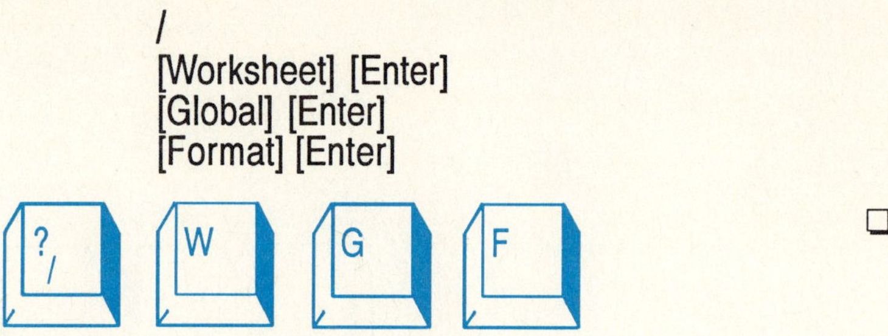

Your screen should match the one shown in Figure T3-20.

FIGURE T3-20

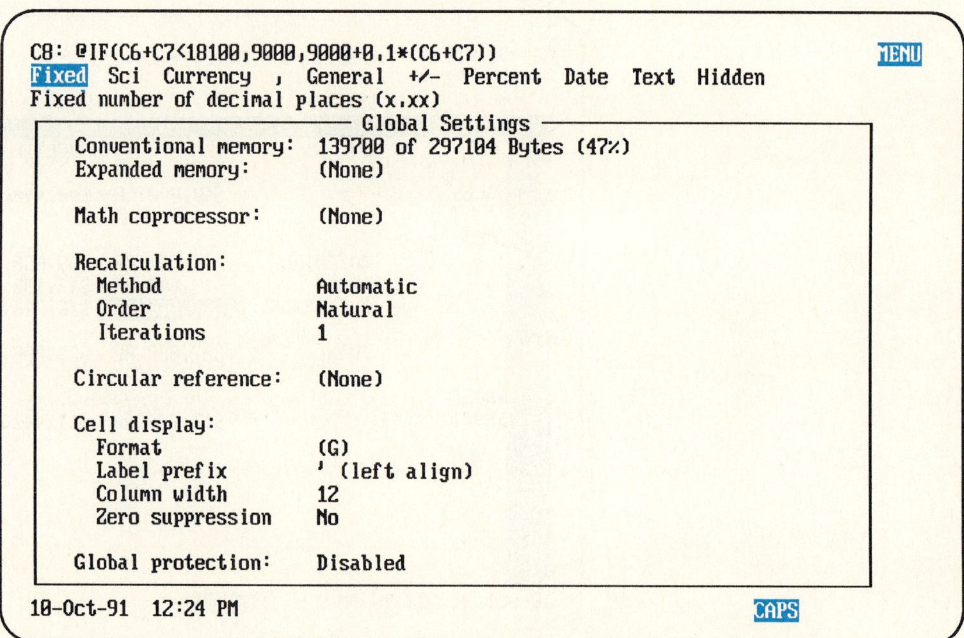

Although many options are displayed on this screen, only two are of concern to us now, Fixed and Currency. The difference between these two is that the Fixed option is concerned only with the number of decimal places. Commas or dollar signs are not inserted. The Currency option, on the other hand, not only allows us to control the number of decimal places but also automatically inserts a dollar sign and commas between successive groups of three digits. Let's choose the Currency option with two decimal places. Enter

[Currency] [Enter]
[Enter]

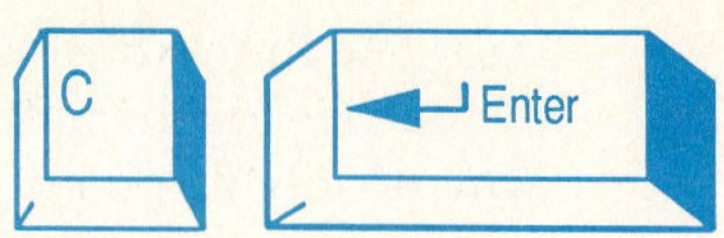

If you have carried out these operations correctly, your spreadsheet display should duplicate the one shown in Figure T3-21. If your spreadsheet does not appear as shown in Figure T3-21, get into the READY Mode by depressing the [Esc] key as many times as necessary and correct it by entering

/
[Worksheet] [Enter]
[Global] [Enter]
[Format] [Enter]
[Currency] [Enter]
2 [Enter]

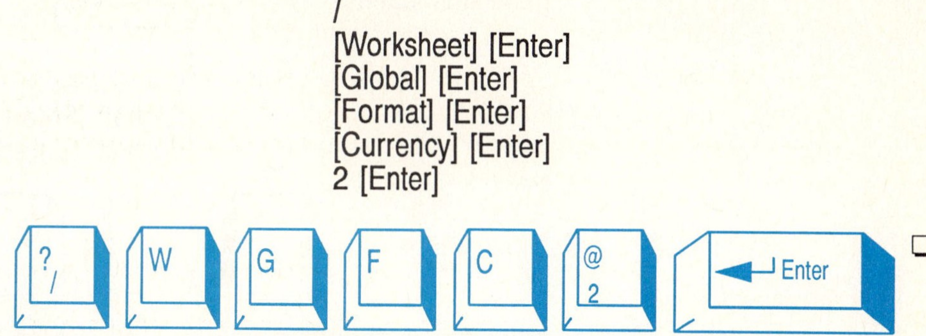

FIGURE T3-21
Spreadsheet with Currency Format.

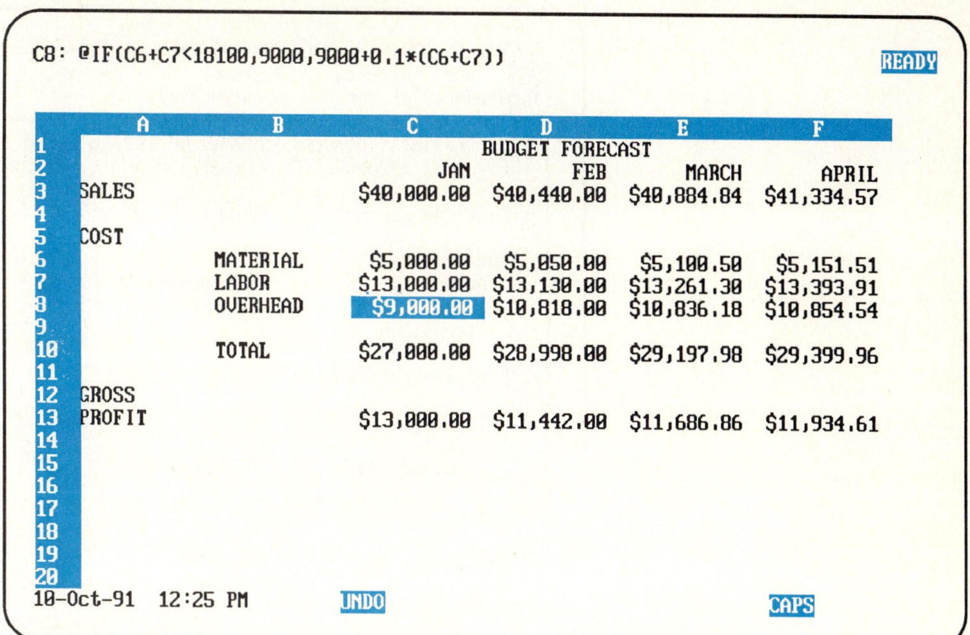

C8: @IF(C6+C7<18100,9000,9000+0.1*(C6+C7)) READY

	A	B	C	D	E	F
1				BUDGET FORECAST		
2			JAN	FEB	MARCH	APRIL
3	SALES		$40,000.00	$40,440.00	$40,884.84	$41,334.57
4						
5	COST					
6		MATERIAL	$5,000.00	$5,050.00	$5,100.50	$5,151.51
7		LABOR	$13,000.00	$13,130.00	$13,261.30	$13,393.91
8		OVERHEAD	$9,000.00	$10,818.00	$10,836.18	$10,854.54
9						
10		TOTAL	$27,000.00	$28,998.00	$29,197.98	$29,399.96
11						
12	GROSS					
13	PROFIT		$13,000.00	$11,442.00	$11,686.86	$11,934.61
14						
15						
16						
17						
18						
19						
20						

10-Oct-91 12:25 PM UNDO CAPS

What If?

Spreadsheets similar to our model are developed to help provide some approximate figures to look at when considering future trends. Changing some of the initial values will obviously have an effect on the computed results. This allows the user to ask "what-if" questions.

For example, *what* would happen to profits *if* sales were adjusted in some way? If sales increased by 1.5 percent instead of 1.1 percent, the profits would obviously increase. If you change the initial value in the original formula from 1.011 to 1.015, all cell values affected by this figure will be altered to reflect the change.

Assuming your spreadsheet display is like the one shown in Figure T3-21, test this "what if" by entering

[F5] D3
1.015*C3

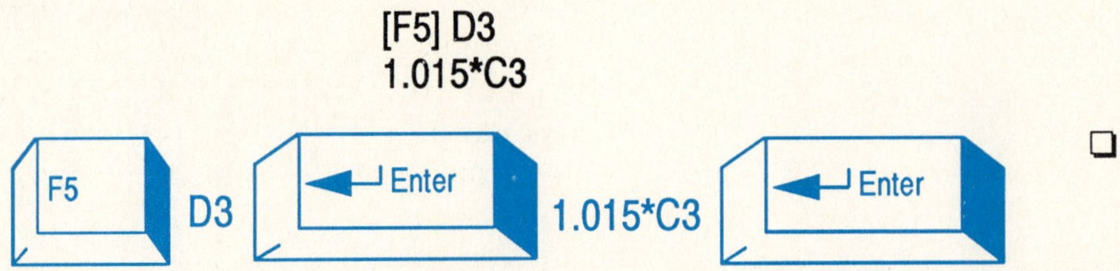

Notice that you did not have to use the Copy command. Lotus 1-2-3 automatically adjusted the other row entries and the corresponding column totals. Thank you, Lotus. Your spreadsheet should now appear as the one shown in Figure T3-22.

FIGURE T3-22
Sample Spreadsheet with "What-If" Modifications.

D3: 1.015*C3 READY

	A	B	C	D	E	F
1				BUDGET FORECAST		
2			JAN	FEB	MARCH	APRIL
3	SALES		$40,000.00	$40,600.00	$41,046.60	$41,498.11
4						
5	COST					
6		MATERIAL	$5,000.00	$5,050.00	$5,100.50	$5,151.51
7		LABOR	$13,000.00	$13,130.00	$13,261.30	$13,393.91
8		OVERHEAD	$9,000.00	$10,818.00	$10,836.18	$10,854.54
9						
10		TOTAL	$27,000.00	$28,998.00	$29,197.98	$29,399.96
11						
12	GROSS					
13	PROFIT		$13,000.00	$11,602.00	$11,848.62	$12,098.15
14						
15						
16						
17						
18						
19						
20						

10-Oct-91 12:20 PM UNDO CAPS

Let's undo our "what-if" experiment and get back to our original spreadsheet. How do you think we might do this?

There are two correct procedures you could follow. You could use 1-2-3's Undo feature, or you could move the cursor to cell D3 and reenter the original formula 1.011*C3. Let's choose the manual method to undo the previous procedure. To manually undo the "what-if" experiment, move the cursor to cell D3 and enter

Good. Now let's change the width of the columns back to 9 characters. Enter the commands

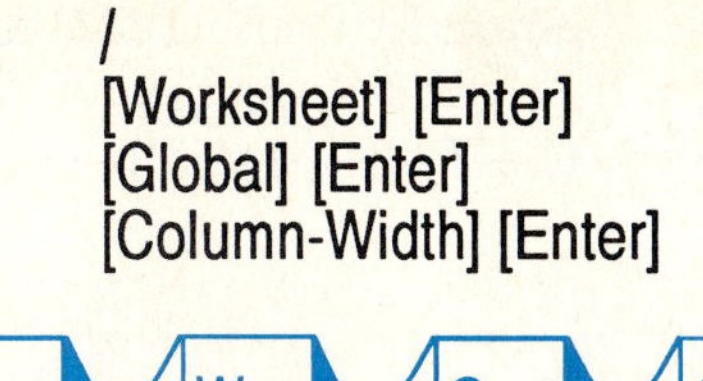

❑

and in response to

```
Enter global column width (1..240):12
```

enter

❑

What happened? Your screen should be filled with rows of asterisks, as shown in Figure T3-23.

FIGURE T3-23
Spreadsheet with Field Widths Too Small.

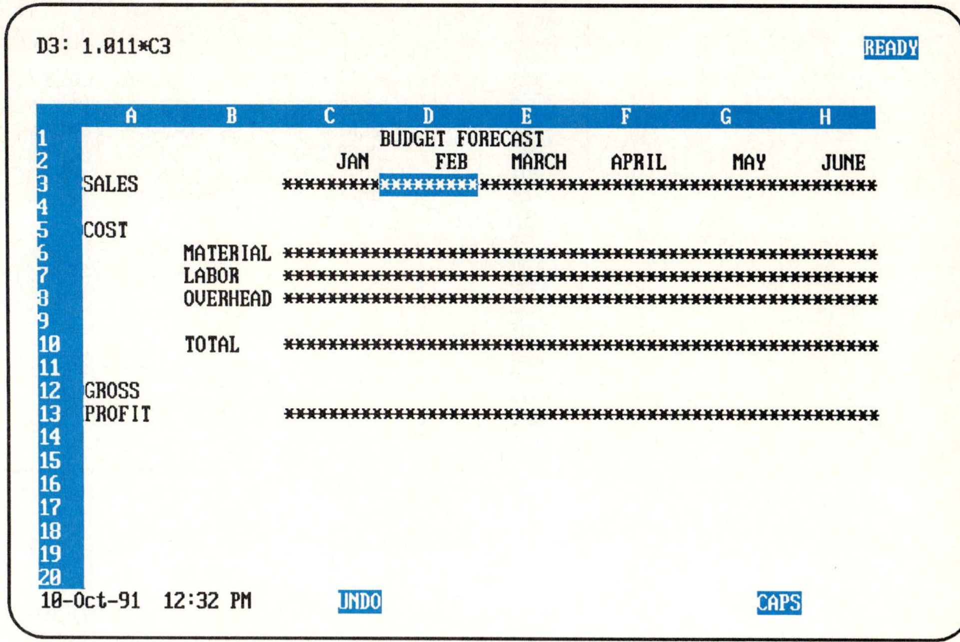

This is 1-2-3's way of telling you that the values stored could not be displayed in the space provided and in the format specified. Ah! Remember the $ and , characters that resulted from our previous Currency format specification. How would you change this to a Fixed, two-decimal-place format? The correct command sequence is shown below. Enter

/
[Worksheet] [Enter]
[Global] [Enter]
[Format] [Enter]
[Fixed] [Enter]

and in response to

```
Enter number of decimal places (0..15):2
```

press

Your screen should now appear the same as shown in Figure T3-24. Let's move on to bigger and better things.

FIGURE T3-24
Finalized Spreadsheet.

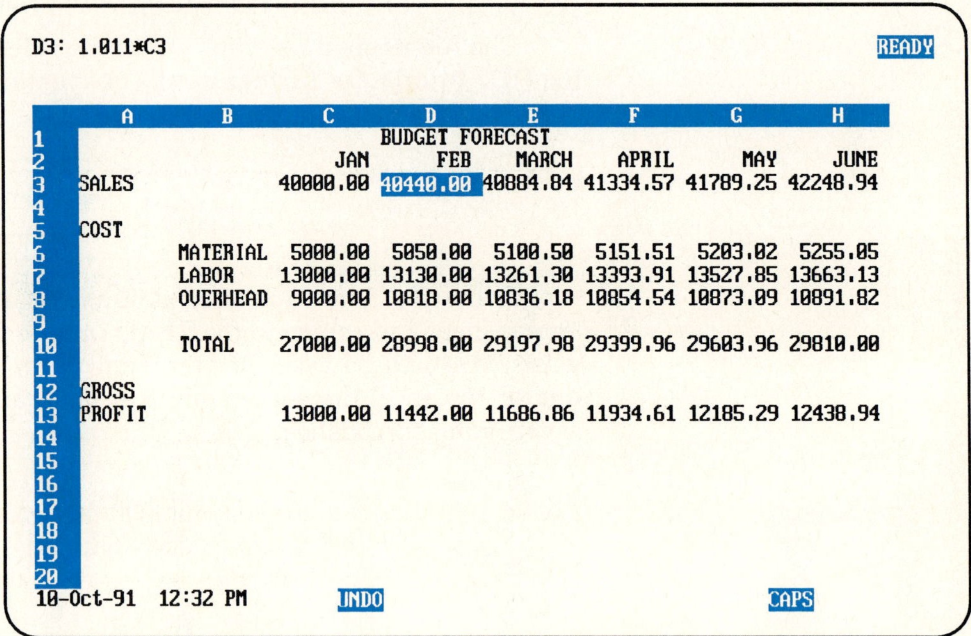

Saving, Printing, Erasing, and Loading

Once your spreadsheet looks the way you want it to, you may want to save it on diskette.

Saving a Spreadsheet on Diskette

To save your spreadsheet, you must use the Save command. Make sure you have a formatted disk in drive B:. To see how this command works, enter

/
[File] [Enter]
[Save] [Enter]

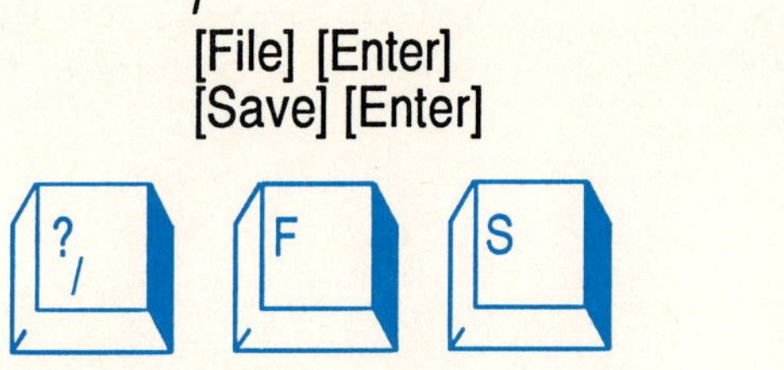

and you should see the prompt

```
Enter name of file to save: A:\
```

If you see a file name listed after the " \ ", this indicates that your file has already been saved. In this case, press the [Enter] key and the [R] key for Replace in response to the next prompt displayed.

This prompt is asking you to enter a file name for your spreadsheet. If you have never saved this spreadsheet, the area to the right of the first colon will contain the prompt **B:** or **A:**, or, if you are using a hard drive, you may see **C:\LOTUS**. Any of these prompts indicate that your copy of Lotus has been programmed to save to the drive listed. If *.WK1 appears after the backslash, this indicates that there are spreadsheet files saved on your storage media.

Let's name the file. Depending on your hardware configuration, you may have to enter the drive specification, followed by the spreadsheet file name. Lotus will automatically add the extension WK1. Our file name will be prefixed by B: to indicate the B drive (you can use A: or C:\Lotus\, depending on your hardware).

If you have the correct drive specified, you need not remove it; however, if the wrong drive specification is displayed, depress the [Backspace] key until the A:\ (or B:\ or C:\Lotus) disappears. Then enter the appropriate drive specification, A:\, B:\, or C:\LOTUS.

The file name must conform to the rules for forming DOS names (see the DOS tutorial for further details on creating DOS file names). Our choice is BUDGET. Enter

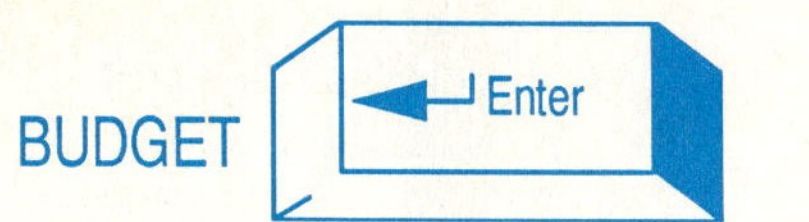

If the file name specified doesn't already exist, 1-2-3 will save your spreadsheet and return to the READY mode. However, if this name already exists, you will be asked if you want to replace the old one with the new one or to cancel the save request. If you want to be certain that 1-2-3 has saved your spreadsheet, reenter the commands

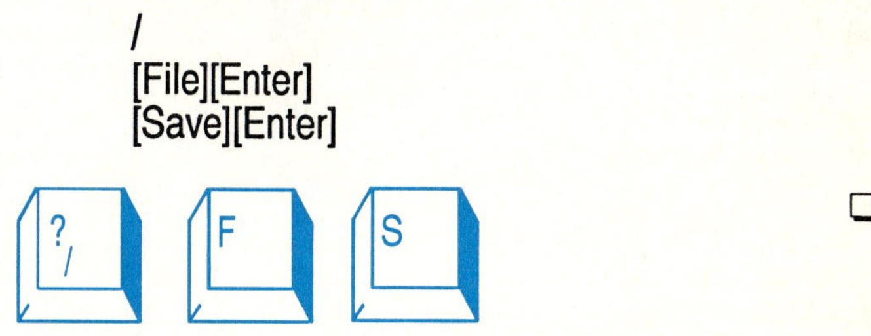

and 1-2-3 should indicate that the previous spreadsheet saved is the one you just saved. The screen indicating this is shown in Figure T3-25.

Press

The Backup option is not available in earlier releases of Lotus.

and Lotus will request you *Cancel* the command, *Replace* the previously stored file, or *Backup* the existing file.

Depress

to cancel the command.

Once you have saved a spreadsheet, you may desire to print it out.

FIGURE T3-25

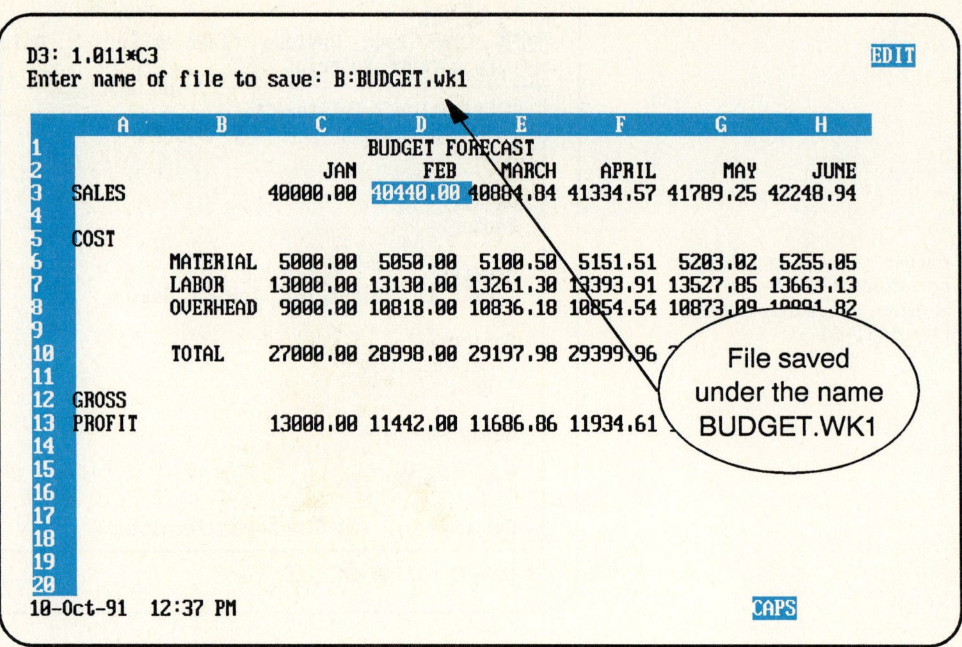

Printing a Spreadsheet

All or a portion of a spreadsheet may be printed. You may even direct the data you want to print to be saved on a file for later printing. Let's assume that you wish the current spreadsheet printed now. This can be accomplished by entering

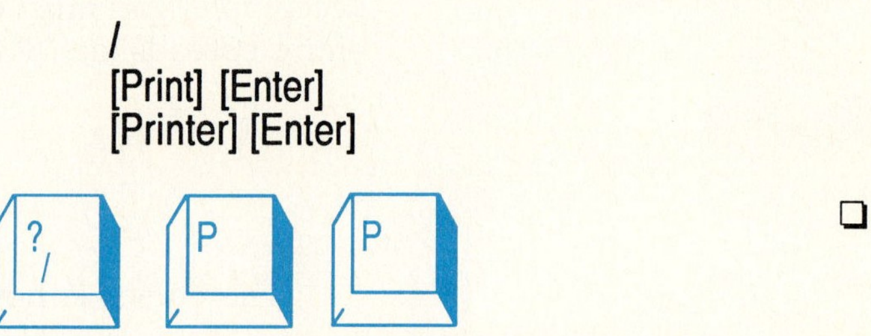

❑

Do this now, and verify that your screen is like the one shown in Figure T3-26.

On this screen, there are a number of options open to us. **Range** allows us to specify the portion of the spreadsheet to be printed; **Line** and **Page** control the advancement of the paper; **Options** allows us to set headers, footers, margins, and so on; **Clear** resets one or more printer settings; **Align** facilitates the alignment of the page; **Go** causes the designated portion of the spreadsheet to be printed; and **Quit** exits the Print command.

Since you have not indicated the portion of the spreadsheet that you want printed, do it now. Type

❑

to select the [Range] command. You should now be prompted to

Enter print range: D3

FIGURE 3-26

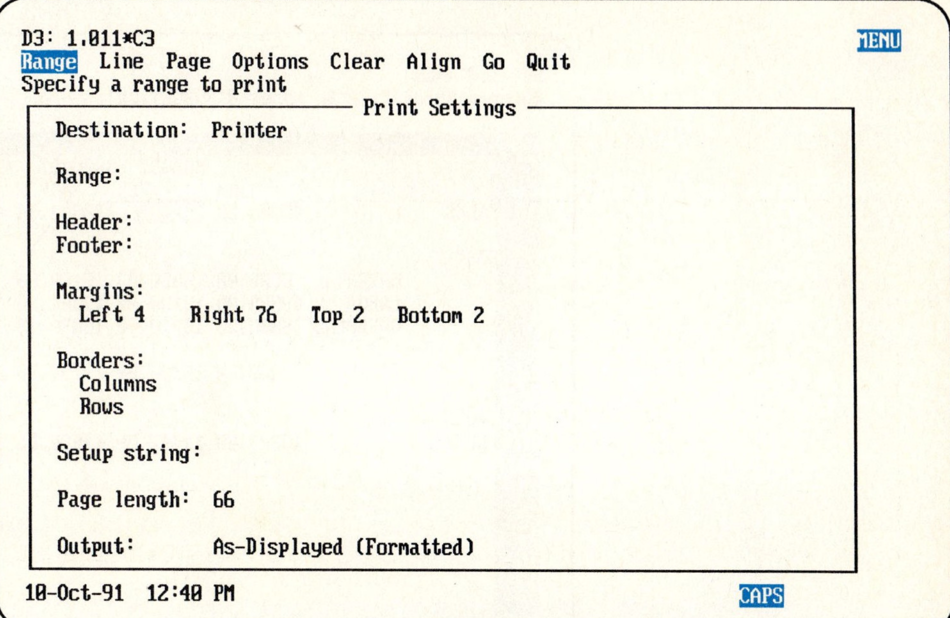

Earlier releases of Lotus do not support the Print Settings sheet displayed in Figure T3-26.

The default range indicated (D3) represents the present cursor position. The segment of the spreadsheet that will be printed is a box defined as a single cell or as a two-cell range. Remember, if it is defined as a two-cell range, the first cell listed defines one corner of the box and the second cell listed defines the diagonally opposite corner. If the default range is not acceptable, you must enter the desired range. Because you want to print the entire spreadsheet, you must enter the desired range as

The cursor is now pointing at Range. Press

to view the specified range. The entire block should now be highlighted, confirming the selected range.

If this is the correct range to be printed, depress the [Enter] key; otherwise correct the range and then depress the [Enter] key.

To print the indicated portion of the spreadsheet, select the [Go] command by typing

and it should print immediately. The printed copy should appear as shown in Figure T3-27. After the printing has been completed, type

to select [Quit]. This will return you to the READY Mode. You will see the word READY in the upper right corner of the screen.

FIGURE T3-27
Printed Copy of the Spreadsheet.

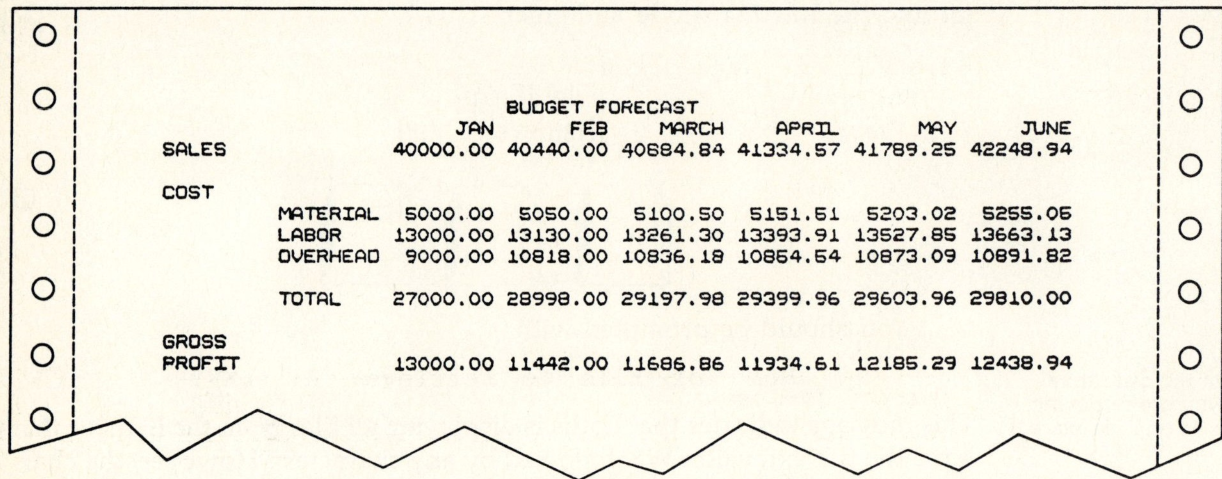

BUDGET FORECAST

		JAN	FEB	MARCH	APRIL	MAY	JUNE
SALES		40000.00	40440.00	40884.84	41334.57	41789.25	42248.94
COST							
	MATERIAL	5000.00	5050.00	5100.50	5151.51	5203.02	5255.06
	LABOR	13000.00	13130.00	13261.30	13393.91	13527.85	13663.13
	OVERHEAD	9000.00	10818.00	10836.18	10854.54	10873.09	10891.82
	TOTAL	27000.00	28998.00	29197.98	29399.96	29603.96	29810.00
GROSS PROFIT		13000.00	11442.00	11686.86	11934.61	12185.29	12438.94

If you wish to experiment with any of the other print options on your own, first ask 1-2-3 for help. Remember how to get help? You simply depress the [F1] Function key.

Erasing a Spreadsheet

Are you finished with your old spreadsheet, and do you want to begin work on a new one? Get into the READY mode (Remember? Use the [Esc] key) and enter

/
[Worksheet] [Enter]
[Erase] [Enter]
[Yes] [Enter]

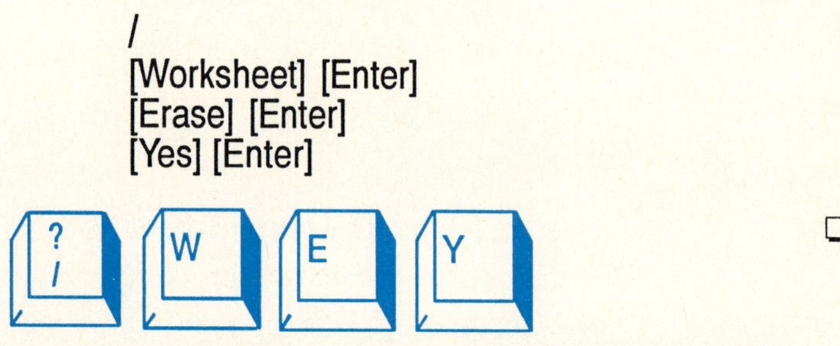

If you wish to utilize one of Lotus' other capabilities, you could enter

/
[Quit][Enter]
[Yes][Enter]

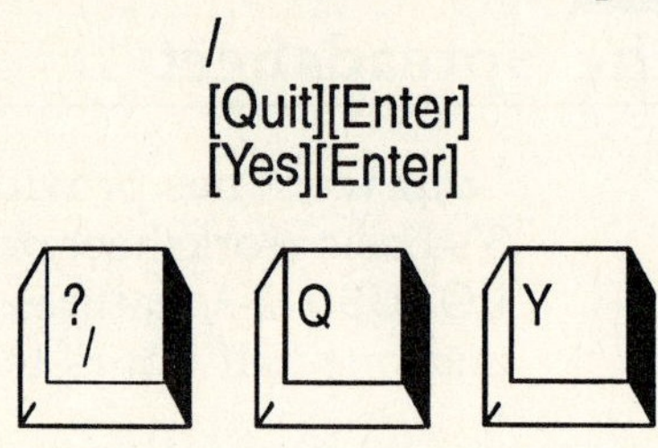

This would return you to Lotus' initial menu. Then, to create a new spreadsheet, you would press

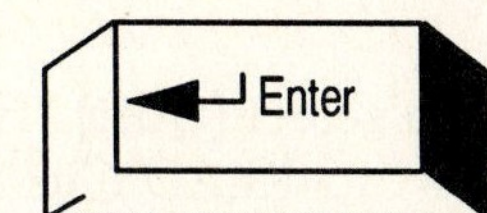

and the copyright screen would appear.

Loading a Spreadsheet File

To load a spreadsheet into memory that was previously saved on diskette, get into the READY mode and enter

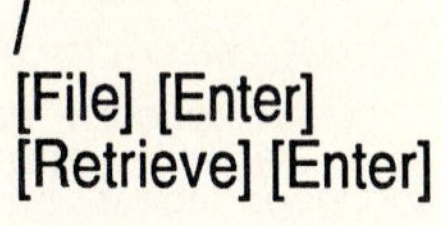

You should be prompted with

Depending on the disk drive from which you are retrieving, you may see A: or C: in place of B:.

```
Name of file to retrieve: A:\*.WK?
```

This message indicates that Lotus is displaying all files from the B: drive that have the file extension **WK** followed by any character. However, the characters that are significant to Lotus are **S, 1,** and **3. WKS** Lotus files are created from saving Lotus Release 1A spreadsheet files, while **WK1** Lotus files are created from saving Lotus Release 2.X spreadsheet files. The **WK3** Lotus files are created from saving Lotus Release 3.0 spreadsheet files.

The command summary line just below this prompt line in the control panel should list the spreadsheet file names in your library. If you saved your spreadsheet as suggested above, the name BUDGET.WK1 should be the first name present. Because the cursor is on this filename, you need only press the [Enter] key to retrieve this file. If several filenames are present, you can move the cursor to the desired file and then press the [Enter] key. To access BUDGET.WK1, press

The spreadsheet in this file should immediately be displayed on the screen.

Part II Beyond the Spreadsheet

Your work has provided you thus far with an understanding of Lotus 1-2-3's basic worksheet procedures. Let's focus our attention on some advanced LOTUS 1-2-3 features. This part of the tutorial will take approximately one and one-half hours to complete.

Graphing Your Output

One of the advantages of using an integrated software package is that several procedures or capabilities are provided in the package and they can be used together. One of the features provided with 1-2-3, in addition to what we have already seen and used, is its graphics ability. 1-2-3 allows us to graph or plot the output that we obtained earlier. *You can see the graphics output displayed only if you have a graphics board installed in your computer.* Otherwise, you will have to save your graph with a **G**raph **S**ave command and print it on your printer using the GRAPH program. An explanation of this program is beyond the scope of our presentation. The choices available with 1-2-3's graphics option are numerous and varied. We do not have the time here to discuss them all, but we will demonstrate how this option can be used to display a very simple bar graph.

A Simple Bar Graph

We will simultaneously plot the sales, cost, and gross profit values for each of the months January through June. Are you game? Here we go!

The graphics option is accessed from 1-2-3's command menu. Do you remember how to bring up the command menu? Get into the READY mode and type

❑

If all is well, you should be in the MENU mode viewing the command menu. If you are, enter

[Graph] [Enter]
[Type] [Enter]
[Bar] [Enter]

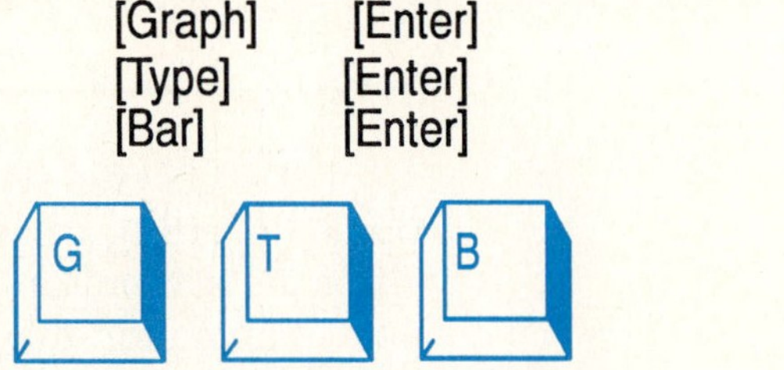

❑

Now we must tell 1-2-3 the cell ranges that we want plotted. Since we are plotting three ranges (SALES, COST, and GROSS PROFIT), we will have to provide 1-2-3 with each of these ranges. We do this one range at a time. Let's begin with the SALES range. Enter

[A] [Enter]
C3..H3 [Enter]

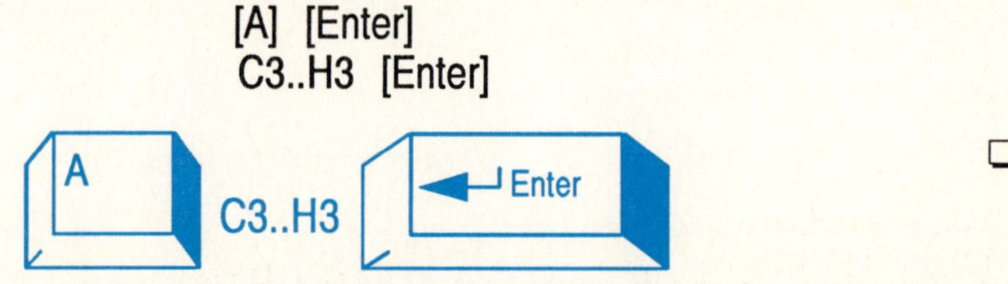

❑

Thus, the A range encompasses all cells to the right of the label SALES. Similarly, to input COST and GROSS PROFIT ranges, enter:

[B] [Enter]
C10..H10 [Enter]
[C] [Enter]
C13..H13 [Enter]

That's all there is to it. Let's view our masterpiece. Type a V to select the [View] option and your screen should appear as shown in Figure T3-28.

FIGURE T3-28
Display of a Bar Graph of the Spreadsheet.

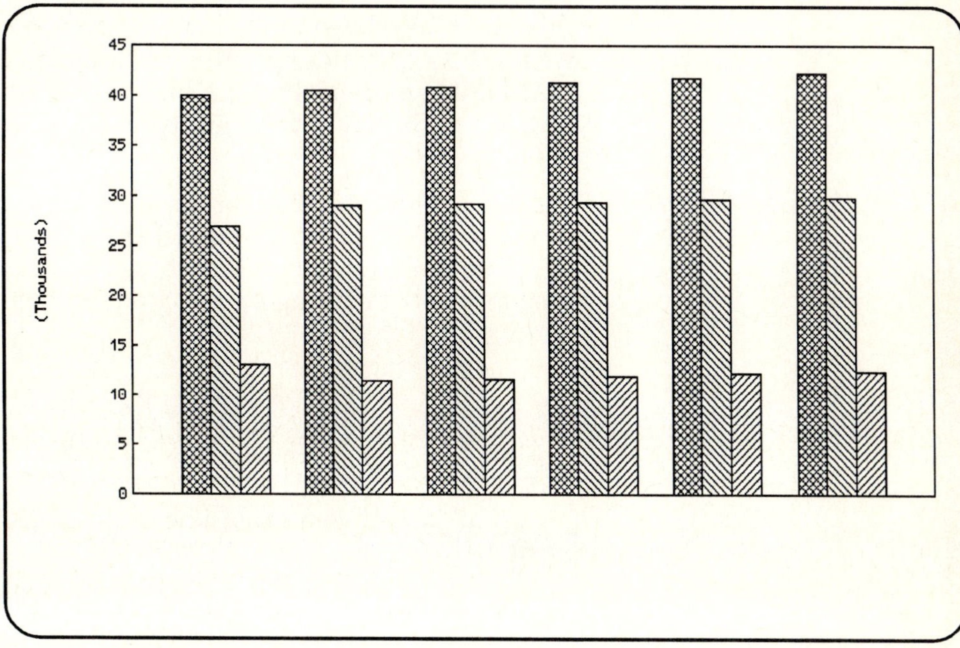

Let's go one step further. Let's put some color into our graph. Of course, inserting color is rather difficult if your computer is not equipped with a color monitor. So, if you don't have a color monitor, read on and let your imagination take over.

Adding Some Color

To get color, we must go back to the previous menu. Do you remember how to return to the previous menu? Correct; simply depress the [Esc] key

You should be viewing the Graph Settings sheet (see Fig. T3-29).

Now enter

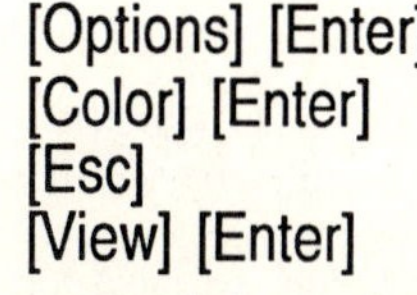

Pressing the [Esc] key brings you to the previous menu.

Earlier releases of Lotus do not support the Graph Settings sheet.

```
D3: 1.011*C3                                                          MENU
Type  X  A  B  C  D  E  F  Reset  View  Save  Options  Name  Group  Quit
View the current graph
                               Graph Settings
 Type: Bar                     Titles: First
                                       Second
 X:                                    X axis
 A: C3..H3                             Y axis
 B: C10..H10
 C: C13..H13                                  Y scale:      X scale:
 D:                                    Scaling Automatic    Automatic
 E:                                    Lower
 F:                                    Upper
                                       Format  (G)           (G)
 Grid: None          Color: No         Indicator Yes         Yes

    Legend:                  Format:   Data labels:         Skip: 1
 A                           Both
 B                           Both
 C                           Both
 D                           Both
 E                           Both
 F                           Both

10-Oct-91   12:55 PM                                       CAPS
```

FIGURE T3-29
The Graph Settings Sheet.

Like magic, you have living color! Your screen should appear as shown in Figure T3-30.

FIGURE T3-30
Display of a Bar Graph of the Spreadsheet in Color.

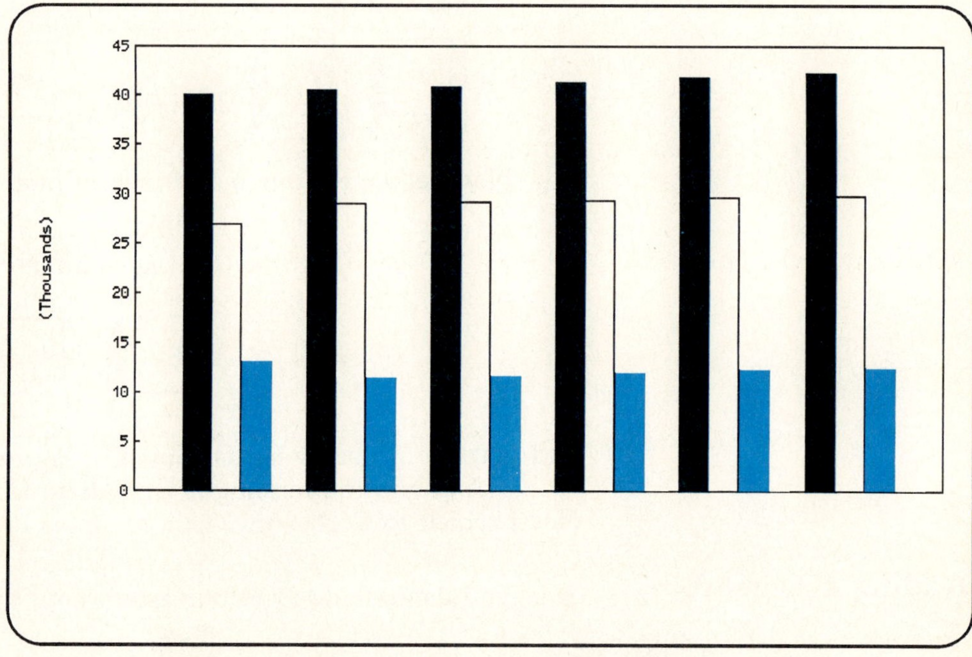

Let's add some titles.

Adding Titles

Let's assume that we wish to title our graph BUDGET FORECAST on the first line and to add the date, MARCH 15, 1991, on the second line. Enter

[Esc]
[Options] [Enter]
[Titles] [Enter]
[First] [Enter]
BUDGET FORECAST [Enter]
[Titles] [Enter]
[Second] [Enter]
OCTOBER 10, 1991 [Enter]

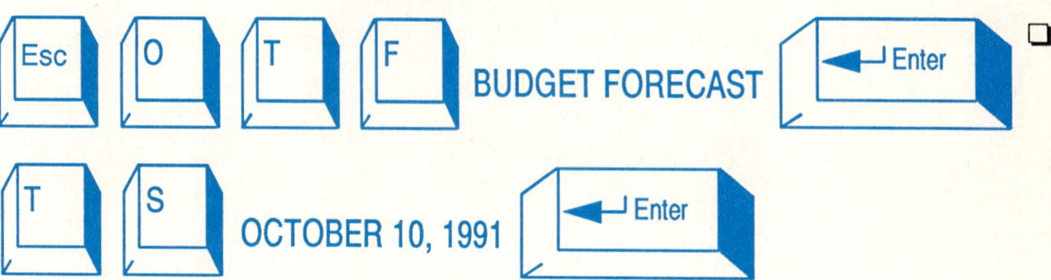

Now let's add titles to the X- and Y-axes. Let's make the X-Axis title FISCAL HALF YEAR and the Y-Axis title DOLLARS. Enter

[Titles] [Enter]
[X-Axis] [Enter]
FISCAL HALF YEAR [Enter]
[Titles] [Enter]
[Y-Axis] [Enter]
DOLLARS [Enter]

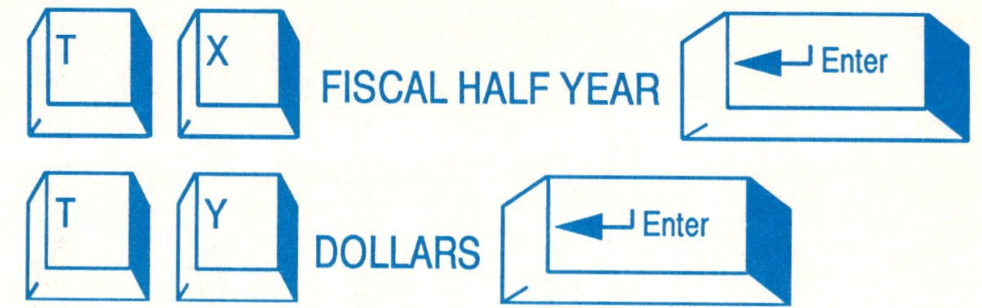

Now let's view our masterpiece. Enter

[Esc]
[View] [Enter]

and you should see what is shown in Figure T3-31.

The only thing missing is legends to tell us which bar corresponds to Sales, which to Cost, and which to Gross Profit.

Adding a Legend

A legend can be added to our graph with the following entries:

[Esc]
[Options] [Enter]
[Legend] [Enter]
[A] [Enter]
Sales [Enter]
[Legend] [Enter]

[B] [Enter]
Cost [Enter]
[Legend] [Enter]
[C] [Enter]
Gross Profit [Enter]
[Esc]
[View] [Enter]

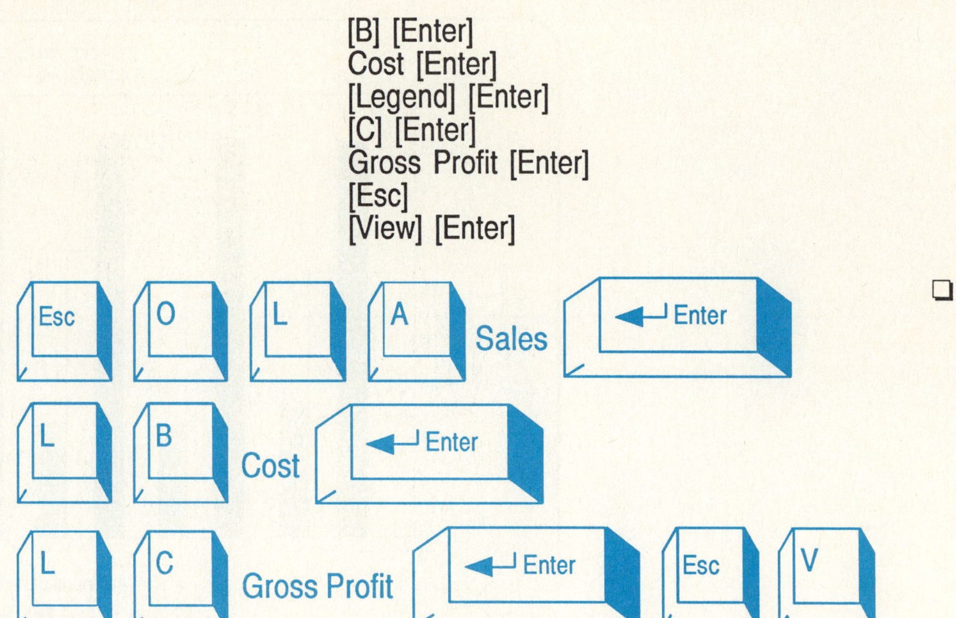

❑

FIGURE T3-31
Display of a Bar Graph of the Spreadsheet in Color with Titles.

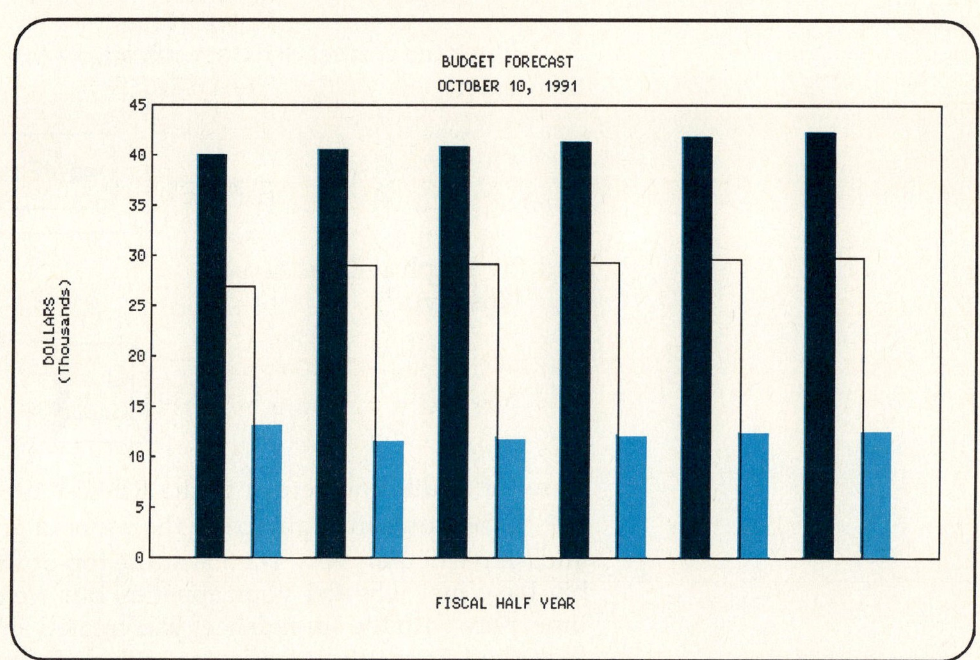

Your graph should look like the one in Figure T3-32. Isn't it beautiful and well worth the time and effort necessary to produce it? Let's save this graph so that you can print it at some future date. Enter

[Esc]
[Save] [Enter]

❑

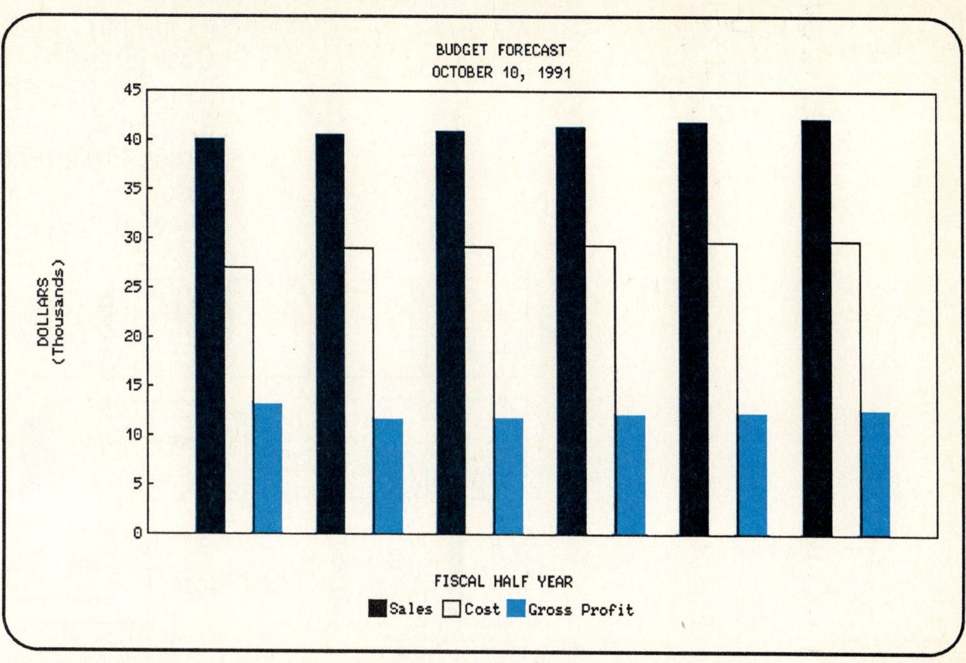

FIGURE T3-32
Display of a Bar Graph of the Spreadsheet in Color with Titles and Legend.

Enter the correct drive specification (A:\, B:\, C:\LOTUS), if necessary, then enter

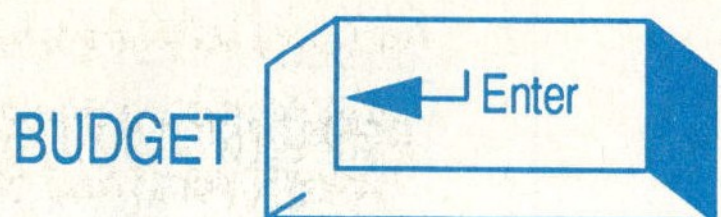

❑

and the graph will be saved.

Now type

❑

to select [Quit] and return to the READY mode and your spreadsheet.

Now you can begin to see the value of an integrated software package and, in particular, why 1-2-3 is at the top of the proverbial heap. We probably have just whetted your appetite, but we must move on. In your spare time, play with the spreadsheet you created and try plotting it in forms other than the bar graph. Experiment with different spreadsheets. Have fun.

Working with the Date

When you first boot up your computer system, you enter the current date and time if this is not provided for automatically by a built-in clock calendar. There are a number of occasions when you might like to access this date, for example, to include on a printed report or to use to determine the number of days since some previous date. This capability is provided to us with 1-2-3's **@NOW** Function.

The @NOW Library Function allows you to enter the current date into a cell. Once it has been entered into a cell, this date can be used in arithmetic computations to determine *future dates* or *the number of days between two dates.*

Let's see how this function works. Begin by pressing [Esc] key until you are in the READY mode. Now enter the commands

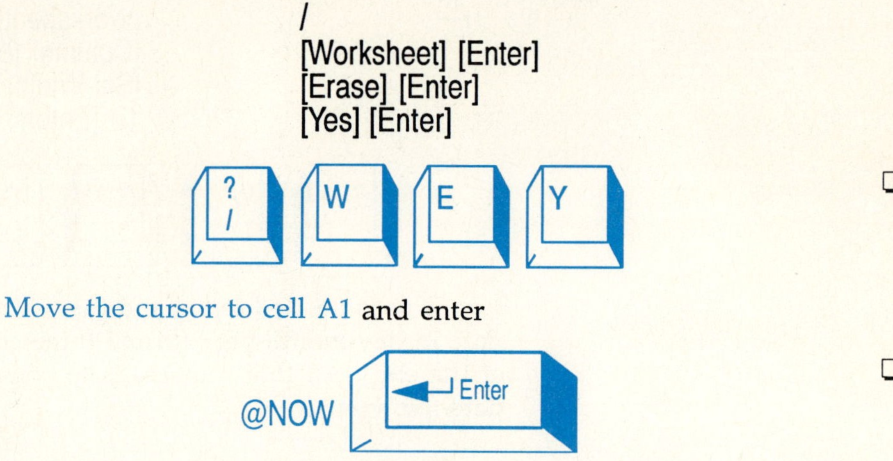

❑

Move the cursor to cell A1 and enter

@NOW [Enter]

❑

and you should see the screen shown in Figure T3-33.

FIGURE T3-33
Screen Produced by Lotus 1-2-3's @NOW Command.

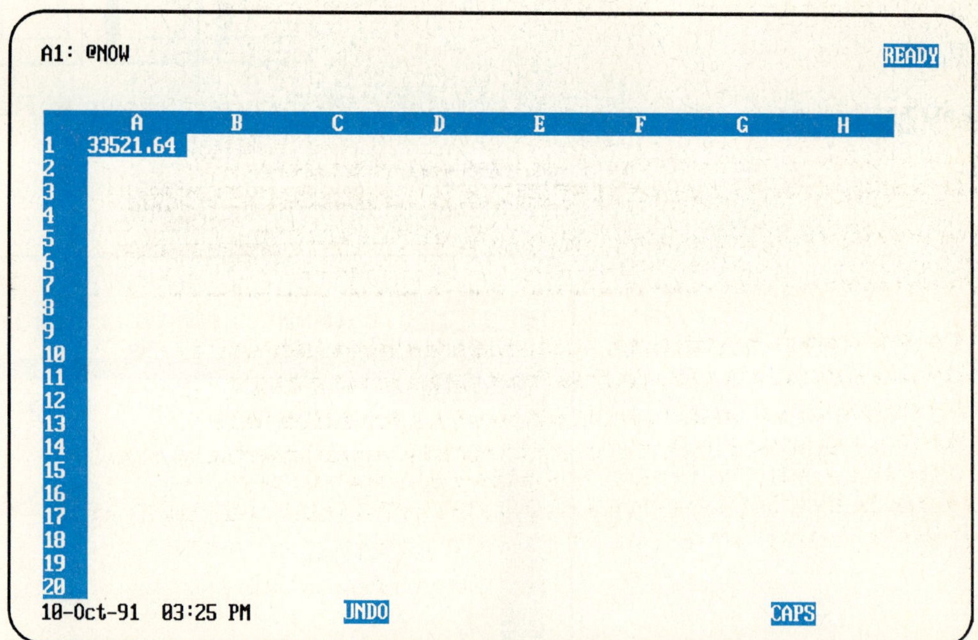

Notice that instead of seeing today's date, you see a number. This number is referred to as a **serial number**, and it contains two pieces of information. The integer, or whole number, portion of the serial number represents the number of days from January 1, 1900, to now. For example, on June 29, 1991, the integer portion of the serial number would be 33418. The decimal, or fractional, portion of the serial number indicates the current time as a fractional part of a day (the day's time).

Clearly, the serial number is not of much value in its current form. However, it is a simple matter to convert the serial number to a readable date by formatting the cell containing the serial number. Let's do that now.

At this point, the cursor should be on cell A1, and this cell should contain the serial number that represents today's date. If this is not the case, repeat the steps shown previously. Now enter

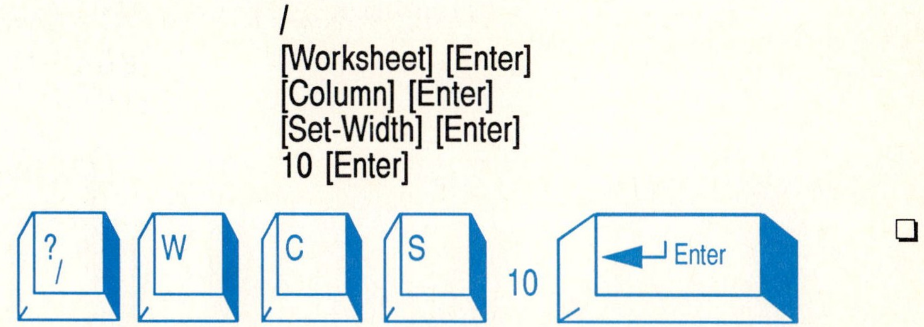

This is needed to expand the width of the cell to provide room for the date in day-month-year format (nine characters for the date and one space at the end). All that remains is to convert the serial number to a readable date. Now enter

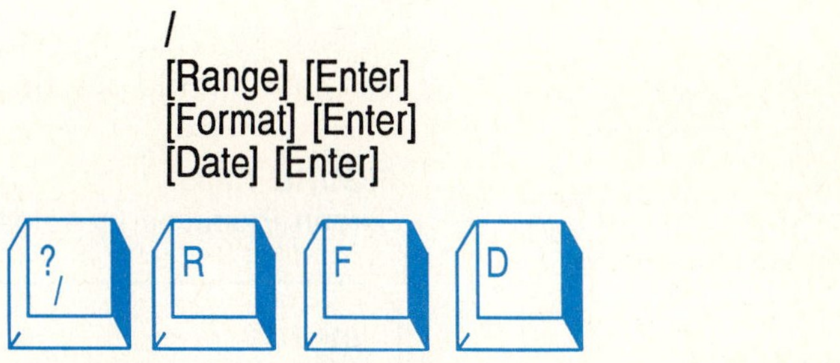

1-2-3 responds with the screen shown in Figure T3-34.

FIGURE T3-34
Screen Showing Date Format Options.

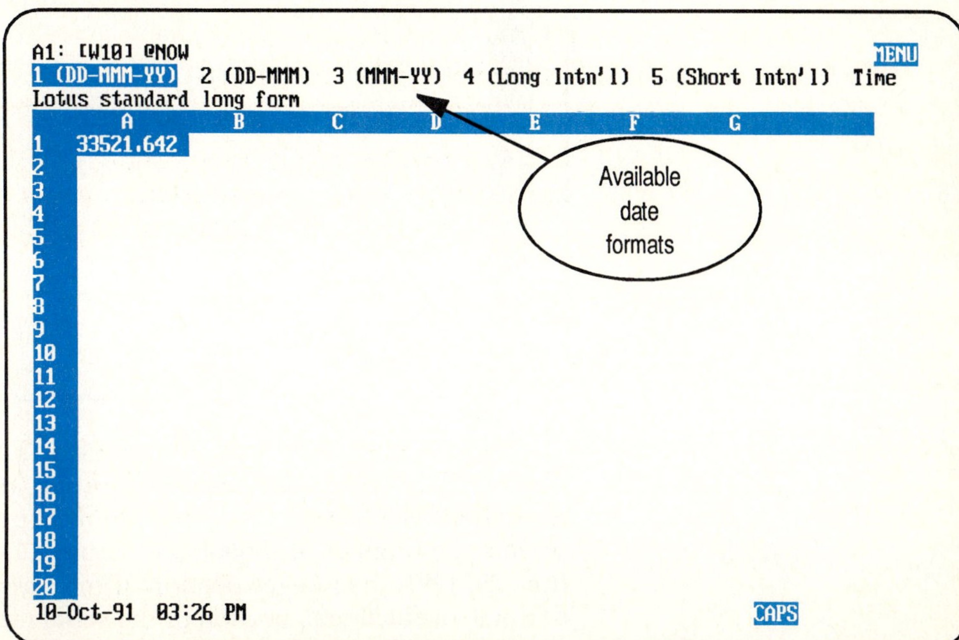

The menu at the top indicates that we have five possible formats in which to display the date: (1) day-month-year (DD-MMM-YY), (2) day-month (DD-MMM), (3) month-year (MMM-YY), (4) Long Intn'l (MM/DD/YY), and (5) Short Intn'l (MM/DD). In the same manner that we previously expanded the width of cell A1 to accommodate the date in Format 1, enter

[1 (DD-MMM-YY)] [Enter]
[Enter]

FIGURE T3-35
Screen Showing Today's Date After Being Converted by the DATE Command.

Unless the actual date is October 10, 1991, your date will be different from the one shown in Figure T3-35.

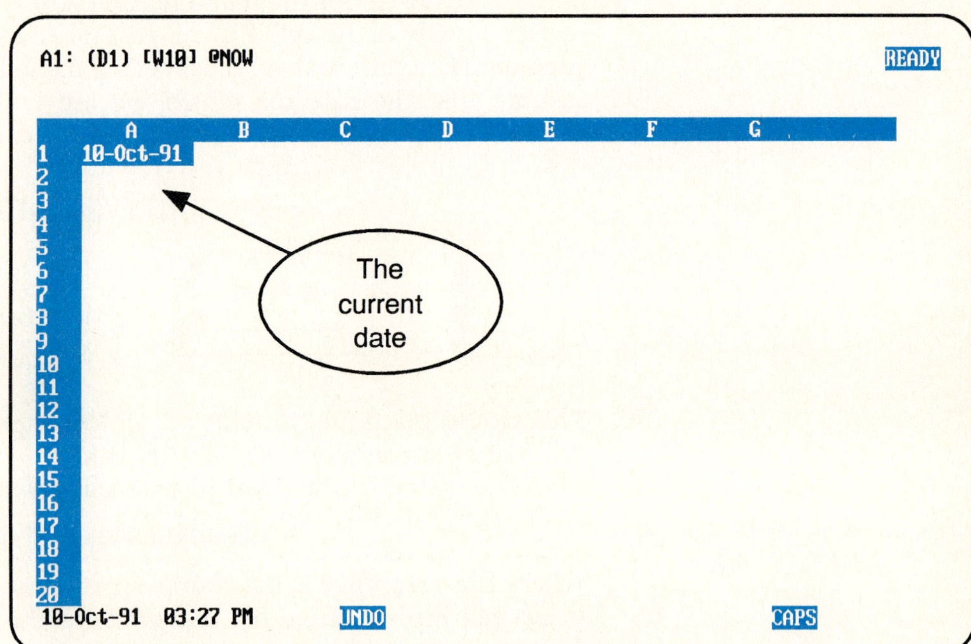

Examination of the screen shown in Figure T3-35 will verify that the serial number has been converted to today's date in a readable form.

Now we need to do some arithmetic. Move to cell C1. There, enter the formula

You now are looking at a serial number that represents the date 60 days hence. Can you remember the commands to convert this number to an actual date in MM/DD/YY format? Enter

/
[Range] [Enter]
[Format] [Enter]
[Date] [Enter]
[4 (Long Intn'l)] [Enter]
[Enter]

and observe that the date displayed is actually the date 60 days from now.

File Linking

1-2-3 offers an efficient method of sharing data between spreadsheet files. You can include a special formula format in your **target** spreadsheet, the spreadsheet that receives the data. Then you can have 1-2-3 find the data you want to include in your target spreadsheet by looking in the **source** spreadsheet file, the file that contains the original data to be shared.

For example, let's assume that we have a spreadsheet saved on a disk in the B: drive under the name ALLISLAN.WK1 and that we are currently working with it. In cell F10 of ALLISLAN.WK1, we are to enter a rate contained in a different spreadsheet file named B:\COUNTY.WK1. Let's also assume that the rate for which we are looking is located in cell F9 of COUNTY.WK1. This could be accomplished by entering

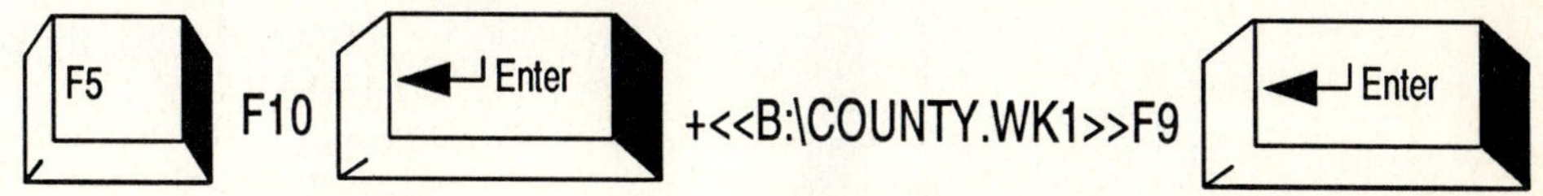

This would place the contents of cell F9 of spreadsheet COUNTY.WK1 into cell F10 of spreadsheet ALLISLAN.WK1.

The general form used to pass data from one file to another is

This feature is not available in earlier releases of 1-2-3.

+<<file-reference>>cell-reference

where **file-reference** is the source spreadsheet file name and **cell-reference** is the cell in the source file that contains the data to be shared.

Sorting

With 1-2-3's sorting facility, you can change the order of the data within a spreadsheet. We can sort a row or column alphabetically, numerically, or chronologically.

In order to demonstrate the sorting facility, we will need a sample spreadsheet. Do you remember how to create a spreadsheet? If you are not sure, review the material at the beginning of this tutorial. Now enter the commands

/
[Worksheet] [Enter]
[Erase] [Enter]
[Yes] [Enter]

to erase our present spreadsheet. Now, create a sample spreadsheet with the following data. Do this now.

	A	B	C	D	E
1			DENT MOTORS		
2	NUMBER		NAME		HOURS
3	1		SMITH		34
4	2		GIOIA		42
5	3		FUORI		28
6	4		JONES		7
7	5		ABBOT		19

If you have entered the data correctly, your screen should appear as the one shown in Figure T3-36. Correct any errors and save your spreadsheet.

FIGURE T3-36
Spreadsheet for Dent Motors before Sorting Operation.

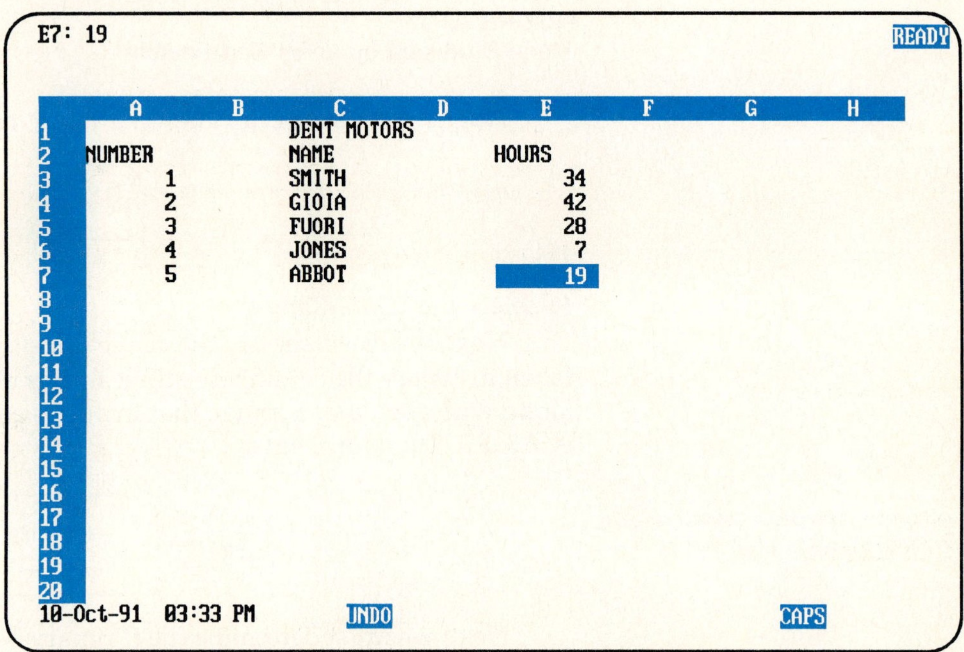

Now let's sort the spreadsheet. Let's assume that we wish to sort it alphabetically. Begin by entering the commands

/
[Data]
[Sort] [Enter]

Your screen should appear as the one shown in Figure T3-37.

Earlier releases of Lotus do not support the Sort Settings sheet.

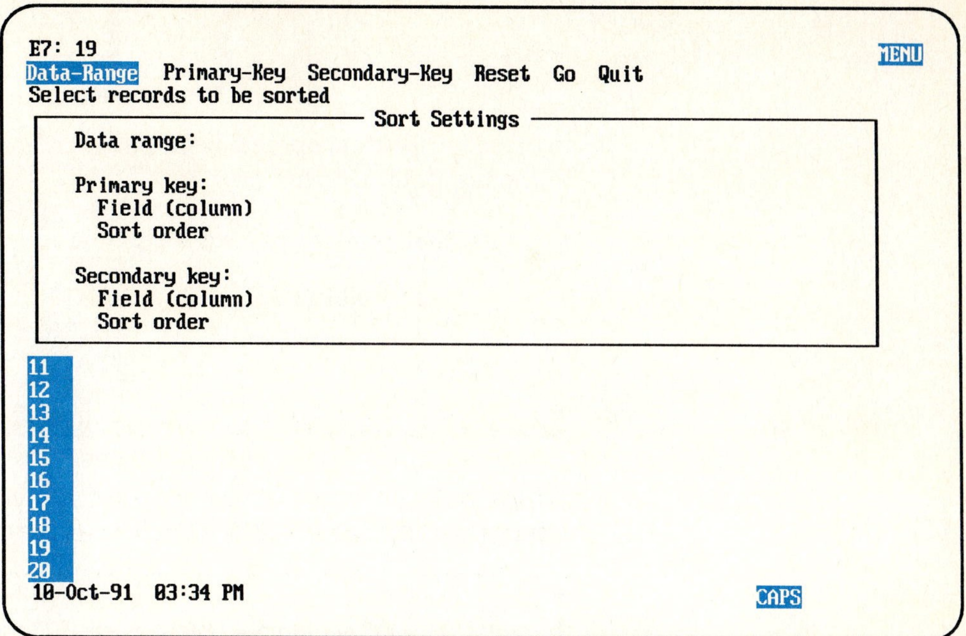

FIGURE T3-37
Menu Produced by Lotus Sort Feature.

Now we must specify the data range of the cells to be sorted. Type

to select the [Data-Range].

Next, we must specify the range of cells we wish to sort. Care must be taken to *exclude* the column headings in this range so that they are not sorted along with the data. A range that includes each row and excludes the titles is A3..E7. Therefore, enter

Next, we must determine the [Primary-Key], the field on which the data will be sorted. Type

Now enter the address of the cell containing the label of the primary key, the cell containing the label NAME. Enter

In response to the prompt

```
Sort order (A or D): D
```

enter

All that remains is to tell the sort to begin. Let's do it. Type

to select [Go]. You should now see the screen shown in Figure T3-38.

FIGURE T3-38
Spreadsheet for Dent Motors After Sorting into NAME Sequence.

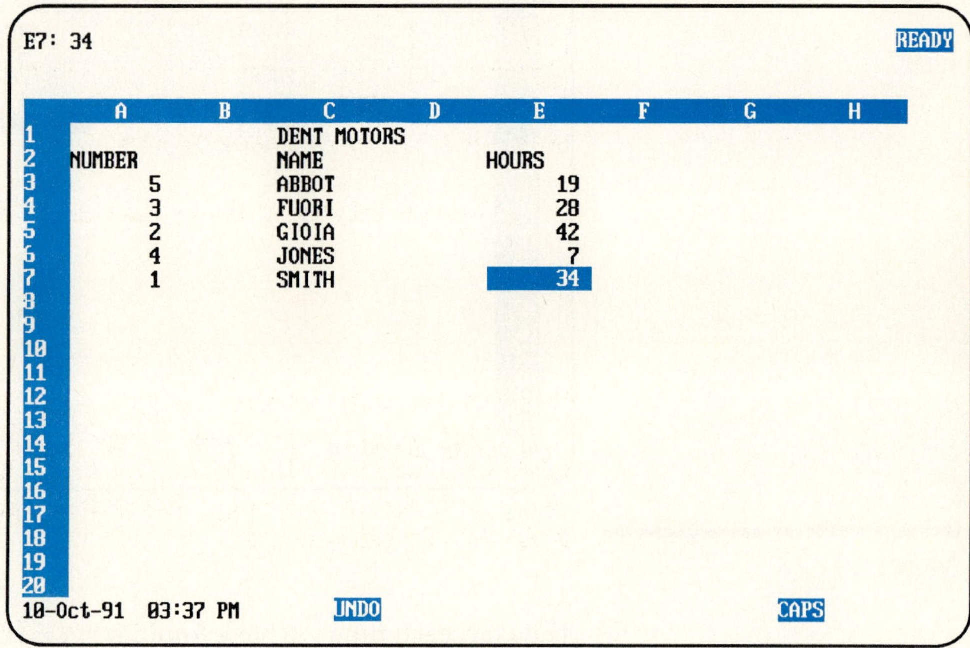

Now let's try sorting the data into descending numeric order by HOURS. Enter the command sequence

/
[Data] [Enter]
[Sort] [Enter]
[Data-Range] [Enter]
A3..E7 [Enter]
[Primary-Key] [Enter]
E2 [Enter]
D [Enter]
[Go] [Enter]

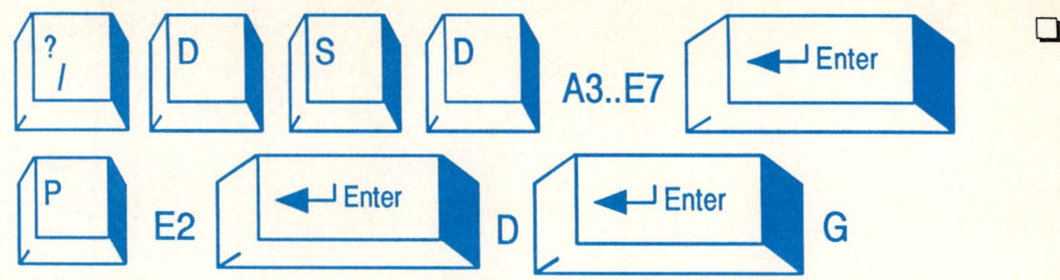

The result is shown in Figure T3-39.

FIGURE T3-39
Spreadsheet for Dent Motors After Sorting into Descending HOURS Sequence.

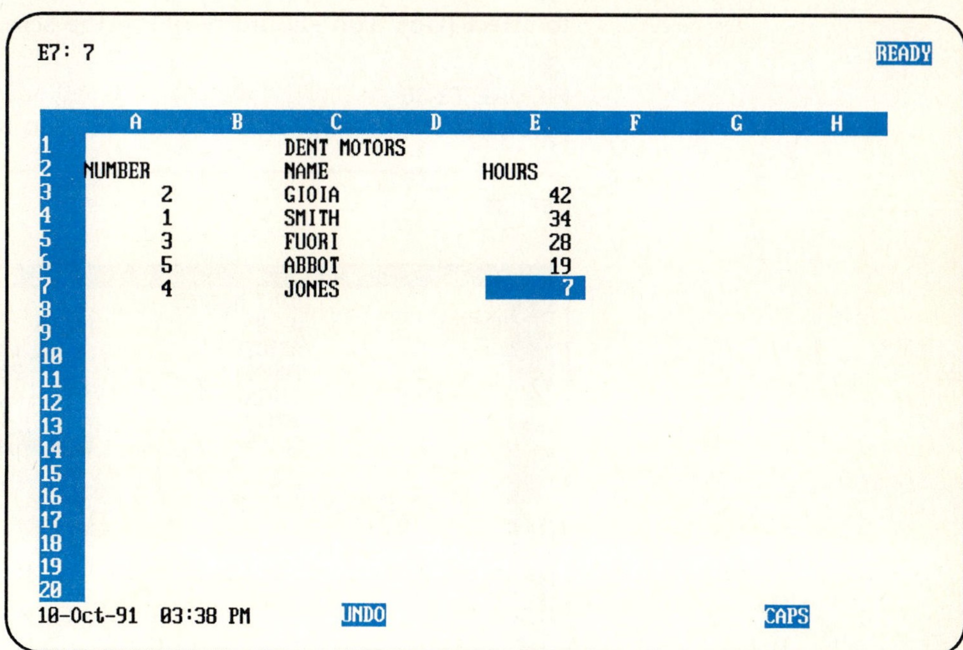

Macros

Thus far, each time we have found it necessary to perform an operation, we keyed in the sequence of commands necessary to accomplish the job. For our purposes this method was both expedient and reasonably efficient. However, were we to find it necessary to key the same **sequence of commands** over and over on a regular basis, this method would be neither expedient nor efficient. Instead, in such situations, we store this *sequence* of commands and then recall them with only a few keystrokes, when and where necessary. This stored sequence of instructions is referred to as a **macro**. We shall now investigate how macros are created and used.

All 1-2-3 functions can be automated using macros. Macros can be used to perform simple tasks from increasing a cell width or erasing the contents of a cell to generating an entire graph.

A macro may be composed of any of the following:

- Function key names
- Keystrokes that select items from command names
- Formulas
- Keystrokes that represent values and labels
- A program command

Let's go through the procedures needed to create and execute some simple macros. First we must erase our spreadsheet. To accomplish this, get into READY mode and type

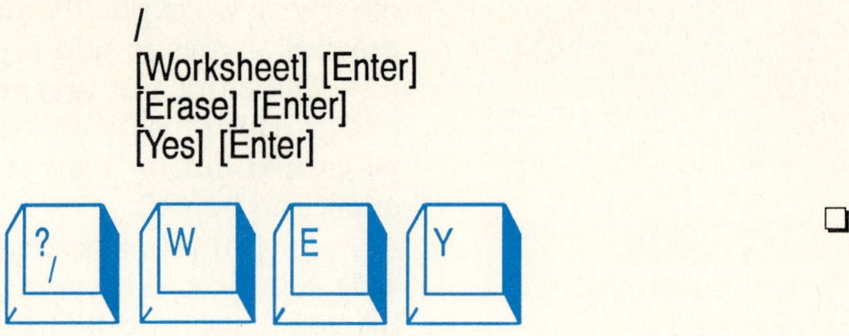

If you are warned that you have not saved your spreadsheet, *respond appropriately.*

Now let's prepare a test spreadsheet. Move the cursor to cell A1 and enter

Then move the cursor to cell B1 and enter

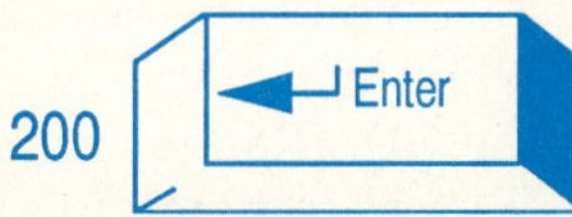

Now continue reading.

Creating a Macro

Let's create a macro to erase the contents of a cell. Three basic steps must be performed when creating any macro:

- Determine the steps that you would carry out if you were to perform the function manually.
- Enter the commands.
- Name the macro.

Step 1: Determine What Has to Be Done. Do you recall how to erase the contents of a single cell? You would move the cursor to the cell to be erased and enter the command sequence

/ [Range] [Erase] [Enter]

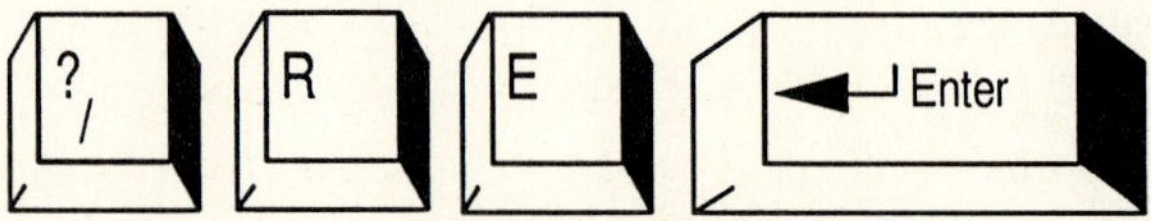

Therefore, our macro must accomplish the same sequence of steps.

Step 2: Enter the Command. Let's enter the commands. But where? We must enter the commands of our macro into our spreadsheet, but somewhere out of view. Common practice is to use the far-right side of the worksheet as a macro writing pad. Therefore, let's go out to cell J1—this is beyond the viewing window of our spreadsheet. Move the cursor to cell J1.

Now to enter our commands. We enter a macro as a string of commands, each represented by a single character. To 1-2-3, a string of characters stored in a cell is a *label.* As with all other labels, it must begin with a label prefix. 1-2-3 will assign a label prefix automatically if the cell entry begins with a letter or with one of a select group of special characters; otherwise we explicitly must enter a prefix. For the time being, it is a good practice always to add a prefix.

Therefore, our first entry in cell J1 will be our label prefix—an apostrophe ('). This must be followed by one letter or symbol for each command to be carried out by the macro. In Step 1 we determined this command sequence to be **/RE**.

An [Enter] is needed to complete the command sequence or macro. This is indicated by using a **tilde** (~). That's all there is to it. Now, input the command in cell J1 by entering

If you see the command menu as you are entering this macro, you forgot to enter the apostrophe (') before the slash (/). In this case, hold down the [Ctrl] key, tap the [Break] key, and then enter the macro again.

Cell J1 of your spreadsheet should contain the entry

/RE~

You have now created a macro to erase the contents of a cell. Note that when this macro is executed, the slash (/) will invoke the command menu, the (R), [Range] command, the E, [Erase] command, and finally the (~), or [Enter] command.

All releases of Lotus support single-letter macro names preceded by the back slash.

Step 3: Name the Macro. All macros must be assigned a two-character name, a back slash (\) followed by a letter of the alphabet. Examples of valid macro names include \A, \K, and \Z. In addition, Lotus Release 2.2 and 3.0 support macro names of 15 characters or less. No back slash (\) can be used in this case.

Let's name our macro \E because the process it carries out is to Erase. We will assign a more meaningful name to the next macro we create. To assign this name to our macro, we position the cursor on the cell containing the macro and enter the command sequence shown next. Position the cursor on cell J1. Now enter

Macros that extend beyond the width of a cell are continued in the next cell below it. This is necessary because a multiple-line macro will execute down. That is, when executed, the first cell containing the macro will execute, then the cell under that, and so on until a blank cell is encountered. A blank cell stops the macro from executing. As a result, it is necessary to name only the first cell in a macro. Always make certain that a blank cell separates two macros located in the same column, otherwise they will both be executed if you execute the one that appears first.

/
[Range] [Enter]
[Name] [Enter]
[Create] [Enter]
\E [Enter]
[Enter]

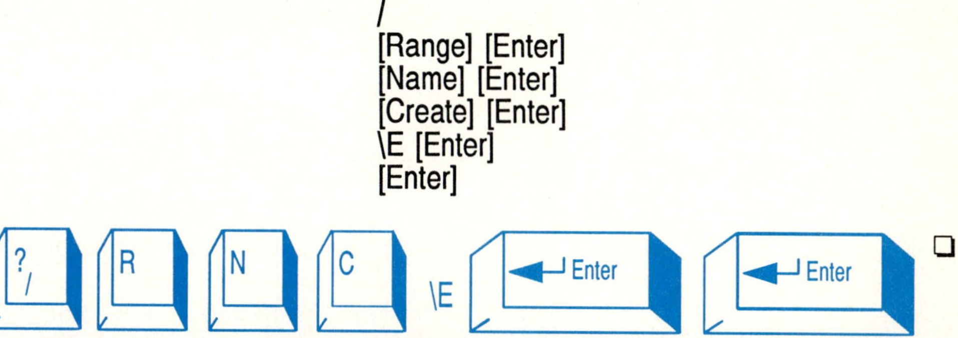

So that we don't forget the name we assigned to our macro, it is a good practice to place the name of the macro in a cell to the left of the cell containing the macro. Let's do this now. Move the cursor to cell I1, the cell to the left of J1. Enter

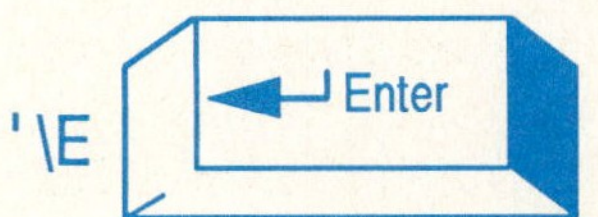

Your spreadsheet should now contain entries in four cells as shown below:

Cell	Entry
A1	100
B1	200
I1	\E
J1	'/RE~

Executing a Macro

Now that we've created and named our macro, let's execute it. The manner in which you execute a macro depends on what you named it. To execute a macro named with the back slash followed by a letter of the alphabet, you simply hold down the [Alt] key and momentarily press the letter key corresponding to the macro name, E in our case. If you choose to assign a more meaningful name to your macro, you will have to use the **Run** key to execute the macro. The keystroke sequence **[Alt]-[F3]** is the Run key. But before executing our macro, we must decide what cell we want to erase.

Let's erase the "100" in cell A1. Move to cell A1. Press and hold the [Alt] key, then type E

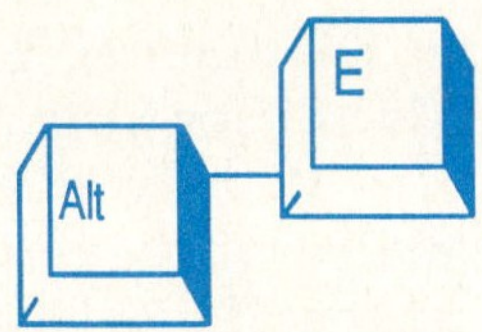

Presto, the "100" is gone. Notice that only two keystrokes were needed to execute our macro. This is true for any macro you write. Now, erase the contents of cell B1.

The steps you should have carried out are (1) moving the cursor to cell B1 and (2) holding down the [Alt] key while typing E.

Several Useful Macros

Can you guess what the macro below does?

/FS~R

If you guessed that it will save the current spreadsheet, replacing any previous version, you would be correct. Just for practice, let's enter, name, and execute this macro.

Enter It. Move the cursor to cell J3. Enter

Users of earlier releases of Lotus should name the macro \S. Thus you must replace the preceding name SAVE with \S and the following name SAVE with '\S.

Name It. Let's assign this saved macro the name SAVE. Can you recall how to do this? Move the cursor to cell J3. Enter

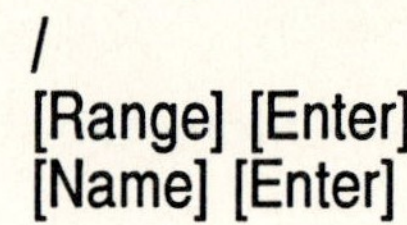

Finally, enter the macro name in cell I3 so you won't forget the macro name. Go to cell I3 and enter:

Execute It. If you named your macro \S, to execute it, you only need hold down the [Alt] key and type the S key. If you named your macro SAVE, you press and hold the [Alt] key and then press the [F3] Function key. This keystroke sequence is called Run. When inputted, Run supplies a list of previously created spreadsheet range names. Placing the cursor on SAVE and pressing the [Enter] key will cause the macro to execute.

However, this will serve no useful purpose now because the macro is intended to replace an old version of a file with a new one, and we have no file to replace.

Save this spreadsheet and name it MACS, using the procedures described in the section "Saving a Spreadsheet on Diskette" discussed earlier in this tutorial. Then execute the SAVE (or \S) macro; see "Executing a Macro" for instructions.

When you are working on your own spreadsheets in the future, this macro will be convenient to save a spreadsheet in stages, as you develop it, so that if you have a momentary power loss or some other unforseen happening occurs, the loss to your spreadsheet will be minimal.

An Interactive Macro

Let's create a macro to format a cell to Currency format with two decimal places. Move the cursor to cell A1 and enter

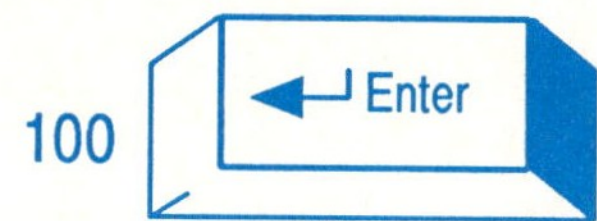

Then move the cursor to cell A2 and enter

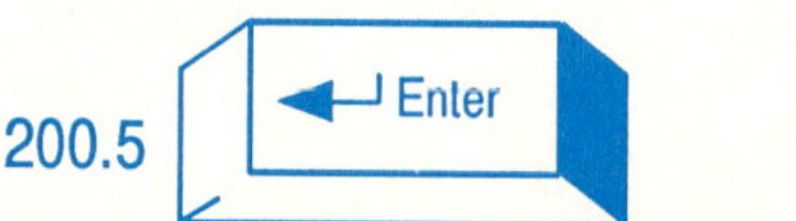

This command requires that we point to the range of cells we want to format. Thus, the macro must stop to allow us the opportunity to point, otherwise we would only be able to format one cell at a time, or the same range. The symbol {?} is used to halt a macro and simultaneously allow us to point, or enter, a response. Accordingly, the correct macro is

/RFC2~{?}~

Move the cursor to cell J5 and enter

Use the /[Range][Name][Create] command sequence to name the macro \C. Type

Be sure to place '\C in cell I5 for documentation purposes.

Finally, execute the macro by pressing and holding the [Alt] key followed by typing C.

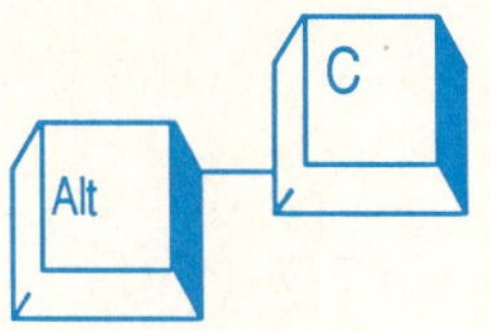

Type the range A1..A2.

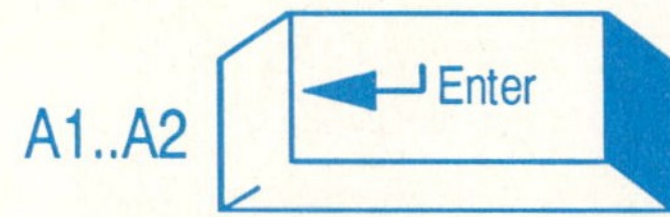

Check your results.

A Macro To Enter Labels

The final macro is designed to enter labels across a page. We would like it to enter the days of the week in adjacent cells. To accomplish this, our macro would have to activate the cursor-movement keys. Move the cursor to cell J7. Enter

Each cursor-movement key has a name. If the name is included in braces and placed in a macro, the cursor will move in the direction specified. The {END}{LEFT} sequence is equivalent to pressing the [End] key followed by the Left Arrow key.

Name the macro \D (remember that you have to name only cell J7), and enter '\D in cell I7. Place your cursor on cell A4 and execute the macro.

You now have the days of the week across the page. As an added bonus, the cursor is in position to enter the data for MONDAY.

This concludes Part II of this tutorial. You can now save your work and exit 1-2-3 or simply exit 1-2-3. If you decide to save your work, execute the SAVE macro.

Now let's exit 1-2-3. Get into the READY mode, enter /[Quit], follow the prompts until you reach the ACCESS menu, then enter [EXIT] to return to DOS.

Lotus 1-2-3 Command Summary

Arithmetic and Logical Operators

Symbol	Function	Order of Preference
( )	Parentheses	8
^	Exponentiation	7
+	Positive	6
—	Negative	6
*	Multiplication	5
÷	Division	5
+	Addition	4
-	Subtraction	4
<	Less than	3
>	Greater than	3
=	Equal to	3
< =	Less than or equal to	3
> =	Greater than or equal to	3
< >	Not equal to	3
#NOT#	Logical NOT	2
#AND#	Logical AND	1
#OR#	Logical OR	1

Label Prefixes

'	Aligns titles on the left side of the cell
^	Centers titles within the cell
"	Aligns titles on the right side of the cell
\	Repeats a single character or a set of characters for the length of the cell

Cursor Control

↑	One cell up
↓	One cell down
→	One cell to the right
←	One cell to the left
Home	To the upper left corner
Pg Dn	One screen down
Pg Up	One screen up
Tab	One screen right
Shift-Tab	One screen left
[F5]	Goto a particular cell

Lotus 1-2-3 Spreadsheet Commands

/Copy Command

Copies a range of cells to a second range of cells.

/File Commands

Admin	Controls worksheet file reservation, creates table of file information
Combine	Adds all or part of a worksheet file to current worksheet
Directory	Changes current directory
Erase	Erases a worksheet file from the data disk
Import	Incorporates a print file into current worksheet
List	Lists all worksheet files and reports disk space
Retrieve	Retrieves a worksheet from the current directory
Save	Saves a worksheet onto the data disk
Xtract	Stores a range of entries from current worksheet

/Graph Commands

Type	Selects Graph type (Line, Bar, Stacked-Bar, XY, or Pie Chart)
X	Sets range for x-axis titles
A B C D E F	Sets ranges for data
Reset	Cancels selected graph settings
View	Views current graph
Save	Saves current graph for printing by PrintGraph disk
Name	Names and saves graph settings with worksheet for viewing
Create	Saves a new graph for viewing
Use	Recalls graph settings
Delete	Deletes a named graph
Reset	Deletes all named graphs
Table	Creates a table of named graphs
Options	Graph formatting
Legend	Sets up a key for the data ranges
Format	Selects Lines, Symbols, Both, or Neither for displaying XY and line graphs
Titles	Sets up main title (First), subtitle (Second), and axis titles (x-axis, y-axis)
Grid	Sets up horizontal or vertical lines
Scale	Formats numeric axis scales (y-axis, x-axis) or x-axis title range (Skip)
Color vs. B&W	Sets for color or black-and-white monitor
Data Labels	Dispays numeric values at data points
Group	Allows you to specify several settings at once

Function Keys

[F1]	Help. Provides on-line help
Alt-[F1]	Compose. Creates characters that cannot be enter directly from the keyboard
[F2]	Edit. Used to edit a cell
Alt-[F2]	Step. Activates step mode, which executes a macro step by step
[F3]	Name. Displays a list of range names in Point mode
Alt-[F3]	Run. Displays a list of range names from which to select a name of a macro to run
[F4]	Absolute. Changes relative cell references to absolute
Alt-[F4]	Undo. Cancels changes made to a worksheet since Lotus was last in Ready mode
[F5]	Goto. Moves cell pointer to any cell
Alt-[F5]	Learn. Activates the learn feature
[F6]	Window. Moves the cell pointer between two windows
[F7]	Query. Repeats the last data query operation
[F8]	Table. Repeats the last data table operation
Alt-[F8]	Activates an add-in program if one has been assigned to the key
[F9]	Calc. Recalculates all formulas in a worksheet
[F10]	Graph. Displays the current graph
Alt-[F10]	Displays add-in menu or activates add-in program assigned to the key

/Worksheet Commands

Column	Changes column width of current column
Delete	Deletes rows or columns
Erase	Clears the entire worksheet
Global	Worksheet default settings
Column-width	Set-default column width (1..72)
Default	Default configuration for printer and disk drive
Format	Format for values; see numeric formatting
Label-Prefix	Changes default format for subsequent titles; see title formatting with label-prefixes
Protection	Enables/Disables Range protect
Recalculation	Sets formula recalculation process (Natural, Columnwise, Rowwise, Automatic, Manual. Iteration)
Zero	Changes the way cells with a 0 value appear
Insert	Inserts rows or columns
Status	Displays current default settings and memory available for worksheet usage
Titles	Sets up titles on part of the worksheet (Horizontal, Vertical, Both, Clear)
Window	Splits/unsplits windows (Horizontal, Vertical, Synchronized, Unsychronized, Clear)
Page	Sets a page break in a worksheet
Learn	Stores macros in a special macro library

/System Command

Leave 1-2-3 temporarily and use the operating system

/Move Command

Moves a range of cells to a new range of cells.

/Print Commands

(Printer must be on line when executing Line, Page, Align, and Go)

Printer vs. File	Print worksheet or saves output in print file
Range	Area of worksheet to be printed
Line	Advances printer one line
Page	Advances printer one page
Align	Sets top of printer page
Go	Starts printing selected range
Clear	Cancels all printer settings
Options	Formats printout
Header, Footer	Adds Utilities
Margins	Sets printer margins (Left, Right, Top, Bottom)
Page Length	Sets page length
Borders	Grafts additional rows and columns to range to be printed
Setup	Sends control codes to printer (compressed print mode)

/Quit Command

Exits from 1-2-3 spreadsheet program

/Range Commands

Format	Formats a range of values; see numeric formatting
Label-Prefix	Formats a range of labels; see title formatting with label-prefixes
Erase	Deletes a range of cells
Name	Assigns a name to a range of cells
Justify	Disables continuous format and justifies text within column of cells in range
Protect	Disallows changes in cells in range
Unprotect	Allows changes in cells in range
Input	Restricts cell cursor to unprotected cells
Value	Converts formulas to their values
Trans	Transpose columns and rows on worksheet
Search	Find and replace

/Add-In Command

Attach	Brings an add-in program into memory
Detach	Erases an add-in program from memory

/Add-In Commands

Invoke	Activates one of the attached add-ins
Clear	Erases all add-ins from memory

/Data Command

Fill	Fills a range with a sequence of values
Table	Creates statistical tables
Sort	Rearranges data in alphabetical or numerical order
Query	Finds and lists data
Distribution	Counts the number of times an item occurs within a range
Matrix	Performs matrix multiplication
Regression	Creates statistical data based on variables
Parse	Converts a column of long labels into smaller ones

Functions

Date Functions

@DATE(yr,mth,day)	Number of specified day (1..73049)
@DAY(date-month)	Day of specified day (1..31)
@MONTH(date-number)	Month of specified day (1..12)
@YEAR(date-number)	Year of specified day (0..199)
@TODAY	Today's number

Financial Functions

@IRR (guess, range)	Calculates iteratively internal rate of return of a series of regular payments (range) Guess should approximate IRR
@NPV(int, range)	Net present value of a RANGE of regular payments at an interest rate of INT
@FV(pmt, int, term)	Future value of an annuity
@PV(pmt,int,term)	Present value of an ordinary annuity
@PMT(prn,int,term)	Mortgage payment for a given principal (prn) at an interest rate (int) for a number of terms (term)

Logical Functions

@FALSE	0 (false)
@TRUE	1 (true)
@IF(cond,x,y)	Returns the value x if cond is true else returns the value y

Mathematical Functions

@ABS(x)	Absolute value of x
@ACOS(x)	Arc cosine of x
@ASIN(x)	Arc sine of x
@ATAN(x)	Arc tangent of x (2 quadrants)
@ATAN2(x)	Arc tangent of x (4 quadrants)
@COS(x)	Cosine of x
@EXP(x)	e (2.178...) raised to the x
@INT(x)	Integer part of x
@LN(x)	Log base e of x (e = 2.718...)
@LOG(x)	Log base 10 of x
@MOD(x,y)	x mod y
@PI	Pi = 3.14159...
@RAND	Returns a random number between 0 and 1
@ROUND(x,n)	Round x to n decimal places
@SIN(x)	Sine of x
@SQRT(x)	Square root of x
@TAN(x)	Tangent of x

Statistical Functions

@COUNT(list)	Number of values in list
@SUM(list)	Sum of all values in list
@AVG(list)	Average of all values in list
@MIN(list)	Minimum value in list
@MAX(list)	Maximum value in list
@STD(list)	Standard deviation of list
@VAR(list)	Variance of list

Exercises

1. What Lotus command or commands or formula or formulas would you use to accomplish each of the following?
   a. Display a number with a dollar sign, comma, and decimal point.
   b. Save a spreadsheet file.
   c. Display the date as a serial number.
   d. Erase the entire spreadsheet.
   e. Sum the values in the range D6..D18.
   f. Subtract the value in cell A5 from cell A9.
   g. Find the date 165 days from today.
   h. Copy a label from cell A1 to cell A5.
   i. Increase the width of a column to 14.
   j. Name a range of cells.

2. Answer true or false to each of the following questions.

   ______ a. A worksheet is created in a spreadsheet.

   ______ b. The label prefix ^ is the default label prefix.

   ______ c. COPY is an example of a lotus command.

______ d. Lotus columns are numbered from 1 to 256.

______ e. To print a spreadsheet, you must first specify a Range of cells to print.

______ f. The address *123 Main Street* when entered into a cell will cause an error.

______ g. The formula +A5–D6 will produce the value 100 if cell A5 contains 200 and cell D6 contains 100.

______ h. The [F5] key is called the GoTo key.

______ i. If the label '10/10/91 appears in cell A1, the formula +A1+60 will produce the serial number of the date 60 days from the date in cell A1.

______ j. A value may have an imbedded space.

3. Describe what each of the following command or commands or formula or formulas do.
   a. /WCS14[Enter]
   b. /RFC2[Enter][Enter]
   c. @SUM(D7..D19)
   d. +C7*F9
   e. +B7/15
   f. /FS[Enter]R
   g. @NOW–95
   h. /QYE
   i. /GTB
   j. /PPR
4. Carry out each of the following short exercises. Be sure you have your Work disk in a disk drive before you start.
   a. Erase the contents of your spreadsheet. Enter your name in cell A1, then save the spreadsheet. Retrieve the spreadsheet.
   b. Enter the first three letters of your first name in four different cells using four different label prefixes.
   c. Enter ten numbers in ten different cells that are not all connected. Enter a formula that will add the ten values you just entered.
   d. Find the date 100 days from today.
   e. Enter the values from 1 to 10 down Column B. Copy these values to Column C.
   f. Enter your full name in any cell. Center it in the cell without typing it again.
   g. Create a bar graph using the numbers 10, 36, -10, and 19 as your A range.
   h. Enter five names in any column. Label the column NAME. Sort in ascending order by NAME.
   i. Create and execute a macro to enter the month names across a row.
   j. Create and execute a macro to format a date serial number to DATE 4 (Long International). You will have to enter a date first to test this.

Hands-On Activities

1. Using our sample spreadsheet BUDGET FORECAST, perform the following operations:
   a. Replace the formula 1.011*C3 in cell D3 with .95*C3, and note the difference in the spreadsheet results.
   b. Using the proper global format commands, change the width of each column to 20.
   c. Obtain a printout of your spreadsheet starting at cell B2 instead of cell A1.
   d. Convert all numbers from dollars and cents to simply dollars.
   e. Instead of writing the word PROFIT beneath the word GROSS, write the words next to each other (GROSS PROFIT) in Row 13.
2. Create a spreadsheet that will compute gross pay for five employees. The gross pay is calculated as the base salary plus the commission amount. The commission

amount is computed as 10 percent of the sales amount. Use the following data. Be sure to format your spreadsheet appropriately. When you are finished, print a copy.

All Island Computers

Name	Base Salary	Sales Amount	Comm. Amount	Gross Pay
SMITH	546	900		
MILLS	680	700		
GIOIA	485	680		
KUSAK	300	2000		
FUORI	700	1300		

3. You are the manager of a small tool-rental store. Your boss has requested that you take the last two years of profit information for each tool and determine the difference between the two years in dollars. Your boss wants the information in the following format (set the worksheet column width to 13):

Tool	Last Year	This Year	Difference	% Change
Lawn mower	480	650		
Tree splitter	270	530		
50-foot ladder	140	140		
Whacker	360	800		
Thatcher	420	135		
TOTALS				

a. Enter the appropriate formulas to calculate the Difference and % Change column entries.
b. Place a total at the bottom of any column containing numeric information.
c. Change the entries to a dollars-and-cents format.
d. What if this year's profits equal 1.25 times last year's profits?

4. Create a spreadsheet with the following data.

Ramco Oil Filters
Inventory Report
4/10/92

Item	Quantity on Hand	Quantity on Order	Unit Cost
PF 49	36	0	2.20
PF 90	21	0	3.75
PF 42	47	0	1.18
PG 13	8	1	1.96
PC 18	9	3	2.53
PD 96	13	9	5.18
PG 24	14	3	1.39
PX 26	26	4	2.25

a. Create a new column called Inventory Value. These values are calculated by multiplying the quantity on hand by the unit cost.
b. Calculate the total inventory value, and place it in an appropriate cell.
c. Create a new column called Selling Price. The selling price is calculated by multiplying the unit cost by a markup rate of 1.25.
d. Use appropriate formatting to display your data.
e. Print the results.
f. Sort the data using ITEM as the key field.

g. Calculate the selling price if the markup rate is 1.33 for items whose unit cost exceeds $2.20, otherwise it remains at 1.25.

5. Scenario: You have been employed as a traveling salesperson since October of last year. This morning your boss called and asked you to drop off your expense log for the first quarter of last year. This log is supposed to reflect your detailed and total expenses, by category, for that period. In addition, you must decide whether you prefer to be reimbursed for your actual auto expenses plus depreciation or be reimbursed at the standard rate of 20.5¢ per mile. You also want to know how many miles per gallon you averaged during this period. Assuming that your records are as follows and that you would be entitled to a yearly depreciation of $1200, prepare a spreadsheet that will satisfy your boss, determine the reimbursement you will receive under each method, and indicate your average miles per gallon during this period. Assume that gas costs $1.30 per gallon.

Expenses

Date	Miles	Gallons	Other Auto Expenses	Meals	Lodging	Tolls
1/5-1/10	1423	75	15.75	118.45	245.50	4.25
2/1-2/15	4752	265	4.75	302.08	895.20	15.45
2/20-2/25	1612	81	0.00	145.12	270.45	2.50
2/28-3/2	709	39	12.75	54.75	62.50	10.10
3/4-3/15	3010	163	45.75	212.00	695.00	23.25

6. Concerning the spreadsheet developed in Activity 5, determine the net change in your expenses had you decreased your average speed by 8 miles per hour. From past experience you know that this will result in a 9 percent increase in your miles-per-gallon rating. And, since the time to complete each trip will increase, you must allow for a 1 percent increase in your total food and lodging costs.

7. Create a spreadsheet that will contain two columns of data. The first column should have a width of 20 and should have the label NAME placed at the top. The second column should be adjacent to the first and have a width of 13. It should have the label PHONE NUMBER placed at the top. Enter the names and phone numbers of friends, family members, and business associates. Sort the data alphabetically by name. Then print your new phone book.

8. Create a spreadsheet that contains macros to carry out the procedures we describe next. Be sure to test to see that they work.
   a. Save and replace.
   b. Change the column width to any acceptable value.
   c. Enter and display the date.
   d. Create any range name.
   e. Print all macros.

Appendix: Lotus Release 3.0

Lotus 1-2-3 Release 3.0 is the advanced worksheet for *organizing, analyzing,* and *presenting* data. It is specifically designed to run on computers equipped with the **INTEL 80286, 80386,** or **80486** microprocessor. It features the most powerful spreadsheet available today and supports true three-dimensional (3-D) spreadsheets. This new technology makes it easier than ever to create and manage complex data. With a 3-D spreadsheet, you can work with up to 256 spreadsheets in a single file each having 256 columns and 8192 rows. Lotus Release 2.2 does not support 3-D spreadsheets.

In addition to 3-D spreadsheets, Lotus Release 3.0 supports an expanded memory of up to 32 megabytes. This allows you to create very large spreadsheet files, much larger than with other Lotus releases.

We suspect that due to the strict hardware requirements of this release, very few of our readers will be using Release 3.0. These hardware requirements include the following:

1. A microcomputer equipped with an 80268, 80386, or 80486 microprocessor
2. DOS 3.X or OS/2 (Note that there are two different versions of Release 3.0, a DOS version and an OS/2 version.)
3. A hard disk
4. A minimum of 1 megabyte of extended memory for users of DOS (3 recommended), or a minimum of 3 megabytes for OS/2 users (4 or more recommended)

As you can see, we have described a rather extensive microcomputer system, and we have not mentioned a monitor, printer, or hard-disk size.

If you will be using Release 3.0 to do this tutorial, differences in Release 3.0 will present no problems for you. The instructions we have provided do not change because of Release 3.0. However, there are a few differences that will appear in your screen displays but not in the illustrations that you see in this tutorial.

First of all, 1-2-3 Release 3.0 displays a worksheet label (A) in the first row of the control panel and above Row 1 (see Fig. T3-40).

FIGURE T3-40
Release 3.0 3-D Spreadsheet.

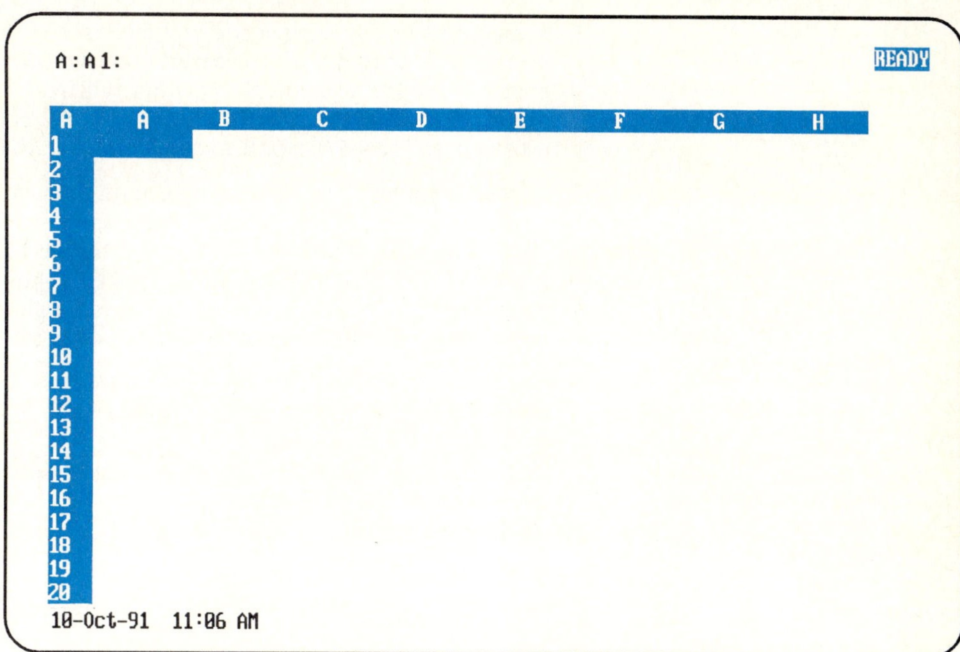

When you start 1-2-3 Release 3.0 you will have one **sheet** on which to work. Sheet is the abbreviation for worksheet. It will be Sheet **A**. If you look at Figure T3-40, you can see

A:A1:

in the first Row of the control panel, and you can also see "A" displayed above Row 1. Both are called worksheet labels and indicate that you are working with Sheet A. If you add a second sheet, it will be Sheet B, a third sheet would be C, and so on. You can move, copy, and erase a sheet or move through sheets. None of the 3-D features are utilized in this tutorial.

A second difference that you will experience relates to the commands you will see displayed when you select the commands presented in this tutorial. 1-2-3 Release 3.0 contains several commands and options that do not exist in Release 2.2. Thus, you may see a command or option appear at the end of a menu that does not appear in the corresponding figure we provide for comparison purposes. For example, consider the Access menu. 1-2-3 Release 3.0 does not have the *PrintGraph* option as Release 2.2 does because you can print a graph directly through the 1-2-3 option of the Access menu using Release 3.0. Several other differences in menus do exist.

Remember that the commands and subcommands we choose to present in this tutorial are fundamental to the creation and manipulation of spreadsheets. As such, they are included with *both* releases.

A third difference occurs with the UNDO option. Release 3.0 does not display UNDO on your display screen. To use UNDO, you must first enable it. The command sequence to do this is /WGDOUEQ. This command sequence should be entered from the READY mode.

Finally, when you save a file or retrieve a previously created file, the file name will be displayed where the date and time are usually displayed.

After reading this, return to the beginning of Part I and continue reading.

4

dBASE III PLUS
Organizing Your Records

This is a step-by-step tutorial that will acquaint you with the dBASE III PLUS file management system (dBASE III PLUS is a trademark of Ashton-Tate, 10150 West Jefferson Boulevard, Culver City, CA 90230).

dBASE III PLUS is a **relational** database management system (DBMS) that uses both commands and menus. As a relational DBMS, dBASE III PLUS organizes data elements into two-dimensional arrays, or tables, consisting of rows and columns. Every row contains information associated with one entry of the database. A row entry is referred to as a **data record**. Every column entry contains a particular fact about the row entry. The column entry is called a **data field**.

dBASE III PLUS contains its own interactive assistance feature, editor, and programming language, permitting a user without prior programming experience to write applications for business as well as for home use.

Since many of the concepts described here are common to most other database programs, this tutorial will also help you to work with virtually any database package. If you do not have immediate access to a computer or to this software package, you will still benefit from the detailed explanations and analyses provided.

This tutorial will take approximately four hours to complete.

Objectives

Upon completing this tutorial you will be able to:

- Create and modify a database file
- Edit, save, and retrieve a database file
- Perform arithmetic operations on database files
- Write a simple program
- Load a database
- Query a database file
- Sort and index a database
- Generate a report

Before You Begin

Review the material concerning database management in Chapter 13.

Follow the Blue

As you follow along, any procedures you must carry out or entries you must make will be printed in *blue* whereas all computer responses will appear as if they were written by a typewriter. *Type only entries or follow only directions that appear in blue.* A ❑ appears at the right of the first line of each sequence of commands you must enter. Check the box when you have completed the instruction as a way of keeping track of your progress as you proceed through the tutorial.

Whenever a special key (any key other than a letter, digit, or special character) is shown printed in blue, you must tap or momentarily depress that key. For example, if the key

were printed in blue, you would be expected to momentarily depress the [Enter] key.

In some special cases, it will be necessary for you to press *and hold down* one special key while momentarily depressing another. To indicate this, the special key or keys to be pressed and held will be printed slightly lower and attached by a thin line to the key to be tapped. If the series of keys

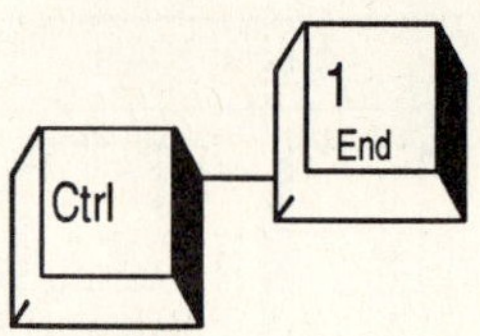

were printed in blue, you would be expected to press and hold down the Control [Ctrl] key, tap the [End] key, and release the [Ctrl] key.

You will also find it necessary to enter combinations of text and special keys. For example, if the entry

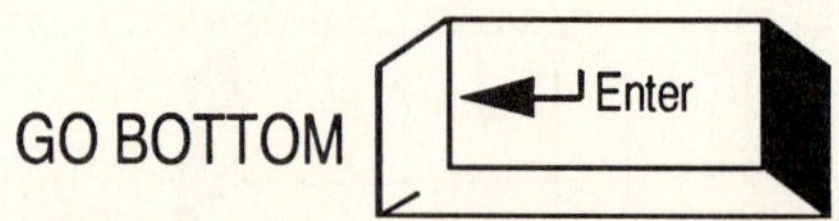

were printed in blue, you would be expected to type **GO BOTTOM** and then depress the [Enter] key.

Required Hardware

dBASE III PLUS works on IBM and compatible microcomputers running under version 2.X, 3.X, or 4.X of the MS-DOS or PC-DOS operating systems with a minimum of 384K bytes of RAM and two 360K disk drives or with one 360K disk drive and a hard disk and an 80-character printer. If you have less than 384K of memory, you cannot use DOS version 3.X with dBASE III PLUS. In this case you must use DOS 2.0 or 2.1

We assume your microcomputer is equipped with two floppy disk drives. If your system is equipped with a hard drive and dBASE III PLUS is stored on the hard drive, some of the procedures you must follow to accomplish the tasks we have for you may vary. When differences arise, we will point them out. The illustrations shown in this tutorial were generated using a microcomputer equipped with dual floppy disk drives.

Required Software

If your computer *is not* equipped with a hard drive, obtain a copy of **DOS** version 2.X or *higher* and an installed copy of **dBASE III PLUS** from your instructor or laboratory assistant. You will need it to start your computer and to begin dBASE III PLUS.

Your dBASE III PLUS system may be contained on one or two disks. If it is contained on two disks, they should be labeled **dBASE III PLUS System Disk 1** and **dBASE III PLUS System Disk 2**. Your instructor may have created a copy of the dBASE III PLUS System Disk 1 that contains the DOS operating system. This disk can be used to start your computer. If you have such a disk, you will use it both to start your computer and to begin dBASE.

If your computer *is* equipped with a hard drive, DOS and the required dBASE III PLUS files are, in all likelihood, stored on it. Thus, you do not need to obtain any other software.

We suggest that you format a floppy disk so you can save your work when finished. Formatting a disk prepares it so that the computer can write data onto it. Every disk must be formatted before it can be used. If you are not familiar with this process, refer to the DOS tutorial. Henceforth, your *Work disk* will mean a formatted floppy disk.

For the remainder of this tutorial, **dBASE** will mean an *installed* copy of dBASE III PLUS.

Special Keys

The use of special keys can greatly simplify the task of creating documents with dBASE. Some of the more commonly used ones are listed next. You should familiarize yourself with them.

Special Keys	Function
8 ↑, 2 ↓, 4 ←, 6 →	The four Arrow keys move the cursor up, down, left, or right without altering text in any way.
↵ Enter	The [Enter] key transmits a line into memory.
Backspace	The [Backspace] key moves the cursor to the left one place (similar to the Left Arrow key), but in the process it erases a character.
Caps Lock	Toggle this key "on" if you desire capital letters. Toggling this key again will return the keyboard to the lowercase mode.

Getting Started with dBASE III PLUS

Starting Your Computer and dBASE

The method for starting your computer will vary depending on whether you have a two-disk drive system or a hard drive and one floppy disk drive. If you have a hard drive, skip to the section titled "Starting Your Computer and dBASE from a Hard Drive"; otherwise read on.

Starting Your Computer and dBASE from a Floppy Disk Drive

Be sure that your computer is turned off before you begin.

Place your DOS/Startup disk (or bootable dBASE System Disk 1) in disk drive A: (the left-hand drive, or top drive) and your Work disk in the B: drive (the right-hand drive, or bottom drive). Be sure the drive doors are closed. Locate your computer's power switch or switches. Turn on your computer.

dBASE depends on DOS for the correct date and time. Thus, always be sure to enter the correct date and time when you start your computer. Computer systems equipped with clock calendars should automatically have the correct date and time logged in when they are started. In this case, it is not necessary for you to enter the date and time.

In a few moments you will hear some disk activity. Then either you will be requested to enter the correct date and time, or the correct date and time will automatically be entered for you. If you are requested to enter the correct date and time, do so now; otherwise read on.

You should see the system prompt

For convenience, we would like all entries to appear capitalized. Thus you should now place the [Caps Lock] key on. Press

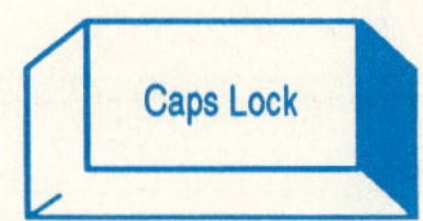

To start dBASE, remove your DOS disk from the A: drive and place the installed dBASE System Disk 1 in disk drive A:. Place your formatted Work disk in disk drive B:. Enter

If the program loads correctly, you should see the screen shown in Figure T4-1.

Depress

and the message

```
Press [Enter] to assent to the License Agreement and
begin dBASE III PLUS.
```

will be replaced by

```
Insert System Disk 2 and press ENTER,or press Ctrl-C
to abort.
```

Replace System Disk 1 with System Disk 2 and press

to see dBASE III PLUS's initial screen as displayed in Figure T4-2. Now skip to the section titled "Assistance from dBASE."

FIGURE T4-1
The dBASE Copyright Screen.

```
dBASE III PLUS Version 1.1
This Software is Licensed to:
J. Q. Public
All-Island Computing
0000000-00

Copyright (c) Ashton-Tate 1985, 1986. All Rights Reserved.
dBASE, dBASE III PLUS and Ashton-Tate are trademarks of Ashton-Tate

You may use the software and printed materials in the dBASE III
PLUS package under the terms of the Software License Agreement;
please read it. In summary, Ashton-Tate grants you a paid-up,
non-transferable, personal license to use dBASE III PLUS on one
computer work station. You do not become the owner of the
package nor do you have the right to copy (except permitted
backups of the software) or alter the software or printed
materials. You are legally accountable for any violation of the
License Agreement and copyright, trademark, or trade secret law.

Command Line ||<A:>||

Press ←┘ to assent to the License Agreement and begin dBASE III PLUS.
```

FIGURE T4-2
The Initial dBASE ASSIST Screen.

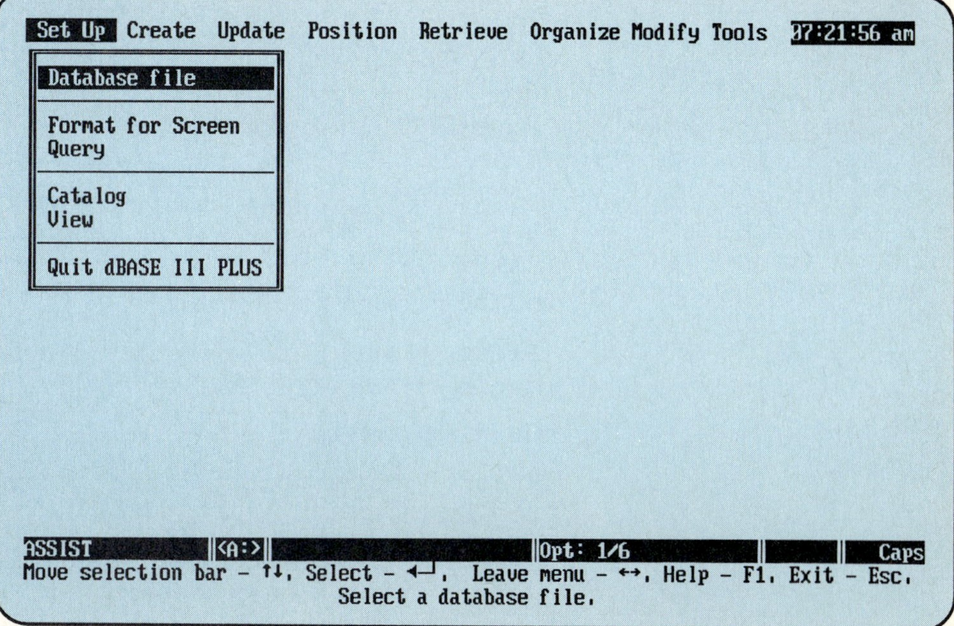

Starting Your Computer and dBASE from a Hard Drive

Be sure that your computer is turned off before you begin. There is no need to place the DOS disk in the A: disk drive because DOS is already stored on the hard disk.

Locate your computer's power switch or switches. Turn on your computer.

dBASE depends on DOS for the correct date and time. Thus, always be sure to enter the correct date and time when you start your computer. Computer systems equipped with clock calendars should automatically have the correct date and time logged in when they are started. In this case, it is not necessary for you to enter the date and time.

In a few moments you will hear some disk activity. If you are requested to enter the correct date and time, do so now; otherwise read on.

You should see the familiar system prompt

```
C>
```

For convenience, we would like all entries to appear capitalized. Thus you should now place the [Caps Lock] key on. Press

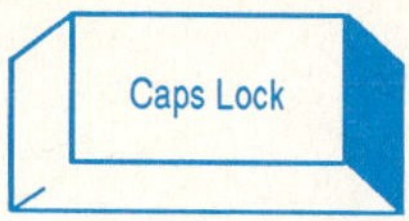

To start dBASE, change the current directory to the subdirectory that contains the dBASE program files. For example, if your dBASE files are stored in a subdirectory called dBASE, from the C> prompt, you would type **CD C:\DBASE [Enter].** If you will be saving your work to the floppy disk drive, place your Work disk in either your A: or B: disk drive.

Assuming you have placed yourself in the subdirectory containing the dBASE software, enter

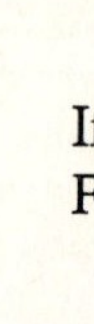

Hard-disk users will find that the figures presented in this tutorial vary slightly from what they will see. Specifically, the differences occur when a disk drive is specified. Since our figures are generated from a two-disk drive system, the screen shown in this tutorial refers to the A: or B: drive. Your screens will refer to the C: drive. However, this should not affect your work with this tutorial.

If the program loads correctly, you should see the screen shown in Figure T4-1.

To the message

```
Press [Enter] to assent to the License Agreement and
begin dBASE III PLUS.
```

press

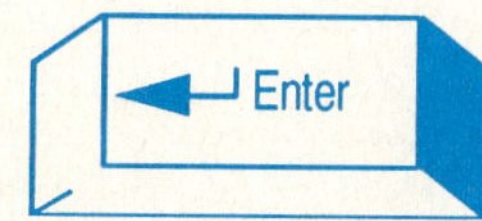

and in a moment you should see dBASE III PLUS's initial screen as displayed in Figure T4-2.

Now that you have started dBASE successfully, you can continue with the tutorial.

Assistance from dBASE

dBASE is ready and willing to provide you with assistance at all times. The initial screen shown in Figure T4-2 was produced by the **ASSIST MENU** feature of dBASE III PLUS. If you do not see this screen but you do see a screen similar to that shown in Figure T4-10, press the [F2] Function key to obtain the initial screen. This feature supports interaction between you and dBASE by displaying a series of menus from which you can choose a particular action or function, eliminating the need for you to remember the exact sequence of commands necessary to perform a given task. Let's take a close look at the components of the ASSIST MENU.

The components of the ASSIST MENU are

1. The menu bar
2. The submenus
3. The action line
4. The status bar
5. The navigation line
6. The message line
7. The current time

See Figure T4-3 to locate these areas.

FIGURE T4-3
Components of the dBASE ASSIST MENU

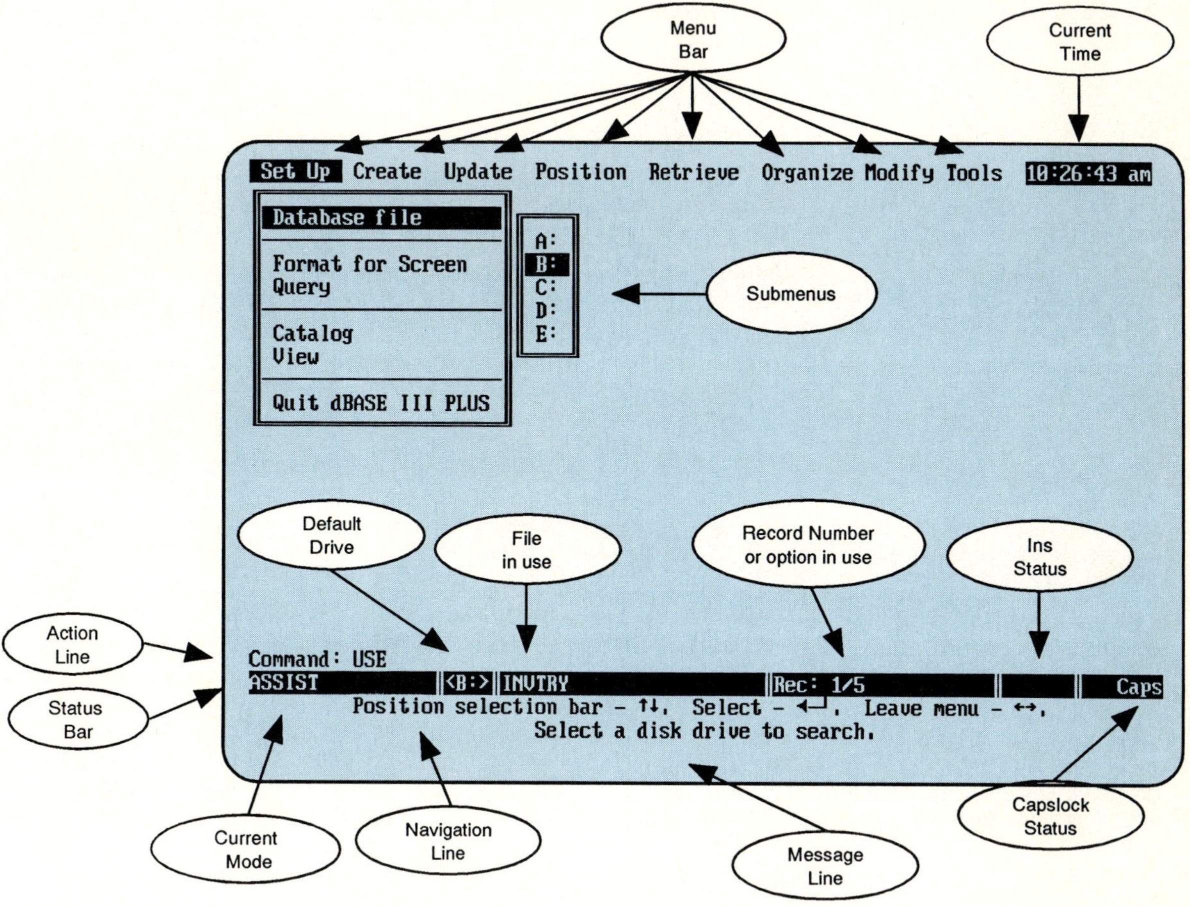

To select a menu option, place the cursor on the desired main menu option. A submenu should appear. Using the Up and Down Arrow keys, select the desired submenu option by placing the cursor on it; then press the [Enter] key.

The **menu bar** displayed at the top of Figure T4-3 displays the options available for your use. The active menu option is always displayed in reverse video. You can move from option to option by pressing the Left and Right Arrow keys. As you do this, the **submenus** change. The submenu options are displayed below the main menu option. To move from submenu option to option, you use the Down and Up Arrow keys. The active submenu option is also displayed in reverse video.

The **action line** appears below the submenus. It displays the menu and submenu options as you select them. The **status bar** provides several valuable pieces of information. Most notable are the mode you are in (ASSIST or Command), the default disk drive, the file in use, and the current record number. In addition, the status bar indicates whether the [Ins] or [Caps Lock] keys have been pressed. The **navigation line** shows how to move between menus and submenus. All dBASE messages to you are displayed in the **message line**. Finally, the **current time** is displayed at the top right of the display.

dBASE can support either the **interactive** (**ASSIST MENU**) **mode** or the **Command-driven (dot prompt) mode**. Experienced dBASE users prefer to enter commands directly using the Command-driven mode, whereas beginners prefer the interactive mode. We will begin our work in this tutorial by using the ASSIST MENU; then we will move to the dot prompt.

dBASE Files

dBASE uses several different file types. A complete dBASE **file name** consists of two parts. The first part, commonly referred to as the **filename**, must begin with a letter and contain only letters, digits, or embedded underscores. The name of the file is followed by the file **extension**, a three-character second part. Thus two files can have the same filename or first part provided that they have different extensions or second parts. This is similar to members of the same family who have different first names but the same last name. The filename, or first part, is the responsibility of the programmer, whereas the file extension, or second part of the file name, is automatically assigned by the dBASE program. For example, in the file name INVTRY.DBF, INVTRY was selected by the programmer and the extension DBF was assigned by dBASE. The extension assigned by dBASE identifies the nature of the file. Table T4-1 lists the extensions that identify common dBASE file types. Don't be upset if you don't fully understand the significance of the file types used by dBASE. We will carefully explain *what* you should know *when* you must know it.

TABLE T4-1
Common File Types Used by dBASE III PLUS

Extension	File Type
DBF	Files that are used to store user databases. These files are specially formulated by dBASE and should not be altered by any program other than dBASE.
NDX	Index files are DBF files that are created by the INDEX command.
PRG	Program files that consist of dBASE programs.
FMT	Format files that can be used by one or more programs to create screen forms.
FRM	Form files that can be used by the report-program generator to create reports.
MEM	Memory files that are used to store variable information temporarily.
TXT	Text or log files that can be used to keep a log of every record sent to the screen or printer.
LBL	Label files that can be used with a database to generate labels.
DBT	Memo files that are designed to store large chunks of text.
CAT	File catalog that is actually a database with a CAT extension.

Creating a dBASE File

A **database** is a set of logically related files containing all data relevant to a system or company. As mentioned earlier, dBASE is an example of a relational database. You will learn how to create a relational database file.

A relational database file consists of two distinct parts, the **file structure** and the **data**. Each file within a database must have a definite structure. That is, each record within a database file is made up of fields, and the description and position of each field within each record of that file is the same. The placement and description of the fields within each record of a file is referred to as the file structure. When creating a database file, the file structure must be created first.

The data represents the raw materials of the database. Data will be organized in the database to produce information. Once the structure of the database file is created, the raw data can be entered.

To illustrate the difference between dBASE's interactive and Command modes, we will create a file structure using each mode.

Creating a File Structure in Interactive Mode

To create a file structure beginning with the initial menu shown in Figure T4-2, we must move the cursor, the highlighted rectangle at the top of the screen, from **Set Up** to **Create**. Do this by depressing

❑

Your display should be as shown in Figure T4-4.

FIGURE T4-4
The dBASE ASSIST Create Screen.

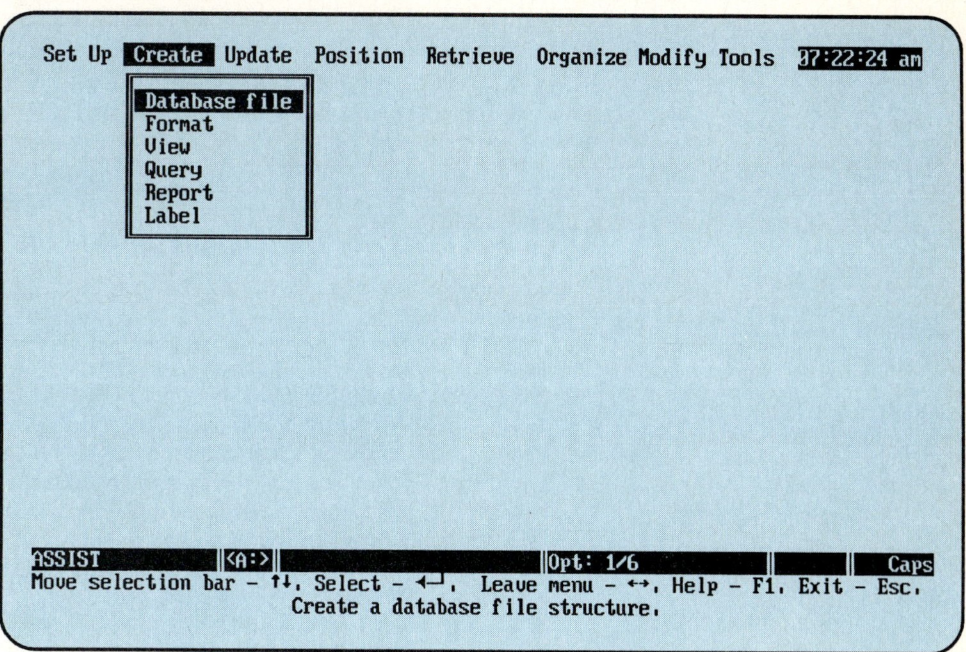

Once *Create* and *Database file* are highlighted, which is what we wish to do, we only need to press

❑

dBASE responds by adding a disk drive menu to the display (see Fig. T4-5). This menu will vary with the disk drives available on your computer system.

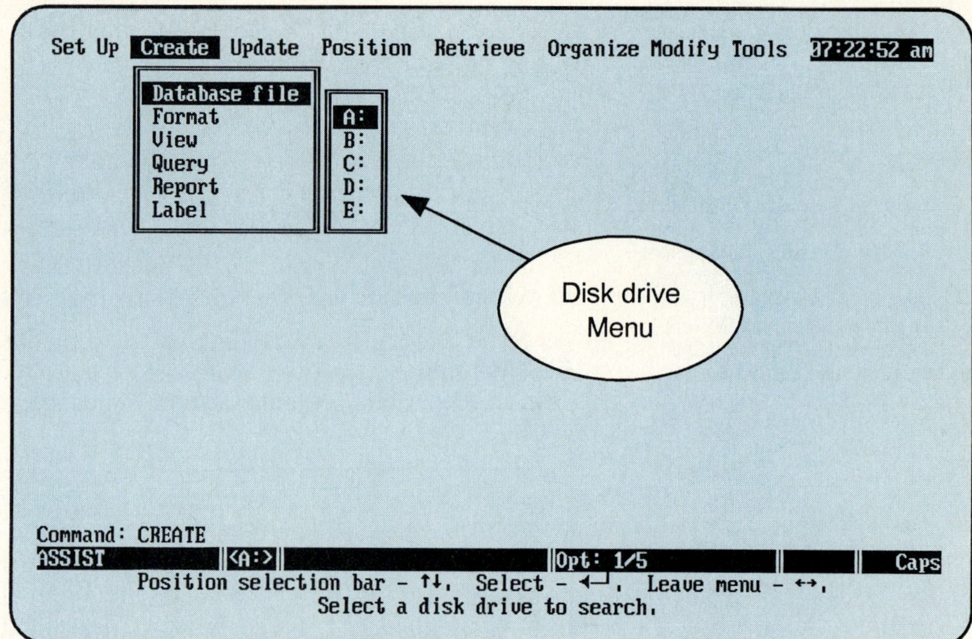

FIGURE T4-5
The dBASE ASSIST Create Screen Requesting the Disk Drive To Be Searched.

If you are a hard-disk user and if you will be saving your work to a drive other than B:, specify that drive in place of B:.

To tell dBASE that we will be saving our work on drive B:, press

❏

FIGURE T4-6
The dBASE ASSIST Create Screen Requesting a File Name.

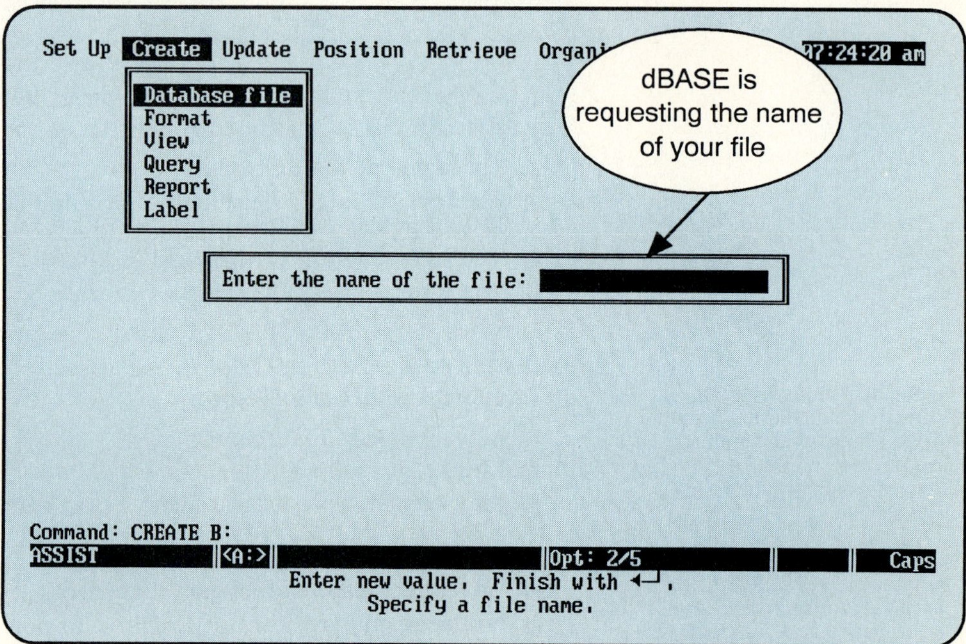

Figure T4-6 appears, and the message line displays

```
Specify a file name.
```

Let's name the file **INVTRY**.

Now enter

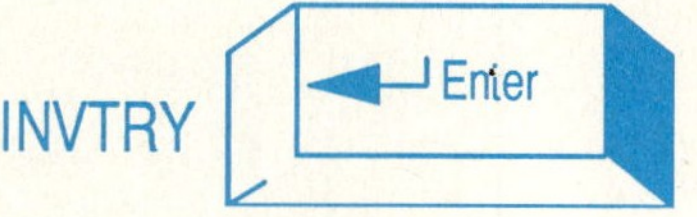

❑

If you wish to correct an error made while typing the name INVTRY, use the [Backspace] key and correct it before you press the [Enter] key. If you already pressed the [Enter] key, press the Escape [Esc] key until you return to the main menu. Then repeat the process described before.

to which dBASE will respond with the screen shown in Figure T4-7.

FIGURE T4-7

The dBASE ASSIST Create Screen Requesting the Individual Fields and Descriptions.

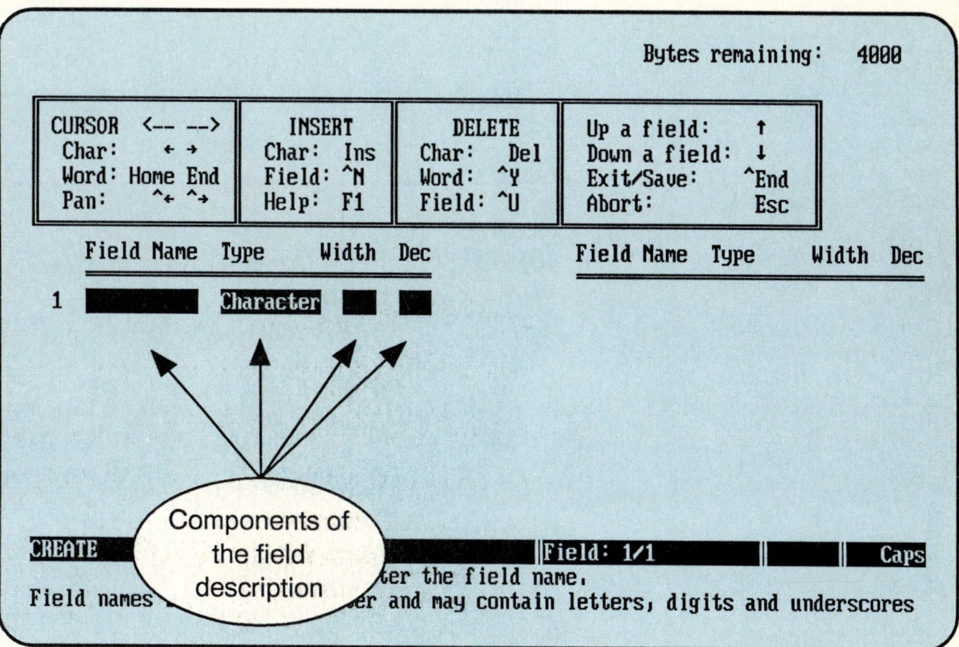

dBASE is requesting that you describe each field in the database. Specifically, dBASE is waiting for you to enter

- The name of the first field
- The type of data to be contained within this field (that is, Character, Numeric, Date, Logical, or Memo)
- The size or width of this field in bytes
- The number of decimal places, if any

There are a number of restrictions that apply to these four entries. Let's consider some of them now.

A field name is entered directly from the keyboard. Field names will be stored in uppercase characters regardless of the form in which they are entered.

A dBASE III **field name**

- May not exceed ten characters
- Must begin with a letter
- May contain only letters, digits, or an embedded underscore (_)

Character is the default data type. This means that unless you specify otherwise, dBASE automatically assigns the character data type to any field you create.

Allowable **data types** are

- **Character** (may contain any characters)
- **Numeric** (may contain any positive or negative number (integer or decimal))
- **Date** (a date in the form mm/dd/yy)
- **Logical** (a value T, t, F, f, Y, y, N, or n)
- **Memo** (the name of a file containing a memo or text file)

Once in the Type column, you can select a data type by entering the first letter of the data type (C, N, D, L, or M) or by depressing the space bar until the desired option is displayed in the Type column and then pressing the [Enter] key to record the indicated data type.

Decimal places can be specified only when Numeric data types is selected. For Date and Logical data types, dBASE automatically sets the field width to 8 or 1, respectively.

The **field width** specified for a particular data type

- Should be no more and no less than is needed for the data to be stored
- Should not violate any of the limits for that data type (A summary of these limits is given in Table T4-2).

TABLE T4-2
dBASE Restrictions by Data Type

Date Type	Type Code	Number of Characters	Allowable Characters	Special Restrictions
Character	C	1-254	Any	
Numeric	N	1-19	Digits	0–15 decimal places and at least two less than the field width
Date	D	8	mm/dd/yy	
Logical	L	1	T, t, F, f, Y, y, N, n	
Memo	M	10	Letters, digits, embedded underscore	Defines the name of a text and file containing 1 to 5,000 characters

Let us assume that we agree on the fields and descriptions shown in Table T4-3.

TABLE T4-3
Fields and Descriptions for INVTRY

Field Description	Field Name	Data Type	Field Width	Decimal Places
Item number	ITEMNO	C	4	
Item description	DESCR	C	24	
Quantity on hand	QTY	N	4	0
Cost to produce	COST	N	7	2
Selling price	SELPR	N	8	2

Each field must be entered as a separate line on the screen. If, after specifying a field description, space remains in the field, depress the [Enter] key to move to the next characteristic. If the characters entered fill the field, pressing the [Enter] key is not necessary since the cursor automatically will move down a line and be ready to accept the next field description.

Begin by entering the data name of the first field. Enter

❑

If you make an error in a field, use the Arrow keys to move the cursor to the source of the error and retype the remainder of that entry. You may go back to a previous characteristic or even to a previous field description entry. If you attempt to enter an illegal character in a field description entry, dBASE will let you know by sounding a beep.

Let's complete the field description for ITEMNO now. To confirm the Character data type, press

❑

and for the field width, enter

❑

Your screen should look like the one shown in Figure T4-8.

FIGURE T4-8
dBASE ASSIST Create Screen After Entering the Field Description for ITEMNO.

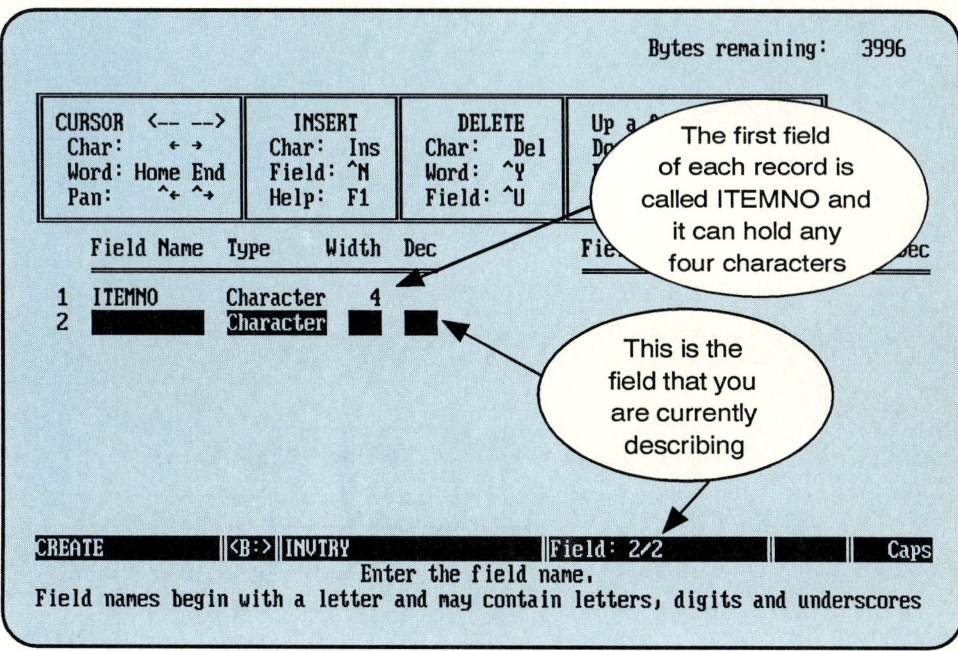

Now we will complete the second field description. Enter the sequence of commands

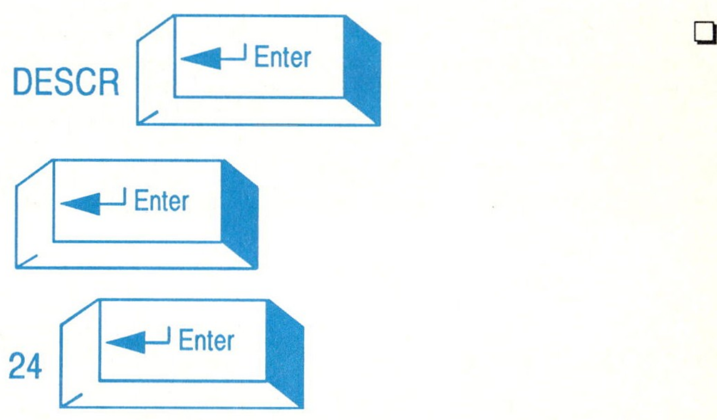

❑

Very good. We'll also do the next field description together because it concerns a different data type. Begin by entering

❑

Now, we must indicate that our field is Numeric and not Character. We do this by depressing the space bar until "Numeric" appears under the cursor. Don't worry if you depress the space bar too many times and pass by the Numeric data type; dBASE will cycle back if you keep pressing the space bar. In our case press the space bar once and "Numeric" should appear. To select this option press

Now finish the field description by entering

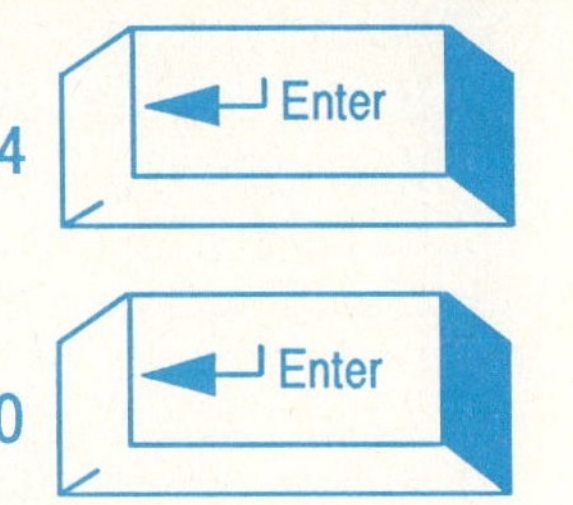

Enter the specifications for the two remaining fields shown in Table T4-3. After the fifth field specification has been entered, your screen should look like the one in Figure T4-9.

You may type a 0 or simply press the [Enter] key to tell dBASE that you do not want any decimal places in a Numeric field.

FIGURE T4-9
The dBASE ASSIST Create Screen After Entering the Field Description for All Fields.

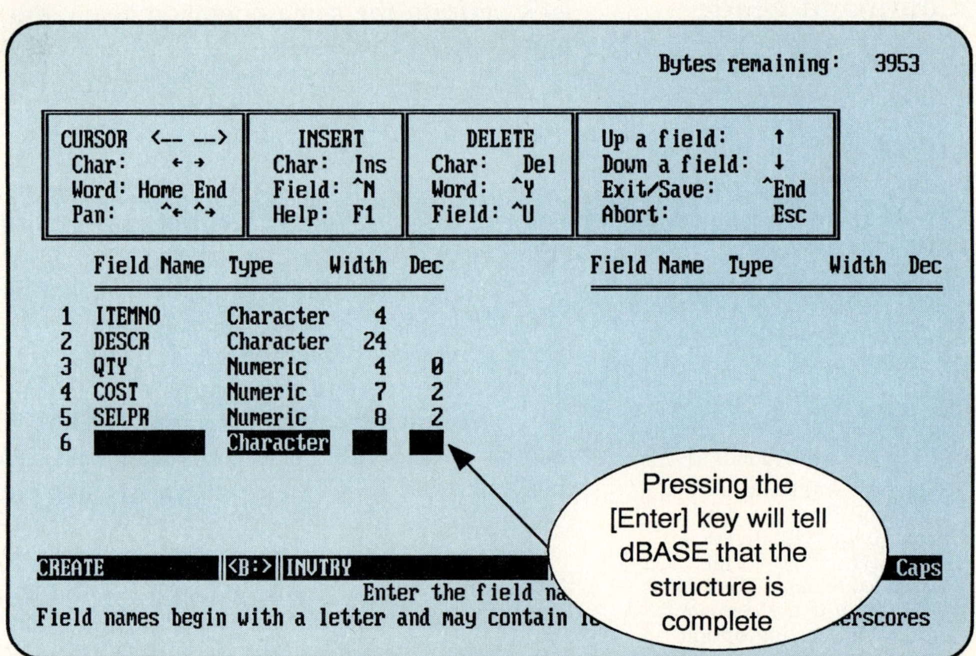

In response to the message line

```
Enter the field name.
```

press

and in response to the message

```
Press ENTER to confirm. Any other key to resume.
```

Press

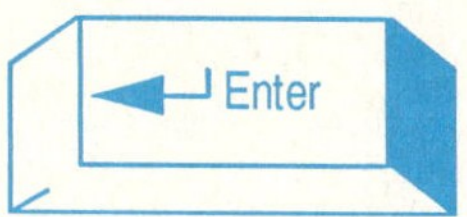

❑

dBASE will now issue the prompt

```
Input data records now? (Y/N)
```

If you type Y, dBASE will display a blank record and permit you to enter data. We will load the records with data shortly. If, however, you enter N, dBASE will save your file, exit the creation routine, and display the initial create screen. For the moment, type

N ❑

If you inadvertently type Y, press the the [Esc] key.

The database structure is now saved. You might be wondering how it could be saved if you didn't issue a **SAVE** command. Well, rest easy; when you pressed the [Enter] key to confirm the preceding message, your structure was automatically saved. It could have also been saved by pressing ^W (the ^ is the symbol for the [Ctrl] key) or ^[End].

Switching to Command Mode

You just created a database in interactive mode. For purposes of comparison, let's perform the same operation again, only this time we'll do it in Command mode. Press

❑

Anytime you want to switch to Command mode (dot prompt) from interactive mode (ASSIST menu), you only need to depress the [Esc] key. To return to the ASSIST menu from the dot prompt, you can type ASSIST and press the [Enter] key or press the [F2] Function key without pressing the [Enter] key.

You are now looking at the dot prompt at the bottom of your screen (see Fig. T4-10).

Can you identify the action line, status bar, and message line? If not, refer to Figure T4-3 for their locations. All dBASE commands, including those available through ASSIST, can be entered from the dot prompt. You simply have to type the command with the correct dBASE syntax.

Before we can create a new INVTRY.DBF database file (DBF is the file extension that dBASE automatically assigns to a database file), we must delete the old INVTRY.DBF file. Even though we didn't actually enter any data into this file, a file structure was created and saved.

The ERASE command can be used to erase files of all types. However, it cannot be used with an open, or currently used, file. Therefore, since INVTRY.DBF was just created, and thus opened, we must close it before we can erase it. To close and erase INVTRY.DBF, enter the commands

When we want you to type a command from the dot prompt, we will always display the " . " followed by the command. *Don't type the.*, just type the command and accompanying options, if any. If you make a mistake typing a dBASE command, you will probably see the error message

***Unrecognized command verb
?
Do you want some help? (Y/N)

You can get help by typing Y or continue by typing N or by simply pressing the [ENTER]

❑

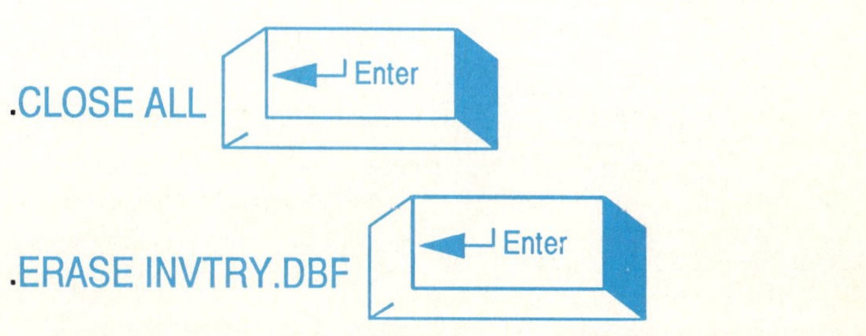

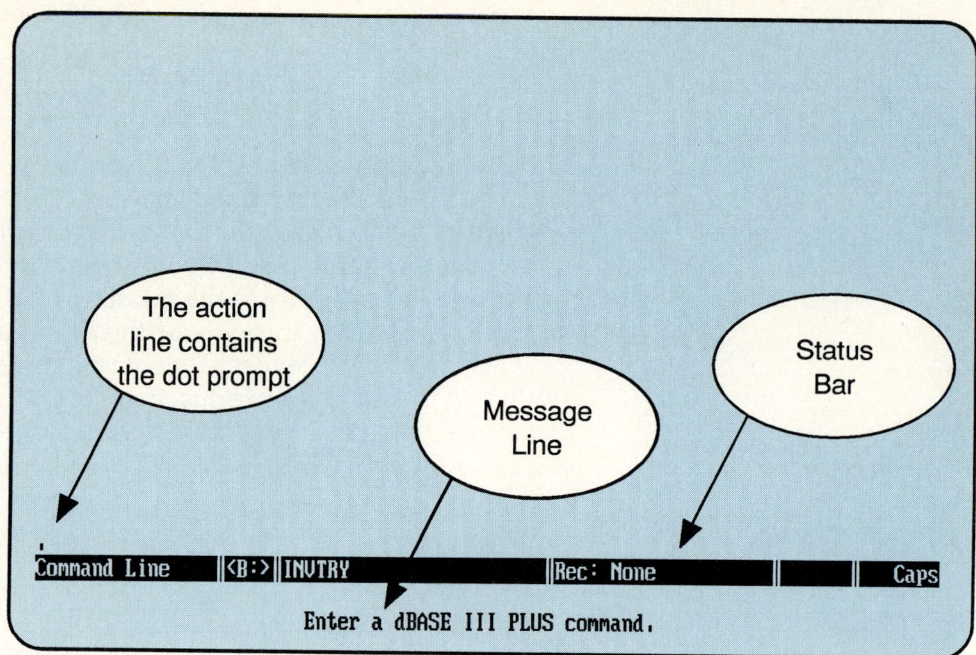

FIGURE T4-10
The Dot Prompt.

dBASE responds with

```
File has been deleted.
```

Note that we included the file extension (DBF) when we displayed the file name—this is necessary or your computer will respond

```
File does not exist.
```

when we attempt to erase it.

Creating a File Structure in Command Mode

To create a file structure in Command mode, you must enter the command CREATE and the file name next to the dot prompt. For example, we could enter the command

The B: prefix would tell dBASE that we want to write this file to the disk in drive B:. An alternative method to declaring the drive each time we refer to the file is to change the default drive to B: at the beginning of the session. To accomplish this, enter

If you leave dBASE, you must enter this command again for it to be in effect. For purposes of this tutorial, we will assume that the preceding SET command is entered each time dBASE is initiated. However, your instructor or laboratory assistant may have installed dBASE to identify automatically the B: drive as the default drive. In this case, you will not have to type the preceding command. One way you can tell if B: is the default drive is to look at the Status Bar. When you start dBASE and see B: appear in the Status Bar, this means B: is the default drive.

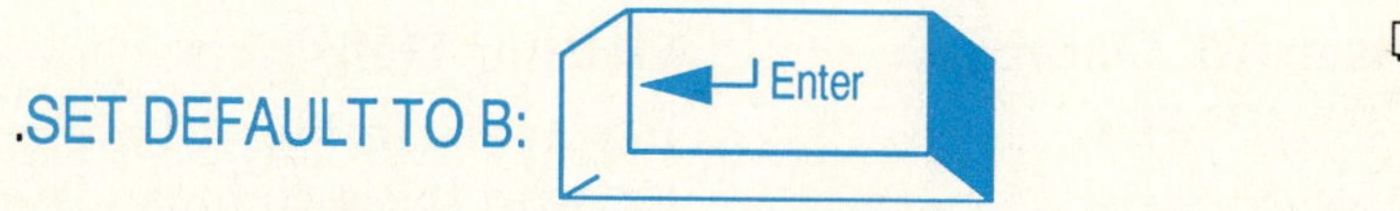

❑

If you will be saving to a drive other than B:, specify that drive instead of B:.

Now, enter the command

and you should see the screen illustrated in Figure T4-7.

The CREATE command, as any dBASE command, can be entered simply by typing in only the *first four letters* of the command. That is, we can accomplish the same result by entering CREA B:INVTRY [Enter].

However, to reinforce the meaning of each command, we will illustrate complete commands throughout this tutorial.

The dBASE procedures for entering field descriptions in the Command mode and the displays produced are identical to those used in the interactive mode. Enter the five field descriptions as they appear in Table T4-3, as you did in interactive ASSIST mode. When you reach field 6, press

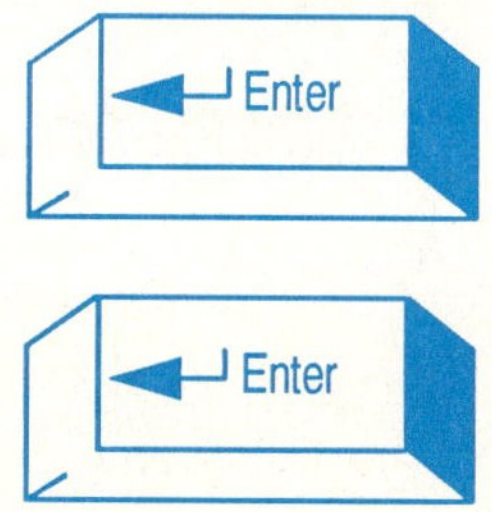

To the prompt

```
Input data records now? (Y/N)
```

enter

N

You should be back at the dot prompt and viewing the message

```
Enter a dBASE III PLUS command.
```

at the bottom of a blank screen (see Fig. T4-11).

Clearly, the Command mode is quicker and more direct than the ASSIST mode. Therefore, we will use the Command mode for the remainder of this tutorial.

The History Buffer

dBASE stores 20 of the most recent commands you've entered in a temporary storage area referred to as a **history buffer**. With this feature you can either examine or reissue commands without having to type them a second time. To activate the history buffer, you press the Up Arrow key. This action displays the last command you typed. Had you pressed the Up Arrow key twice, the next previous command would appear, and so on. Once the command you are looking for appears next to the dot prompt, press the [Enter] key to execute it.

Helpful Database Procedures

Getting Help

If you are feeling a little apprehensive, take heart. You will become familiar with these commands quite quickly as you move through this tutorial, and you will soon feel confident and comfortable using them. Should you ever need ASSISTance, simply enter

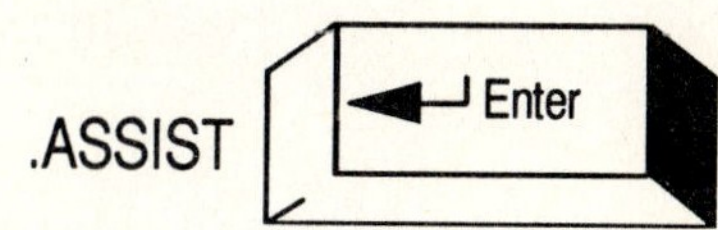

Pressing the [F2] Function key will achieve the same result.

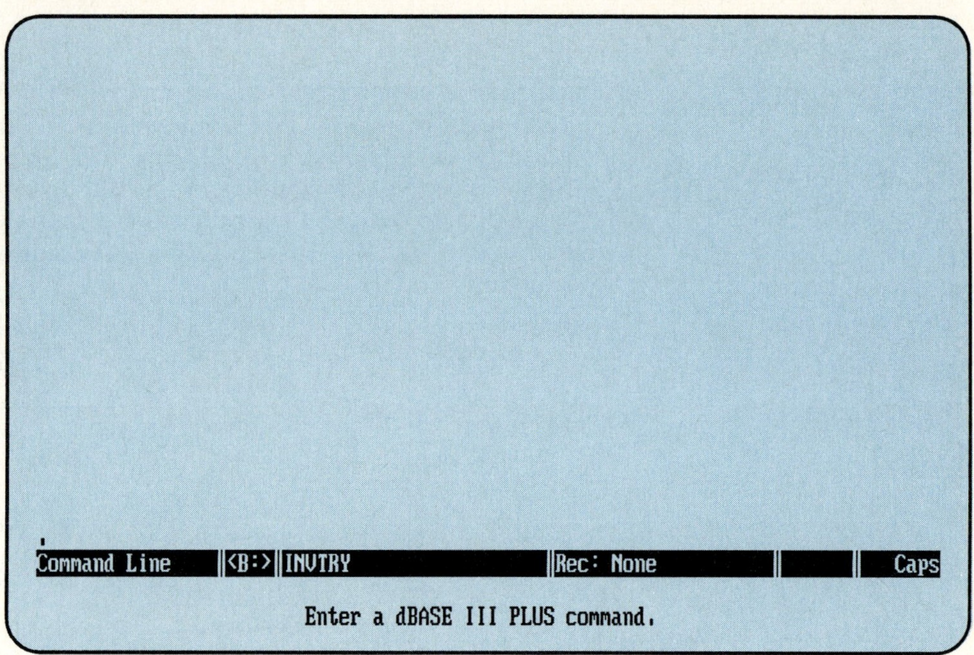

FIGURE T4-11
The dBASE Screen Display After All Field Descriptions Have Been Entered.

and you are back in interactive mode. Strike the [Esc] key and, at the speed of light, you're back in Command mode.

While in Command mode, all you need do is to enter

Pressing the [F1] Function key will achieve the same result.

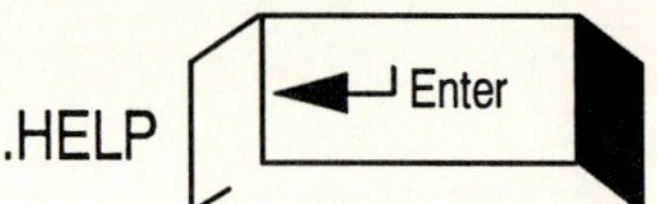

for general help or enter

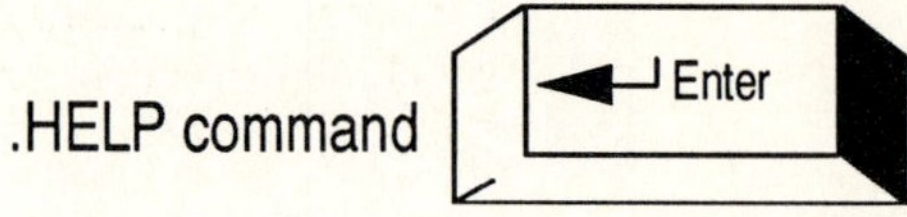

for help with a particular command. The name of the particular command must be typed after the word HELP and before you press [Enter]. dBASE will respond with on-screen assistance.

Clearing the Screen

From time to time before you commence your next operation or procedure, you will find it desirable to clear the screen of extraneous information that may have resulted from a previous operation or display. dBASE provides us with a very simple way to erase the screen of everything except the dot prompt. Enter

and the screen is erased. The dot prompt still appears at the bottom of the screen.

Viewing Your Structure

Let's take a look at the structure of our database. The first thing that we must do is to make certain the file containing the desired structure is open. That is, we must direct dBASE to access the file from storage, if this has not been done previously. This function is performed by the **USE** command. In addition to opening a new file, the USE command also closes any old file or files still open. Once we have the file open and ready for use, we can use the **LIST** or **DISPLAY** command to list the structure. For now, we will assume that the LIST and DISPLAY commands perform the same basic functions. Enter

❑

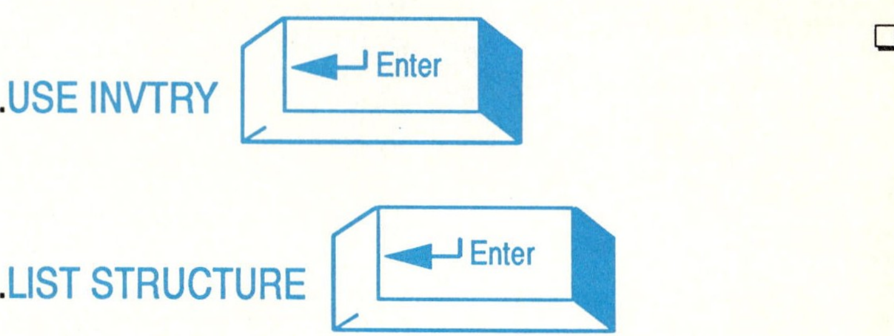

Pressing the [F5] Function key will achieve the same result.

Figure T4-12 shows the results. Note that we did not have to include the drive specification B: because we previously had entered the command SET DEFAULT TO B:.

FIGURE T4-12
Listing of the Completed Structure.

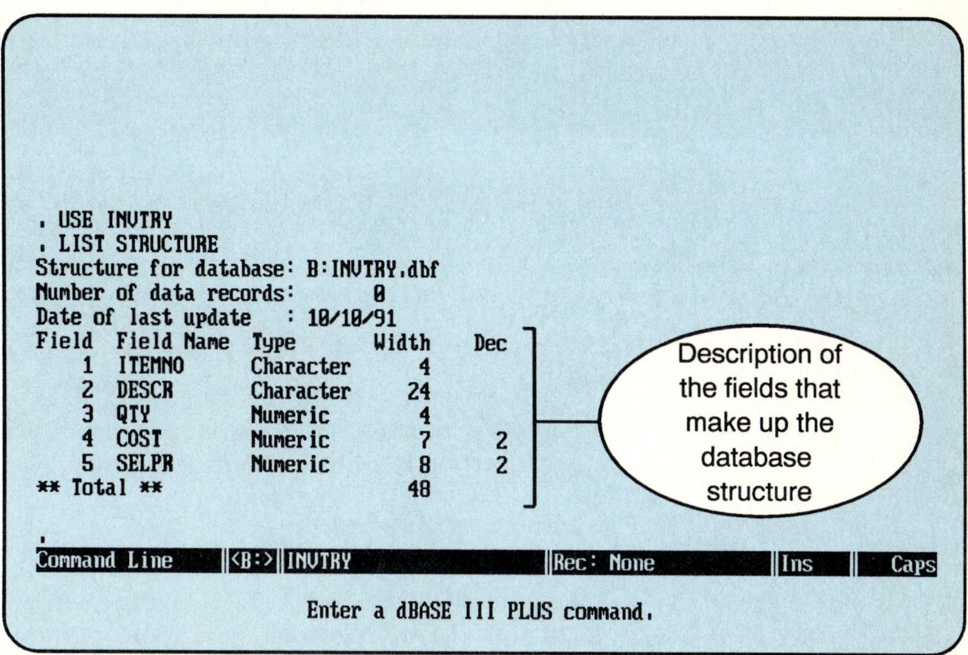

Modifying a File Structure

If you find it necessary to change or modify the structure of a database file you have already created, dBASE provides a command—**MODIFY STRUCTURE.**

To make certain that you don't inadvertently modify the wrong file, you should first designate the file to be used. This is accomplished with the **USE** command. Enter

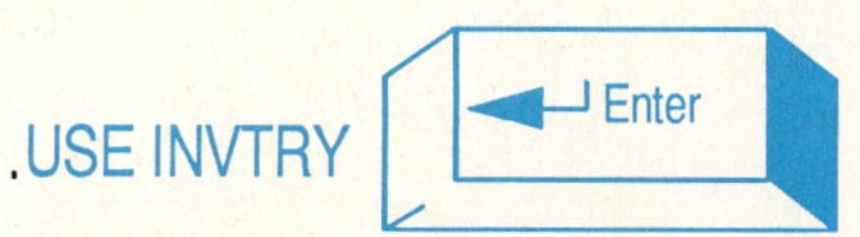

This guarantees that only this file will be accessed. Now enter

and view the screen as shown in Figure T4-13.

FIGURE T4-13
Screen Produced by MODIFY STRUCTURE Command.

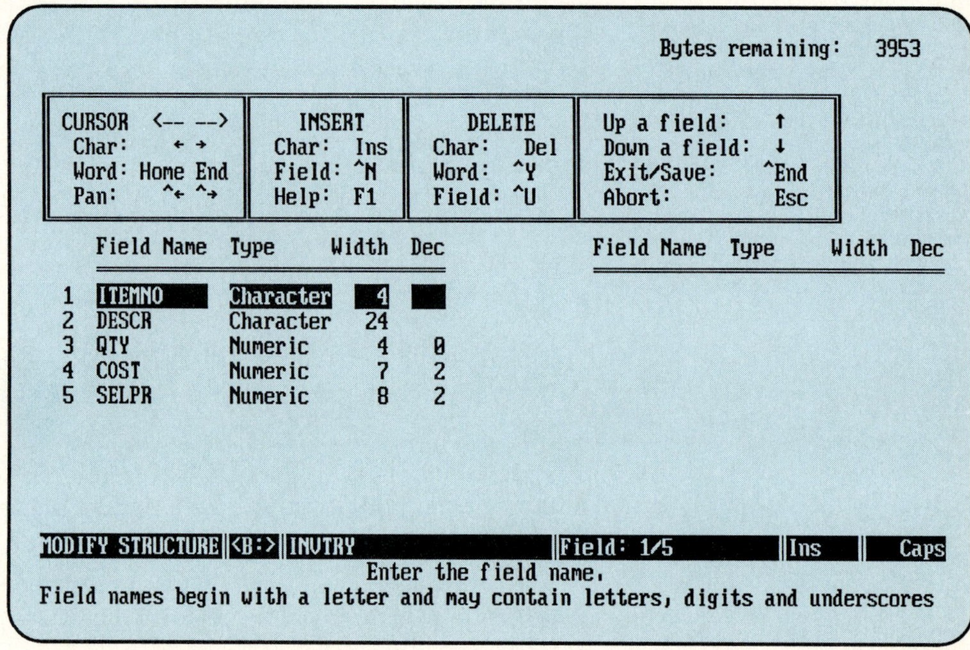

You can now change any of the field descriptions. Just use the Arrow keys to move the cursor and reenter. When using MODIFY, you may also use the control codes shown in Tables T4-4 and T4-5.

^ means hold the [Ctrl] key down. Thus ^E means hold the [Ctrl] key down and momentarily press E. Be careful not to hit the [Shift] key.

TABLE T4-4
Control Codes Used with All Commands

Control Code	Function
^E or ^A	Moves the cursor up to the previous field
^X or ^F	Moves the cursor down to the next field
^S	Moves the cursor left one character
^D	Moves the cursor right one character
^Y	Clears the field to blanks
^V	Turns INSERT on or off ([Ins] key may also be used.)
^G	Deletes the character under cursor
^Q	Aborts the screen APPEND operation without adding a record
^W	Ends the screen APPEND and adds record, if any, or goes to the next record entry
^P	Toggles the printer on and off

TABLE T4-5
Control Codes Used with MODIFY

Control Code	Function
^N	Moves all fields down one line from the present cursor position to allow the user to insert a new field definition
^Q	Exits, leaving the database structure in its original state with no alterations
^T	Deletes the field at the cursor position and moves up the fields below the field just deleted
^W	Exits, changing the structure to include all changes
^Y	Clears the current field to blanks to the right of the cursor position without affecting other fields

It is important to know the consequences of modifying the structure of a database that already has data entered. If you should make the field width smaller than what was originally specified, you may lose some data. Also, changing the field type can be disastrous and thus should be avoided. The best security against having to modify the structure of a database is to *do it right the first time.*

Experiment! Try moving the cursor around using the Arrow keys or some of the control codes shown in Table T4-4 and making some changes. To get the original database structure back again, enter

^Q ❑

and in response to the prompt

```
Are you sure you want to abandon operation? [Y/N]
```

enter

Y ❑

This will get you out of the MODIFY STRUCTURE command, restoring your structure to what it was. If you want your changes incorporated, enter ^W instead of ^Q.

Want To Stop?

You should never exit dBASE by simply turning off your computer while still in the dBASE environment. This action could damage your data and the software. The only safe way to exit the software is by using the QUIT command from the dot prompt or by selecting **Set Up** from ASSIST and then choosing the **Quit dBASE III PLUS** option.

If at any time you want to take a break and continue at a later date, just do the following

- At the dot prompt, type Quit and press the [Enter] key.
- At the DOS prompt A>, remove your disks.

To continue, if you have a two-disk drive system,

- Put DOS in drive A: and boot up.
- Press the [Caps Lock] key.
- At the A> prompt, replace DOS with the dBASE System Disk 1 and enter DBASE [Enter].
- Press the [Enter] key.
- Replace dBASE System Disk 1 with dBASE System Disk 2.
- Press the [Enter] key to bring up dBASE's initial ASSIST screen.
- Press the [Esc] key to leave the interactive mode and enter the Command mode. At the dot prompt, enter

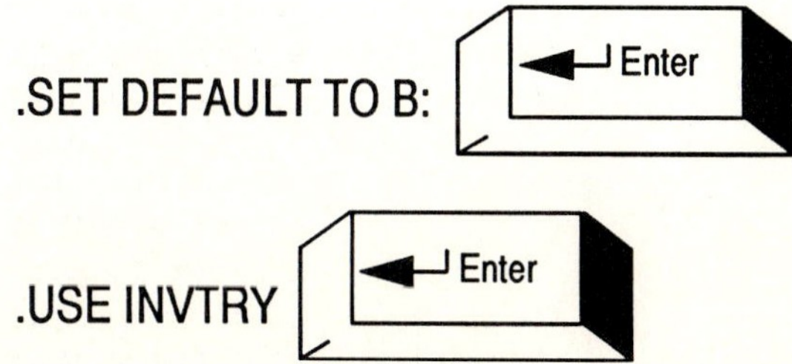

and pick up where you left off.

For all you hard-drive users, fear not. We didn't forget you.

- Turn on your computer.
- At the C> system prompt, press the [Caps Lock] key.
- Change the current directory to the directory containing the dBASE program files.
- Enter DBASE [Enter] [Enter].
- When you are at the ASSIST MENU, press the [Esc] key to leave the interactive mode and enter the Command mode.
- At the dot prompt, if necessary, change the default directory to the directory containing your database file or files by entering SET DEFAULT TO followed by the drive specification and pressing the [Enter] key. Then enter

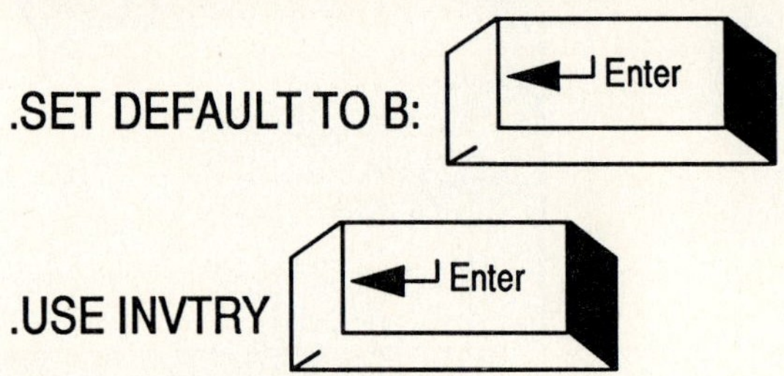

and pick up where you left off.

Loading a Database

Now it's time to enter our data. We could have entered our data earlier when dBASE asked us if we wanted to *Input data records now? (Y/N)*. Do you remember? We chose not to at that point. However, under normal circumstances you would enter the data immediately after you create the database structure.

The easiest way to add records to a database is with the command **APPEND**. At this point, we have only a structure for our database; the records are still empty. To load the database, enter

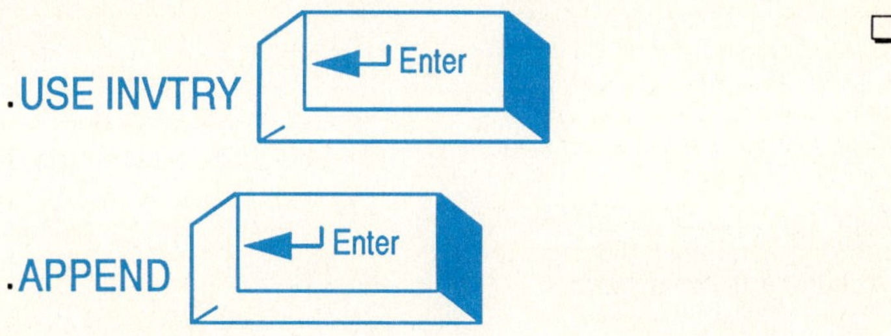

Pressing the [F9] Function key will achieve the same result.

This will display a blank record with empty fields (see Fig. T4-14).

Enter the first data record as shown in Table T4-6, pressing the [Enter] key as needed to advance from field to field. If the data you type fills a field to capacity, dBASE will automatically advance you to the next field. If you make a mistake, simply use the Arrow keys to move the cursor to the source of the error and *retype* the entry. The first record should be typed this way:

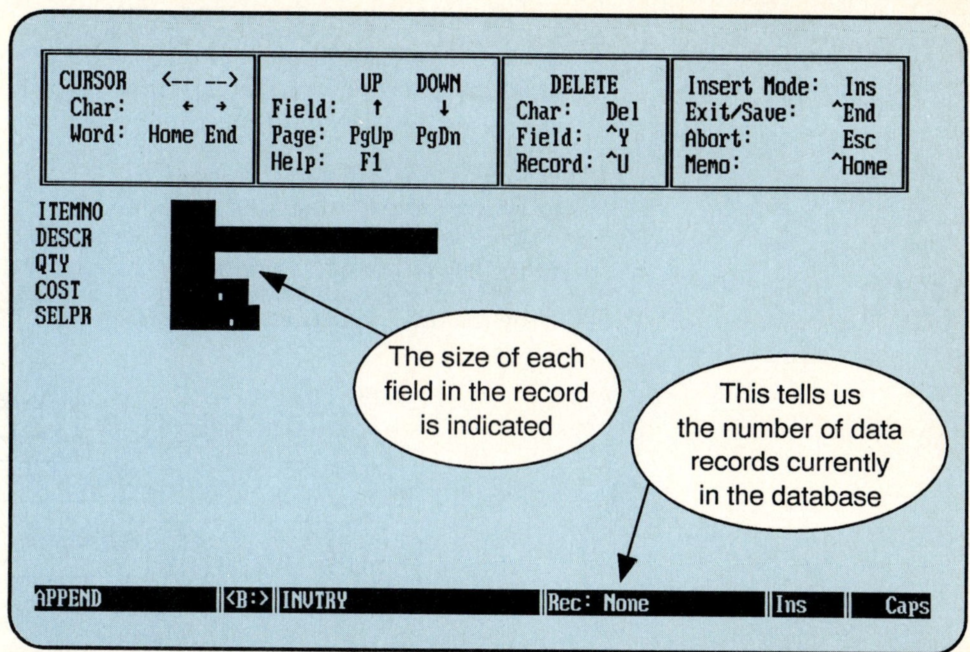

FIGURE T4-14
dBASE APPEND Screen.

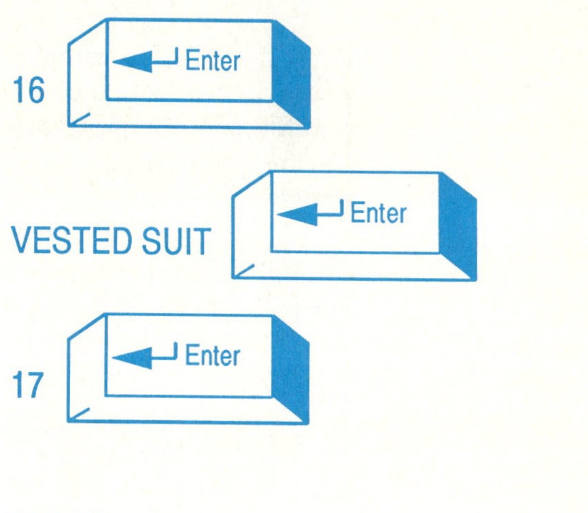

Type the decimal point when entering a number that contains a decimal point.

248.95

311.19

Can you see that it was not necessary to press the [Enter] key in order to move from the COST field to the SELPR field or to move from the SELPR field to the second record? This is because dBASE issues an [Enter] automatically after a field has been filled to capacity. Because only two decimal places are allocated in the COST and SELPR fields, after the second decimal place is entered in each field, dBASE recognizes the field is filled and automatically issues an [Enter].

TABLE T4-6
Data To Be Included in INVTRY Database File

Record Number	Item Number	Description	Quantity	Cost Price	Selling Price
1	16	VESTED SUIT	17	248.95	311.19
2	12	COTTON SLACKS	10	35.50	44.38
3	03	BATHING SUIT	20	18.00	22.50
4	14	SUMMER COAT	6	145.90	194.05
5	05	FLANNEL SHIRT	112	20.00	22.00

After entering the first record, your screen should look like the one in Figure T4-15.

FIGURE T4-15
Screen After APPENDing First Data Record.

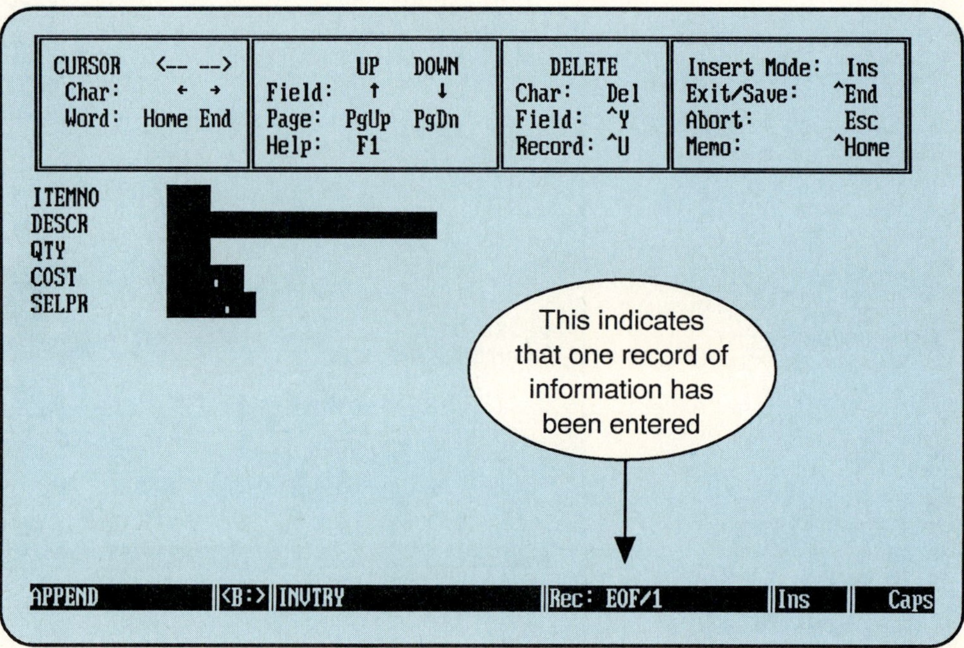

Enter the remaining four data records now. If you detect an error after entering a record, use the Arrow keys or the Page Up [Pg Up] and Page Down [Pg Dn] keys to go back, or *keep going and don't worry*. We will learn shortly how to edit the database.

After the fifth record is entered, press

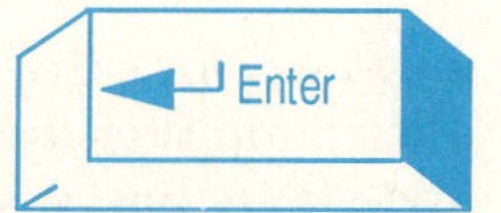

❑

dBASE saves data on a record-by-record basis. Immediately after the last field of a record is completed, the record is added to the database.

This will save your work and return you to the dot prompt.

Saving could have been accomplished by pressing and holding the [Ctrl] key while momentarily pressing the [End] key. [Ctrl]-[End] saves the *displayed* data record as well as all *prior records* entered. If you decide to press [Ctrl]-[End] with all data fields empty, an empty record will be added to your database. You will then have to remove the empty record.

Issuing the command QUIT and pressing the [Enter] key will close this file and all other open files, save these files to disk, and exit dBASE III PLUS. It also cancels any SET commands such as SET DEFAULT TO B:.

Before we go further, let's take a look at our data. Enter

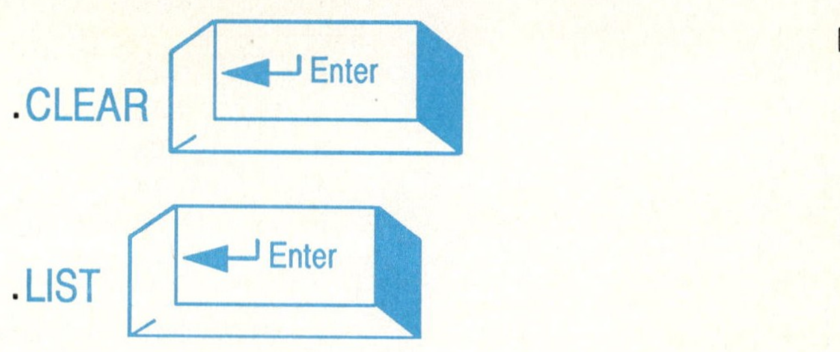

Depressing the [f3] Function key will achieve the same result.

You should see Figure T4-16 on your screen.

FIGURE T4-16
Screen After APPENDing All Five Data Records.

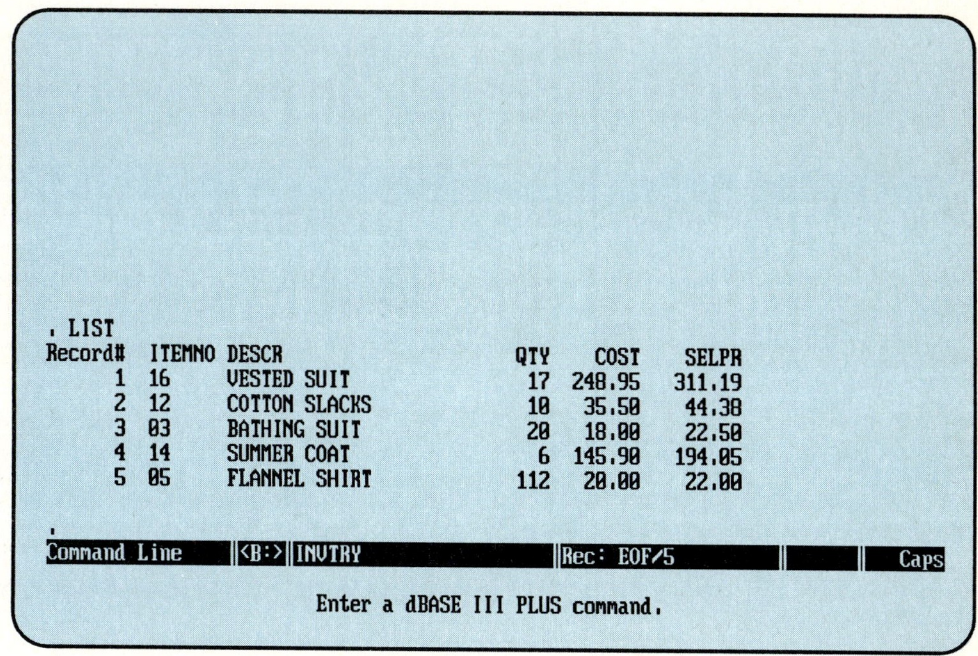

If your screen looks different, don't worry. You will have an opportunity to correct your errors in a moment.

Moving around Your Database

Let's explore the ways we can move within a database. dBASE utilizes a record pointer that keeps track of the current record number. If you look at the status bar, you can see that it displays *Rec: EOF/5*. This indicates that the record pointer is pointing to the End Of a File of five records, not Record 5. Enter

The status bar now displays

```
Rec: 3/5
```

This means that the record pointer is pointing to Record 3 of a total of five records. To move the record pointer to a particular record, you need only type the record number and press the [Enter] key.

Enter

The last record in a database may not always be the record having the largest record number. Similarly, the first record may not always be the record having the smallest record number. As you will learn later, the order in which records are displayed can be changed from the order in which they were created to a numeric order, alphabetic order, or chronological order. Any of these processes could place Record 5 at the top of the database, and Record 1 at the bottom.

Notice that you moved to the last record in the database, Record 5. Type

Now you are back at the first record, Record 1.

These simple procedures for moving around a database are very important to what will follow. Remember them.

Editing a Database

It is often necessary to change or update the contents of one or more fields within a database file or even to add or remove records from the database. You have already seen the APPEND command in action and understand that it is used to add records to a database. Now we will learn about dBASE commands that perform other editing functions.

For example, let us assume that we wish to change the selling price of FLANNEL SHIRT from $22.00 to $21.50. In short, we wish to edit this file. To accomplish this, we use the **EDIT** command. Before using this command, let's make certain that we will be editing the file INVTRY by issuing the command

Editing a Single Record

Now that we're certain we've accessed the right file, let's try editing it. Since we want to change or edit Record 5, enter

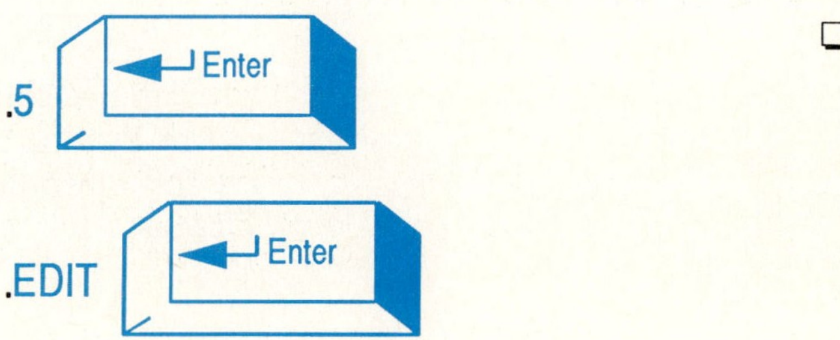

You should see the screen shown in Figure T4-17.

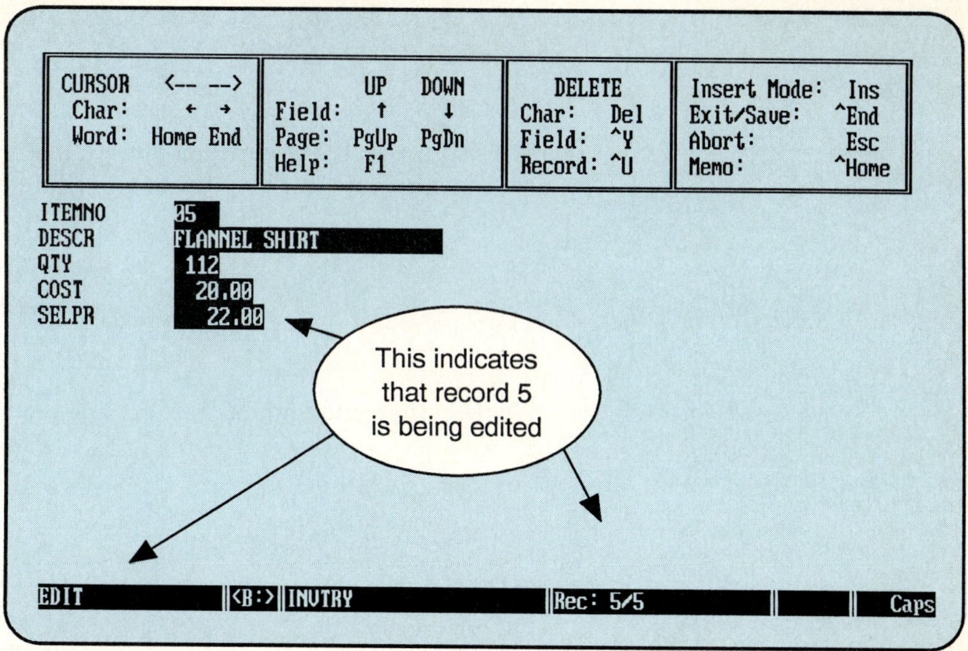

FIGURE T4-17
Screen After Issuing the Command EDIT 5.

Our procedure was simple: First we positioned the record pointer to the record we wanted to edit; then we executed the EDIT command.

If the EDIT command is used without a record number, dBASE will simply display the record accessed by a previous command or, if no record was accessed by a previous command, it will display the record currently being pointed to by the record pointer.

In order to move around within the record from field to field while editing, you may use the Arrow keys or any of the control codes shown in Table T4-4. Additional control codes are shown in Table T4-7.

TABLE T4-7
Control Codes Used with EDIT

Control Code	Function
^C	Changes the record in memory and advances to the next record or returns the dot prompt if there is no next record
^R	Changes the record in memory and backs up to the previous record or returns the dot prompt if there is no previous record
^U	Toggles the record deletion mark on and off

You can use control codes or the Arrow keys to move the cursor to the last field in Record 5 and change its contents to 21.50.

Try this operation now using the Arrow keys and the regular Number keys. Depress

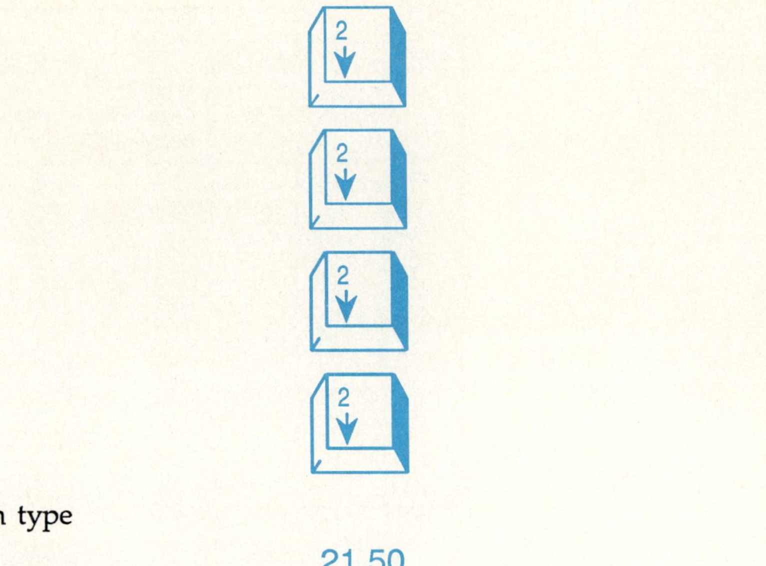

Then type

21.50

You should be at the dot prompt.

Full Screen Editing with BROWSE

You just saw how the EDIT command permitted us to access and edit a single record. Now let's examine a command that can be used to access and edit a screen full of records—the **BROWSE** command. BROWSE allows you to edit up to 17 records at once and as many fields as will fit across your display. Fields that are not displayed can be viewed by using the **Pan** option of the BROWSE menu. This feature will be discussed shortly.

When executed, the BROWSE command will display a set of records beginning with the current record as indicated by the status bar. At this point, you can use the BROWSE menu displayed at the top of your screen to assist in changing the contents of a field or fields, add a record, or delete a record. The BROWSE menu can be displayed or removed, depending on its current status, by pressing the [F1] Function key.

For example, let's begin editing with Record 3. Enter

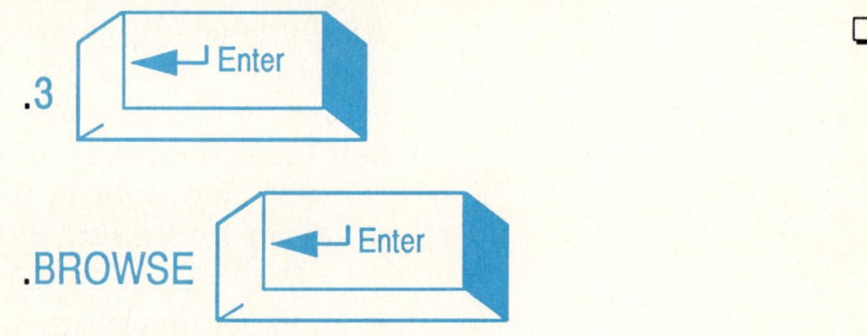

The screen produced is shown in Figure T4-18.

The Arrow keys or any control codes from Tables T4-5 and T4-7 may be used with the BROWSE command.

This will locate and display Record 3 and all other records to the end of the file or until the screen is full. Assuming that no changes have to be made due to errors, we can get back to the dot prompt by entering

If you make corrections that you want to save, enter ^W or ^[End] instead of ^Q.

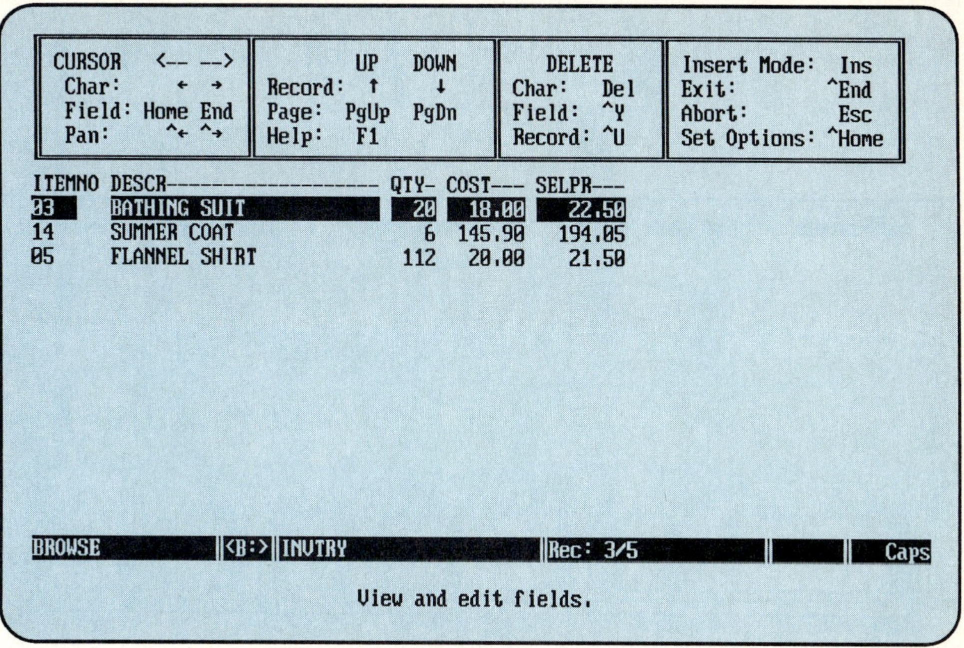

FIGURE T4-18
Screen Produce by the BROWSE Command.

Browsing Large Records

In cases where the record is so large that it exceeds the 80-character screen width, the scope of the BROWSE command can be limited to selected fields within the record. This is accomplished by following the word BROWSE with the word FIELDS and with a list of the names of the selected fields to be viewed, separated by commas. For example,

accomplishes full-screen editing of only the QTY and COST fields.

Alternatively, we can use the pan feature of BROWSE. Entering ^B will pan, or move, the viewing window right one field, possibly exposing a field that was otherwise out of view, whereas entering a ^Z pans, or moves, the window one field to the left. In our case, panning would have no effect, since our entire record is less than 80 characters.

At this point, if your database contains typing errors, use the BROWSE or EDIT commands to make the corrections and save the file. Make sure that you do not change the SELPR for FLANNEL SHIRT to 22.00.

❑

Deactivating and Removing Records

If you are tired of those unsightly records and are having trouble getting rid of them, try **DELETE**. It's guaranteed to work fast. Enter

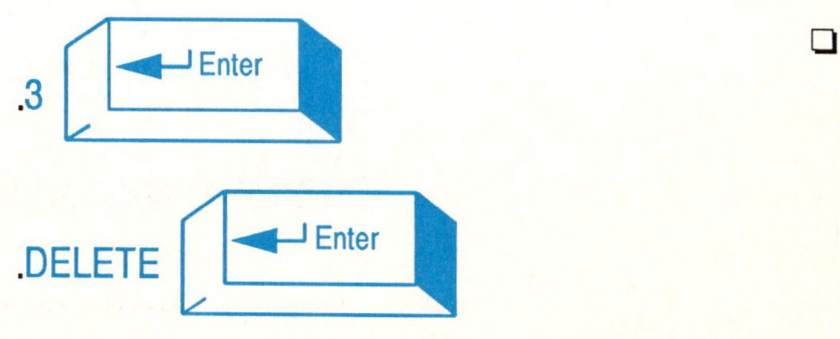

dBASE responds with

```
1 record deleted
```

Enter

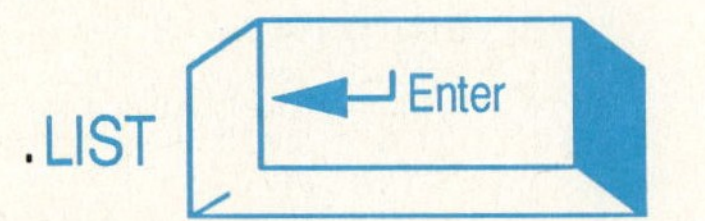

❏

Can you see the asterisk by Record 3? You have just marked Record 3 for deletion. To remove Record 3 permanently, you must enter the **PACK** command. Don't do it. We need Record 3. However, you may have a blank record or two you would like to remove. In a minute we will give you the opportunity to remove them permanently.

When a record is deleted using the DELETE command, an asterisk is placed before it. This indicates that the record is marked for deletion. However, the record will still be an active part of the database. If you PACK the database, the record will permanently be removed from the database and the records will be renumbered.

dBASE can be directed to skip over records marked for deletion until directed to do otherwise. This is accomplished with the **SET DELETED ON** command. To see this, enter

❏

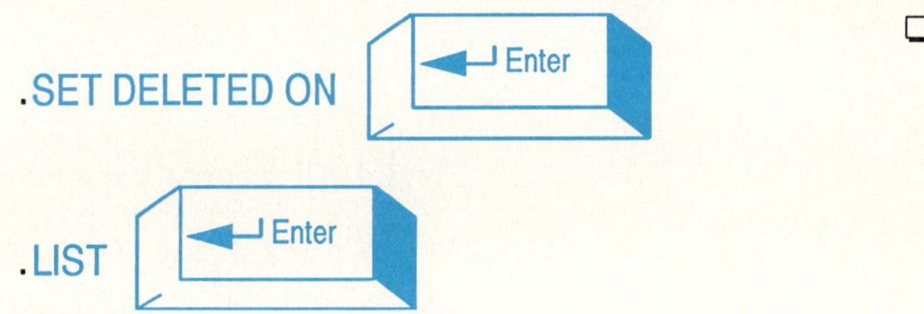

You now see Figure T4-19.

FIGURE T4-19
Listing of Database with SET DELETED ON.

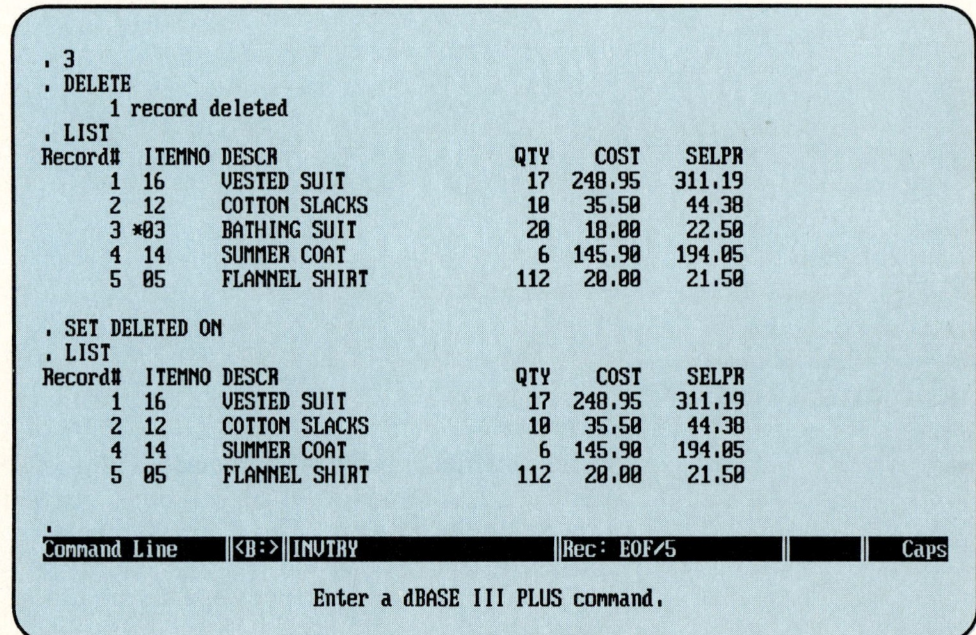

```
. 3
. DELETE
      1 record deleted
. LIST
Record#  ITEMNO DESCR                          QTY   COST    SELPR
      1  16     VESTED SUIT                     17  248.95   311.19
      2  12     COTTON SLACKS                   10   35.50    44.38
      3 *03     BATHING SUIT                    20   18.00    22.50
      4  14     SUMMER COAT                      6  145.90   194.05
      5  05     FLANNEL SHIRT                  112   20.00    21.50

. SET DELETED ON
. LIST
Record#  ITEMNO DESCR                          QTY   COST    SELPR
      1  16     VESTED SUIT                     17  248.95   311.19
      2  12     COTTON SLACKS                   10   35.50    44.38
      4  14     SUMMER COAT                      6  145.90   194.05
      5  05     FLANNEL SHIRT                  112   20.00    21.50

.
Command Line  |<B:>|INVTRY              |Rec: EOF/5  |    |    Caps

                    Enter a dBASE III PLUS command.
```

If you compare the listings shown in Figure T4-19, you should see that Record 3 is missing from the second listing. The SET DELETED ON command served its purpose—it directed dBASE to ignore all records marked for deletion. Thus the LIST command ignored Record 3. To activate Record 3 again, enter

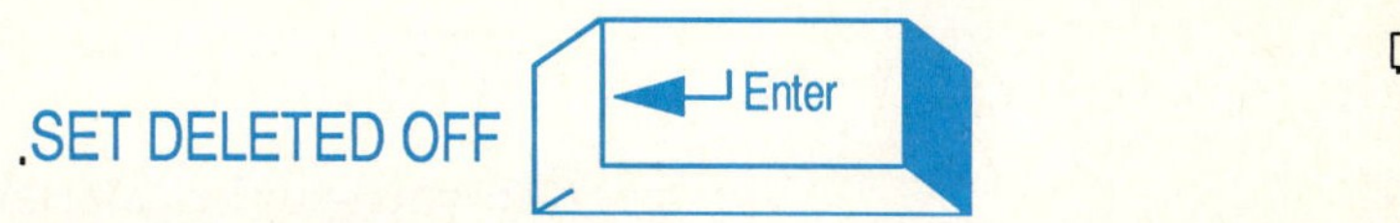

It is also possible to recall a record that has been marked for deletion using the **RECALL** command. Executing RECALL will remove the asterisk from Record 3 and return it to active status. Enter

You could type RECALL ALL to recall all records that have been marked for deletion.

to which the computer responds with

```
1 record recalled
```

Enter

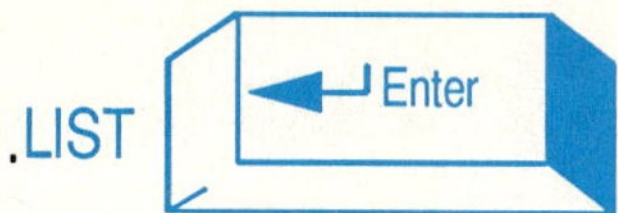

Presto! All records are active.

If you have blank records or if you have records that were incorrectly entered or edited, you should mark them for deletion using the DELETE command and then PACK the database; otherwise read on.

Now, enter

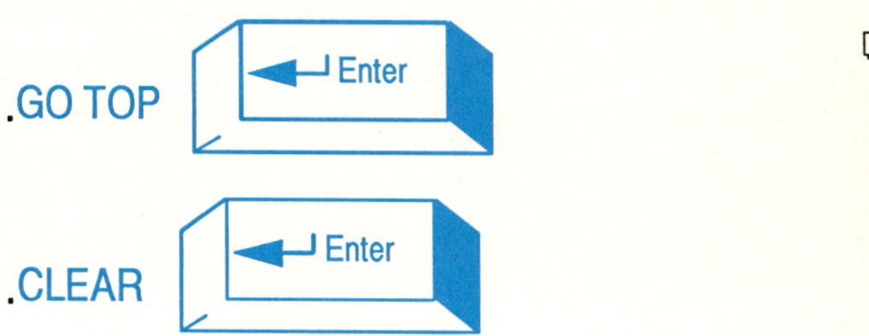

LIST and DISPLAY

The contents of records are viewed with the **LIST** and **DISPLAY** commands. The LIST command, when executed, continuously lists all fields of each record in the database. The DISPLAY command, on the other hand, normally lists only the record that is displayed in the status bar. It can be expanded to display 20 lines of data by specifying the ALL option. We'll have more on this later.

Let's examine the DISPLAY command. Begin by entering

If the database is positioned at end-of-file, DISPLAY will show only the headings.

Your screen should appear as shown in Figure T4-20.

FIGURE T4-20
DISPLAY Command Displaying Record 1.

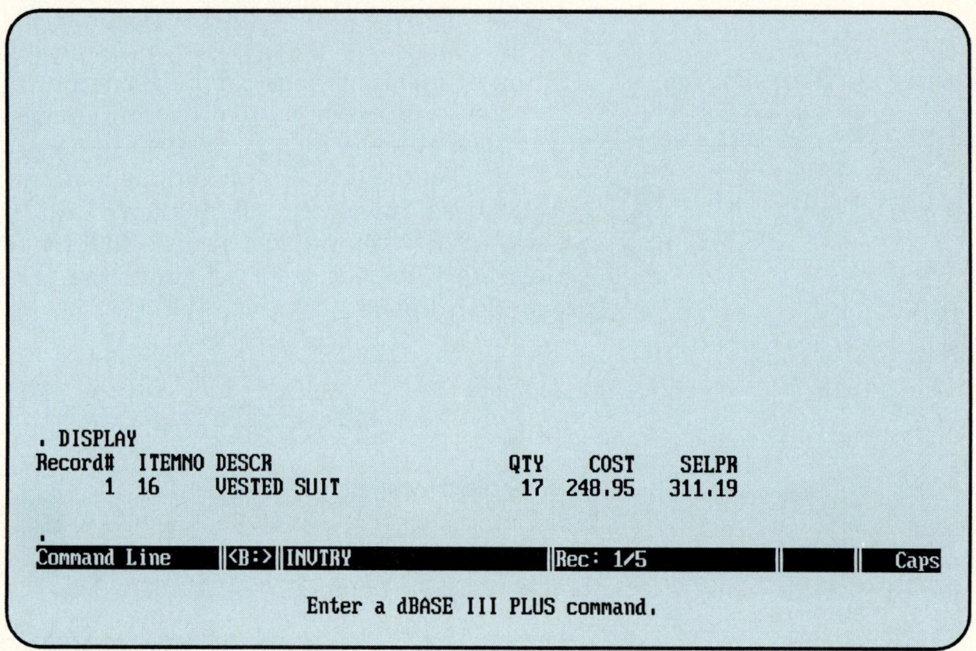

Since the record pointer was on Record 1, you see Record 1 displayed. Thus, if you know the record number, you can go to that record and then DISPLAY it. However, if you do not know the record number, you could enter LIST or DISPLAY ALL. If you have many records, DISPLAY ALL is preferred. Let's try it. Enter

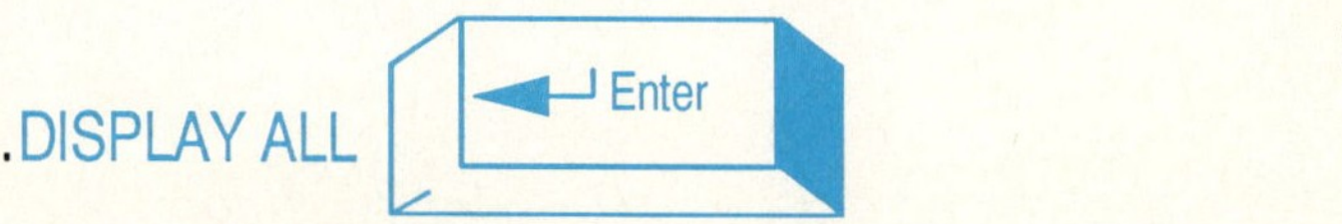

Your five records are displayed and you're back at the dot prompt. Record 1 should still be displayed in the status bar. Had our database contained 30 records, for example, DISPLAY ALL would have paused after displaying 20 lines of data. Directions regarding how to continue would then have been provided.

There are other options available with the LIST and DISPLAY commands. For example, the OFF option can be used to suspend the listing of record numbers. Enter

Notice, that *the record numbers are missing*. We can limit the display to specified fields only. For example, enter

We can also use the DISPLAY command to list selected fields or have the records listed without record numbers. However, to have the scope of the DISPLAY command affect all records, we must use the ALL option. An example is DISPLAY ALL ITEMNO, QTY.

.LIST ITEMNO, QTY

and note that only the fields specified, ITEMNO and QTY, are displayed. Since the OFF option was not specified, record numbers appeared.

Now, clear your screen. Enter

.CLEAR

Doing Arithmetic

Arithmetic manipulations can be carried out using the LIST and DISPLAY commands. For example, two numeric fields of a record can be multiplied to produce a new value.

Let's list the description and the total inventory value of each record in our database. Since the total inventory value is not a field within the record, we will have to compute it. Assume that the total inventory value of an item equals the COST of the item times the QTY on hand. The command to accomplish this is

.LIST DESCR, QTY*COST

You should now see Figure T4-21.

FIGURE T4-21
Listing of DESCR and QTY*COST.

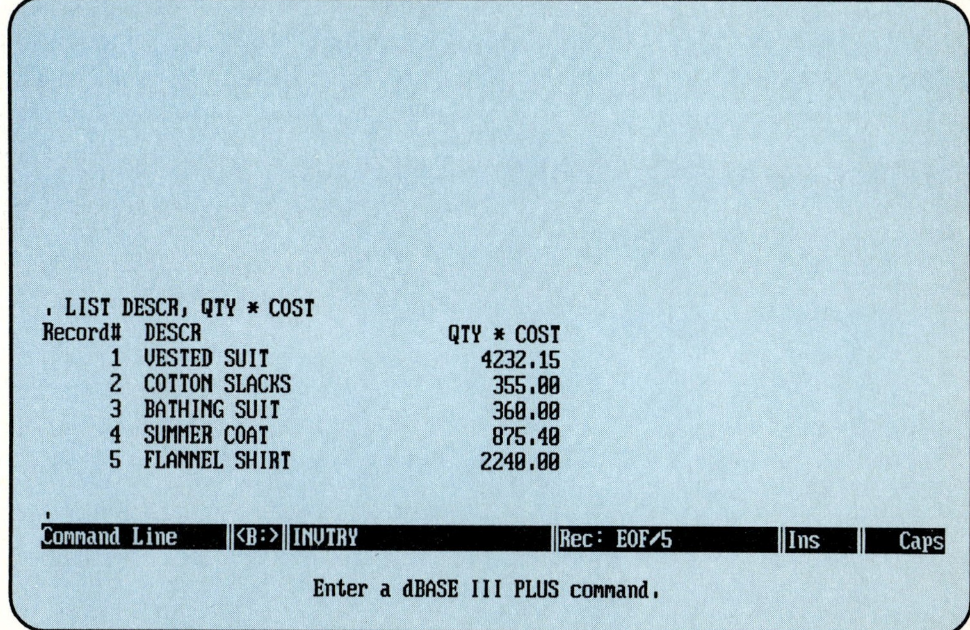

When you have finished viewing your output, CLEAR your screen.

The arithmetic operators displayed in Table T4-8 can be used to create your own arithmetic formulas.

TABLE T4-8
Arithmetic Operators

Operator	Function
( )	Parentheses for grouping
*	Multiplication
/	Division
+	Addition
–	Subtraction

Why don't you try creating a formula? Here is what we want you to do. List all ITEMNOs and profit margins. Profit margins are computed as SELPR – COST.

If you did it correctly, you entered the command LIST ITEMNO, SELPR – COST, and your display should appear as shown in Figure T4-22.

FIGURE T4-22
Listing of Profit Margins.

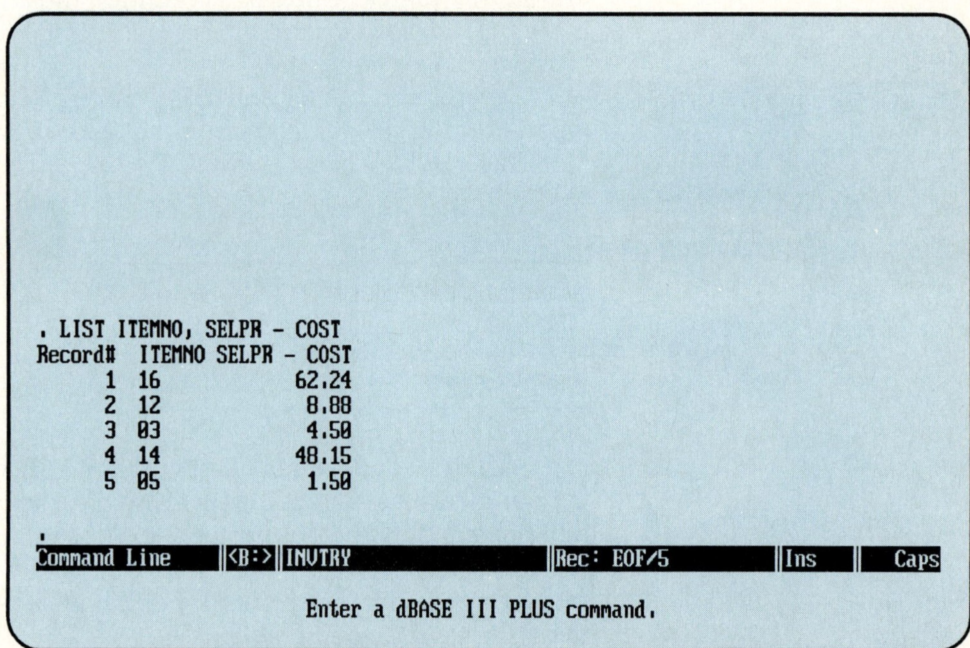

When you have finished viewing your output, CLEAR your screen.

Creating Conditions

Suppose we want to list only those records whose COST exceeds $100. To accomplish this, we must add a **condition** to the LIST command.

A condition specifies a **logical relationship** between two data items of the same type. A data item can be a Numeric field or one or more fields combined into an arithmetic expression or function that evaluates to a numeric value. Data items used in conditions can also be Character, Date, and even Logical fields. Each of the following six data items could be used to form a logical relationship.

400
SELPR – COST
– 10

Notice that a *character value* (value stored in a field of type Character) is preceded and followed by a single quotation mark.

'VESTED SUIT'
DESCR
0

Logical relationships use **logical operators**. The logical operators you can use in conditions are shown in Table T4-9.

TABLE T4-9
Logical Operators

Operator	Condition Being Tested
=	Equal
<	Less than
>	Greater than
<=	Less than or equal to
>=	Greater than or equal to
<>	Not equal to

Thus a condition consists of two data items separated by a logical operator. The **logical value** of a condition must be either *true* or *false*. It is true if the relationship expressed is true; it is false if the relationship expressed is false.

Several conditions and their corresponding logical values are shown next. The logical values shown are based on the field values: DESCR = VESTED SUIT, QTY = 5, PROFIT = 20, SELPR = 100, COST = 50.

Condition	Logical Value
DESCR = 'VESTED SUIT'	True
QTY > 13	False
PROFIT < SELPR – COST	True
SELPR <> 100	False

When a condition is used with a BASE command to specify that only certain records are to be affected by the command, this condition is generally preceded by the keyword **FOR**. For example, a command might contain the condition FOR QTY > 10. The command would then be directed only to those records for which this condition is true—records where the value in the QTY field is greater than 10.

With respect to our earlier problem, to list only those records whose COST exceeds $100 would require the condition

FOR COST > 100

If we include this condition as an option in a LIST command, only those records for which this condition is true will be listed—exactly what we want.

Now let's put what we learned into practice. Let's list only those items that cost more than $100. Enter

and your display should appear as shown in Figure T4-23.

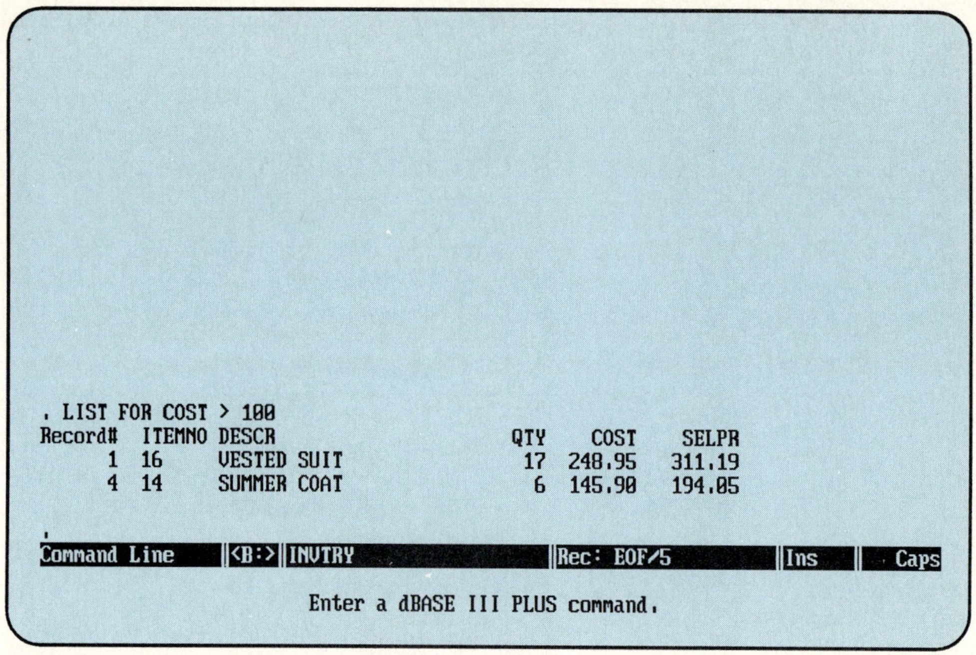

FIGURE T4-23
Screen Produce by LIST Statement with Search Condition.

When you have finished viewing your data, CLEAR your screen.

Now its your turn. List all records whose SELPR is less that $100. Check your results with Figure T4-24.

FIGURE T4-24
LIST with Search Condition of SELPR < 100.

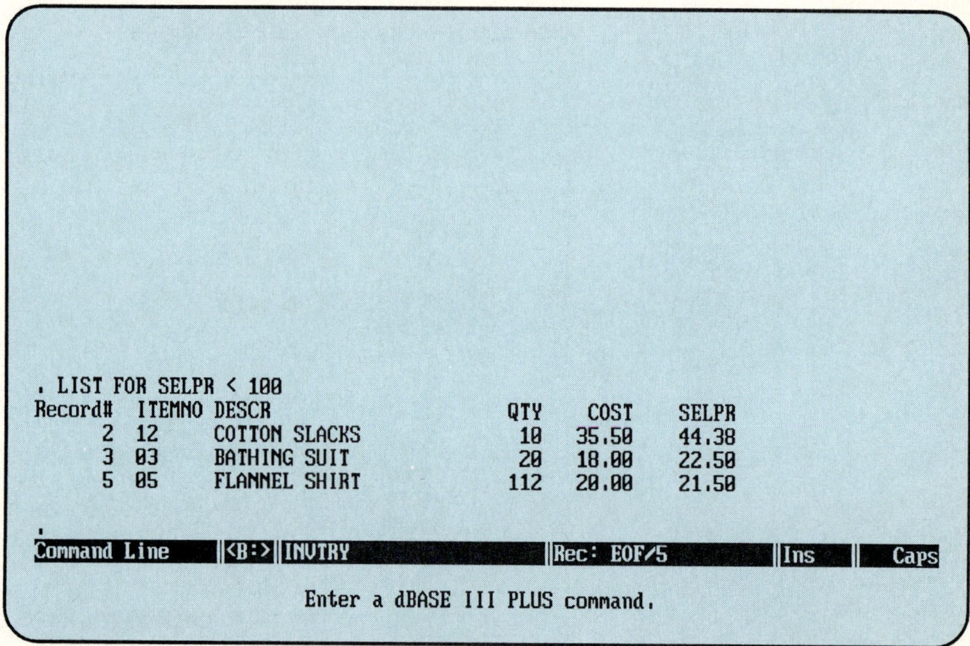

When you have finished viewing your data, CLEAR your screen.

Compound conditions can also be used in dBASE. A **compound condition** is formed from several simple conditions. To form a compound condition, another set of **logical operators** must be used. They are shown in Table T4-10.

TABLE T4-10
Logical Operators

Operator	Function
( )	Parentheses for grouping
.NOT.	Boolean not
.AND.	Boolean and
.OR.	Boolean or

Let's try one. Type

❑

How about trying another? Enter

.LIST OFF ITEMNO, DESCR FOR ITEMNO = '05' .OR. QTY < 15 ❑

The output from the preceding two commands is shown in Figure T4-25.

FIGURE T4-25
Screens Produced by LIST Commands.

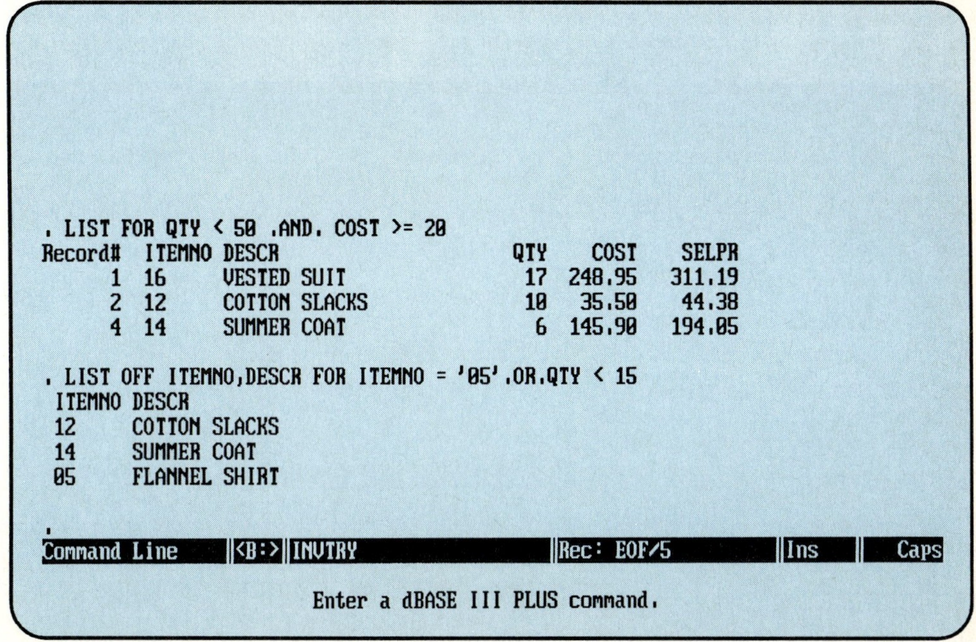

```
. LIST FOR QTY < 50 .AND. COST >= 20
Record#  ITEMNO DESCR                          QTY    COST   SELPR
      1  16     VESTED SUIT                     17  240.95  311.19
      2  12     COTTON SLACKS                   10   35.50   44.38
      4  14     SUMMER COAT                      6  145.90  194.05

. LIST OFF ITEMNO,DESCR FOR ITEMNO = '05'.OR.QTY < 15
 ITEMNO DESCR
 12     COTTON SLACKS
 14     SUMMER COAT
 05     FLANNEL SHIRT

.
Command Line  ||<B:>||INVTRY          ||Rec: EOF/5        ||Ins   ||  Caps

                     Enter a dBASE III PLUS command.
```

The reason we used '05' instead of '5' is because we defined ITEMNO to be a two-position Character field (enclosed within quotes). A '5' is the same as '5 '.

Before moving on, let's clean up our screen. Enter

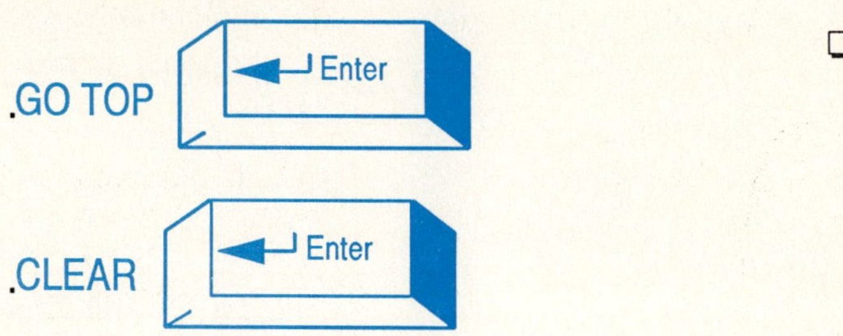

Printing Your File

If at any time you would like a printout of your database file or structure, you can obtain it with just a few keystrokes. All you would have to do is turn on your printer and type

^P

From this point on, and until you type another ^P to cancel, everything displayed on the screen will be echoed to the printer. For example,

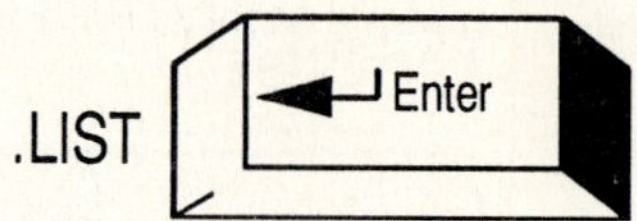

would both display and print each record in your database. To turn off the print echo, you would enter

.^P

A second method of getting a printout is to *append* the keywords **TO PRINT** to the dBASE command from which you want printed output. For example, to get printed copy of the output from the command, you would enter

. LIST FOR COST > 100

Before you attempt to print, be sure that your printer is on-line. Also, if your computer shares a printer with other computers, you may be connected to a printer switch box. If so, be sure the switch box is set for your computer.

Turn on your printer and enter

You will immediately hear your printer tapping out the results.

Arithmetic Operations on a Database File

Earlier we saw that dBASE can perform arithmetic operations on numeric data fields. Now we can use this capability to determine the value of one field by using an expression and the values contained in one or more other fields. For example, we could instruct dBASE to multiply COST by 1.25 and store the product in SELPR for *each* record in the INVTRY database.

Let's do it. Enter

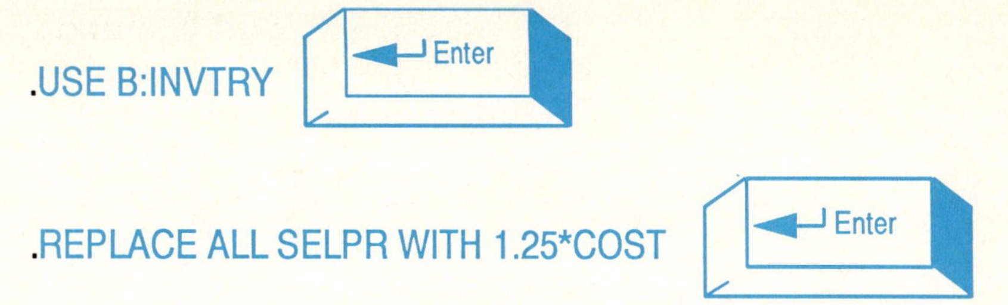

dBASE displays

```
5 records replaced
```

To see the changes, enter

The results are shown in Figure T4-26. When you have finished viewing your data, CLEAR your screen.

FIGURE T4-26
Listing of INVTRY File After Executing the Command REPLACE ALL SELPR WITH 1.25*COST.

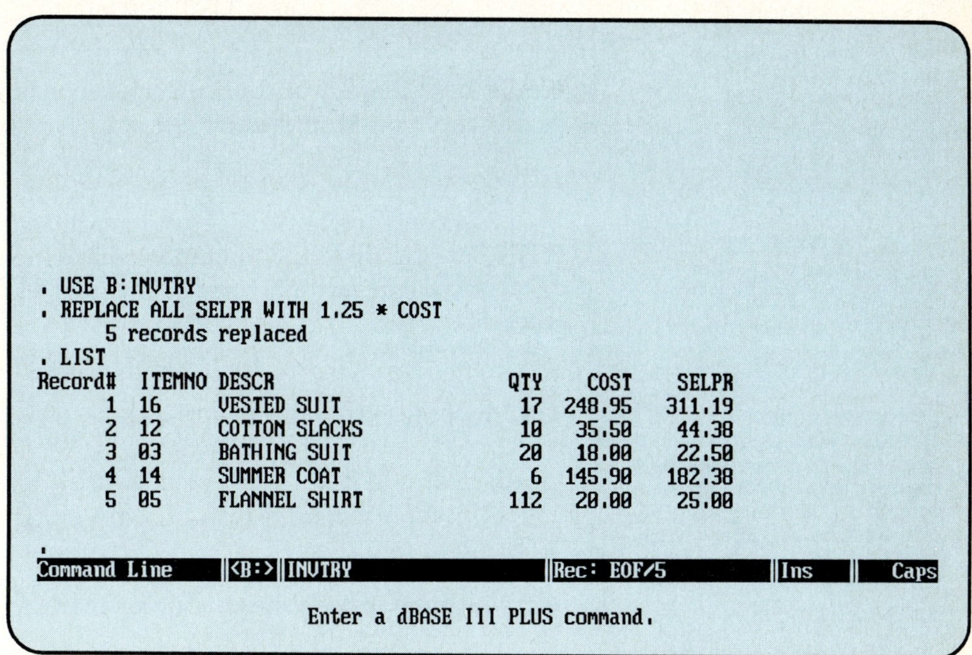

```
. USE B:INVTRY
. REPLACE ALL SELPR WITH 1.25 * COST
      5 records replaced
. LIST
Record#  ITEMNO DESCR                  QTY    COST    SELPR
      1  16     VESTED SUIT             17  248.95   311.19
      2  12     COTTON SLACKS           10   35.50    44.38
      3  03     BATHING SUIT            20   18.00    22.50
      4  14     SUMMER COAT              6  145.90   182.38
      5  05     FLANNEL SHIRT          112   20.00    25.00

.
Command Line   <B:> INVTRY             Rec: EOF/5       Ins     Caps
                       Enter a dBASE III PLUS command.
```

Here we specified that SELPR was to be replaced in ALL cases. By eliminating the keyword ALL, we could reduce the effect of the command to the extent that it would apply to only one record, the current record as specified in the status bar. We can also confine the effects of the REPLACE command to only those records satisfying one or more conditions, as we did earlier with the LIST and DISPLAY commands. Let's look at some examples. Enter

.REPLACE SELPR WITH 1.20*COST– 2.00 FOR ITEMNO = '05' ❑

You should see

```
1 record replaced
```

To verify the results of this replacement, enter

.LIST ❑

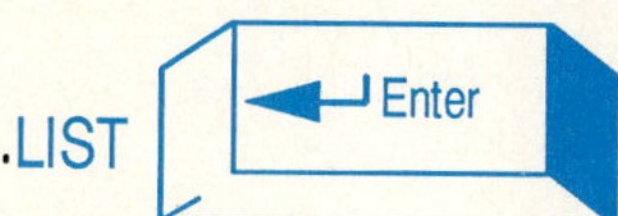

Try another example. Enter

.REPLACE SELPR WITH 1.25*COST FOR QTY <= 20 ❑

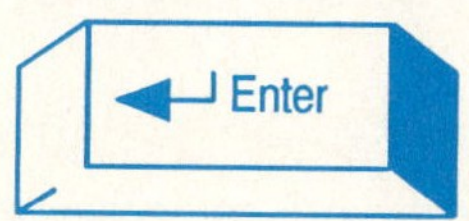

and you should see

```
4 records replaced
```

Enter

.LIST ❑

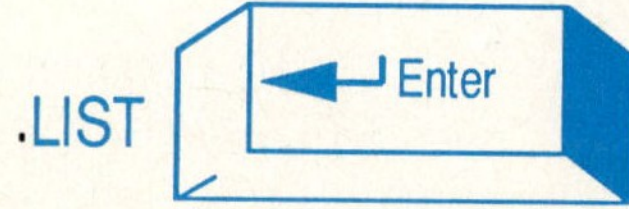

and verify the replacements.

Now, let's return our database to its original form. Do you remember how to change the contents of records? You could use either the EDIT or BROWSE command to change the SELPR value in each record to the one shown next.

ITEMNO	SELPR
16	311.19
12	44.38
03	22.50
14	194.05
05	21.50

Begin with Record 1. Enter

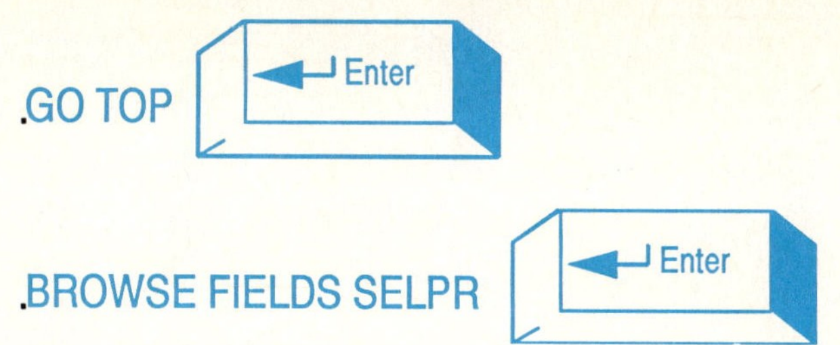

Now, restore all records to the values listed previously. When you reach the end, you may be asked if you want to *Add new records*. If necessary type N. To save your changes, enter

^W means press and hold the [Ctrl] key and tap the W.

^W

CLEAR your screen.

The SUM Command

The **SUM** command is used to instruct dBASE to total the values in one or more fields. For example, enter the statement

and all the COST values and all the SELPR values will be summed. The sums will be displayed as follows:

```
5 records summed

  COST      SELPR
468.35     593.62
```

As with the REPLACE command, we can specify a *FOR condition* with a SUM command. For example, the scope of the command

```
.SUM COST, SELPR FOR QTY > 10
```

would total the COST and SELPR fields of all records FOR which the QTY > 10.

Before moving on, enter

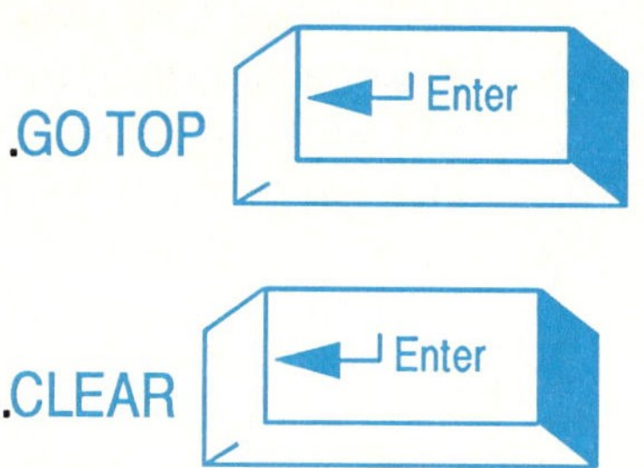

Creating a Database Filter

We saw earlier that we can specify a FOR condition in the LIST, DISPLAY, REPLACE, and SUM commands. Sometimes, however, it becomes necessary to apply the same condition to a sequence of commands. In these cases, it is not always possible to include the FOR condition in each command. The solution is to use the **SET FILTER** command to establish the condition. Once a condition has been established by a SET FILTER command, it will remain in effect and apply to each command issued subsequently until it is changed or withdrawn by another SET FILTER command.

For example, enter the command

Let's verify that it worked. Enter

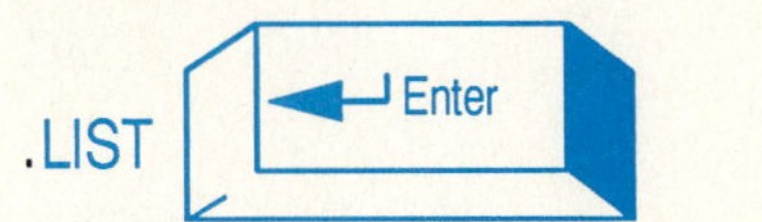

You should see the same records listed that are shown in Figure T4-23.

To remove a filter, enter

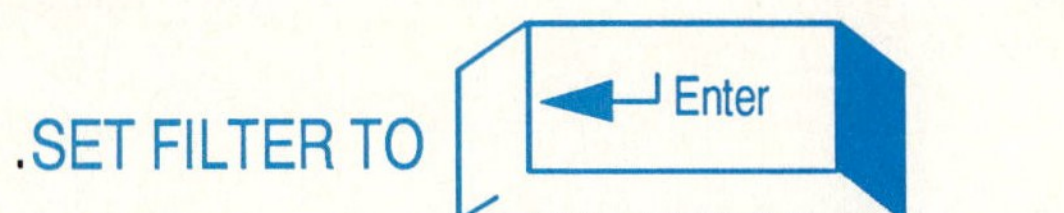

with no condition specified. Now, CLEAR your screen.

Sorting or Indexing a Database File

dBASE allows the user to sort or order the records within a file. Records can be put in alphabetic, numeric, or chronological order. dBASE provides two commands that can be used to order a file, **SORT** and **INDEX.** Both cause new files to be created, but the contents of these newly created files are somewhat different.

The SORT command creates an entirely *new database* file containing the same records but in ascending sequence (unless DESCENDING is specified) by the key field specified. INDEX, on the other hand, creates a *new index* file containing only the record numbers from the original file and an *index* for each record. The index reflects the position of the corresponding record in the ordered database file. Only ascending sequence is possible with the INDEX command. If, for example, Record 00005 were assigned an index of 3, this would mean that Record 00005 is the third record in the ordered sequence. Note that the newly created index file contains no data other than record numbers and their corresponding index numbers. Thus an index file must always be processed in conjunction with a database file, which contains the actual data fields. The file produced by SORT may be processed without the original database file, since it contains all the data fields. Changes made to a database with an APPEND command will be reflected automatically in the index file if it is in use at the time of the change. This is not the case with files produced by the SORT command. If the database is added to or deleted from, a new sort file must be created in order to reflect these additions or deletions.

The SORT Command

Now let's look at the SORT command. We said earlier that the SORT command physically rewrites the data records. As a result, a second, sorted file is created and must have a different name. The only difference between the original and the sorted file is that the sorted file will be in ascending order based on the key field selected. Let's get some practice sorting our records. Make certain the disk in the B:, or default, drive contains the INVTRY.DBF file. Now, enter

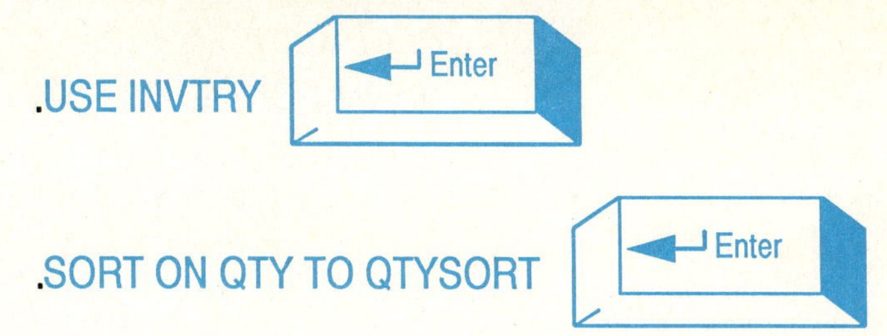

dBASE responds with

```
        100% Sorted          5 Records sorted
```

We can now list the new sorted file. Enter

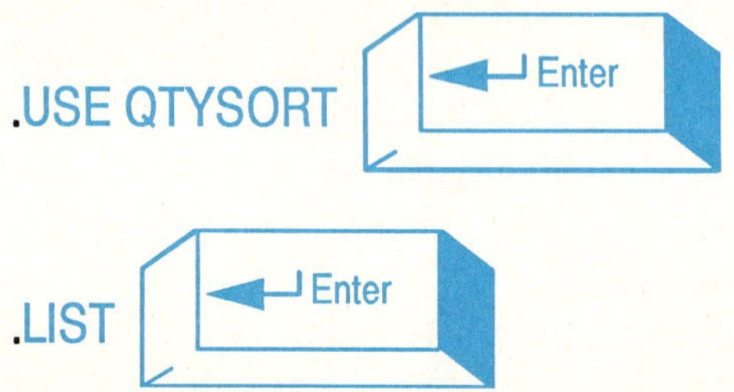

Compare your results with those shown in Figure T4-27.

FIGURE T4-27
Listing of INVTRY File Sorted into Sequence by QTY.

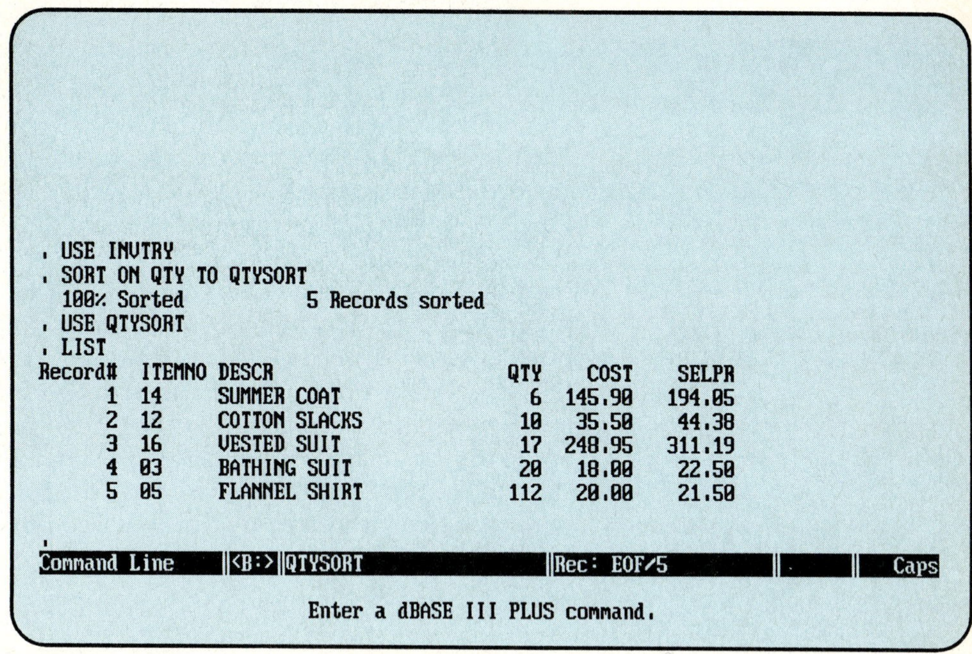

```
. USE INVTRY
. SORT ON QTY TO QTYSORT
  100% Sorted           5 Records sorted
. USE QTYSORT
. LIST
Record#  ITEMNO DESCR                    QTY    COST   SELPR
      1  14     SUMMER COAT                6  145.90  194.05
      2  12     COTTON SLACKS             10   35.50   44.38
      3  16     VESTED SUIT               17  248.95  311.19
      4  03     BATHING SUIT              20   18.00   22.50
      5  05     FLANNEL SHIRT            112   20.00   21.50
.
Command Line    ||<B:>||QTYSORT          ||Rec: EOF/5     ||      ||    Caps
                    Enter a dBASE III PLUS command.
```

When you have finished viewing your data, CLEAR your screen.

The INDEX Command

Let's experiment with the INDEX command. Assume that we wish to set up an index file for our database file INVTRY and that the key field is to be ITEMNO. Enter

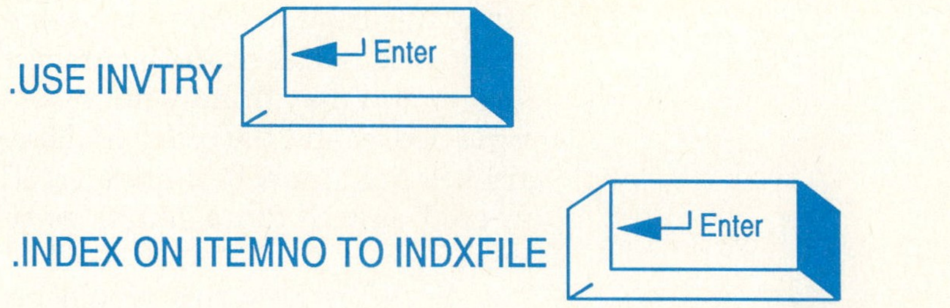

and dBASE will respond with

```
100% indexed          5 Records indexed
```

The new index file will be stored under the name INDXFILE.NDX on the disk in drive B:. Remember, you may not use this index file without the original database because it contains only a record number and index number for each record in the file.

Let's list our original file INVTRY in key field (ITEMNO) sequence. Enter

The results are shown in Figure T4-28.

FIGURE T4-28
Listing of Indexed INVTRY File.

```
. USE INVTRY
. INDEX ON ITEMNO TO INDXFILE
  100% indexed          5 Records indexed
. USE INVTRY INDEX INDXFILE
. LIST
Record#  ITEMNO DESCR                      QTY    COST   SELPR
      3  03     BATHING SUIT                20   18.00   22.50
      5  05     FLANNEL SHIRT              112   20.00   21.50
      2  12     COTTON SLACKS               10   35.50   44.38
      4  14     SUMMER COAT                  6  145.90  194.05
      1  16     VESTED SUIT                 17  248.95  311.19
.
Command Line  ||<B:>||INVTRY             ||Rec: EOF/5       ||Ins  ||  Caps

                    Enter a dBASE III PLUS command.
```

dBASE does not support INDEXing fields in descending order. This doesn't stop us from INDEXing in descending order. To index a Numeric field in descending order, create the index file with the key (numeric) field multiplied by -1. For example, we could enter INDEX ON -1*SELPR TO SELDESC. This creates an index file that, when listed, will display the record having the largest SELPR first and the record having the smallest SELPR last.

CLEAR your screen.

When sorting or indexing a file, one should always consider the possibility that two or more records may have the same key field value. In some cases, this is impossible—for example, if the key field in a payroll file is the employees' social security number. However, in other cases this is a real possibility and may or may not be of concern. If duplicate key field values are a possibility and the order of the concerned elements is important, a secondary key field must be stipulated. This secondary key field value will be considered only in those situations when the primary key field values are the same.

Let's see how this would be handled. For example, suppose that we wish to index INVTRY on the key field DESCR. Should there be two fields with the same description, index them on ITEMNO. We could accomplish all this by entering the statements

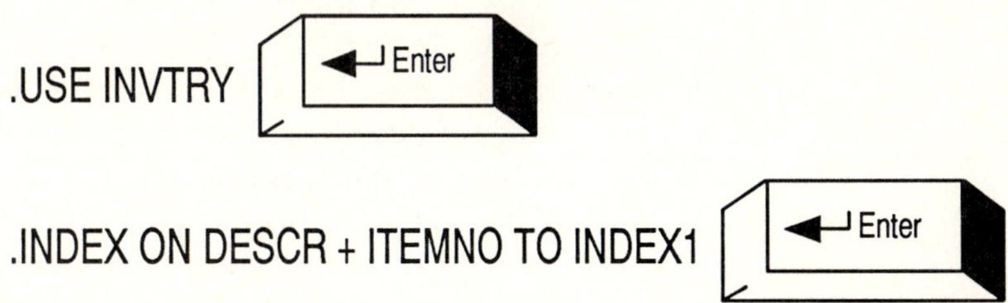

Activating an INDEX File

Sometimes, we already may have selected the database and only need to activate an index file or change the index file if a database is associated with more than one index. This can be accomplished with the SET INDEX TO command. For example, SET INDEX TO INDXFILE will activate INDXFILE for the database file currently in use. To restore the natural order of the database, enter SET INDEX TO without specifying an index file name. Enter

SET INDEX TO {INDEX file name} command can be only used when the database to which the INDEXed file applies is already active.

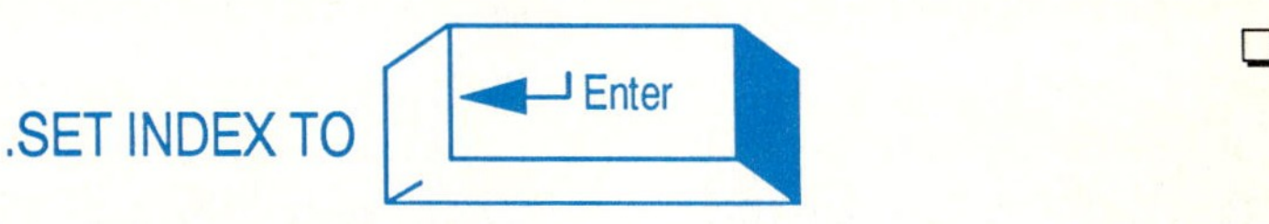

Locating Records in an INDEXed File

A major benefit of an indexed file is that it allows you to use the **FIND** command. For example, on typing

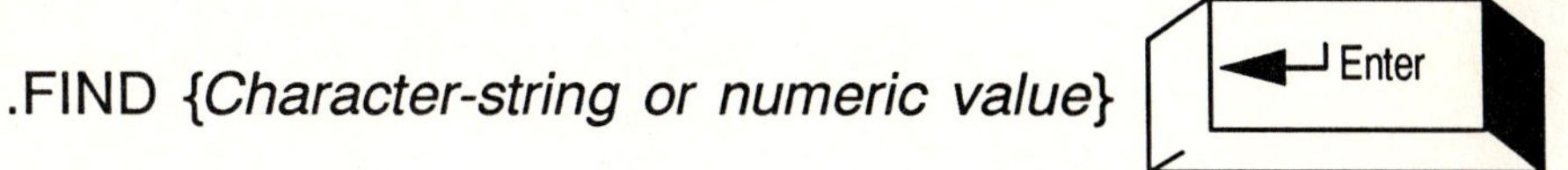

where *character-string* is all or the first part of a field, dBASE will search for the matching record from within the indexed field. However, for this command to work, an index file must be in use and its index key field must be the one you are searching. The **SEEK** command is similar to the FIND command except that it can be used with any valid expression. Enter

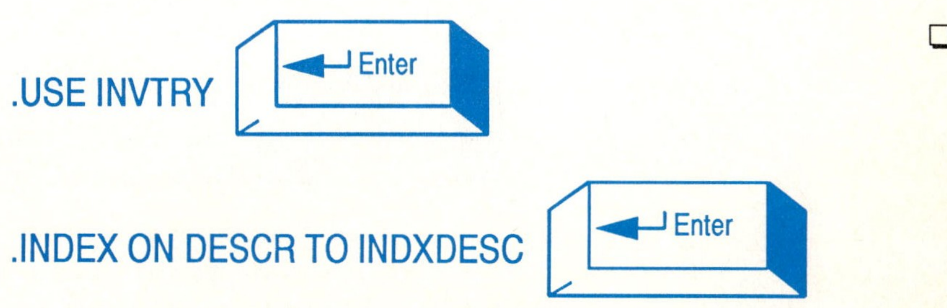

to which dBASE will respond

```
100% INDEXED    5 RECORDS INDEXED
```

Now, enter

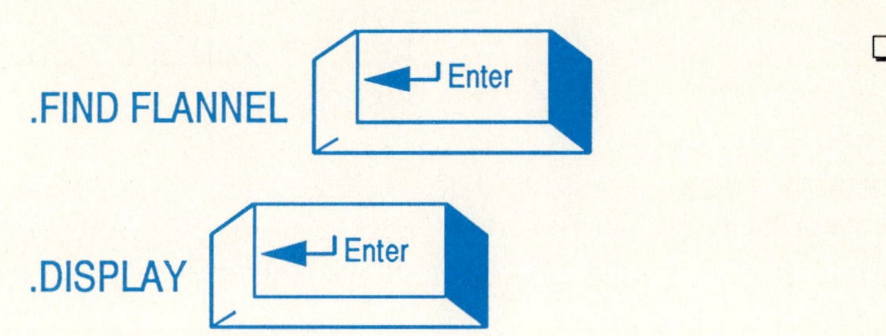

You should now see Record 5 displayed.

Note that if Flannel, flannel, or any other combination of uppercase and lowercase characters except FLANNEL had been entered, dBASE would have issued a *No Find* message. This is simply because when we entered the data originally, we used all uppercase letters. dBASE will find only an *exact* match.

The **LOCATE** command can be used with database files that are not indexed. With LOCATE, you must specify a valid search condition. For example, LOCATE FOR DESCR = 'BATHING SUIT' will move the record pointer to Record 3. However, unlike the FIND and SEEK commands, you cannot specify part of the field value for which you are searching. You must specify the entire and exact value. That is, the command LOCATE FOR DESCR = 'FLANNEL' would produce a *No Find* message. Also, the LOCATE command is extremely slow when compared with the FIND or SEEK commands. When speed is necessary, use FIND or SEEK over LOCATE. But don't forget that to use FIND or SEEK, the database file must be indexed and the *key* index field must also be the *search* field.

To Sort or To Index

In summary, there are advantages and disadvantages to both sorting and indexing. Indexing allows for a substantial savings in storage space compared to sorting and can be completed three to four times faster than sorting. Indexing also allows for the FIND and SEEK commands and for the addition or deletion of records to be reflected automatically in the index file. Still, there are situations where sorting is preferred over indexing. An example would be when you need to access each record in turn, as in printing labels. It is faster to use a file that has already been sorted into the desired sequence because all the records are physically in that order. dBASE has to perform fewer disk operations to retrieve the sorted records.

At this point enter

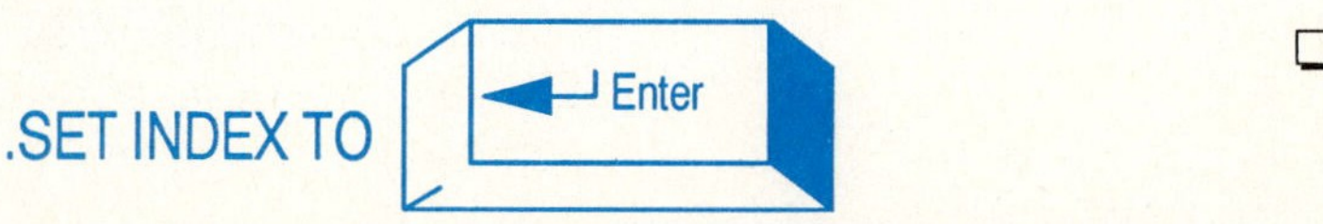

If you want to take a break, enter QUIT and press the [Enter] key. When you return, start your computer, press the [Caps Lock] key, start dBASE, set the default drive to your default drive (use SET DEFAULT TO), and then continue reading.

Generating a Report

To generate standardized reports, dBASE provides a **report generator**. This feature can take care of virtually all your report needs. To see how the REPORT generator works, let's create a report with the layout shown in Figure T4-29.

FIGURE T4-29
Layout for a Sample Report.

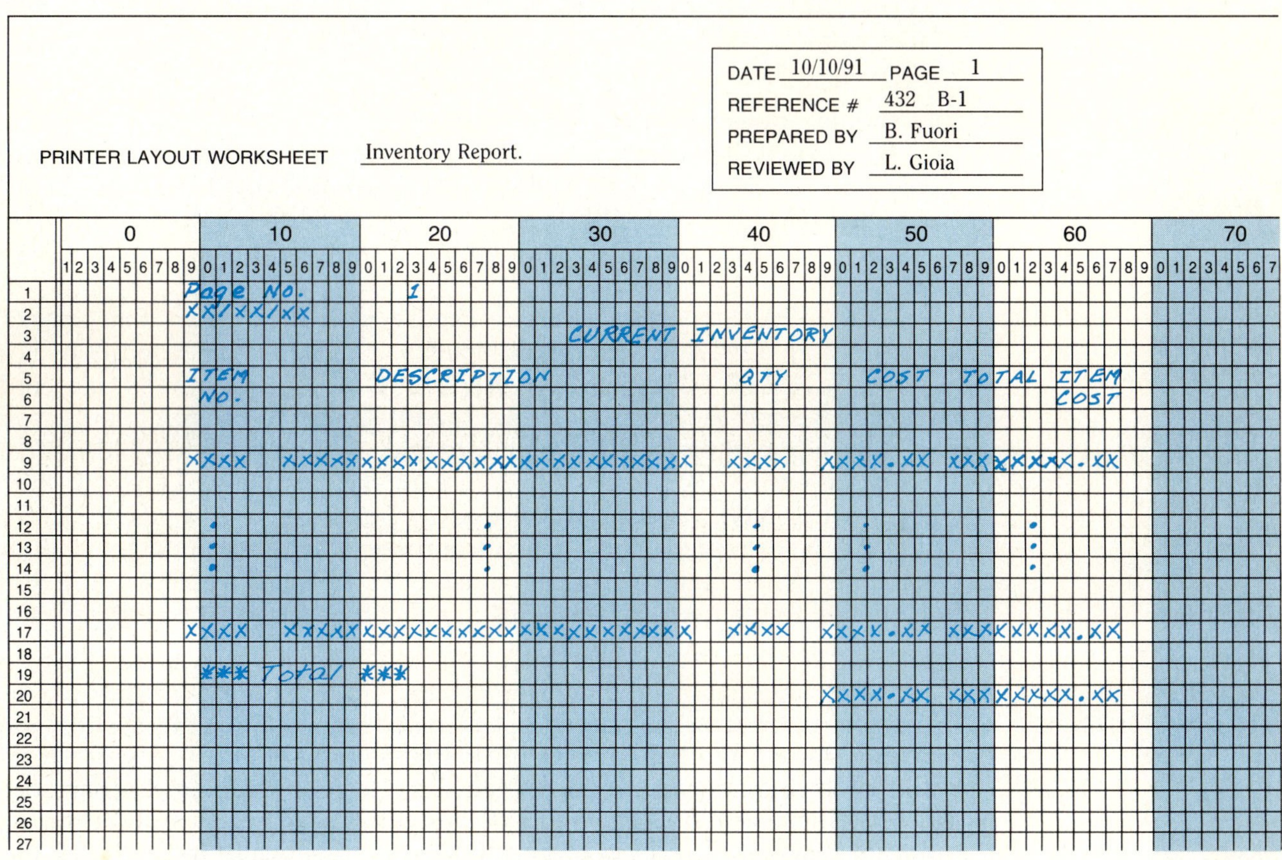

Calling dBASE's Report Generator

As with creating a database file, a **CREATE** command must be used to create a report file. Begin by typing

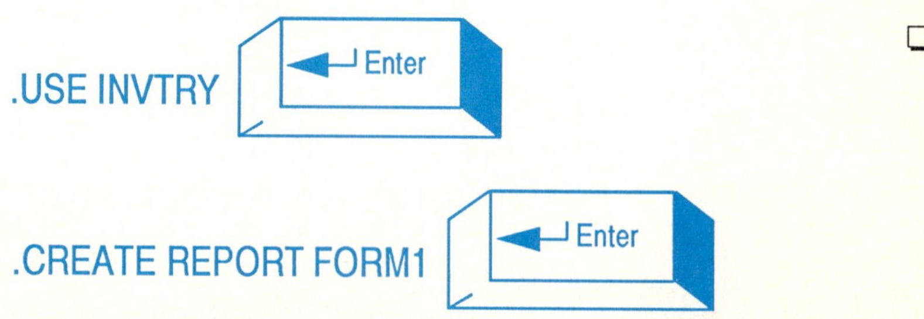

The **CREATE REPORT** command will access dBASE's report generator, a feature that allows you to define the report's structure and guides you step by step through the process. The results will be stored in the report form file FORM1.FRM.

Laying Out Your Report

dBASE confirms access to the report generator by presenting the screen shown in Figure T4-30. We will use this screen to describe the general layout of our report.

FIGURE T4-30
The Initial Report Generator Screen.

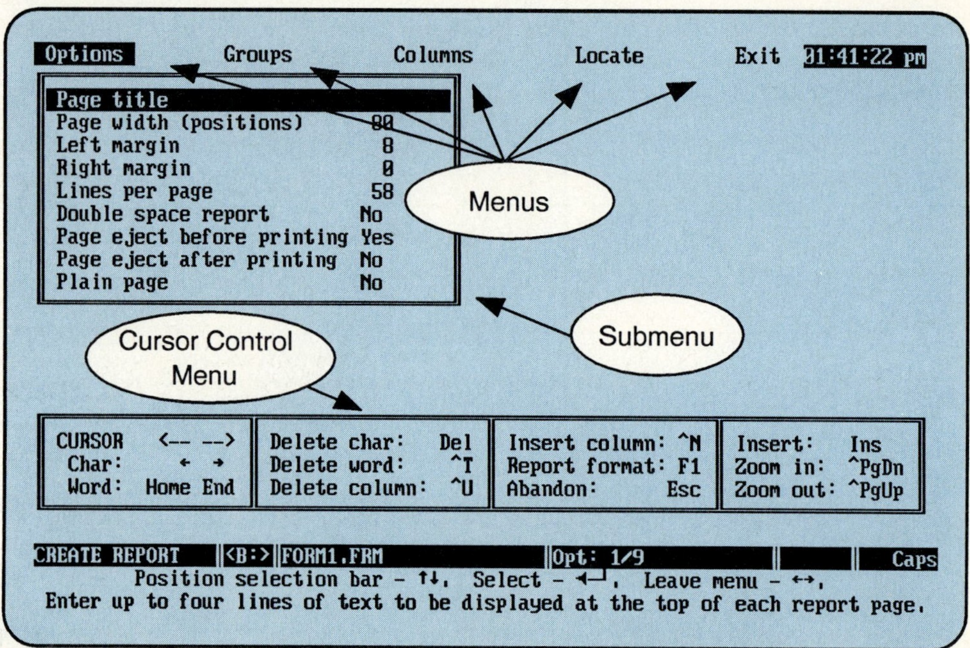

Moving Around

The Left and Right Arrow keys are used to choose among the menu options appearing at the top of the screen, and the Up and Down Arrow keys are used to select items from the corresponding submenus. Experiment. Move the menu cursor to each menu and the submenu cursor to each submenu item. Then return the cursors to the position shown in Figure T4-30.

Did you notice that the bottom window changed? The window at the bottom of your display changed from the *Cursor-control* help menu to the *Report Format* help menu. This is shown in Figure T4-31.

The *Report Format* help window is currently blank because we have not entered any titles or structure for the report. The [F1] Function key toggles between the *Report Format* and the *Cursor-Control* windows. Depress

❑

and observe how the Cursor-control window toggles in an out. The other way to change the window is by moving around with the Arrow keys.

Entering a Title

The first item on the Options submenu is *Page title.* Make certain the submenu cursor is positioned over Page title and press

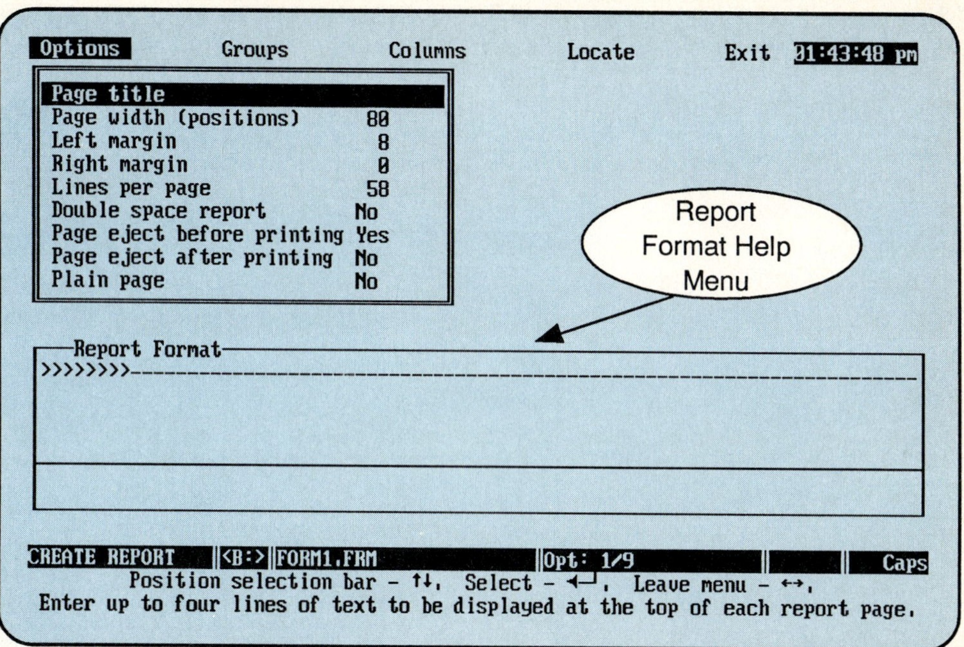

FIGURE T4-31
The Initial Report Generator Screen After Moving Around with the Arrow Keys.

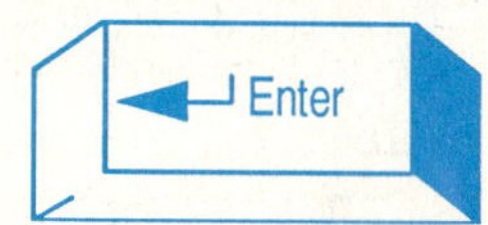

This tells dBASE you want to enter a page title. A small *Print-title* window, into which you type your report title, appears at the right, and a large Report Format help window appears at the bottom of the display. Remember, the Report Format window can be replaced by the Cursor-control at any time by simply depressing the [F1] Function key. The Print-title window, at the right of the screen, provides space for a four-line title and will pan right to accommodate longer entries (up to 254 characters). dBASE will automatically center the title.

Type

CURRENT INVENTORY

but *do not* press the [Enter] key. Your screen should now appear as shown in Figure T4-32.

Don't worry about making errors while typing. You can always correct them later by using the MODIFY REPORT command.

The instructions at the bottom of this screen *(Exit - Ctrl-End)* direct us to press and hold the [Ctrl] key and tap the [End] key to exit this operation. Therefore, enter

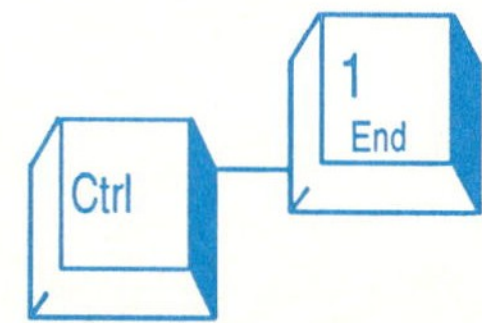

The report generator uses the same cursor commands throughout: [Enter] to select an option and [Ctrl]-[End] or [Enter] to finish the option and return you to the submenu. [Ctrl]-[End] is used with titles and headings, and [Enter] is used with all other entries.

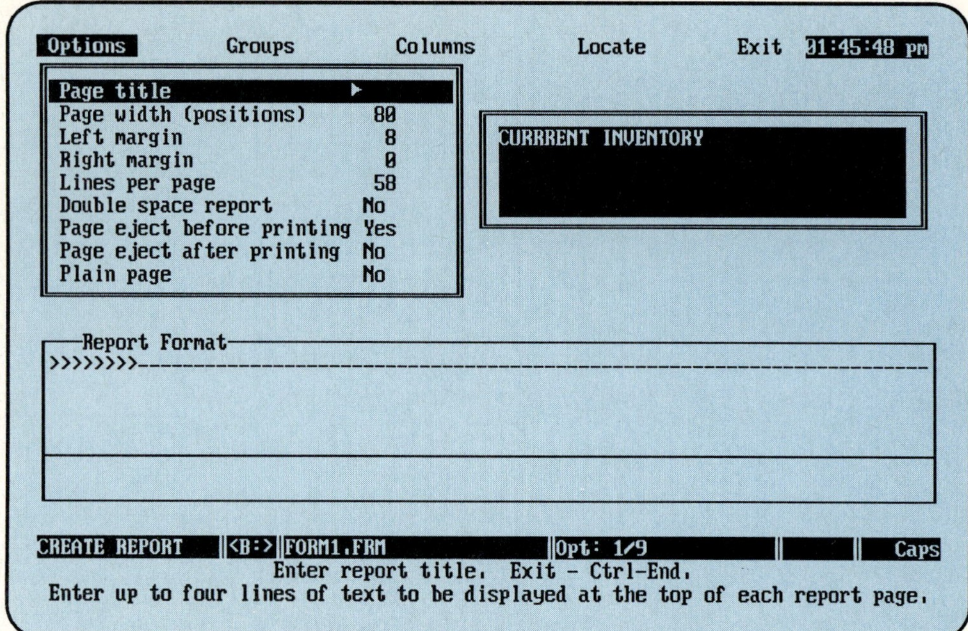

FIGURE T4-32
The Page Title Report Generator Screen

Page Numbers and the Date

dBASE automatically places the page number on the first line of each report page and the date on the next line. No entry is required by you to activate this feature.

Changing Other Initial Screen Values

Page width can be changed if you have a 132-character printer or if your printer is capable of printing in a compressed mode. For our purposes, the 80-position default value is satisfactory.

The *Left margin* and *Right margin* options are generally left at the 8 and 0 settings until the report layout is completed and you know how much space is used for data and how much remains for margins. However, since we know this information now (see Fig. T4-29), let's practice and set the right margin to 8. To do this now, move the cursor down to Right margin and enter

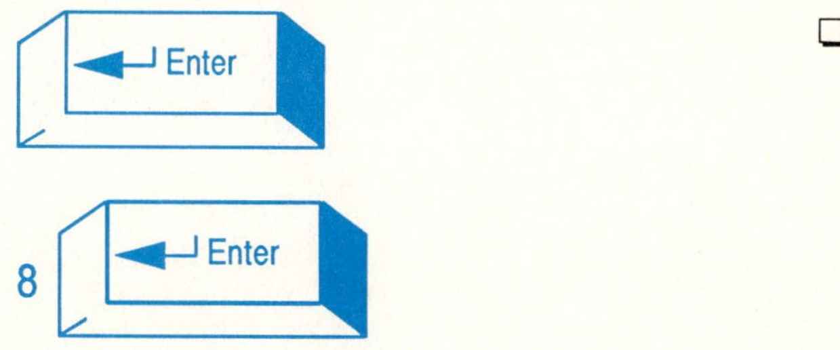

❑

The *lines per page* default value of 58 provides 6 lines per inch, the standard for most printers.

The *Double space report* default is *No*. This value can be changed by pressing the [Enter] key. To double-space our report, simply move the cursor to Double space report and press

The *Page eject before printing* and *Page eject after printing* options are self-explanatory. Leave them unchanged.

Plain page is set to *No* and should remain so unless the output is to be directed to the screen only. If you have a printer available, leave this option unchanged; otherwise, move the cursor to Plain page and press the [Enter] key.

The final screen should appear as shown in Figure T4-33.

FIGURE T4-33
The Report Generator Options Screen After the Last Field Has Been Specified.

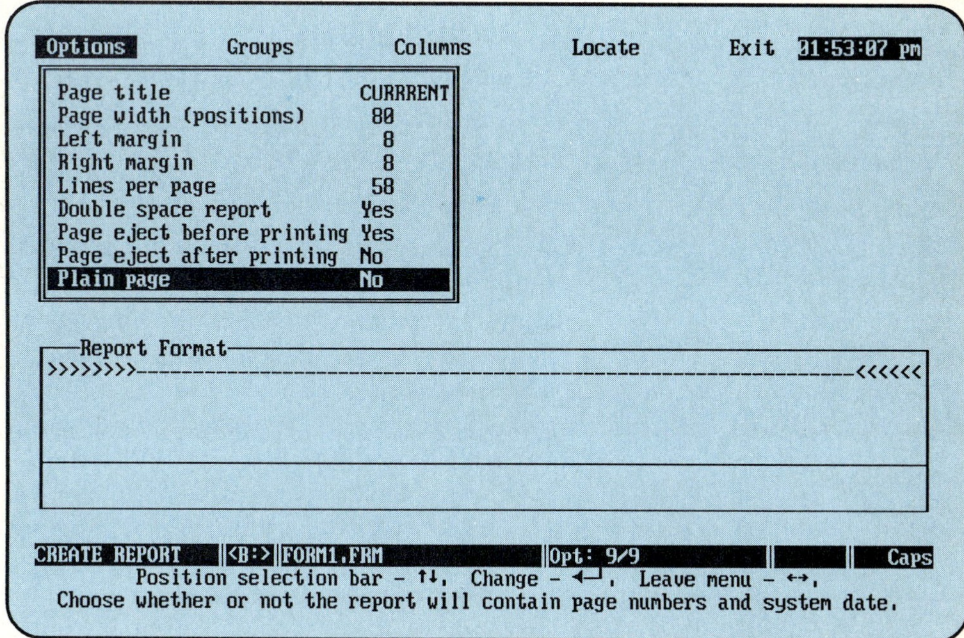

Report Groups

This option is used when you desire to present separately one or more groups (and subgroups, if desired) of selected records within a report. The records to be selected are those containing the same information in one or more specified fields—for example, group all records having a description beginning with SHIRTS. Since this feature is most useful in reports applied to large databases containing many fields, we will not discuss it further in this tutorial.

Report Columns

The Column menu allows you to specify the contents, headings, width, and totals to be included in each column in the report. To access this menu, move the menu cursor to *Columns* by pressing

You should see a screen containing a Column submenu and a Report Format window at the bottom (see Fig. T4-34).

FIGURE T4-34
The Columns Report Generator Screen.

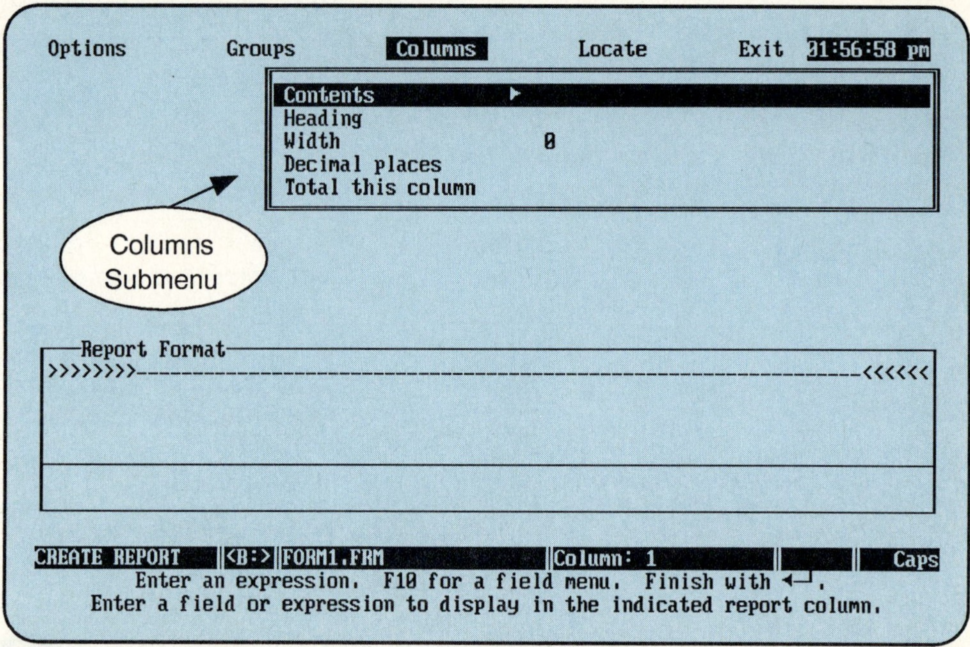

Column Contents

To enter the contents for our first column, position the submenu cursor on *Contents* and press

❑

Observe the arrowhead pointing to the entry area at the right. If you need more space than is provided in this area, the area will automatically pan to the right. The contents of a column can be a single field or an expression involving several fields. For example, the expression

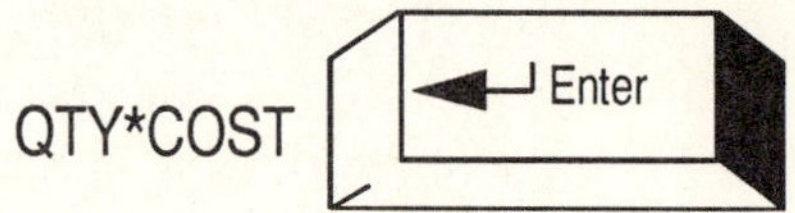

would place the product of the QTY and COST field values in this column, whereas the expression

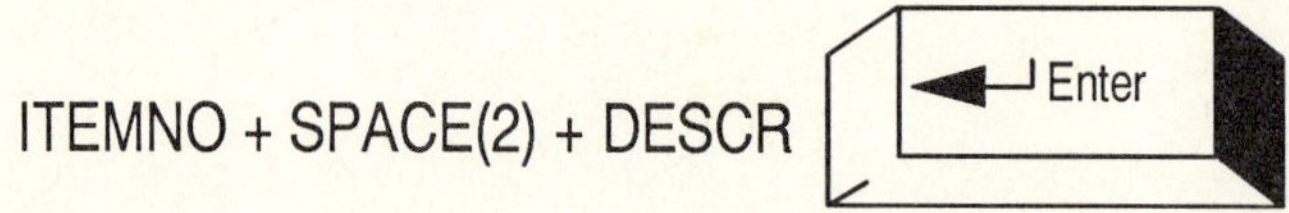

would establish a 30-position field consisting of the item number (4 positions), two spaces, and the item description (24 positions).

For our inventory report, the first column is to contain item numbers (see Fig. T4-29). Therefore, all we need do is enter

ITEMNO 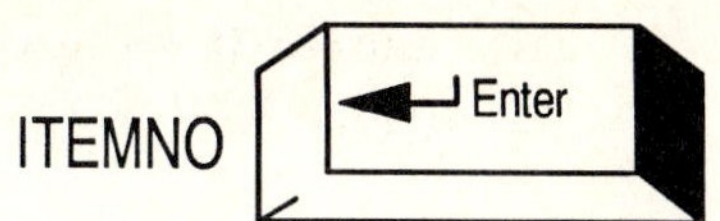

However, if we need help in recalling field names or descriptions for the file in use, simply press

which will produce the screen shown in Figure T4-35.

FIGURE T4-35
The Columns Report Generator Field-Name Menu.

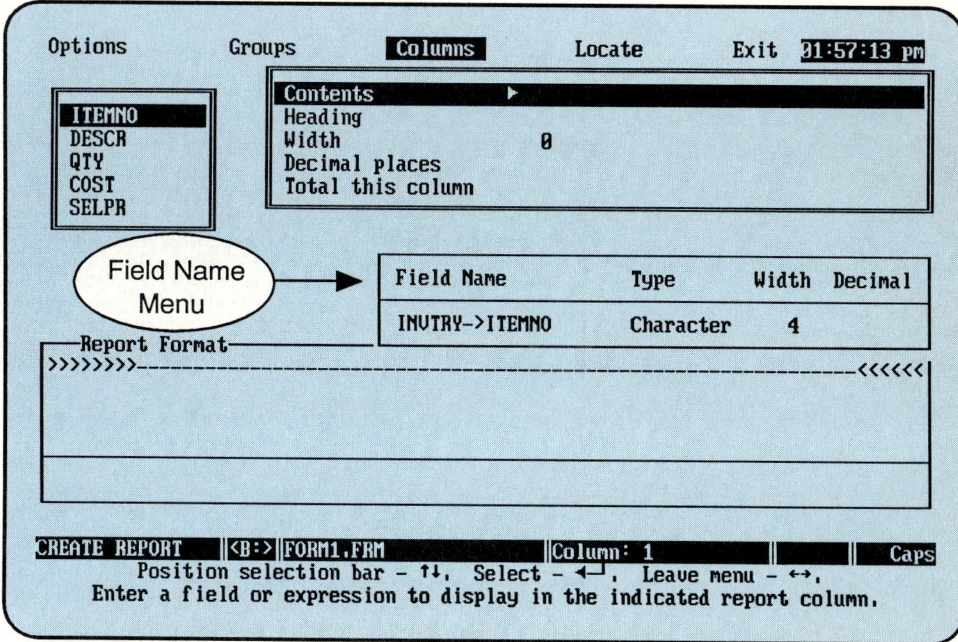

From this screen we can select any field within the database in use (INVTRY.DBF). We can also leave the field-name menu by pressing either the Right or Left Arrow keys.

Use the Up and Down Arrow keys as necessary to move the field-menu cursor to ITEMNO and press the [Enter] key. This will cause **ITEMNO** to be entered automatically as it will cause the field contents and the field-name menu to be exited. Complete the entry by pressing

Press the Down Arrow key once to move the submenu cursor to *Heading.* Then press

This will bring up a column-heading window. Enter the two-line column title

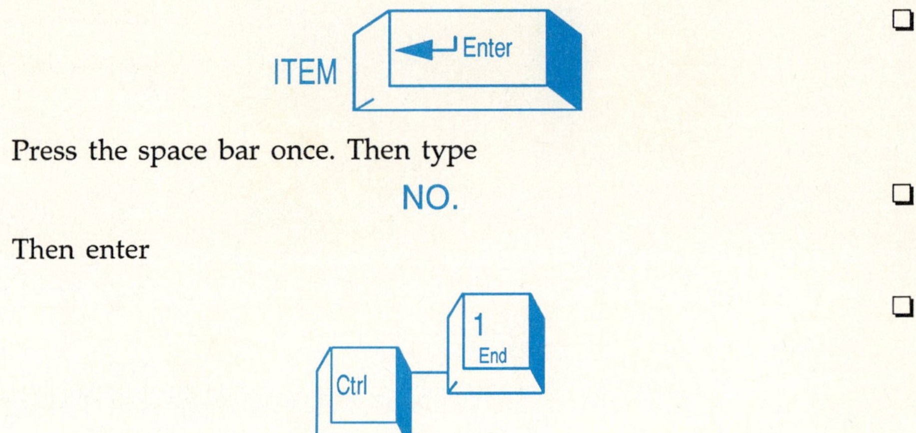

Press the space bar once. Then type

NO.

Then enter

Observe in Figure T4-36 that the column heading you just entered appears in the Report Format window.

FIGURE T4-36
The Columns Display After the First Column Heading Has Been Entered.

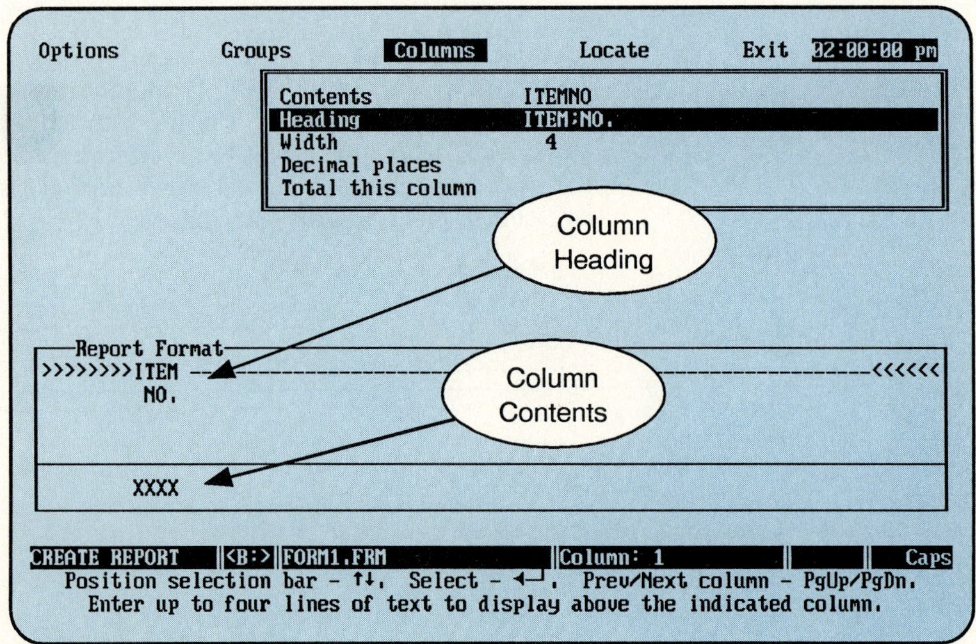

Press the Down Arrow key to move the submenu cursor to *Width*. dBASE determines the field width needed to accommodate the largest possible item and automatically enters it. You can override this width, if desired, by pressing the Up Arrow key (to increase it) or the Down Arrow key (to decrease it). You might want to adjust the field width when the data contained in a field occupies fewer positions than the field width provides space for or when more space is needed to accommodate a column total or separate the column from the column before or after.

Increase the field width from 4 to 5 positions by entering

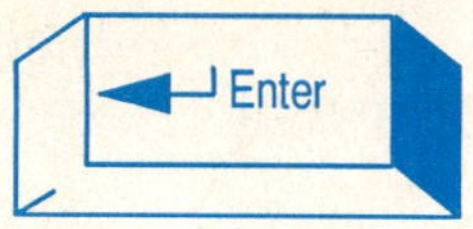

5

Then press

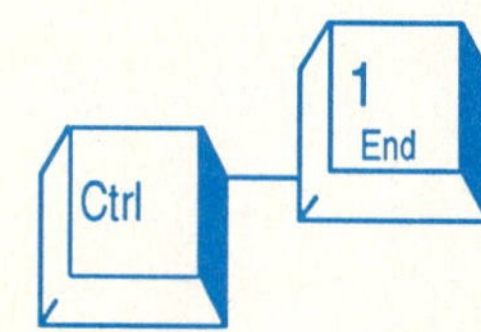

This provides two spaces at the end of the field (character data is left-justified in a field) as a separator between this column and the description column. dBase will automatically provide a space between columns.

Our first column is now completed. Proceed to the next column by depressing

Complete the remaining column entries on your own by referring to Figure T4-29 and Table T4-11. Remember that (1) headings in numeric fields are always right-justified; (2) the contents of the fifth column must be expressed as QTY*COST; (3) to activate an option, the cursor must be placed on it and the [Enter] key pressed; and (4) the [Ctrl]-[End] keys must be pressed to save an entry and move on.

TABLE T4-11
Column Entries for Report Form Form1

	Column 1	Column 2	Column 3	Column 4	Column 5
Contents	: ITEMNO	: DESCR	: QTY	: COST	: QTY*COST
Heading	: ITEM bNO.	: bbbbbbDESCRIPTION	: QTY	: bbbCOST	: bTOTALbITEM bbbbbbbCOST
Width	: 5	: 26	: 4	: 7	: 11
Decimal places			: 0	: 2	: 2
Total this column			: NO	: YES	: YES

Note: b refers to a blank space.

After entering Column 5, if your screen appears as shown in Figure T4-37, you're doing wonderfully.

The meaning of the symbols shown in the Report Format is given in Table T4-12.

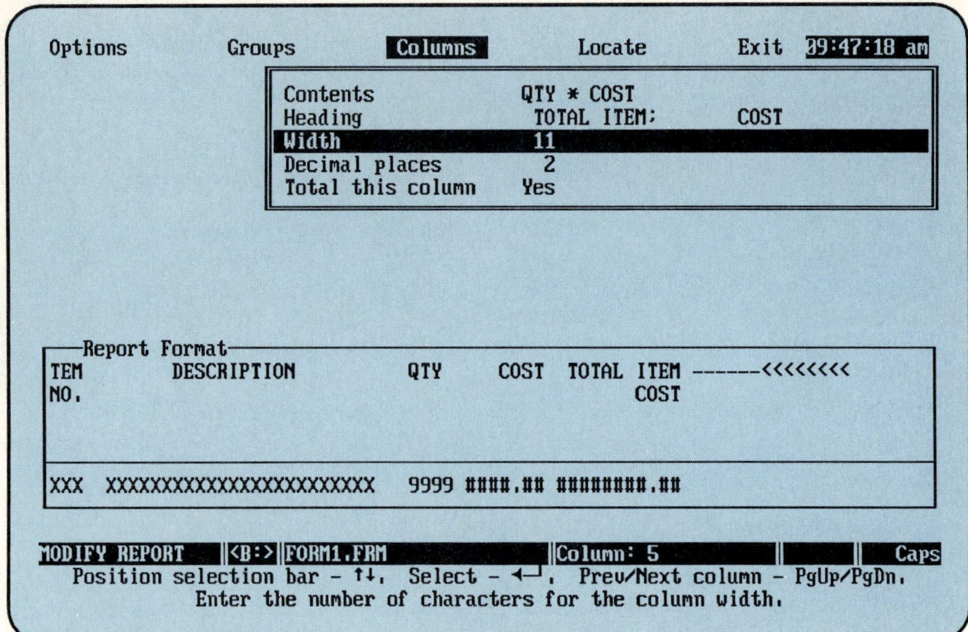

FIGURE T4-37
The Columns Report Generator Screen After All Column Entries Have Been Made.

TABLE T4-12
Meaning of Report Format Symbols

Symbol	Meaning
X	Position in character report column
9	Position in a numeric report column with no total
#	Position in a numeric report column with total
.	Decimal point in numeric report column
>	Space reserved for left-hand margin
<	Space reserved for right-hand margin
-	Unused positions after the last column and before the right-hand margin

Correcting Column Errors

If your screen does not look like Figure T4-37, move the menu cursor to the *Locate* menu. This will display a menu of all field contents. Use the Up and Down Arrow keys to position the submenu cursor on the field contents to be modified. Depress the [Enter] key, and the cursor will be transferred automatically to that column menu. Refer to Table T4-11 to view the correct specifications.

If you need help recalling which cursor-control keys to use, depress the [F1] Function key while in the Column menu and replace the Report Format, referred to as the *blackboard*, inset window with the cursor-control menu. You may toggle between these two help features by depressing the [F1] Function key.

Saving Your Report

After all the columns have been described, you should save your report. To do this, use the Arrow keys as needed to move the menu cursor to *Exit*. Make sure the Save option is highlighted and press

to terminate the report definition, save the FORM file under the name specified, and exit the report generator. You now should see the dot prompt.

Displaying a Report

To see the results of all your labors, enter

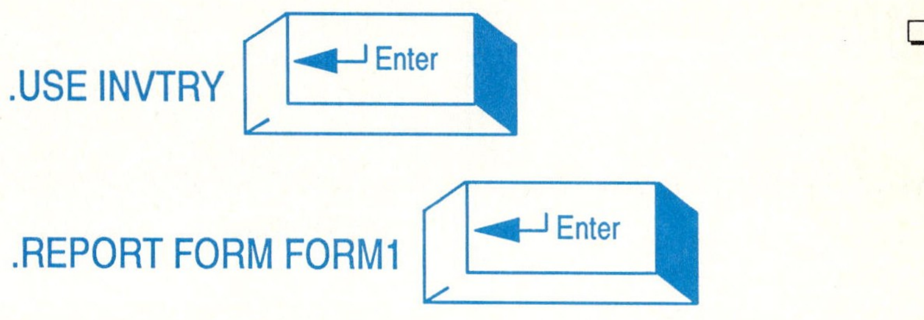

You can place a search condition in the REPORT statement. For example, you could enter REPORT FORM FORM1 FOR QTY > 15. This will create a report based only on those records whose QTY is greater than 15.

The displayed report should appear as shown in Figure T4-38.

FIGURE T4-38
The Screen Display of Report FORM1.FRM.

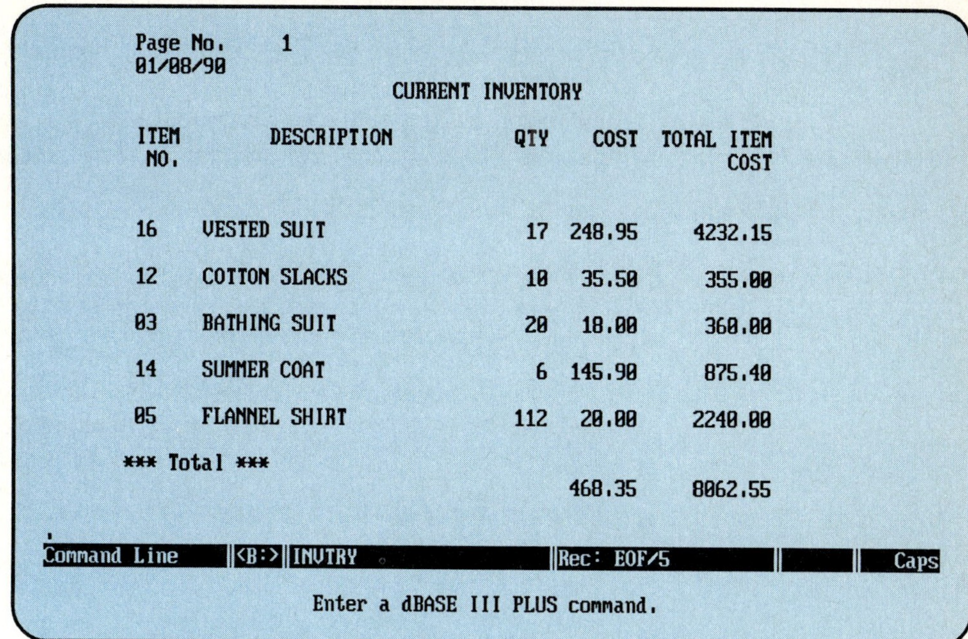

```
Page No.     1
01/08/90
                    CURRENT INVENTORY

ITEM         DESCRIPTION          QTY    COST   TOTAL ITEM
 NO.                                                  COST

16     VESTED SUIT                 17  248.95      4232.15

12     COTTON SLACKS               10   35.50       355.00

03     BATHING SUIT                20   18.00       360.00

14     SUMMER COAT                  6  145.90       875.40

05     FLANNEL SHIRT              112   20.00      2240.00

*** Total ***
                                       468.35      8062.55

.
Command Line   ||<B:>||INVTRY          ||Rec: EOF/5   ||    ||  Caps

              Enter a dBASE III PLUS command.
```

To make a printout, turn on your printer and enter the commands

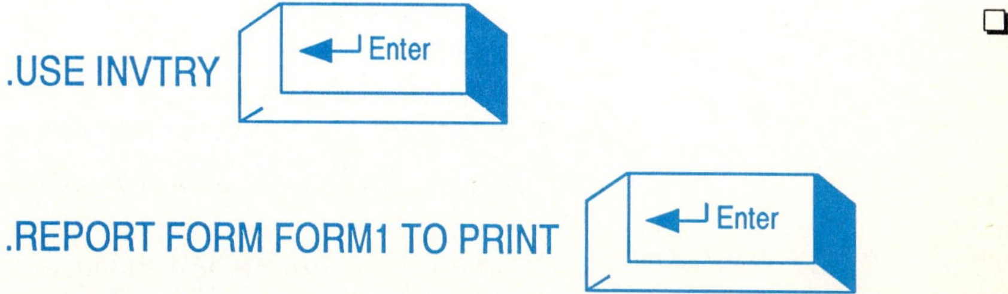

The printed report should appear the same as it does on the screen display.

Changing the Order of the Records in a Report

If you want the data in your report displayed in an order other than the physical order in which they were created, you can enter the commands

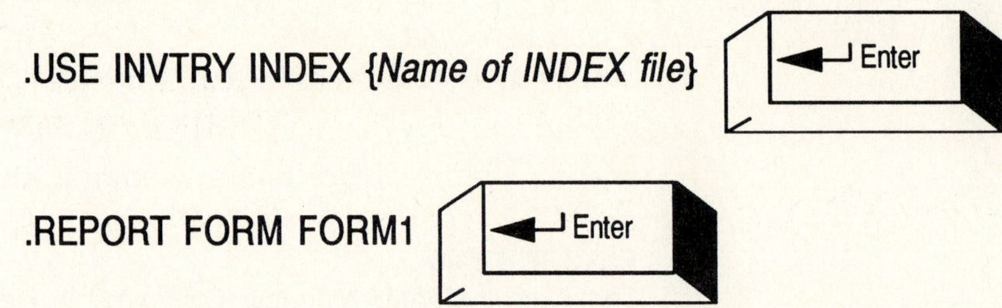

The *name of the INDEX file* must be a previously created index file.

Modifying a Report

If, after creating a report, you desire to change any part of it, you can enter the commands

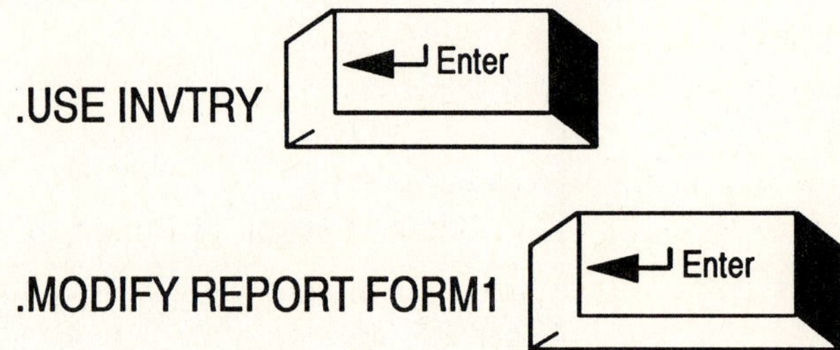

This will access dBASE's report generator and present the initial screen shown in Figure T4-33. The report form can then be modified using the same menus and commands as we used to create the form.

Writing a Program

For many situations, the standard, formatted report obtained from the report generator is sufficient. If you must have output that differs at all from that which the report form provides or that uses more than one database file, you will have to use the dBASE programming language and write your own program. A full discussion of dBASE programming is beyond the scope of this tutorial, but we will present two short programs.

Sample Program 1

Figure T4-39 shows a sample dBASE program.

Each line in a dBASE program contains one valid dBASE command, comment, or program statement.

FIGURE T4-39
Sample dBASE Program I.

```
USE INVTRY
LIST
WAIT 'PRESS ANY KEY TO CONTINUE'
CLEAR
```

After you enter this program, we will show you how to execute it. Then, we'll discuss it. Enter the command

If your program is to be saved on a drive other than B:, you must specify that drive.

.MODIFY COMMAND B:SAMPLE1 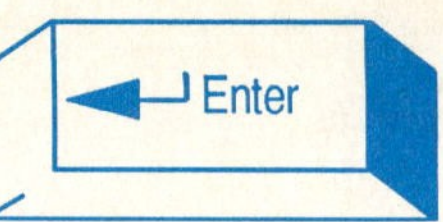

and dBASE will respond by displaying the message

```
Edit: B:SAMPLE1.prg
```

and a Cursor-control menu as shown in Figure T4-40.

FIGURE T4-40
The Cursor-Control Window Displayed in Response to MODIFY COMMAND for a New Program.

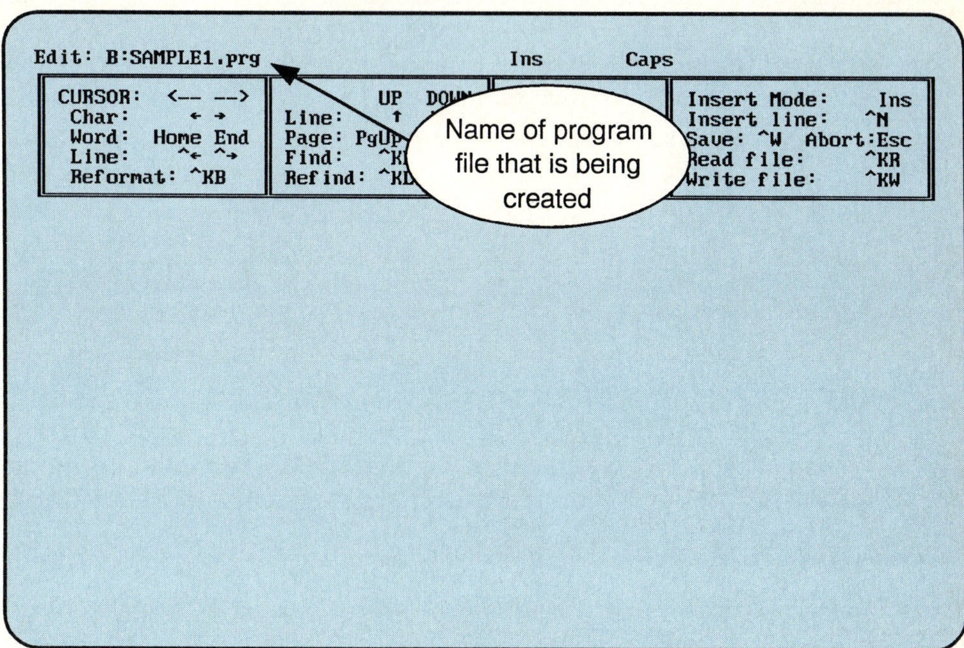

This is dBASE's way of telling you that this program doesn't already exist and that you may begin entering it. So, enter it. Use the Cursor-control menu to assist you in moving from instruction to instruction during the process to correct any keying errors.

When you have finished entering the program, enter

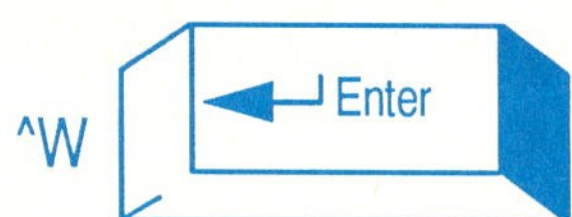

to save the program.

To execute the program, simply enter

The DO command is used to execute a dBASE program file.

and follow the directions provided by the program.

Let's analyze what happened as each command in SAMPLE1 was executed (see Fig. T4-39).

First, the command USE INVTRY accessed the INVTRY database file from the default drive and prepared it for use. Second, the LIST command listed the entire database. Third, the command WAIT 'PRESS ANY KEY TO CONTINUE' printed the message PRESS ANY KEY TO CONTINUE and caused the computer to pause until a key was depressed. Last, the display was cleared. And, all this was accomplished by entering a single dBASE command.

Sample Program 2

Figure T4-41 contains a second and more complex dBASE program. Let's give it a try.

FIGURE T4-41
Sample dBASE Program 2.

```
SET TALK OFF
SET DEFAULT TO B:
*  SAMPLE.PRG  3/1/91   AUTHOR - ANN AUFIERO
*  PROGRAM USES A MENU TO SELECT COMMANDS,
*          WORKS WITH FILE - INVTRY.DBF
*
*
USE INVTRY
*         DISPLAY THE MENU
CLEAR
?
?
? '        INVENTORY SYSTEM'
?
? '     A =  APPEND'
?
? '     B =  LIST'
?
? '     C =  PURCHASE QUERY'
?
*  ASK THE QUESTION
*
ACCEPT 'WHAT WOULD YOU LIKE TO DO?' TO AMT
*
IF AMT = 'A'
     APPEND
ENDIF
*
IF AMT = 'B'
     LIST
ENDIF
*
IF AMT = 'C'
*
*  PRINT OUT ALL INVENTORY ITEMS THAT ARE LESS THAN 20 IN NUMBER'
CLEAR
?
?
? '  LISTING OF INVENTORY ITEMS WITH A QUANTITY LESS THAN 20'
?
? '  ITEM NUMBER        QUANTITY ON HAND          PURCHASE'
?
    DO WHILE .NOT. EOF()
    *
       IF QTY < 20
           STORE 20 - QTY TO AMT1
           ? '        ', ITEMNO, '              ', QTY, '          ', AMT1
           ?
       ENDIF
       SKIP
    ENDDO
*
ENDIF
```

Enter the command

and dBASE will respond by displaying the message

```
Edit:  B:SAMPLE2.prg
```

and a Cursor-control menu similar to that shown in Figure T4-40, except that it has the name SAMPLE2.prg.

dBASE is telling you that this program doesn't already exist and that you may begin entering it. Go ahead now; enter the program. Use the Cursor-control menu to assist you in moving from instruction to instruction during the process to correct any keying errors.

When you have finished entering the program, enter

❑

to save the program.

To execute this program, simply enter

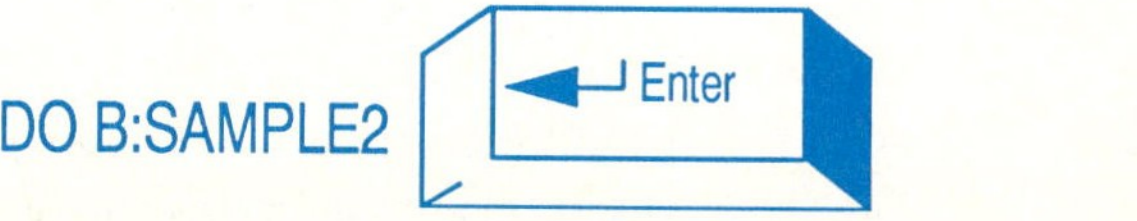

❑

The program will now display three options: type A to APPEND, B to LIST, and C to make a PURCHASE QUERY. Enter

❑

Your output should be as shown in Figure T4-42.

FIGURE T4-42
Output from the dBASE Program SAMPLE2.PRG If Option B Is Chosen.

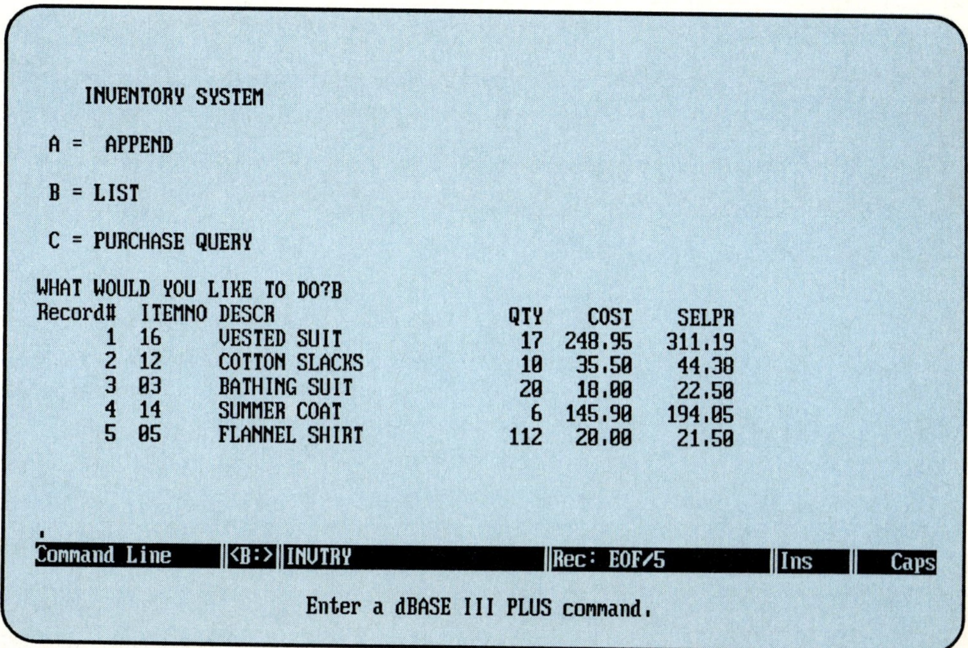

```
   INVENTORY SYSTEM

 A =  APPEND

 B = LIST

 C = PURCHASE QUERY

WHAT WOULD YOU LIKE TO DO?B
Record#  ITEMNO DESCR                    QTY   COST    SELPR
      1  16     VESTED SUIT               17  248.95  311.19
      2  12     COTTON SLACKS             10   35.50   44.38
      3  03     BATHING SUIT              20   18.00   22.50
      4  14     SUMMER COAT                6  145.90  194.05
      5  05     FLANNEL SHIRT            112   20.00   21.50

Command Line  ||<B:>||INVTRY          ||Rec: EOF/5   ||Ins  ||  Caps
                  Enter a dBASE III PLUS command.
```

If you like, execute SAMPLE2 again and choose Option C.

Explanation of the Program

We begin by running our program, B:SAMPLE2.

TALK is a debugging tool. If it is on, the result of every command execution will be displayed. Entering **SET TALK OFF** turns this option off. To help you debug, you can turn this option on by entering

.SET TALK ON 

The * in Column 1 of a line makes that line a comment. It is similar to a REM statement in BASIC. What we put here makes no difference to the computer. By convention, we use comments to include the program name SAMPLE2.PRG, date, author, and purpose of the program.

The **CLEAR** command clears the screen. Every dBASE program should begin with CLEAR.

The **?** is used to display the contents of field names, variables, numeric values, and text on the screen or printer. It is similar to PRINT in BASIC.

Text or **string values** are enclosed within single quotation marks (').

The **ACCEPT** command accepts a *character* string from the terminal and assigns it to a memory variable.

The **IF** is a conditional statement. If the condition specified (QTY < 20) is met (logical value = true), the next statement or statements will be executed. If the condition is false, execution continues after the **ENDIF** delimiter.

DO WHILE initiates a loop. As long as the condition stated is true (an End Of File is not reached), the program will loop through the DO WHILE to the **ENDDO** statement.

The **STORE** function stores a value into a specified memory variable. STORE 20 to AMT1 places the number 20 into the variable AMT1.

SKIP causes the computer to skip forward or backward through the current file. SKIP as used in our program causes the next record to become the current record.

^W saves the program to disk.

To run this program, use the **DO** command. As mentioned earlier, DO is used each time you want to execute a dBASE program.

In Conclusion

It will take time, effort, and practice to become proficient in the use of dBASE III PLUS, but your efforts will be well worth it. We have just scratched the surface, but if you have successfully mastered this tutorial, you have made a good start.

To exit dBASE enter

❑

Remove your disks and turn off your printer, monitor, and computer. You have done very well.

dBASE III PLUS Command and Function Summary

Commands

? [exp]
?? [exp]
@ [row,col] [SAY [exp] [PICTURE [clause]]] [[GET [variable] [PICTURE[clause]]] [RANGE [exp, exp]]][CLEAR]
ACCEPT [[prompt]] TO [memvar]
APPEND [BLANK]
APPEND FROM [file name] [FOR [exp]] [SDF] [DELIMITED]
ASSIST
AVERAGE [exp list] [[scope]] [FOR/WHILE [exp]] [TO [memvar list]]
BROWSE [FIELDS [field list]]
CANCEL
CHANGE [[scope]] [FIELDS [FIELD LIST] [FOR/WHILE [exp]]
CLEAR
CLEAR ALL
CLEAR GETS
CLEAR MEMORY
CLOSE [ALTERNATE/DATABASES/FORMAT/INDEX/PROCEDURE]
CONTINUE
COPY FILE [file name] TO [file name]
COPY TO [file name] [[scope]] [FIELDS [field list]] FOR/WHILE [exp] [SDF/DELIMITED [WITH [delimiter]]]
COPY STRUCTURE TO [file] [FIELDS [field list]]
COUNT [[scope]] [FOR/WHILE [exp]] [TO [memvar]]
CREATE [.dbf file name]
CREATE LABEL [.lbl file name]
CREATE REPORT [.frm file name]
DELETE [[scope]] [FOR/WHILE [exp]]
DIR [[drive:]] [[path]\] [[skeleton]]
DISPLAY [[scope]] [FIELDS [field list]] [FOR/WHILE [exp]] [OFF]
DISPLAY MEMORY
DISPLAY STATUS
DISPLAY STRUCTURE
DO [.prg file name]/[procedure name] [WITH [parameter list]]
DO CASE.CASE.[OTHERWISE] . . . ENDCASE
DO WHILE. [commands] . . ENDDO
EDIT [[RECORD] [n]]
EJECT
ERASE [file name]
EXIT
FIND [character string]
GO/GOTO [BOTTOM/TOP/[expN]]
HELP [[keyword]]
IF. . [ELSE] . . ENDIF
INDEX ON [exp] TO [.ndx file name]
INPUT [[prompt]] TO [memvar]
INSERT [BLANK] [BEFORE]
JOIN WITH [alias] TO [new file] FOR [condition] [FIELDS [field list]]
LABEL FORM [.lbl file name] [SAMPLE] [[scope]] [FOR/WHILE [condition]] [FIELDS [field list]] [OFF]
LIST [OFF] [[scope]] [expression list]] [FIELDS [field list]] [FOR/WHILE [condition]] [TO PRINT]
LIST MEMORY [TO PRINT]
LIST STATUS [TO PRINT]
LIST STRUCTURE [TO PRINT]
LOCATE [[scope]] FOR [condition]
LOOP
MODIFY COMMAND [file name]
MODIFY LABEL [.lbl file name]
MODIFY REPORT [.frm file name]
MODIFY STRUCTURE
NOTE/* [undelimited character string]
PACK
PARAMETERS [parameter list]
PRIVATE [ALL [LIKE/EXCEPT [skeleton]]] [[memory variable list]]
PUBLIC [memory variable list]
QUIT
READ
RECALL [[scope]] [FOR/WHILE [condition]]
REINDEX
RELEASE [[memvar list]] [ALL/LIKE/EXCEPT [skeleton]]]
RENAME [current file name] TO [new file name]
REPLACE [[scope]] [field] WITH [exp] [,[field2] WITH [exp2],...]
REPORT FORM [.frm file name] [[scope]] [FOR [exp]] [PLAIN] [HEADING [character string]] [NOEJECT] [TO PRINT] [TO FILE] [file name]
RESTORE FROM [.mem file name] [ADDITIVE]
RETURN [TO MASTER]
RUN [command]
SAVE TO [.mem file name] [ALL LIKE/EXCEPT [skeleton]]
SEEK [expression]
SET SELECT [n/alias]
SET ALTERNATE TO [[file name]]
SET ALTERNATE on/OFF
SET BELL ON/off
SET CARRY on/OFF
SET COLOR TO [standard display] [,[enhanced display]] [,[border]]
SET CONFIRM on/OFF
SET CONSOLE ON/off
SET DEBUG on/OFF
SET DECIMALS TO [n]
SET DEFAULT TO [drive]
SET DELETED on/OFF
SET DELIMITER TO [[character string]] [DEFAULT]
SET DELIMITER on/OFF
SET DEVICE TO SCREEN/print
SET ECHO on/OFF
SET ESCAPE ON/off
SET EXACT ON/off
SET FILTER TO [condition]
SET FIXED on/OFF
SET FUNCTION [key#] TO [character string]
SET FORMAT TO [.fmt file name]
SET HEADING on/OFF
SET HELP ON/off
SET INDEX TO [.ndx file list]
SET INTENSITY ON/off
SET MARGIN TO [n]
SET MENUS ON/off
SET PATH TO [[path list]]
SET PRINT on/OFF
SET PROCEDURE TO [,procedure file name]

Commands

SET RELATION TO [key] INTO [alias]
SET SAFETY ON/off
SET STEP on/OFF
SET TALK ON/off
SET UNIQUE on/OFF
SKIP [n]
SORT TO [new file name] ON [field] [/A] [/D] [,[field2] [/A] [/D. . .] [[scope]] [FOR [condition]]
STORE [exp] TO [memvar] [,memvar list]]
SUM [[scope] [[expression list] TO [memvar list]] [FOR/WHILE [condition]]
TEXT. . ENDTEXT
TOTAL TO [file name] ON [key] [[scope]] [FIELDS [field list]] [FOR/WHILE [condition]]
UPDATE [RANDOM] ON [key field] FROM [alias] REPLACE [field] WITH [EXP] [,[field2] WITH [exp2]...]
USE [[.dbf file name]] [INDEX [.ndx file list]] [ALLIAS [alias]]
WAIT [[prompt]] [TO [memvar]]
ZAP

Function Name	Description	Input Data Type	Output Data Type
&	Macro substitution	C	C
AT	Substring search	C	C
ASC	Character to ASCII code conversion	C	N
BOF	Beginning of file		L
CDOW	Day of week	D	C
CHR	ASCII code to character conversion	C	C
CMONTH	Calendar month	D	C
COL	Current screen column position	·	N
CTOD	Character to date conversion	C	D
DATE	System date	·	D
DAY	Day of month	D	N
DELETED	Deleted record	·	L
DOW	Day of week	D	N
DTOC	Date to character conversion	D	C
EOF	End of file	·	L
EXP	Exponential (ex)	N	N
FILE	FIle existence	C	C
INT	Integer	N	N
LEN	Length of character string	C	N
LOG	Logarithm	N	N
LOWER	Uppercase to lowercase conversion	C	C
MONTH	Month of year	D	N
PCOL	Printer column position	·	N
PROW	Printer row position	·	N
RECNO	Cunrent record number	·	N
ROUND	Rounds off	N	N
ROW	Current screen row position	·	N
SPACE	Generates blank spaces	N	C
SQRT	Square root	N	N
STR	Numeric to character conversion	N	C
SUBSTR	Substring selection	C	C
TIME	System time	·	C
TRIM	Removes trailing blanks	C	C
TYPE	Validates expression	C	C
UPPER	Lowercase to uppercase conversion	C	C
VAL	Character to numeric conversion	C	N
YEAR	Year	D	N

Functional Classification	Function Name	Description
Date and time	CDOW CTOD CMONTH DATE DAY DOW DTOC MONTH TIME YEAR	Day of week Character to date conversion Calendar month System date Day of month Day of week Date to character conversion Month of year System time Year
Mathematical	EXP IN LOG ROUND SQRT	Exponential (ex) Integer Logarithm Rounds off Square root
Character manipulation	& AT LOWER SPACE SUBSTR TRIM UPPER	Macro substitution Substring search Forces lowercase Generates blank spaces Substring selection Remove trailing blanks Forces uppercase
Specialized tests	BOF COL DELETED EOF FILE LEN POOL PROW RECNO ROW TYPE	Beginning of file Current screen column position Deleted record End of lile File existence Length of character string Printer column position Printer row position Current record number Current screen row position Validates expression
Conversion	ASC CHR LOWER STR UPPER VAL	Character to ASCII code ASCII to character code Uppercase to lowercase Numeric to character Lowercase to uppercase Character to numeric

Exercises

1. What dBASE command or commands would you use to accomplish each of the following?
   a. Create a database file.
   b. Sum the values in a Numeric field.
   c. Activate an index file named INDEX2.
   d. Clear the display screen.
   e. Change a field in one record.
   f. Edit on a full screen.
   g. Close all database files.
   h. Change the default disk drive.
   i. Run a dBASE program file.
   j. Change the natural order of records in a database file.

2. Answer each of the following questions with either true or false.

_______ a. To create an index file, a database must be activated first.

_______ b. A field name can have an imbedded space.

_______ c. The output of a DISPLAY command cannot be printed.

_______ d. Once a filter is in place, it cannot be removed.

_______ e. The top record in a sorted database will always be Record 1.

_______ f. The BROWSE command cannot be used to add records to your database.

_______ g. Once the structure of a database is created, it can be modified as much as you like.

_______ h. The ASSIST MENU must be used to create the structure of a database.

_______ i. A record that is marked for deletion remains an active member of the database until SET DELETED ON is entered.

_______ j. Once a database is PACKed, the records that have been marked for deletion are removed from the database.

3. Describe what each of the following commands does:
   a. INDEX ON AMT TO AMT
   b. SET INDEX TO
   c. EDIT RECORD 5
   d. LIST FOR AMT < 30
   e. CREATE ALLISLAN
   f. DO MYPROG
   g. DISPLAY TO PRINT
   h. MODIFY COMMAND GOGO
   i. BROWSE FIELDS QTY, AMT
   j. LIST OFF

4. Answer each of the following questions as best you can:
   a. Explain the differences that occur when using the dBASE ASSIST MENU and the dot prompt.
   b. Name the command or commands you would use to perform the following operations:

      ■ Create a file structure
      ■ List your file structure
      ■ Modify an empty file
      ■ Load a database
      ■ List all or part of a database

   c. Describe the SORT and INDEX commands. Explain how they are different. What are the advantages and disadvantages of each?
   d. List the commands you would use to create a standard report using a file called PAYROLL. Call your report file FORM-P. Assume your file is on disk drive B:.
   e. Referring to Figure T4-29, notice how the heading CURRENT INVENTORY is centered whereas the body of the report is not. Using MODIFY REPORT B:FORM1, change the necessary parameters so the entire body of the report is shifted to the right, resulting in a more centered report layout.
   f. How would you enhance the program B:SAMPLE2 so it contained the option to use the SORT command? Write the necessary code to SORT the file INVTRY using COST as the KEY field. (*Hint:* Use MODIFY COMMAND SAMPLE2.)
   g. How might a database management program be used to process a company's payroll?
   h. Modify program SAMPLE1 so that only those records whose COST is in excess of 100 are listed. (*Hint*: Use MODIFY COMMAND SAMPLE1.)

Hands-On Activities

1. Create a database structure for the database B:CUSTOMER.DBF to be used as a customer file.

Field	Name	Type	Width	Dec
001	FIRST	C	10	
002	LAST	C	15	
003	ADDRESS	C	25	
004	CITY	C	15	
005	STATE	C	2	
006	ZIP	C	9	
007	AMOUNT	N	7	

   a. Load the database B:CUSTOMER. The first record to be loaded should be:

   RECORD #00001
   FIRST :Thomas
   LAST :Hennessy
   ADDRESS :14655 Fernwood Ct.
   CITY :San Diego
   STATE :CA
   ZIP :10076
   AMOUNT :800.00

   Now add four more records.

   b. List your file.

   c. Using the SORT command, sort your database into alphabetic order using LAST as the key field. Store the sorted file as B:SORTNAME.

   d. Use the INDEX command to index your file on the key field AMOUNT. Use the index filename B:AMTINDEX.

   e. Query your database to produce a listing of all records whose AMOUNT field is over 500.

   f. Find the sum of the AMOUNT values.

2. Activate the database file CUSTOMER.DBF you created in Activity 1. Use the REPORT command to access dBASE III PLUS's report generator, and create a report of your own design based on the file CUSTOMER. Store your report file in B:REPORT1. After specifying your report parameters, print out a copy of the report.

3. Create a database of two-character fields. Enter the names and phone numbers of friends, family, and business associates into these fields. Index the database by name. Create a report that will print your new phone book.

4. Carry out each of the following steps as directed:

   a. Create the database you see displayed next. However, remember that commas are not valid parts of numeric fields.

NAME	DEPARTMENT	SALARY	PHONE EXCHANGE
MILLS	MKT	35,635	368
JACKOBS	MKT	54,328	332
SMITH	SLS	23,234	242
GIOIA	MKT	78,293	662
FUORI	SLS	12,432	212
BROWN	MIS	32,234	345

b. Print the structure of the database.

c. Print only those names of people in the marketing department whose salaries exceed 35,500.

d. For anyone who earned less than 25,000, give them a 10 percent raise and print their names and adjusted salaries.

e. Print the names of the individuals whose phone exchanges are between 340 and 380 inclusive, and print their phone exchanges.

5. Index the database created in Activity 4 by SALARY in descending order. Then create a report that displays the name and salary only in index-file order.

6. Carry out each of the following steps as directed.

a. Create the following database:

State	City	Last Name	Rental Price
DC	Washington	Lewis	789.50
VA	Fairfax	Hiller	768.90
DC	Washington	Gioia	890.00
DC	Washington	Fuori	679.00
CA	Ventura	Brown	678.00
CA	Burbank	Ewing	500.00

b. INDEX on two key fields, State and City.

c. Set a filter that will display only those people whose Rental Price is greater than 680.00.

d. List the Last Name, State, and City in the order contained in the index file you created in Part b of this question.

e. List the Last Name, State, and Rental Price. The Rental Price should have 10 percent added to it if the State is CA (California).

7. Create a command program file that will carry out Activity 6, Parts c, d, and e.

8. Create a database of the courses you have taken or are currently taking. The database should include the following fields. *(Hint: We placed the field type after the field.)*

Course number (C)	Final grade (could be N or C, you decide)
Course name (C)	Elective/required (L)
Course description (C)	Semester taken (C)
Instructor (C)	Number of credits (N)

Create your own data. When you are finished, answer each of the following questions.

a. What is the total number of credits you have taken in courses you have passed? Don't include credits for courses you have failed or from which you have withdrawn.

b. Create a report form that will print your transcript. The transcript should include your name, course number and name, description, and final grade. Also the total number of credits accrued should be at the bottom of the report.

c. Print the report only for the science courses.

d. Print the report only for general liberal arts courses.

Index

E

F

G

H

I

J

K

L

M

P

Q

R

S

T

U

V

W